THE ECONOMICS AND REGULATION OF UNITED STATES NEWSPAPERS

THE COMMUNICATION AND INFORMATION SCIENCE SERIES
Series Editor: **BRENDA DERVIN**, The Ohio State University

Subseries:
Progress in Communication Sciences: Brant R. Burleson
Interpersonal Communication: Donald J. Cegala
Organizational Communication: George Barnett
Mass Communication/Telecommunication Systems: Lee B. Becker
User-Based Communication/Information System Design: Michael S. Nilan
Cross-Cultural/Cross-National Communication and Social Change: Josep Rota
International Communication, Peace and Development: Majid Tehranian
Critical Cultural Studies in Communication: Leslie T. Good
Feminist Scholarship in Communication: Lana Rakow
Rhetorical Theory and Criticism: Stephen H. Browne
Communication Pedagogy and Practice: Gerald M. Phillips
Communication: The Human Context: Lee Thayer

THE ECONOMICS AND REGULATION OF UNITED STATES NEWSPAPERS

Stephen Lacy
and
Todd F. Simon

Michigan State University
East Lansing, MI

ABLEX PUBLISHING CORPORATION
NORWOOD, NEW JERSEY

Copyright © 1993 by Ablex Publishing Corporation

All rights reserved. No part of this publication may be reproduced, stored in a retrieval system, or transmitted, in any form or by any means, electronic, mechanical, photocopying, microfilming, recording, or otherwise, without permission of the publisher.

Printed in the United States of America

Library of Congress Cataloging-in Publication Data

Lacy, Stephen, 1948–
   The economics and regulation of United States Newspapers / by Stephen Lacy and Todd F. Simon.
     p. cm.—(Communication and information science)
   Includes bibliographical references and index.
   ISBN 0-89391-753-2
   1. Newspaper publishing—United States—Finance. 2. Newspaper publishing—Government policy—United States. 3. Press law—United States. I. Simon, Todd F. II. Title. III. Series.
PN4888.F6L34 1992
338.4'70705722'0973—dc20   91-36511
                                                CIP

Able Publishing Corporation
355 Chestnut Street
Norwood, New Jersey 07648

Stephen Lacy:
For Leslie and Lois

Todd Simon:
In memory of Bernie Simon

Table of Contents

Preface **ix**

Acknowledgments **xi**

1 OVERVIEW OF THE NEWSPAPER INDUSTRY **1**
   What is Economics? **2**
   What is Regulation? **3**
   What is a Newspaper? **4**
   The Process of Running a Newspaper **7**
   The Nature of the U.S. Newspaper Industry **9**
   Of Newspapers and Shoes **16**
   Summary **19**

2 NEWSPAPER DEMAND **23**
   Demand in the Information Market **23**
   Demand in the Advertising Market **40**
   Demand in the Intellectual Market **48**
   Summary **50**

3 NEWSPAPER SUPPLY **55**
   Economic Theory **55**
   Newspaper Supply and Costs **62**
   Newspaper Supply and Demand **76**
   Summary **87**

4 COMPETITION IN THE NEWSPAPER INDUSTRY **91**
   Newspaper Market Structure **91**
   Direct Competition **94**
   Intercity Competition **112**
   Intermedia Competition **119**
   Summary **123**

5 NEWSPAPER OWNERSHIP   **131**
    Trends in Newspaper Ownership   **132**
    Ownership Goals   **136**
    The Impact of Ownership on Newspaper Markets   **141**
    Summary   **156**

6 NEWSPAPERS AND TECHNOLOGY   **163**
    Technology and the Newspaper Industry   **163**
    Technology's Impact on Newspaper Markets   **166**
    The Future of Newspaper Technology   **181**
    Summary   **183**

7 ANTITRUST AND MARKET REGULATION OF NEWSPAPERS   **187**
    Background of Federal Antitrust Law   **188**
    Newspapers, Antitrust, and the First Amendment   **190**
    Overview of Newspaper Antitrust Cases   **193**
    Antitrust Claims Against Newspapers   **199**
    The Newspaper Preservation Act   **207**

8 NEWSPAPER ECONOMICS AND ANTITRUST   **215**
    The Economics of Antitrust Laws   **215**
    Impact of Newspaper Monopoly Power   **220**
    Summary   **233**

9 BUSINESS REGULATION OF NEWSPAPERS   **237**
    Tax Laws and Newspapers   **238**
    Labor Laws and the Press   **246**
    Newspapers and the Postal Laws   **253**
    Newspaper Distribution, Circulation, and Recirculation   **256**
    Summary   **260**

10 CONCLUSIONS   **265**
    The Impact of Market and Regulatory Constraints   **265**
    Policy Issues in the Newspaper Industry   **274**
    Summary   **283**

Author Index   **287**

Subject Index   **291**

Preface

In a way, this book started more than 30 years ago with a debate published in the pages of *Journalism Quarterly*. In the Summer 1959 issue, Edmund Landau and Scott Davenport argued that traditional economic theory was limited because of its concentration on price as the important variable in determining supply and demand. Fred Currier countered in the Spring 1960 issue that existing theory could be adequate in dealing with newspaper economics. The underlying assumption of this book is that Landau and Davenport had a valid argument. Although existing economic theory is useful in analyzing some of the behavior of newspaper firms, new theory explaining newspaper readers' behavior is needed. A second assumption is that government regulation of all businesses, but especially the newspaper industry with its First Amendment protection, should be based on adequate economic analysis.

Research into newspaper economics has followed the direction set by both sides of the argument about the applicability of traditional economic theory. This book will not try to end the debate, but it will attempt to present newspaper economic research in a systematic manner, to relate that research more closely to scholarship on regulation, and to suggest some new ideas and directions for the future.

To date, a book concentrating specifically on newspaper economics is unavailable. A well-written book by Jon Udell, published in 1978, had newspaper economics in its title, but its contents were oriented more toward business practices of newspapers than toward the more abstract analysis that usually falls under the heading of economics.

Because of the absence of books on newspaper economics, this particular effort is a compromise. Its summary nature could make it useful to anyone unfamiliar with the research in this area. As a compromise effort that seeks to span such a large area of interest, we aimed at upper-level undergraduate and masters-level students. However, we hope some of the ideas will be of interest to more advanced readers. The first chapter is an effort to acquaint unfamiliar readers with the newspaper industry.

Readers familiar with the newspaper industry may not need to go over this material.

Two other assumptions of the authors are important for the reader to know. First, we picture the social role of newspaper journalists as similar to that of a mechanic. They work to keep the society moving as efficiently as possible toward achieving its goals. They are not engineers who redesign the society, although they can and should suggest ways of improving the way it works.

A second assumption is that a newspaper firm can produce an adequate profit for survival and still produce a newspaper that makes a valuable and worthwhile contribution to its readers and society. Profit need not mean an inferior commodity. In fact, it is the underlying assumption of the market system that the users of a commodity—the readers, in the case of newspapers—are best prepared to determine how useful and worthwhile the commodity is. This mechanism is far from perfect, but without a belief in its long-term success, support of the democratic process and the corresponding press system seems hypocritical.

Acknowledgments

We would like to thank our colleagues and students for the ideas and information we have absorbed during the hours of discussion and debate. Specifically, we would like to thank Bill Blankenburg for his comments and suggestions early in this project.

We also are grateful to staff members at Michigan State University, especially Dee Dee Johnson, for their help in preparing the manuscript for this book.

Stephen Lacy thanks his teachers and colleagues James Tankard and Alfred Smith for helping revive his interest in economics. Todd Simon thanks his teachers and colleagues Warren Francke and Sanford Katz.

A special thanks goes to Leslie Lacy for her help with the manuscript and for putting up with the complaining that seems a natural part of producing a book.

1

Overview of the Newspaper Industry

Each day people in the United States spend more than 100 million hours reading newspapers. Despite this great expenditure of time, the average reader has little understanding of the nature of newspaper work. Even people who create newspapers sometimes fail to understand fully the forces that shape and direct their work. Reporters often contend they serve as watchdogs, serving the readers by keeping an eye on the abuses of government and business. Yet newspaper publishers will sometimes say these same watchdogs are more like ungrateful family mutts who bite the hand that feeds them.

Whatever the strengths and weaknesses of newspapers in the United States, there is no doubt that they have been given a special role in this country. The First Amendment to the Constitution, despite varying interpretations, clearly defines a societal role for newspapers. This role clearly separates newspapers from other businesses, but it is the fact that newspapers are businesses that generates so much controversy about how well they fulfill that role.

As businesses, newspapers are expected to make a profit. As organizations that affect the political direction of the United States, newspapers are expected to be above mere commercial concerns. This potential, and often actual, conflict has characterized the newspaper industry for more than 150 years and will continue to do so. This conflict has become even more complex with the expansion, since the 1930s, of government regulation concerning the business side of newspaper firms, an expansion explicitly approved by the U.S. Supreme Court.

These forces have created a tug-of-war between the business and journalism concerns of newspapers, and between the business concerns of newspapers and government. Which interest wins in a given situation affects what the public reads during those 100 million hours a day spent with newspapers. The struggles among these three elements—profit role, social role, and government regulation—form the basis for this book.

As with most books about economics, this one starts by defining terms.

2   THE ECONOMICS & REGULATIONS OF U.S. NEWSPAPERS

Unlike other economics books, this one must also define a specific commodity—newspapers. It may seem silly to define a newspaper; after all, millions of people read them every day. However, this ordinary nature of newspapers makes such a definition important. People often fail to analyze fully what they so often use; they rarely consider the people and processes involved in writing and editing their newspapers until the content upsets them. This book concentrates on the economic nature of these processes because all processes at newspapers have economic implications. The term "economic" simply involves a point of view that differs from, but is related to, other viewpoints, whether they be sociological, ethical, or organizational.

In addition to economics, the role of some government regulation will be examined. Governments affect newspapers in many ways, from tax laws to postal laws. Since the main focus of this book is economics, the role of antitrust law will also be included. Antitrust is a form of regulation that is based on inappropriate economic behavior.

WHAT IS ECONOMICS?

In its simplest form, economics deals with the behavior of deciding how resources are used to obtain goals. More specifically, *economics is the analysis of the process and outcome of allocating scarce resources.* This definition focuses on three concepts: the process of allocating, the results of allocating, and scarce resources.

Economics must involve scarce resources. If resources are not limited in some way, allocation is unnecessary. If news of political activities or of a recent basketball game could be acquired with no expenditure of money or time, newspapers or television would not be needed. In fact, acquiring information costs time and money. Newspaper organizations act as intermediaries. They make the spending of time and money more efficient and effective by dividing the cost among large numbers of people.

Scarce resources take many forms, including people, money, equipment and time. From an economist's viewpoint, these types of resources are fairly interchangeable. If one has money and needs time, people are paid for their time. The exact forms of resources necessary to produce a commodity vary with the industry. Newspapers, like most industries, use all forms of resources, but gathering news and selling advertising is labor intensive. So, despite the growing use of technology by newspapers, people remain the most important resource.

Newspapers combine resources through several processes to create a product and perform services. Managers set up these processes to achieve goals. These goals can be organization-wide; they can involve subdivisions of the organization; or they can be held by individuals within the organization. For example, a newspaper organization's overall goal may be to make a certain level of profit, while the news-editorial department's goal is to produce a comprehensive report of events and issues that might interest its readers. If all works well, both goals will be achieved. If not, one goal will be sacrificed to achieve the other.

Organizational processes vary from industry to industry, but they also vary within an industry. These variations within the newspaper industry sometimes go unnoticed by people outside the industry. A key to understanding an industry lies in examining the intraindustry variations in allocating resources. These variations usually involve time of publication, extent of geographic market, and structure of the newspaper organization.

While the process of allocating resources is important for understanding, the outcome of the process is just as important. After all, the printed material called a newspaper is what people buy and read. Since the content influences people and allows the newspaper firms to make money, the achievement of goals by a newspaper firm ultimately depends on the content of the newspaper itself.

Economics is concerned with studying the allocation of scarce resources in an abstract form. Economic analysis is interested in individual cases only as a way of getting at a more general understanding of behavior. Particular incidents that receive attention concern issues of management more than issues of economics. Perhaps the best distinction between economics and management is that economics involves drawing generalizations to explain why and how something happens, rather than how something should happen.

WHAT IS REGULATION?

While both economic factors and government regulation affect the performance of newspaper firms, they differ in that *economic factors constrain behavior, while regulations prescribe behavior.* A society imposes regulations on groups and individuals for various reasons. This book is concerned with economic and societal-based regulations that involve newspaper firms. This includes areas such as antitrust law, postal and labor regulation, and tax law.

Regulations dictate behavior, such as the postal requirement for a certain percentage of space to contain news for newspapers to have a second-class mail permit. They can also be applied as punishment. For example, the Sherman Act provides for punishing those who fix prices and share profits under certain conditions.

Governments create regulations in response to what they see as societal values or economic inefficiency. Antitrust legislation became law because of the growth of monopolies that were inefficient in resource distribution and that discriminated in pricing to the detriment of consumers. Whatever the reasons for creating regulations, they limit the discretionary power of managers and owners. The value of regulations may be disputed, but their impact cannot be ignored. This impact helps determine the process of producing and delivering newspapers. Regulation even has an indirect effect on content because of its relationship to allocating money.

Ultimately, regulation concerns the allocation of scarce resources. The key difference from economics is that regulation requires legislators, administrative officials, and judges to focus on individual cases. As a result, regulation is fact- and context-specific. While courts may consider generalized effects in laws and regulations, they need not do so, and only the U.S. Supreme Court has generalization of constitutional standards as a mission.

It might properly be said that regulation *reallocates* scarce resources. The postal subsidy for newspapers, for example, is largely paid by higher first class rates, a transfer of resources from one part of society to another. Regulation may be direct—provisions for overtime pay, for example—or it may be indirect, as exempting retail sales of newspapers from sales tax, which requires nothing of the firm.

WHAT IS A NEWSPAPER?

Even those who work at newspapers dispute the answer to this question. A standard lament of some newspaper reporters and editors is that newspapers have become a product. By the word *product*, they mean something to be produced and sold in the same way as shoes and soap. As Doug Underwood said:

> So maybe we shouldn't be worried as the pressures grow on newspapers to treat their readership as a market—to use the words of business consultants who have proliferated throughout the industry—and the news as a product to appeal to that market.
>
> Well, after spending more than a dozen years as a reporter with *The Seattle Times* and the Gannett Company, I'm plenty worried.[1]

Some journalists believe being a "product" cheapens a newspaper. They argue that newspapers serve the public with important political information. This importance is illustrated by the protection newspapers receive from the First Amendment. Calling a newspaper a product removes the special feeling that motivates some journalists.

At the heart of the journalists' concern is what Udell calls the "profit controversy."[2] Some journalists believe the need for profits at newspapers will interfere with the constitutionally protected service of providing public information. The concept of newspapers as products represents the profit approach, while the newspaper as service represents the public information approach. As Udell points out, the controversy need not exist. He says producing a newspaper that serves the public means the newspaper will be profitable in the long run. He adds that cutting editorial expenses for a quick profit will hurt circulation and profits in the long run because the paper will no longer serve the public adequately.

Whatever the answer to the "profit controversy," the debate continues as to whether a newspaper is a product or service. In reality it is both. An analogy can be found in physics. For years a debate raged as to whether light spread in waves or particles. Eventually, theories developed that included both behaviors. Newspapers have dual characteristics. They are tangible because a reader can hold a copy in his hand. So, papers are physically a product. Reading turns this tangible product into services called information and entertainment. To avoid confusion, this book will use the term *commodity* to describe newspapers, with the understanding that it encompasses newspapers as products and as services.[3]

As commodities, newspapers function in two types of marketplaces: an *economic market* and an *intellectual market*. The economic market is subdivided further into an *information market*, where a newspaper sells information (news, editorials, and advertising) to readers, and an *advertising market*, where the attention of these readers to advertising information is sold to advertisers. These two economic submarkets interact because readers use advertising as information. Also, advertisers would not be interested in buying newspaper space if they did not get attention from these readers.

The *intellectual market* has been called "the marketplace of ideas."[4] The modern expression of this concept is traced to John Milton.[5] The concept holds that ideas compete in a market for attention and acceptance by the public. Just as the consumers in an economic market will buy the commodity that best meets their demands, voters and officials will favor the ideas that work best for a society. Supply and demand in Milton's marketplace of ideas work basically the same as the "invisible hand" worked in Adam Smith's market for goods.[6]

Theoretically, ideas can enter the intellectual market through interpersonal communication or mediated communication. But, as a society's population increases, media become more important for gaining access to this market. A person with an idea can tell it directly to only a limited number of people. This interpersonal limitation contributes to the important role the First Amendment plays as a barrier to government closing access to the intellectual market through political control of the press.

Because mass media must have money to exist, the economic markets are inherently related to the intellectual market. This leads to an assumption that underlies this book: newspaper economic markets are as important to the U.S. society as the intellectual market. Economically weak newspapers can be manipulated and eliminated more easily than newspapers with adequate financial resources. However, economic strength alone will not guarantee adequate contributions to the intellectual market. Understanding the newspaper industry is crucial if the public wants to influence that industry to serve the intellectual market adequately.

This assumption does not necessarily apply to societies other than the United States, nor does it mean only commercial media companies should prosper in the United States. It is accepted here because the majority of newspapers in this country are commercial enterprises. Since this book is an effort to explain behavior within and among these firms, recognition of the fact that papers are businesses is a starting point. Arguments about whether society is served well by this system are beyond the domain of this examination.

While economic and intellectual markets differ in how they work, they share some limitations. *Newspapers in the United States tend to be geographically specific.* Each paper serves a primary area that is usually defined geographically, politically, or both. Historically, geographic limitations resulted from technological and financial constraints. The entire United States is difficult to serve because of its size. The few newspapers that do, such as *USA Today* and *The Wall Street Journal*, require large sums of money and elaborate production and distribution systems.

The role politics plays in the geographic limits of newspaper markets results from the relatively decentralized form of government in the United States. An individual in the United States is affected by a layered system of governments. Residents face laws and ordinances passed by federal, state, county, and city governments. They may also face government by school boards, township commissions, water districts, and other official bodies. People in Madison, Wisconsin usually do not care for news about the East Lansing, Michigan city council because the decisions of the East Lansing government rarely affect the residents of Madison. The governmental system creates a need for geographically specialized information markets.

In addition to being categorized by the types of markets, newspapers can also be broken down into physical characteristics. As commodities, newspapers can provide specialized information and advertising, or they can bundle several different types of information and advertising into one physical product. *Specialized newspapers* include financial newspapers, which concentrate on business, and ethnic newspapers, which deal with concerns of a certain group of people. Copies of *general circulation newspapers* are collections of information. These collections may also include sections of specialized information. For example, the average general circulation newspaper issue has a front section that includes international, national, state, and some local news. The paper usually includes a more locally oriented section about the city, county, or metropolitan area. In addition, such newspapers usually include sports and feature sections. Along with these news/feature sections will be an editorial section and a section of classified advertising. Increasingly, newspapers are adding even more specialized information, such as business and science sections.

Specialized newspapers have limited circulation, with advertising aimed only at that narrow group. General circulation newspapers, however, appeal to larger groups with people buying newspapers for sections of information that are of particular interest to them. The ability to divide a newspaper into specialized sections adds to its attraction. General circulation newspapers are bundles of information that allow readers to select what and when they want to read.

Although general circulation newspapers are designed to serve many narrowly defined groups of readers, these newspapers do not necessarily serve all groups within their geographic market. An ongoing criticism of U.S. newspapers, and news media in general, is that they neglect the needs of ethnic minorities. The 1969 Kerner Commission saw this as a failure to fulfill the societal role of the press.[7] Despite some improvement in coverage, critics charge that newspapers still need improvement in this area.[8]

THE PROCESS OF RUNNING A NEWSPAPER

Understanding the newspaper industry requires knowledge of how individual newspaper organizations work. Newspapers usually have up to five departments: the news-editorial, advertising, circulation, production, and business departments. Sometimes these departments may be combined. For example, the business and advertising departments are often one department. *These departments engage in six interrelated processes: preparing information, reproducing information, distributing information, promoting the newspaper to readers and advertisers, financing operations of the newspaper firm, and coordinating the other five processes.*

First, both news-editorial and advertising information must be prepared. The advertising, news-editorial, and business offices are involved in this process. The advertising department sells space and produces or processes advertisements. The news-editorial department produces news and editorial material. The business office distributes space between advertising and news-editorial information.

Once the advertising and news-editorial departments have prepared information, it must be reproduced and distributed. The production department reproduces copies of the newspaper. This involves the back shop, where the information from advertising and news-editorial are combined, and the pressroom, where the presses reproduce the newspaper. After reproduction, the circulation department distributes the copies. Newspaper firms have various types of circulation departments, but the most common are independent distributors, who are contracted by the circulation department, and in-house distributors, who work directly for the newspaper. Four common types of distribution are home delivery, coin-operated boxes, store and newsstand sales, and mail delivery.

Producing copies of a newspaper is not enough. People must be aware of what a newspaper has to offer them before they will buy copies or advertising space. This requires promotion. Promotion takes many forms, including advertising, making newspaper employees available as public speakers, providing newspapers to students in public schools, and sponsoring community-oriented events. Promotion in the information market aims to get people to read the newspaper and acquire a habit of doing so over an extended period. Promotion in the advertising market aims to get business executives to see newspaper advertising as more efficient at increasing sales than other forms of advertising.

As with the creation of information, the business department acts as a coordinator of the production, distribution, and promotion processes. Managers in the business office directly coordinate activities in other departments, but they also affect other processes by helping to determine the budgets for all departments.

Financing the newspaper firm is a process shared by three of the departments. Circulation collects money for the newspaper copies, while the advertising department bills its customers through the business department. The business department ultimately handles all revenues and pays all expenses.

These six processes are applicable to all media organizations, although the nature of each may changes. For example, public television has all six processes, but the financing comes from individual contributions and organizational grants.

Most newspaper organizations have some variation of the five departments and six processes, but size will determine how independent they are. At a small weekly newspaper, the publisher may sell advertising, write news stories, and collect bills. Size and nature of the medium define how departments are set up and how processes are carried out.

THE NATURE OF THE U.S. NEWSPAPER INDUSTRY

Newspapers can be classified in several ways. Publication cycle is the simplest. Newspapers can be *dailies*, which means they are published five or more days a week, but the majority of newspapers publish once or twice a week. These nondailies are usually grouped under the heading of *weeklies*. The United States had 1,626 dailies and 7,606 weeklies in 1989.[9] As shown in Table 1.1, the number of weeklies and dailies has declined compared to 1960, although the number of weeklies actually increased between 1970 and 1980.

The daily newspapers can be further divided into those that have Sunday editions, which included about 847 dailies in 1989, and those without. Dailies circulate either in the morning or evening, although some large ones publish throughout the day. The number of morning dailies and dailies with Sunday editions have increased since 1960, while the number of evening dailies has declined (see Table 1.1). The type of newspaper a city has depends primarily on the city's population, its proximity to other cities with newspapers, and the social and economic conditions of the population.

In addition to publication cycle, newspapers are often classified by the type of ownership. Newspapers owned by companies with more than one newspaper or other media organizations are called *group newspapers*. Nongroup newspapers are called *independents*. Even groups differ in their ownership makeup. *Publicly owned groups* sell stock to the public. *Privately owned (or "closely held") groups* do not sell stock to the public. Groups also differ on the basis of what other types of companies the parent corporations owns. *Media conglomerates* are corporations that own dif-

Table 1.1. Trends in Number of Newspapers from 1960 to 1989

Year	Total Number of Weeklies	Morning Dailies	Evening Dailies	Total* Dailies	Sunday Editions
1960	8,174	312	1,459	1,763	563
1965	8,061	320	1,444	1,751	562
1970	7,612	334	1,429	1,748	586
1975	7,612	339	1,436	1,756	639
1980	7,954	387	1,388	1,745	735
1985	7,704	482	1,220	1,676	798
1989	7,606	530	1,125	1,626	847

Note: Weeklies include both paid and free circulation newspapers.
*There were 29 all-day newspapers in 1989. They were listed in both the morning and evening columns but only once in the total column.
Sources: Editor & Publisher and National Newspaper Association, published in *Facts About Newspapers '90*, American Newspaper Publishers Association.

ferent types of media companies. Conglomerate generally refers to any corporation that owns a number of companies involved in different businesses.

A third classification of newspapers involves the number of newspapers in a given geographic market. Cities with two or more separately owned and operated newspapers are called *directly competitive* markets. In 1989, about 20 cities had directly competitive general circulation daily newspapers.[10] Another 21 cities had two newspapers that operated under *joint operating agreements*. The Newspaper Preservation Act, which passed Congress in 1970, allows joint operating newspapers to exist by exempting them from some aspects of antitrust laws. These joint operating agreement (JOA) newspapers share all processes except the creation of news and editorial material. The remaining dailies are in single-newspaper cities. These newspapers are often called *monopoly* newspapers, although this term is not strictly applicable. Figures for competitive weekly markets are unavailable, but one study of 901 suburbs found that 166 had nondailies and 20 of these had two or more nondailies.[11]

Circulation

In 1989, morning circulation totaled 40.7 million copies a day, while evening newspapers circulated 21.9 million copies. Sunday circulation topped 62 million in 1989, and weekly newspaper circulation averaged about 53 million per week.[12] While circulation grew in 1989 compared to the previous year, the overall trend revealed in Table 1.2 is a leveling off of circulation since 1960. This trend is misleading for a couple of reasons. First, if the nearly one and a half million circulation of *USA Today* is subtracted, the total 1989 daily circulation is below its 1970 level. Second, the population continues to grow as circulation stagnates. In 1987, one copy of a daily paper was printed each day for every 3.9 people, compared to one copy for every 2.8 people in 1946.

However, the downward trend in percentage of population who actually read newspapers may have leveled off. In 1987, a survey by the National Opinion Research Center found that 65 percent of adults said they read a newspaper the previous day. This was up from 63 percent in 1985, but was below the 78 percent response rate in 1970.[13] Readership often is measured by *penetration*, which is the percentage of households within a geographic area that buys newspaper copies.

Even if the trend in declining penetration has leveled, the number of people reading newspapers daily remains a concern for newspaper managers. The number of newspapers sold peaked in the 1920s and dropped below one per household in 1970.[14] The reasons for the decline are numerous and represent basic changes in how people get information.

Table 1.2. Trends in Newspaper Circulation from 1960 to 1989

Year	Total for Weeklies	Morning Dailies	Evening Dailies	Total Dailies	Sunday Editions
1960	20,974,338	24,028,788	34,852,958	58,881,746	47,698,651
1965	25,036,031	24,106,776	36,250,787	60,357,563	48,600,090
1970	27,857,332	25,933,783	36,173,744	62,107,527	49,216,602
1975	35,892,409	25,490,186	36,165,245	60,655,431	51,096,393
1980	42,347,512	29,414,036	32,787,804	62,201,840	54,671,755
1985	48,988,801	36,361,561	26,404,671	62,766,232	58,825,978
1989	52,919,846	40,759,016	21,890,202	62,649,218	62,008,154

Note: Weeklies include both paid and free circulation newspapers after 1980.
Sources: Editor & Publisher and National Newspaper Association, published in *Facts About Newspapers '90*, American Newspaper Publishers Association.

Weekly newspapers have fared better with circulation than dailies in recent years (see Tables 1.1 and 1.2). The paid and free circulation of weeklies in 1989 increased by 8 percent compared to 1985. This represents an upward trend from 1960, when the 8,174 weeklies averaged only 2,566 circulation per week. In 1989, weeklies averaged 6,958 copies per week. This growth resulted from several factors, including the increase of free circulation newspapers and the growth of suburbs as population centers where weeklies can prosper.

Prices for newspaper copies increased steadily between 1965 and 1989. The average daily newspaper cost 8 cents in 1965, with most newspapers selling for 10 cents. By 1980, the average had increased to 20 cents, with most selling for 20 or 25 cents. Nine years later, the average price of a daily was 30 cents, with 776 selling for 25 cents and 688 selling for 35 cents.[15]

Advertising

Trends in advertising involve bad news and good news for newspaper managers, as shown in Table 1.3. The bad news is that in 1989 newspapers received only 26 percent of all advertising dollars in the United States, compared to almost 39 percent in 1940 and about 28 percent in 1980. The good news is that advertising dollars spent on newspapers totalled $32.4 billion in 1989, which was up from $15 billion in 1980. The change in percentage during the past half century is accounted for primarily by the development of television, which had only 3 percent of all advertising expenditures in 1950 and 22 percent in 1988.[16]

Despite the decline in readership and shares of advertising shown in Table 1-3, newspapers still perform well financially. Of 14 publicly held newspaper groups reporting net income for 1987, 13 saw increases compared to 1986.[17]

Table 1.3. Shares of National Advertising Expenditures

	1960		1980		1989	
	Dollars (Millions)	% of Total	Dollars (Millions)	% of Total	Dollars (Millions)	% of Total
Newspaper	3,681	31	14,794	28	32,368	26
Television	1,627	14	11,469	21	26,891	22
Direct Mail	1,830	15	7,596	14	21,945	18
Radio	693	6	3,702	7	8,323	7
Magazines	909	8	3,149	6	6,716	5
Other	3,220	26	12,840	24	27,687	22
Total Dollars (Millions)	11,960		53,550		123,930	

Source: McCann-Erickson, Inc.

The geographic emphasis of newspaper advertising also has changed during the past half century. The percentage of advertising revenue from national advertisements has slipped with the growth of television. As national newspaper advertising has declined in importance, local advertising has grown. In 1989, 88.5 percent of newspaper advertising came from local sources, up from 75 percent in 1950.[18]

While dependence on local advertising has been growing, the distribution of that advertising among categories has changed. Local retail advertising made up only 40 percent of newspaper advertising in 1986, down from 56 percent in 1960. As this advertising has decline in importance, the use of preprinted inserts and the volume of classified advertising have increased. The growth in newspaper total advertising space between 1970 and 1980 can be accounted for almost entirely by the growth of inserts.[19] An example of classified advertising importance is a Midwest group of 12 suburban newspapers for which more than 50 percent of 1987 advertising income came from classified advertising.

Recent growth in advertising through the mails, known as *total market coverage*, is seen by many managers as a threat to local advertising revenue for newspapers. Between 1988 and 1989, the percentage of all advertising dollars spent on direct mail declined slightly from 17.9 to 17.8, but the total amount of dollars spent increased by 5 percent.[20] However, the percentage of all U.S. local advertising dollars given newspapers has remained stable at about 23 percent during the mid-1980s.

Advertising prices vary greatly. They are affected by such factors as level of competition, size of market, and economic activity within the market. For example, the largest 20 newspapers in the United States increased their ad rates by 8 percent at the beginning of 1988.[21] Yet a study of smaller daily newspapers found that the advertising rates adjusted for inflation were actually lower in 1980 than in 1959.[22] Because of variations in markets, generalizations about ad rates can be misleading.

Readers

The question of who reads newspapers is crucial to the newspaper industry. Newspaper managers must have the answer in order to know the needs and wants of their readers. Advertisers consider the answer important because different types of readers have interest in different types of goods and services. Even placement of advertising within a newspaper can depend on who reads what section. Not every reader of a general circulation newspaper is in the market for a Mercedes Benz, but the readers of some sections, such as business, may be more likely to fit this category.

Knowing who reads newspapers is important for understanding the economic markets of newspapers, but it is also important from the standpoint of understanding who receives information in the intellectual market. The political process in this country depends on people who participate in the intellectual market as consumers or suppliers. Scholars have expressed fear that our society is developing "knowledge gaps."[23] These gaps result when one class of citizen has more access to information than another and pose a danger of some groups going unrepresented in the political process. Newspapers can play a role in creating or removing these gaps.

Researchers usually describe readers by using *demographic* data. As Stone said in his summary of newspaper research, "Very little in the entire realm of mass communication research is as certain as this single finding: older, more educated and higher income individuals are the most likely newspaper clients."[24] These three demographic measures dominate as correlates of newspaper readership. When age, income, and education are taken into account, race and sex cease to be good predictors of readership.

In addition to demographics, readers are often categorized by *psychographics*, their psychological lifestyles. Studies in this area have shown that newspaper readers tend to be more active in church and community affairs and depend less on other people for their information.[25] Several studies found that readers tend to be more politically active and have different information demands compared to nonreaders.[26]

However, it would be a mistake to conclude from this research that newspapers are just read by older, wealthier, and more educated people. Since almost two-thirds of adults in a 1986 survey said they had read a newspaper the day before,[27] obviously age, income, and education alone do not determine readership. It may be that age, income, and education predict frequency of readership. The poor, young, and less educated may turn less frequently to newspapers because of the availability of television and radio news at no cost or because they feel uncomfortable with the level of newspaper writing.

Historical Trends in the Industry

Five economic trends in the newspaper industry stand out during the 20th century. Newspaper competition has declined, while group ownership has grown. Third, technology has reshaped newspaper organizations, content, and markets. Fourth, the growth of suburbs has restructured the industry. Fifth, the development of broadcast media has intensified competition for advertising.

In 1909-1910, more than half of all cities in the United States with dailies had directly competitive daily newspapers. Twenty years later this figure had fallen to about 20 percent. Only three percent of the cities had separately owned and operated daily newspapers by 1968.[28] This decline continues. As a result, most cities have only one general circulation newspaper. While these newspapers are not monopolies in the strictest sense of the term, the lack of direct newspaper competition gives the firm a high degree of *monopoly power*, which is discretionary power for making decisions. The greater the monopoly power, the less responsive a firm must be to users of its commodity. With newspapers, this power can have negative effects on a community's economic and intellectual markets.[29]

As competition has declined, group ownership has increased. Thirteen groups owned 62 dailies in 1910, which was about three percent of all dailies. By 1968, 159 groups owned 828 dailies, which was 47 percent of all dailies.[30] The number of groups shrunk slightly to 143 in 1987. Groups owned 76 percent of all dailies and controlled 82 percent of the daily circulation in 1989.[31] In 1989, Gannett was the largest group in terms of circulation with 82 dailies and total daily circulation of about six million.[32] Thomson, a Canadian firm with newspapers in the United States, had the greatest number of dailies in 1989, with 122.[33]

Not only have newspaper groups been growing, but they also have been buying other media firms. In 1987, Gannett owned 8 television and 18 radio stations. Knight-Ridder owned 8 television stations and one book company in addition to its 34 dailies and seven nondailies. The Times Mirror Company, which published *The Los Angeles Times* and seven other dailies in 1987, also owned more than 70 cable companies and 10 magazines.[34]

This growth of group ownership has created the concern among some critics that group concentration may affect the nature of the industry. Some fear that a few groups will own most or all of the newspapers and may purposefully manipulate what people read throughout the United States. Ownership in the U.S. newspaper industry is not very concentrated compared to other industries, such as the automotive and airlines industries. But critics point to Canada, where two groups owned half of all the daily newspapers in 1986,[35] as an example of what can happen.

Another possible ownership problem arises from *cross-ownership* within a market. In this situation, a company owns more than one type of media firm within the same geographic area. For example, a company may own the newspaper and a television station. Research indicates that this type of ownership may result in poorer media performance and less knowledgeable citizens.[36] The Federal Communications Commission has barred this cross-ownership, and the number of "grandfathered" markets with cross-ownership has been declining.

Concern also has developed during the past quarter century about conglomerates that own businesses other than newspapers. Examples of this type of corporation are Westinghouse and Gulf & Western. The fear is that corporate management will prevent their media companies from pursuing stories about their nonmedia companies. In effect, this allows business concerns in nonmedia industries to limit newspapers' contributions to the intellectual market. While conglomerates had not acquired newspaper companies to any great degree by the end of of the 1980s, the high profit level of some newspaper groups have made them excellent targets for acquisition by other types of corporations.

A corollary concern of conglomerate ownership is the interconnection among boards of trustees that control corporations. Many of the same people sit on more than one board. Thus, trustees that sit on an oil company board and a media company board may try to influence a media company to limit coverage of environmental issues related to the oil industry. Such behavior is difficult to detect but holds the potential for limiting information in the intellectual market.

A third trend, which holds true for almost all industries, concerns the impact of technology. The very existence of newspapers as a mass medium depends on the ability of presses to print a large number of copies in a short period. The development of linotype machines during the 19th century, the increasing speed and capacity of presses during the 19th and 20th centuries, and the development of offset printing during this century all affected the physical nature of newspapers.

More recently, the use of computers for writing and typesetting and the development of satellite transmission of content have changed the industry. Computers have bridged the writing and editing of news and the creation of the plates that go on the presses. Satellite transmission allows national newspapers to exist. *USA Today*, *The Wall Street Journal*, and *The New York Times* beam their newspaper content to printing plants across the country and deliver copies of the same newspaper in Los Angeles and Washington, D.C. on the same day. This ability to print at distant locations can redefine the geographic market and relates to the fourth major trend in the newspaper industry—growth of the suburbs.

Technological change and development of suburbs as population centers have redefined the meaning of local news. Traditionally, local news meant information about the city and, to some degree, the county in which a newspaper was published. Now, with many residents of large metropolitan areas living in one city and working in another, local has a much broader meaning. A daily in a metropolitan central city no longer can be designed just for one city. It increasingly must cover the suburbs, where it faces competition from dailies and weeklies. Add the national newspapers to the suburban newspapers and the metropolitan area has become a more competitive and dynamic newspaper market during the past 25 years.

Many editors and publishers consider competition among newspapers in different cities within and around a metropolitan area to be an important factor in the survival of their newspapers.[37] This type of intercity competition has been called *umbrella competition* because each larger newspaper forms an umbrella of coverage and competition over the smaller ones below.[38]

The fifth significant trend of the 20th century is the development of broadcast media as competitors for advertising. Both radio and television have affected the distribution of advertising revenues among media, but television affected newspaper more than radio did. Radio took some advertising from newspapers, but the overall impact on the newspaper industry was limited.[39] This may have resulted from radio's limited life span as a true mass medium. The development of television in the early 1950s made radio a fragmented medium that functions primarily as a specialized entertainment service and adjunct to the sound recording industry.

Television is a different matter. The distribution of advertising revenue given earlier in the chapter shows the movement of national advertising from newspapers to television. Some researchers suggest that most or all of the advertising television has captured came from newspapers.[40] Others contend that television actually generated advertising revenues that would not have been spent otherwise.[41] The strength of television for advertisers has been its national mass audience. Predictably large audiences for network shows as an every night occurrence are a thing of the past as more homes connect to cable systems and acquire video cassette recorders. These two developments have created the potential for television to follow the path taken by radio toward becoming a more specialized and fragmented medium. If that occurs, newspapers could profit. The growth of newspaper groups and the development of national newspapers makes the industry more attractive as a national mass medium for advertising.

OF NEWSPAPERS AND SHOES

Growing concentration in the newspaper industry is similar to that in other industries. Such developments in the oil, steel, and railroad industries during the late 19th century contributed to the development of antitrust laws because of concerns about the impact of concentration on consumers. These concerns become even more important with newspapers because of the role they play in the intellectual market. The First Amendment protects newspapers from most government intervention, but this protection is not total. Antitrust laws cover competition in the newspaper economic markets, while the intellectual market benefits from unequivocal First Amendment protection, which means newspapers have special responsibilities. Society does not consider newspaper firms to be the same as shoe companies. Participatory government is not dependent upon good footwear.

The Supreme Court affirmed First Amendment protection for newspapers in the intellectual market in Miami Herald v. Tornillo.[42] In this case, the Court ruled Florida's "right of reply" law unconstitutional. The law required newspapers to publish replies by political candidates who had been attacked by the newspaper. The plaintiff argued that most newspapers have monopolies, which limit access to the intellectual market of politics. In the decision against Tornillo, who was a candidate for the Florida legislature, Chief Justice Warren Burger quoted an earlier case, which said:

> The power of a privately owned newspaper to advance its own political, social, and economic views is bounded by only two factors: first, the acceptance of a sufficient number of readers—and hence advertisers—to assure financial success; and, second, the journalistic integrity of its editors and publishers.[43]

Despite the observation of the courts, another possible constraint on newspapers has developed. Scholars have argued that the concentration of newspapers, and the corresponding limited access to the intellectual market, creates a *social responsibility* to cover all sides of a controversial issue.[44] Although this responsibility is not accepted by all scholars,[45] and certainly not practiced by all newspapers, it has become part of the newspaper industry's culture. The role of this responsibility can be seen in the standard of "objectivity" applied by many newspapers.

The social responsibility concept for the intellectual markets developed as a response to concentration in the economic markets. Recently, some have argued that social responsibility can actually help increase profits in the information and advertising markets.[46] This argument asserts that social responsibility basically involves a return of service to society by the press for the special protection it receives.

The First Amendment is not the only reason the newspaper and other industries differ. Other differences result from the nature of newspaper's economic markets. Newspapers are joint commodities, and they tend to be natural monopolies.

A newspaper is a joint commodity because it serves two economic markets with one physical product. This relationship complicates matters. Shoes are made and sold to whoever will pay a price that covers the cost of making them. Subscription prices for newspapers usually bring in less revenue than the cost of collecting and printing the news. However, the attention of readers that the news brings can be sold to advertisers. The revenue from advertising must cover the cost of selling and printing advertising, cover the excess cost of gathering news, and provide a profit.

This joint commodity nature is related to the tendency of newspapers to acquire monopoly power within a narrow geographic market. Some scholars have argued that newspapers are natural monopolies. *A natural monopoly occurs when one firm is so efficient that all other firms within the geographic market go out of business.* Economists attribute natural monopoly to *economies of scale*, which means the more of a product you produce the less each additional unit costs. Newspapers appear to have economies of scale with printing.[47] Much of the printing cost of a newspaper must be paid just to print the first copy (see Chapter 3). After that first copy, the average cost of each additional copy drops quickly. Thus, it is more efficient for one newspaper company to print all of the issues for a market than for two newspapers to do so using two presses. Some newspapers also receive scale economies for pages in an issue. The costs of adding pages to an issue declines quickly after a certain number.

Although the economies of scale contribute to the monopoly power in newspaper markets, the joint commodity nature of newspapers plays a greater role in the absence of direct newspaper competition within a city. The fact that readers buy and read newspapers for advertising means increases in advertising lead to increases in circulation. The newspaper with more advertising in a market tends to attract more readers. Because it attracts more readers, it has more reader attention to sell to advertisers. This means it attracts more advertising, which in turn attracts more readers, and so on. The result is a tendency for newspapers that trail in advertising to fall even further behind as time passes. Since advertising accounts for about 70 to 80 percent of newspaper revenue, the leading newspaper gets a larger proportion of the revenue in a market. The interaction of circulation and advertising is called a *circulation spiral*.

The impact of this circulation spiral on revenue is enhanced by competition's effect on expenses. Newspapers in markets with separately owned newspapers must keep the quality of their commodity competitive. This means spending more money on news and editorial content than they would if they were the only newspaper in the market.[48] This increase in cost for the leading newspaper can be offset by economies of scale savings, but the trailing newspaper does not have this advantage.

As a result of several economic forces, only one daily newspaper survives the competition within most cities. After one of two dailies goes out of business, the high cost of starting a large general circulation newspaper keeps other companies from entering the market. These costs create *high barriers to entry.*

A handful of cities continue to have direct competition because a few circumstances exempt markets, often only temporarily, from these economic forces. A booming economy with its growing advertising base can support two newspapers for as long as the base continues to grow. A densely populated metro area, such as New York, has enough residents within a given geographic area that a newspaper can find a niche to serve. In effect, two newspapers do not really compete for the same group of readers. One serves one type of reader, while the other serves a different type. The population density helps to hold down delivery costs. The failure of *The Bulletin* in Philadelphia, the closing of the *Los Angeles Herald Examiner*, and the JOA formed between *The Detroit News* and *Detroit Free Press* indicate a city must be as densely populated as Boston or as large as Chicago to support newspapers with separate niches. The third possibility for continued direct competition is a subsidy from another source. For example, *The Washington Times* is not self-supporting. Its excess of costs over revenues is paid by its owners. From a practical viewpoint, these three exceptions don't hold much hope for those who would like to see continued direct competition. Economies don't boom forever and few organizations are willing to pay the high subsidies needed for large general circulation newspapers.

An example of entrepreneurship brightened hopes for a revival of competition briefly in 1989, as the Ingersoll company started a second daily in St. Louis. The effort to generate competition within a large city gained much attention in the industry but ended on April 25, 1990, less than a year after it started, with the last edition of the *Sun.*

SUMMARY

Newspaper companies do not exist in vacuums. They are open subsystems within larger systems. The newspaper subsystem has five departments with six processes that produce a commodity. The larger system is an environment where the social, economic, cultural, and political needs of society interact with newspaper companies. The interaction occurs in two types of markets: economic and intellectual. Economic markets fall into two types: the information market for readers and the advertising market for advertising space.

The interaction of newspaper firms with the market and society has created and been affected by several trends within the 20th century. The trends concerning readers, advertisers, ownership technology, regulation, and competition will determine the nature of newspapers in the next century. These trends form the basis for the other chapters in this book, where they will be developed further.

Newspapers influence society and their market with the commodities they produce. In turn, the society and their markets influences them with constraints on the actions of owners and managers. This type of symbiotic relationship defines and controls the content readers receive daily as a reflection of the their world. Understanding the relationship will help one better understand the accuracy of that reflection.

ENDNOTES

1. Doug Underwood, "When MBAs Rule the Newsrooms," *Columbia Journalism Review*, March/April 1988, pp. 23-30.
2. Jon G. Udell, *The Economics of the American Newspaper* (New York: Hastings House, Publishers, 1978).
3. Using the term "commodity" instead of product or service for a newspaper was suggested by Bill Blankenburg. The authors appreciate his suggestion. The development of the term in this book does not necessarily represent Professor Blankenburg's use of "commodity."
4. The authors thank Bill Blankenburg for suggesting "intellectual market" as a term for the marketplace of ideas concept. The ideas related to this term that are developed in this book do not necessarily reflect Professor Blankenburg's use of the term.
5. John Milton, *The Prose Work of John Milton*, ed. J. A. St. John, Vol. 24 (London: George Bell & Sons, 1883).
6. J. Edward Gerald, *The Social Responsibility of the Press* (Minneapolis, MN: The University of Minnesota Press, 1963).
7. Kerner Commission, *Report of the National Advisory Board on Civil Disorders* (New York: Bantam, 1968).
8. See Carolyn Martindale, "Changes in Newspaper Images of Black Americans," *Newspaper Research Journal*, Winter 1990, pp. 40-50; Mary Alice Sentman, "Black and White: Disparity in Coverage by Life Magazine from 1937 to 1972," *Journalism Quarterly*, 60:501-509 (Autumn 1983); Carolyn Martindale, "Coverage of Black Americans in Five Newspapers since 1950," *Journalism Quarterly*, 62:321-328, 438 (Summer 1985); and Carolyn Martindale, *The White Press and Black America* (Westport, CT: Greenwood Press, 1986).
9. American Newspaper Publishers Association, *'90 Facts About Newspapers* (Washington, DC: American Newspaper Publishers Association, 1990).
10. *1990 Editor & Publisher International Year Book* (New York: Editor & Publisher, 1990).
11. Stephen Lacy, Walter E. Niebauer, James M. Bernstein, and Tuen-yu Lau, unpublished data, 1987.

12. *'90 Facts About Newspapers, op. cit.*
13. Gene Goltz, "Reviewing A Romance With Readers Is the Biggest Challenge For Many Newspapers," *presstime*, February 1988, pp. 16-22.
14. Leo Bogart, *Press and Public: Who Reads What, When, Where and Why in American Newspapers* (Hillsdale, NJ: Lawrence Erlbaum Associates, Inc., 1981).
15. *'90 Facts About Newspapers, op. cit.*
16. Robert J. Coen, "Estimated Annual U.S. Advertising Expenditures 1935-1989," report prepared for *Advertising Age*, McCann-Erickson, Inc., 1990.
17. Andrew Radolf, "Annual newspaper group financial reports," *Editor & Publisher*, March 5, 1988, pp. 16-17, 19, 45.
18. Coen, *op. cit.*
19. Bogart, 1981, *op. cit.*
20. "Circulation Results Mixed, Advertising Up Slightly in 1989," *presstime*, May 1990, p.90.
21. "Ad Rates Up 8 Percent," *presstime*, March 1988, p. 50.
22. B. E. Wright and John M. Lavine, "The Constant Dollar Newspaper: An Economic Analysis Covering the Last Two Decades," Inland Daily Press Association, Chicago, IL, 1982.
23. P.J. Tichenor, G. A. Donohue, and C.N. Olien, "Mass Media Flow and Differential Growth in Knowledge," *Public Opinion Quarterly*, 34:159-170 (1970).
24. Gerald Stone, *Examining Newspapers: What Research Reveals About America's Newspapers* (Newbury Park, CA: Sage Publications, 1987).
25. Bruce H. Westley and Werner J. Severin, "A Profile of the Daily Newspaper Non-reader," *Journalism Quarterly*, 41:45-50 (Winter 1964).
26. Stone, *op. cit.*
27. Goltz, *op. cit.*
28. Raymond B. Nixon, "Trends in U.S. Newspaper Ownership: Concentration with Competition," *Gazette*, 14:181-93 (1968).
29. Bruce M. Owen, *Economics and Freedom of Expression* (Cambridge, MA: Ballinger, 1975).
30. Nixon, *op. cit.*
31. *90'Facts About Newspapers, op. cit.*
32. *Ibid.*
33. *Ibid.*
34. *presstime*, January 1987, p. 29.
35. *1987 Editor & Publisher International Yearbook*, (New York: Editor & Publisher, 1987).
36. Guido H. Stempel III, "Effects on Performance of Cross-Media Monopoly," *Journalism Monographs*, No. 29, June 1973; and William T. Gromley, *The Effects of Newspaper-Television Cross-Ownership on News Homogeneity* (Chapel Hill, NC: University of North Carolina, 1976).
37. Stephen Lacy, "Competition Among Metropolitan Daily, Small Daily and Weekly Newspapers," *Journalism Quarterly* 61:640-44, 742 (Autumn 1984).
38. James N. Rosse, "Economic Limits of Press Responsibility," Discussion paper, Stanford University: Studies in Industry Economics, No. 56, 1975.

39. Stephen Lacy, "Effect of Intermedia Competition on Daily Newspaper Content," *Journalism Quarterly*, 65:95-99 (Spring 1988).
40. Maxwell E. McCombs, "Mass Media in the Marketplace," *Journalism Monographs*, No. 24, August 1972.
41. Roger G. Noll, Merton J. Peck, and John J. McGowan, *Economic Aspects of Television Regulation* (Washington, DC: The Brookings Institute, 1973).
42. *Miami Herald v. Tornillo*, 418 U.S. 241 (1974).
43. *Columbia Broadcasting System, Inc. v. Democratic National Committee*, 412 U.S. 94, (1973).
44. Robert D. Leigh, ed. *A Free and Responsible Press: A General Report on Mass Communication: Newspapers, Radio, Motion Pictures, Magazines, and Books by the Commission on Freedom of the Press* (Chicago: The University of Chicago Press, 1947; reprinted ed., Chicago: Midway, 1974); and Frederick S. Siebert, Theodore Peterson and Wilbur Schramm, *Four Theories of the Press* (Urbana: University of Illinois Press, 1956).
45. John C. Merrill and S. Jack Odell, *Philosophy and Journalism* (New York: Longman, 1983).
46. John M. Lavine and Daniel B. Wackman, *Managing Media Organizations* (New York: Longman, 1988).
47. William B. Blankenburg, "Newspaper Scale and Newspaper Expenditures," *Newspaper Research Journal*, Winter 1989, pp. 97-103.
48. Barry R. Litman and Janet Bridges, "An Economic Analysis of Daily Newspaper Performance," *Newspaper Research Journal*, Spring 1986, pp. 9-26; and Stephen Lacy, "The Effects of Intracity Competition on Daily Newspaper Content," *Journalism Quarterly*, 64:281-290 (Summer-Autumn 1987).

2

Newspaper Demand

Most people initially encounter the concepts of supply and demand as a collection of diagrams drawn by a college professor standing in front of several hundred drowsy sophomores. As uninspiring as the first encounter may be, the concepts are central to understanding commerce in the United States. Both economists and business people are concerned with the very basic questions of what people will buy and how those goods will be provided.

Although the questions are simple, the answers are complex. This complexity exists even more noticeably in the newspaper industry, where the commodity interacts with demand in three different but related markets. This chapter will examine the concept of demand in these three markets. Supply will then be dealt with in the following chapter.

DEMAND IN THE INFORMATION MARKET

In its simplest form, *demand* is how many people in a market will buy a given commodity, product, or service. Economic theory states that four factors affect demand: the price of a commodity, the price of substitutes and complements, the income of the individual, and taste.[1] Just which factor is most important in determining demand depends on the commodity and the market. Of the four factors, taste is probably the most important for newspapers, but the other three still affect demand. Taste includes the demand readers have for various forms of content.

Price as a factor of demand is not as important for newspapers as it is for other commodities for several reasons. First, most newspaper readers do not buy newspapers one at a time. They pay on a weekly, monthly, or yearly basis. Thus, they do not react to newspaper copy price changes in the same way they react to changes in the price of hamburger. Second, most newspapers do not have readily acceptable substitutes. With a few exceptions, cities tend to have only one locally produced newspaper.

Without good substitutes, price comparisons for purchase decisions lose importance. Economic theory of demand is based on the assumption that consumers are indifferent to the homogeneous goods produced by various firms in a market. Thus, only price plays a role in selecting which good to buy. Third, many readers view newspapers as necessities because of their contribution to the intellectual market. They believe a good citizen has a responsibility to keep up with what is happening in government and a newspaper is one of the best ways of doing this. Fourth, many people buy newspapers out of habit, a behavior built up over an extended period of time.

Despite these exceptions, demand in the newspaper information market does respond to some degree to price changes; it simply doesn't happen as often or extensively as it does in markets for other commodities or products. When circulation prices increase, some readers stop subscribing. If there is no ready substitute for a newspaper, which is usually the case, the aggregate impact of a price change may be relatively slight. This means the demand is *inelastic* with respect to price. Elasticity represents the degree to which a change in a factor affects demand.[2] If the percentage change in circulation divided by percentage change in price is greater than one, the commodity is *elastic*. If the ratio is less than one, it is inelastic. If it equals one, the commodity has *unit elasticity*.

Figure 2.1 shows an inelastic demand curve, an elastic demand curve, and a demand curve with unit elasticity for a newspaper's information market. Curve D_1 is inelastic because the decrease in price from P_1 to P_2 results in a less than proportionate increase in circulation from C_1 to C_2. Curve D_2 has unit elasticity. The price decrease from P_1 to P_2 has a proportionate increase in circulation from C_3 to C_4. Curve D_3 represents elastic demand. A decline in prices from P_1 to P_2 creates a disproportionately larger increase in circulation from C_5 to C_6.

The extent of the impact of price is determined by the other three factors mentioned in economic theory. The greater the number of good substitutes for a newspaper, the more elastic the demand curve. Demand also becomes more elastic as the price of the substitute decreases. The more particular the taste, the more inelastic the demand.

The second factor for determining demand is the price of substitutes and complements. *Substitutes* are commodities that can be used in lieu of another commodity. Butter and margarine are substitutes. In mass media, two newspapers in the same market can be good substitutes, while newspapers from separate cities are limited substitutes. Substitutability is a matter of degree and is based on the nature of the commodity. The more similar the newspapers in content and publication cycle, the more substitutable they are. In reality, few perfect substitutes exist in mass media because of variations in the nature of commodities. The nature of

Price

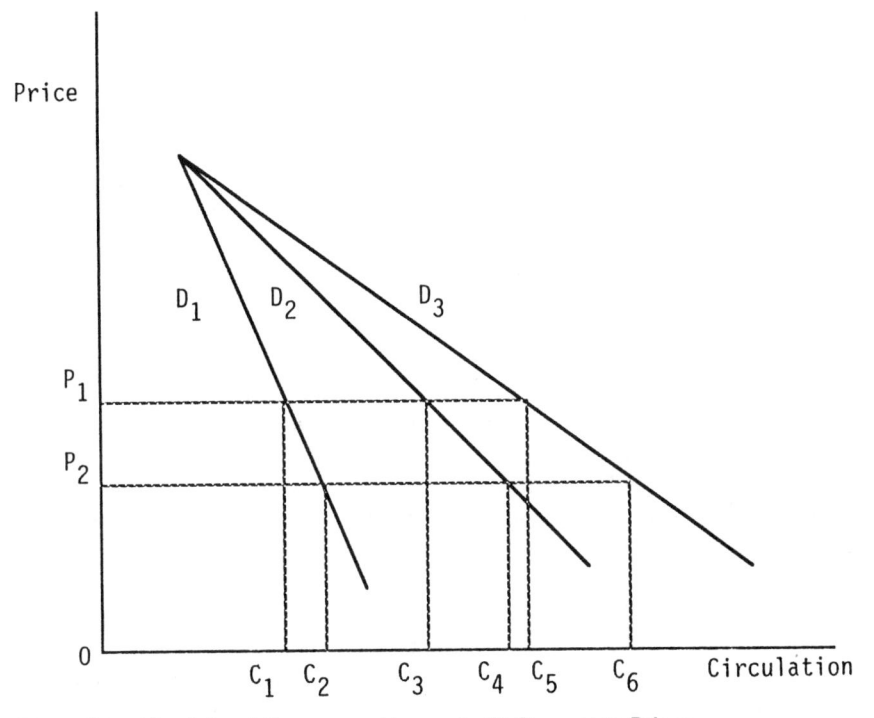

Figure 2.1. Elasticity of Newspaper Demand with Respect to Prices
The change in circulation that results from a change in price from P_1 to P_2 is shown for an inelastic demand curve (D_1), a demand curve with unit elasticity (D_2), and an elastic curve (D_3).

television news makes it an imperfect substitute for newspapers. Some people may substitute local TV news for newspapers, but most will not.

Complementary commodities are used in conjunction with another commodity, or at least have a relationship so that the increased use of one commodity increases the use of another. Some scholars, for example, have argued that radio news in the 1930s and 1940s actually encouraged use of newspapers. Radio news drew attention to an event or issue, and people sought additional information about that issue from newspapers.[3] The complementary role of media will vary from individual to individual, but it is not unusual for people to use more than one medium to collect information about especially pertinent stories.

The relationship between prices of substitutes is positive. As the price for a substitute increases, a commodity's demand will increase and the demand for the substitute will fall. The relationship between prices of complements is negative. As price for a complement increases, demand for the commodity declines and so does demand for the complement. Thus, if the *San Antonio Light* increases its home delivery price and the *San Antonio Express* does not, demand for the *Light* will decline and demand for the *Express* will increase because they are relatively close substitutes.

In a sense, the information and advertising markets are complements. Significant circulation declines can mean advertising demand declines and vice versa, depending upon how much monopoly power a firm holds in a market. The reaction of demand for a commodity when the price of a substitute changes is called the *price cross-elasticity of demand*.[4] The relationships occur as the other three factors remain constant.

The impact of individual *income* on demand is obvious. As a household earns more money, it can buy more of what it already buys and buy commodities that it was not purchasing before. The impact of income is related to price of commodities. It is real income, adjusted for inflation, and not the absolute amount of income that is important. If income increases 5 percent and the average costs of everything goes up 10 percent, the household will have to cut demand rather than increase it.

The fourth factor, *taste*, is a catchall term that represents how a person's background and attitudes interact with the nature and quality of a commodity. A reader's education, occupation, age, and other demographic factors affect his attitude about a commodity. The attitude and perceptions of the commodity's quality can be affected by advertising. While taste may be the most important demand factor in newspaper information markets, it is the least developed by economic theory.[5] Discussion of taste for newspapers often revolves around the concept of newspaper quality. The effect of quality on demand involves the taste of readers in relation to the nature of the newspaper content. Because of the importance of quality in determining demand, reader's taste and the nature of newspaper content will be analyzed separately.

Newspaper Readers

The process readers use to evaluate newspapers is an important aspect of demand. This complex process results from three factors: the varied use of information by readers, whether the content of newspapers is specialized or a collection of information, and the number of people within a purchasing unit who contribute to the purchasing decision. Newspapers meet many different needs and wants and are evaluated along several dimensions. They are usually bought by a household rather than just one individual.

Economists describe the varied uses of information by newspaper readers with the word "taste." But it is difficult to explain just what taste is. Studies in an area of communication research called "uses and gratifications" have tried to answer the question of why people acquire information. Basically, the answer is because they get utility from it. The problem with existing uses and gratifications research, and a source of criticism of this area, is that it has yet to develop an effective theory detailing the actual process of using media content. It is, therefore, difficult to predict and understand individual demand for newspapers in the information market on the basis of uses and gratification research.[6]

Other content use categories preceded uses and gratifications and are sometimes the basis for analyzing why people buy newspapers. One typology deals with the time involved in using information. News can have an *immediate reward* and a *delayed reward*.[7] With immediate-reward news, the reader uses it as it is read, or soon after. Delayed-reward news is useful in understanding one's environment. It is an investment that yields returns across time as information is recalled. The difference between the two types of rewards is not clear-cut or constant. What gives an immediate reward to some will give a delayed reward to others. This approach has some intuitive appeal on an individual basis, but it becomes difficult to apply in the aggregate because the reward nature of news varies from individual to individual.

Another way of defining demand is to identify characteristics of individuals that are associated with reasons for using newspapers. The demographic and psychographic research mentioned in Chapter 1 represents efforts by researchers to understand demand in newspaper information markets. This type of research looks for correlations between people's characteristics and media use. These correlations are then used for predicting who will buy newspapers and in designing promotion campaigns. For example, studies have found a relationship between community ties, such as home ownership, and newspaper readership. Communities with more mobile populations will tend to have lower newspaper use.[8] The underlying process is one of readers needing information to monitor the events that are important to them and to make decisions about these events. In effect, commitment to a community results in a need or want for information about that community.

Based on research in the areas of uses and gratifications and community and civic commitment, the typology presented in Table 2.1 is a handy abstraction of how people use information. It has two dimensions: type of use and timing of use. Type of use has four subheadings and timing has two.

The first type of use is *surveillance*, which is a way of keeping up with what is happening in the reader's environment. Stories about crime and regularly scheduled government meetings usually fit here. Most readers are not affected directly by any one particular crime or meeting, but they want to be aware of events and issues that occur in their neighborhoods and cities. This monitoring type of information use is wide-ranging.

Table 2.1. Dimensions of Information Use

I. Type of Use

    A. *Surveillance*—People use information to check the environment to see what issues and events might interest them. This monitoring can identify new information about old issues and events of interest, or it can identify new areas of interest.

    B. *Decision making*—This is the purposeful use of information to decide on a course of action or to form an opinion or belief. Information that a person encounters is usually judged to be relevant or not relevant to the decisions. This use involves seeking specific information about a specific decision.

    C. *Entertainment*—Information used for entertainment may include, but is not limited to, material that is enjoyable, such as movies, television shows, books, and feature articles. This type of information provides utility to a user from the material itself. The benefits flow just from the acquiring and understanding of the information and not from its application to another process. The entertainment need not be pleasant. For example, a well written feature on a person or an account of a crime might both fit in this category. This use has emotional effects on the user.

    D. *Social-Cultural Interaction*—Communication is a central part of group membership. Social and cultural groups share information in a process that allows members to identify common ground on which they can establish interaction. The exchange may be about serious issues, such as the goals and processes of the group, or about less serious matters, such as shared interest in sports. Such group communication will take many forms. All such communication that helps either to bond members or to separate members from groups fits under this heading.

II. Timing of Use

    A. *Short-term*—Information can be used immediately in the four ways listed above. In one sense it is consumed because the majority of bits of information we receive is used and then forgotten. However, all is not forgotten. Some is retained. Information becomes short-term when it serves its use as it is taken in by the user. Examples are the sports scores and many of the comics in newspapers. It is difficult to define when the short-term ends, but as a rule the term means the time period during which a user is acquiring information from the source of the information. This could be during a television show or during the 20 minutes in the morning a person allots to reading the newspaper.

    B. *Medium-term*—Information that is used at times other than following its acquisition but before it enters long-term memory is considered medium-term in nature. This means information that does not fit into the short-term time frame. A person might read a story about a political campaign. Recalling that information during a discussion later in the day fits this category.

    C. *Long-term*—This information is committed to long-term memory and used at periods more than 48 hours after its acquisition. This type of information is usually used more than once. It includes the type of information used in performing one's work, as well as general information about such things as laws and even spelling. This type of information is crucial to social and cultural interaction.

Particular topics vary with individuals, but some areas, such as weather, have a wide appeal.

The second use of newspaper information is *decision making.* This refers to very specific decisions that readers make. Decisions of any type involve degrees of uncertainty. Uncertainty is reduced by developing information about that decision and its possible outcomes. So, when a person has to decide who to vote for, newspapers become a source for identifying the areas that are important for voting and for finding the information that will help reduce the uncertainty of choosing a candidate.

This process of decision making plays an important role in the utility of newspaper advertising as information. Most newspaper advertising tends to be very specific about what is on sale and how much products and services cost. When a reader needs to buy car tires, for example, the advertisements in the newspaper become useful for deciding where to get the best price. This type of use helps to explain why some readers value advertising content as highly as the news stories in newspapers.

A third type of use for newspaper information is *social-cultural interaction.* Communication is a binding process for any group membership. Communication allows members of groups to evaluate others in that group and to define their relationships with individuals and the group as a whole. The topics of discussion and the positions held about topics play an important role in this integration. Information about these topics often comes from mass media. For example, the Monday morning discussions in an office about the football games or movies watched over the weekend serves not only as a diversion, but as a group affirmation process. Discussion about an area of common interest reinforces individual feelings of group membership. Often, the discussion includes what was read about the games or movies in the newspapers, as well as what was observed while watching. Similar discussions about community issues, business, or movies serve as a way of defining relationships within a group.

The final use of newspaper information is *entertainment.* This term is used here in a broad sense. Entertainment is anything that gives the reader some utility but doesn't fit into the other categories. This use could include something as obviously entertaining as the comics and crossword puzzles, but it might also be a feature story about a local elderly man who collects cold drink cans and gives the money to the United Way. Entertainment deals with emotional reactions to information, while decision making is a more rational use of information.

These four types make up one dimension of newspaper information use; the second dimension involves timing. This idea is drawn from Schramm's immediate-reward and delayed-reward concepts mentioned above. Each of the four types of information can be used during the short term, medium term, or long term.

Short-term use means the information returns its reward during the actual reading. Reading a comic strip might fit this use. Medium-term means the information is recalled after it was read, but it does not enter long-term memory. Immediate discussion following a presidential debate about some of the comments could fit this category, although some such comments may enter long-term memory. Long-term memory involves information that is used more than 48 hours following its reading. Particularly noteworthy comments during a presidential debate would fit this category.

Some long-term information retention is deliberate, such as following the New Hampshire primary in January for a decision about the presidential candidates in November. Other information, such as trivia, just seems to stick in one's brain. It is not intention but actual use that defines these categories.

Combining these two dimensions results in 12 types of information use. These types provide a classification system for the ways people use information in newspapers, but they are not mutually exclusive. Information can have more than one type of use and be applicable both immediately and on a delayed basis. Reading a review of a movie can be entertaining and also useful for deciding later that week if the reader wants to pay $5 to see the movie. Following political campaigns often has immediate value as entertainment and for social-cultural integration, but it may also contribute to voting decisions. The 12 categories are not discrete; they overlap. One could argue that the information that best meets readers' demands is information that serves more than one use. This efficient use of space and time might make one newspaper, or other news medium, more appealing than a competitor's commodity. Television may well be a more appealing news medium for some people because it can provide information that entertains, allows surveillance, and helps with social-cultural interaction all in a short time.

Despite suggestions of classification systems from research, little theory exists to explain and predict individual demand for newspapers. However, economists and managers are more interested in aggregate demand. The traditional economic explanation of consumer demand, which is called utility theory, deals with consumer decisions based on price. Taste is assumed constant. With newspapers, taste plays a more important role. Traditional utility theory is not entirely satisfactory in explaining reader demand.

A model of aggregate demand for news has been developed that emphasizes the quality of the product.[9] In the model, quality is a function of how well the newspaper serves the needs and wants of readers. Wants and needs are specified by the aggregate group of demand attributes held by all readers. Circulation is a function of quality, which is dependent on the newspaper's content. Content quality is related to how much money the newspaper organization spends on the commodity.

The model states that a reader develops an overall impression of the newspaper based on how well its content correlates with his or her group of demand attributes. These attributes are a collection of information needs and wants that can be fulfilled by newspaper content. Readers have a minimal level of acceptable quality for newspapers, based on these attributes. If a newspaper does not meet these minimal standards, a reader will not buy the paper. He will find a substitute or not get the information at all. The minimal level of acceptable quality varies from person to person, but as quality declines, more people have similar minimal levels.

The model also suggests that the demand curve representing the relationship between circulation and quality for a given newspaper is kinked. A kinked curve is one that changes slope at a given point. The demand curve for a given newspaper based on quality is shown in Figure 2.2. To the left of point A, circulation (demand) falls faster with respect to quality than to the right. This is based on the assumption that newspapers may reach a level of quality below point A where readers find the newspaper so inferior that they will either turn to other media or just stop taking the newspaper.

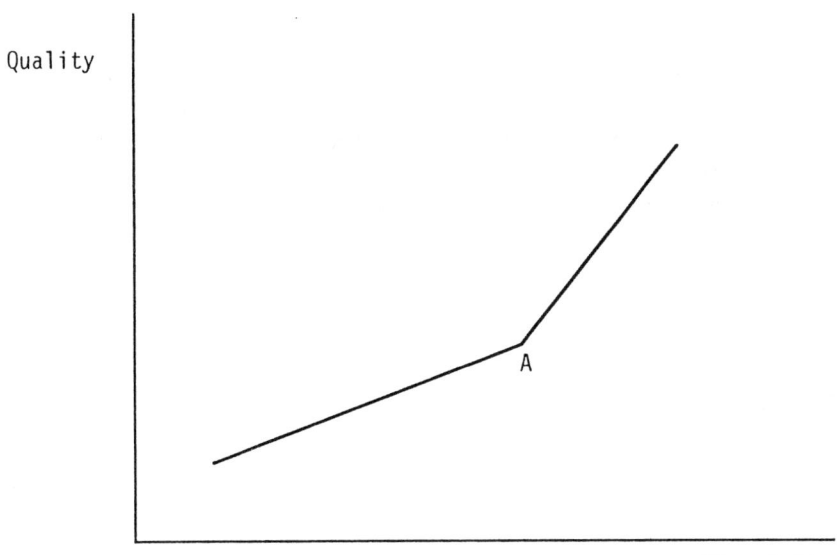

Figure 2.2. Demand Curve with Respect to Newspaper Quality
The upward sloping demand curve for circulation with respect to newspaper quality is kinked at point A. Above point A the curve is in elastic, while below point A the curve is elastic.

To the left, demand is elastic with respect to quality. Quality is so poor that a small increase in quality will result in a large increase in circulation. To the right of the kink, demand is inelastic with respect to quality. So many of the serious newspaper readers are already taking the newspaper that quality must increase greatly to attract marginal readers.

Individuals make demand decisions. The aggregate effect is simply a matter of summing all of the individual decisions. Although this model of newspaper demand is based on existing research, it has yet to be totally tested. However, some research into the relationship between competition and circulation indicates that at least some of the propositions of the model appear to predict behavior in the newspaper circulation market. This aspect of the model will be dealt with in more detail in the chapter on competition.

Content Nature of Newspapers

While information use by readers defines demand, the content of newspapers defines how well the needs and wants of readers are being met. Content can be and has been classified in many ways. Table 2.2 presents a typology for categorizing content attributes that is consistent with existing research.

This typology has four main dimensions: geographic, nature of information, information format, and topic area. These dimensions allow one to develop a profile of the types of information contained in a newspaper. The *geographic* dimension concerns the area covered by content. Its subheadings are local, state, regional, national, international, and nonspecific. Boundaries drawn by governments define the state, national, and international areas, but local and regional categories are defined more by the concerns of a given newspaper's readers. Local need not mean the same thing in all markets.[10] A reader in a suburban city who works

Table 2.2. Dimensions of Newspaper Content

I. Geographic

    A. *Local*—Information about the county, city, or neighborhood in which a reader lives.
    B. *State*—Information about events and issues affecting the state in which a reader lives.
    C. *Regional*—Information about the region of the country in which a reader lives (the Great Lakes region, for example).
    D. *National*—Information about the United States government and other events affecting the country or a part of the country outside the region.
    E. *International*—Information about countries outside of the United States.
    F. *Nonspecific*—Information that has no geographic connection, such as personal advice.

II. Nature of Information

    A. *Advertising*—Information put in the newspaper by a group or individuals in order to influence the reader to take some action or to make the reader aware of an issue, event, product, or service.

        1. Awareness advertising—Information that attempts to bring an event, issue, product, or service to the readers' attention.
        2. Price advertising—Information about the price of a product or service.
        3. Quality advertising—Information about the quality or reliability of a product or service.
        4. Identity advertising—Information that is designed to create a positive image of a product or service in the minds of the readers.

    B. *News*—Information that is prepared by the newspaper's staff or by another news-gathering organization. The news organization does not receive pay for printing this information.

        1. Hard news—Information that deals with disaster and physical or ideological conflict. The emphasis is on a specific event or series of events.
        2. Features—Information that does not involve conflict and disaster. The emphasis is usually on people and interaction among people.
        3. Analysis—Information that is meant to improve understanding of an event, trend, or issue by providing context.
        4. Opinion—Information about someone's or some organization's position concerning events, trends, and issues. This includes editorials, some columns, and letters.

III. Information Format

    A. *Written*—Information conveyed with words.
    B. *Visual*— Information conveyed primarily with visual images and symbols other than words and letters.

IV. Topic Area

    A. *Government*—Information concerning an official governing body, members of a government body, or people seeking to become a member of a government body.
    B. *Business*—Information concerning groups and individuals involved in commerce or trade.
    C. *Sports*—Information about athletic efforts and athletes.
    D. *Science*—Information concerning the natural, applied, and social sciences.
    E. *Schools*—Information about systems of education and members of those systems.
    F. *Crime*—Information about people or groups who violate laws and about people and groups who enforce the laws.
    G. *Leisure activities*—Information about things people do for entertainment and those who provide entertainment.
    H. *Social-cultural activities*—Information about actions that affect the society and culture in which the readers live. This includes information about marriages, deaths, and activities of noncommercial organizations.

downtown may have a different idea of local than a reader who both lives and works in the same suburb.

The *nature of information* dimension concerns whether the information is advertising, which generally is not produced by the news-editorial staff, or news, which is produced as such by the news-editorial staff. Advertising falls into four types of information: awareness advertising, price advertising, quality advertising, and identity advertising. News information is either hard news, feature, analysis, or opinion.

The third dimension is the *format of the information*. It can be either written or visual. Sometimes both are used in conjunction. The growing use of graphics during the 1980s has increased the need for newspaper staffs to understand visual communication.

Topic areas make up the fourth dimension. This involves the subject of the information. The subheadings include government, business, sports, science, schools, crime, leisure activities, and social/cultural activities. These are often-used subheadings, but other divisions could be developed for classifying newspaper information.

Based on the typology in Table 2-2, a reader might take a newspaper because of his interests in price advertising for groceries, in local sports activities, and in national science news. Another reader might take the same newspaper because of her interest in professional basketball, national business activities, local school board activities, and opinion pieces about national politics. Individual demand for various types of information becomes a function of individual attitudes and behavior. A general circulation newspaper with its collection of specific information can serve the demands of a wide range of people with different information needs and wants.

This ability to offer a variety of information is crucial because households tend to take newspapers.[11] If the household includes more than one person, more than one group of demand attributes for a newspaper come into play. If the demand attributes of a husband and wife are consistent or complementary, there is little problem in deciding to take a specific newspaper. If, however, the attributes are not consistent, the decision process is complex and may depend even more on other factors, such as quality and price. For example, if a wife wants politically liberal opinion articles and her husband prefers politically conservative opinion articles, they may have a conflict as to which newspaper to take, or they may have to take more than one. Which option is preferred depends on the price and quality of available newspapers.

Two other factors not mentioned in Table 2-1 affect newspaper content and, therefore, demand. *Timeliness* plays a role in what people expect from newspapers. Timeliness is inherent in some types of news; time defines hard news. When a news event is written about several months after it occurs, it either represents a new hard news development, such as a trial after a crime, or the story emphasizes an analysis or a feature angle of the event.

In addition to time, the *degree of interest* is important. Two people may be interested in the same type of news but one may follow it more intensely than the other. This intensity becomes very important when the newspaper changes its content or price. Someone who is slightly interested in local news may drop the newspaper when prices increase, while someone who is intensely interested will pay the higher price. This intensity applies to several aspects of newspaper content, including comics.[12]

A particular newspaper firm often will include all of the attributes mentioned in this typology every day or even across time. Yet some newspapers will carry a narrow range of content because they serve different functions. The managers of a newspaper decide the type of content their newspaper will carry. Three types of newspaper content classifications are of interest: specialization of information, geographic area of news and editorial coverage, and production cycle. These content classifications also result in categories for the newspapers.

The *specialization of information* results in newspapers being classified as either general circulation or specialized newspapers. General circulation newspapers are meant to attract readers from several social, economic, and geographic groups. These newspapers are bundles of information with sections defined by geographic or topic emphasis. Specialized newspapers are more narrow in scope for both the information and advertising markets and can take several forms.

Specialized newspapers develop primarily because general circulation newspapers and other media cannot, or do not, meet the information demands of all the people in a given geographic market. Just as with general circulation newspapers, the geographic areas served by specialized newspapers will vary. For example, *The Wall Street Journal* is a national business and financial newspaper, while the *San Diego Daily Transcript* is a business publication that concentrates on southern California.

Many large cities have dailies or weeklies that concentrate on business and legal matters. All face fairly specific types of demand for information. A reader's interest in these papers involves surveillance of a topic that is too narrow for adequate coverage in a general circulation newspaper but is still larger than they can monitor personally. These publications may also provide in-depth details about issues of importance to the readers, as well as information for entertainment and social-cultural interaction.

Ethnic and minority newspapers are important specialized newspapers. These newspapers may serve a group of immigrants by publishing in their native language, or they may serve a racial minority not served adequately by the general circulation newspapers. In 1987, *Editor & Publisher International Year Book* listed 178 black newspapers, 237 foreign language newspapers, and 84 religious newspapers in the United States.[13]

Ethnic and minority newspapers provide the type of social, cultural and political coverage of minority communities that is missing from large metropolitan dailies. Specialized newspapers provide coverage somewhat analogous to the coverage in suburban general circulation newspapers. Suburban readers base their demand on geographic limitations, while specialized newspaper readers base their demand on other concerns.

This lack of adequate coverage for smaller groups by general circulation newspapers exists in the information, advertising, and intellectual markets. The extent of inadequate coverage of minority groups in the information and intellectual markets was commented on by the Kerner Commission Report in 1968.[14] The commission said that inadequate coverage by mass media of issues relating to the African-American community contributed to the 1967 summer riots in large cities across the United States.

Another growing area of specialized newspapers is the "alternative press." The United States had about 100 such publications in 1988.[15] These primarily weekly publications appeal mostly to young and educated readers and cover stories that larger dailies either do not cover or devote little space to. Content often concentrates on social, cultural, and entertainment events, although some in-depth stories about local government are often included. Circulation is mostly through bundles of papers placed in stores for free distribution. One newspaper group, Landmark Communications, had a subdivision in 1989 that involved five alternative weeklies.

Publication cycle affects content and demand for both specialized and general circulation newspapers. Less than daily publication will tend to emphasize nonhard news because hard news has an inherent timeliness about it. Weeklies will carry some hard news stories, but these are limited to stories that affect most readers and that happen close to the deadline. Weeklies also tend to have a more local geographic focus.

Geographic specialization has become an integral part of defining newspaper demand. Geographic limits result from both the cost of distribution and the needs of advertisers and readers. The farther away a home is from a newspaper's printing facility, the more it costs to get copies delivered to that home. Also, the farther away a subscriber is from an advertiser's business, the less likely the subscriber is to be a customer. Autonomy of local governments and the sheer size of the United States has resulted in geographically defined interest in governmental news.

This geographic emphasis has generated a functional approach to newspapers called the "umbrella" model.[16] This model proposes four different types, or layers, of newspapers. The metropolitan dailies are regional newspapers that cover large geographic areas, but they also have some news about the city in which they are located. Satellite-city dailies compose the second layer. These dailies are in cities that are not adjacent to the metropolitan central cities but are close enough that metro dailies are bought by readers in the satellite markets. Satellite-city newspapers are more locally oriented than metro dailies but still cover a wider area than lower-layer papers. The third layer contains suburban dailies, which are primarily local. They may also cover the county and carry some wire service material, but they tend not to send reporters to news events outside the county. The fourth layer is composed of weeklies and shoppers. These are almost entirely local and cover the city in which they publish.

Since this model was proposed in 1975, two new layers appear to have developed more extensively. First, a layer of national newspapers has developed. This includes *USA Today*, the national edition of *The New York Times*, *The Christian Science Monitor*, and the *Wall Street Journal*. These papers carry primarily national and international news, with some stories that are of interest to specific states and regions.

Below the suburban-daily layer and above the weekly and shopper layer are group suburban nondaily newspapers. These weekly and twice-weekly newspapers cover several separate suburbs but are printed at one plant. They compose a different layer because they compete more with metro dailies for advertising than do independently owned weeklies. Their ability to cover several suburbs with news and advertising means they can offer more information to several particular suburbs than do metro dailies. The group weeklies combine to cover a larger advertising market than do independents. This puts them in direct competition with metro dailies for large chain retail advertising.

Research in this area of umbrella competition, discussed in Chapter 4, indicates that competition among the layers tends to be for circulation and advertising. News competition is more likely to exist among dailies. Weeklies and dailies are not good substitutes because of publication cycles. Geographic limits affect competition, but it can still be intense as you move toward the lower layers.

Overall, the demand for newspapers in the information market, which is expressed as circulation, is primarily a matter of how well the content meets the needs and wants of the readers. Price can play a role in some markets at some times, as in intensely competitive markets, but it is usually secondary to the nature of content. This content can be categorized in several ways, but the basic question is whether it provides the utility readers want.

While circulation is used often as a measure of demand, it is not the only measure. Penetration is used as well, especially by advertisers. Penetration represents the proportion of the potential market being reached.

As mentioned in Chapter 1, penetration has been declining, even as circulation increased. The relationship between circulation and penetration is not clear. Research has found a positive relationship between quality and circulation, but not between penetration and quality.[17] In fact, quality and penetration were negatively related. It may be that circulation is a function of the quality of the newspaper, while penetration is a function of the nature of the readers. Whether readers in a information market tend to be homogeneous or heterogeneous in their interests will affect penetration. Penetration rates tend to be higher in smaller markets. Smaller markets tend to have fewer institutions and organizations that cater to diversity. This leads to more interpersonal interaction and, thus, a modifying effect on tendencies to move away from group mores and norms. On the other hand, large markets are much more diverse. As absolute number increases, the likelihood of finding individuals with interests that vary from the norm increases.

Figure 2.3 illustrates the relationship between homogeneity of readers and newspaper content. The two curves represent two different distributions of interest for a city's population. The curve with the hatched area underneath is a homogeneous population, where people tend to be very similar in interests. The flatter, nonhatched curve is a more heterogeneous population. The area between the dotted vertical lines marked C_1 and C_2 represents the areas of interest covered by a newspaper's content. The areas under the two curves between C_1 and C_2 are the penetration levels for the two types of markets. The homogeneous population has a much greater penetration level than the heterogeneous population.

Because the attributes that make up an individual's newspaper demand are a function of that person's attitudes and behavior, greater variance in personality types means greater variance in individual newspaper demand. It becomes difficult to produce a newspaper that can meet the great variety of demand in a heterogeneous market. The greater availability of other media in a large market enhances the difficulty of meeting the greater variance in demand because these alternatives can sometimes better serve some subgroups of readers.

As a result of the nature of potential readers, newspapers in large markets cannot realistically expect to obtain penetration rates equal to those in smaller markets. In effect, the cost of providing newspaper issues big enough to meet the diverse demand attributes of a large hetero-

Homogeneous Population

Heterogeneous Population

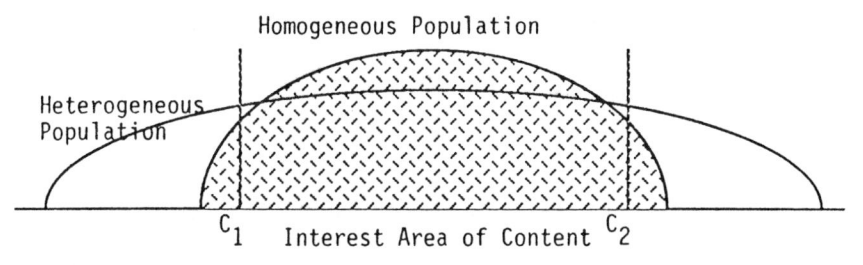

C_1 Interest Area of Content C_2

Figure 2.3. Relationship of Population Homogeneity to Penetration
The vertical axis represents the range of interest in newspaper content. A given newspaper might include the range between C_1 and C_2. This range would better serve the interest of a homogeneous population, which is one with similar information needs, than the much more dispersed interest of a heterogeneous population. Penetration increases as a newspaper serves the interest of a given population.

geneous market tends to exceed the revenue that can be made by doing so. An optimum point exists at which the marginal cost of getting an additional reader equals the marginal revenue from having that reader.

Newspapers facing a heterogeneous market will have a widely diverse aggregate demand. They can accept low levels of penetration, try to promote homogeneity for some topics that they address with their newspaper content, or increase the diversity of content in order to serve a diverse audience.

One way newspapers try to increase diversity of content is through the Sunday newspaper. Sunday newspaper readership and penetration are growing.[18] This seems to result from two factors: A Sunday paper has enough space to better serve heterogeneous audiences, and there is more time to read on Sundays. The problem newspapers face during the week is providing enough daily variety and depth to retain marginal readers who don't have strong newspaper reading habits.

While the heterogeneity of a community affects penetration, so can other factors. The increasing variety of alternative media and other activities from which people may choose seems to limit time available for newspaper reading. The decline in the literacy of United States citizens and the increasing cost of newspapers also seem to affect penetration. In effect, not as high a percentage of people have as strong a newspaper habit as they did at the turn of the 20th century. Whether this habit can be instilled in future generations is a prime concern of the newspaper industry.

If newspaper firms are not content with lower daily penetration rates, they will have to affect demand through education programs and alternative circulation patterns based on more specialized information. If young people learn newspaper reading as a habit, the drop in penetration may reverse itself. Newspaper organizations might make newspaper demand more homogeneous by teaching people what good journalism is and why they should demand good journalism. Of course, newspapers must provide good journalism.

DEMAND IN THE ADVERTISING MARKET

As with information markets, advertising markets are defined geographically. Advertisers want readers in their selling areas. Therefore, businesses interested in buying ads from a newspaper firm generally are located within areas where those newspapers circulate. These areas can be defined any way the newspaper firms want and are related to the geographic areas of the information market. The prime geographic advertising market is the *retail trade zone*. This represents a geographic area including and surrounding a city or cities in which most of the retail activity takes place.

The retail trade zone is important because it represents a concentration of demand for an advertiser's goods and services and, correspondingly, a concentration of demand for advertising from the newspaper firm. Not all advertising comes from the retail trade zone, but most newspapers are local commodities. They depend on local business and people for advertising.

Demand in a geographically defined information market influences demand in the advertising market, and vice versa. If a newspaper does not attract readers in an area from which a business draws its customers, advertising in that newspaper will be of little use to the business. If a business wants to reach a certain type of person, it will tend to advertise in newspapers that appeal to that type of person. In this case, advertisers are not interested in the greatest number of readers but in the greatest number of "attractive" readers. This relationship has led some newspapers to limit their geographic markets for news coverage and delivery of newspaper copies.[19] The managers at these companies reason that these areas do not provide revenue consistent with the cost of servicing them.

As mentioned previously, advertising content is valued by readers,[20] who use it to make purchase decisions and to become aware of the availability of several goods and services. The value of advertising draws circulation to newspapers. One case study found the most important content variable in attracting suburban readers to metropolitan dailies was the amount of advertising from suburban businesses.[21]

The information market can also affect the advertising market. A newspaper that wants to expand its advertising base into a new area will usually do so by increasing or beginning coverage of that geographic market. It must show advertisers in this expanded market that it can attract the attention of the readers there.

Once a geographic market is defined, demand for advertising is based on the same four factors as demand for information: taste, price, price of substitutes and complements, and income. But just as the nature of a medium dictates limitations of news coverage, so it dictates types of advertising that will be successful. Some types of advertising work better in newspapers than they do in other media, while some work better in media other than newspapers.

As defined in Table 2-2, advertising messages fall into four general types: awareness advertising, price advertising, quality advertising, and identity advertising. *Awareness advertising* is simply an effort to make readers aware of something by describing it. For example, employment ads are awareness ads. They contain information about jobs that readers might not be aware of without the newspaper. These ads tend not to sell a reader on a product or service as much as bring it to his or her attention. *Price advertising* gives the reader information about how much a product or service costs. The Sunday newspaper inserts that litter the front porch when the paper is picked up are an example of this type of advertising. The primary purpose is to attract buyers to a store by offering low prices on some goods. Much of newspaper advertising fits into this category.

Just as price advertising is specific to a product, so is quality advertising. *Quality advertising* attempts to convince consumers that a specific product is better than a competitor's product, or that the product is worth the asking price. These advertisements are often vague about what makes the good or service of high quality. Sometimes, particular attributes of the product or service are emphasized in the ad to persuade consumers that the product has quality worth the purchase price.

The fourth type of advertising, *identity advertising*, deals with individual reader's perceptions of a product or commodity. These advertisement try to associate something (or someone) that has a positive image for the consumer with a company's product. For example, television beer commercials often try to associate an image of having an enjoyable time with the advertiser's particular beer. Advertisements that discuss the public service of a particular company are forms of image advertising. The idea is to have consumers identify a positive cause or position with the company. While identity ads are more often seen on television than in print, they can be printed. Magazine ads for cigarettes and "advertorials," which are advertisements that present a certain stance of a company on a topic of public interest, are forms of identity advertising.

Some media hold comparative advantages for certain types of advertising. It is difficult to imagine a grocery store using television instead of newspapers to run their Wednesday sales prices and coupons. While some grocery stores do use television, the price information on television is less cost-effective than in newspapers. It is also impossible to clip coupons from the TV screen.

Television has a similar advantage when it comes to identity advertising. The impact of looking at handsome, healthy smokers on television is greater than the impact of looking at photographs of the same smokers in magazines. That is why cigarette advertising was banned from television.

Because each medium has comparative advantages in some types of advertising, businesses tend to do two things. First, they target certain types of media for certain type of advertising. Second, they tend to use several media for an advertising campaign. This multimedia approach widens their reach and allows the use of all types of advertising where they are most effective.

Newspaper Advertising as a Commodity

Not only does effectiveness of certain types of advertisement change from medium to medium, but so does the nature of the commodity the advertisers buy. Newspaper advertisers buy two things: space and the attention given that space by readers. On the other hand, television advertisers buy attention and time. Space generally is cheaper than time because it is easier to add space to a printed publication than time to a broadcast program. Newspaper firms will add space because of economies of scale from pages per issue. Each additional page costs less to print, which means a reduction in average costs of printing one page as the size of the newspaper increases. Since the price of additional advertising does not decline as quickly as the cost of production, the profit from increased advertising grows with additional space. This is the basis for quantity discounts for advertisers. Part of the increased profit rate is returned as a discount to the advertisers who buy large amounts of space.

This use of attention from newspaper readers means the information and advertising markets are inseparable for most newspapers. This connection is amplified by the fact that advertising serves as information. The connection of the information and advertising markets is expressed through a concept called the *milline rate*. This is the cost of a line of advertising per thousand readers, which incorporates circulation into the price of advertising. Another way to look at the concept is that the milline rate is a way of evaluating the quality of the ad space. As circulation goes up, the quality increases. This relationship with circulation allows a newspaper to increase advertising rates when circulation increases and still maintain an attractive milline rate. It also emphasizes the need for newspapers to have a quality news-editorial commodity that meets the demand in the information market.

The cost per thousand has been a traditional way of evaluating the quality of newspaper ads, but another way is looking at the types of people who read a paper. Advertisers are more interested in having potential customers see their ads than just anyone. Just as newspaper firms use demographics and psychographics to identify demand for their commodities, businesses use the same measures to identify people who are likely to buy their products and services. This emphasis on characteristics, such as age and income, has resulted in a great deal of market research for and by newspapers. For example, certain newspapers, such as "alternative newspapers," may be more likely to reach people with higher incomes and more education, often called "upscale" readers. The demographic identification of readers can even be extended to specific sections of the newspapers. Advertisements for sporting goods stores are likely to run in the sports sections of newspapers for obvious reasons.

The type and number of readers are important considerations in newspaper advertising, but not the only ones. The type of ad that fills the space plays an equally important role. Newspaper advertising generally falls into three categories: display ads, classified ads, and insert ads. *Display ads* include most ads other than classifieds that appear in the news sections. They usually, but not necessarily, have some sort of graphic in the advertisements. The type face generally is larger than that used for news stories and classified ads. When this type of advertising runs in all copies of a newspaper for a given day, it is called run-of-the-paper (ROP) advertising. *Classified ads* run in the classified section. They are usually, but not always, printed in smaller type called agate. They are less expensive and are usually the most effective way for an individual to advertise, although organizations buy them as well. It is possible to combine the impact of display and classified ads by placing larger, more graphically sophisticated, advertisements in the classified sections. Appropriately enough, this hybrid is called a *display classified*. *Inserts* are advertising sheets or booklets that are inserted into the fold of a newspaper. These ads are preprinted and added to the newspaper after it has been printed.

Two of the three types of advertising actually compete with each other, primarily on the basis of price. During the 1980s, newspapers saw a decline in ROP advertising and a growth of insert advertising. Because insert advertisements are preprinted and supplied to the newspapers, they cost the advertiser less than an equivalent amount of ROP advertising. Consequently, inserts produce less revenue and profit for newspapers than do ROP ads.

This movement away from ROP advertising was not welcomed by newspapers, but they could do little about it for two reasons. First, the development of *total market coverage* (TMC) publications provided an alternative for inserts. TMC publications are provided free, usually by mail, to all homes within a geographic area. They began initially as advertising sheets with little news and editorial content. TMCs guarantee the advertiser potential exposure to all the customers in a given area, but, as newspaper managers argue, it does not mean they will be read. The advantage of newspapers is that they attract readers to the commodity with news-editorial information. This argument must have some validity because many TMCs are using more and more news-editorial information to keep people from throwing the publication away.

The second reason newspapers have been forced to accept inserts is that readers use them. The inserts, which are similar to small catalogues, have value as information. If a newspaper refuses to carry inserts instead of ROP, the advertiser will go to a TMC and in doing so reduce the attractiveness of the newspaper to the reader.

Interestingly, newspapers have begun to protect themselves from TMC competition by starting their own total market coverage publications. These publications often contain content from the newspapers of the parent firms. The effectiveness of this defensive action depends on the substitutability of competing TMCs.

Within the three general types of advertising there are subcategories. Classified advertising can cover a wide range of types depending on what is being advertised. *Legal advertising* usually falls into this general classification. Legal ads are those purchased by governmental entities to advertise some proposed action or planned meeting. They are mandated by law in most areas of the United States.

Display advertising is composed of local and national advertising. *Local advertising* involves the businesses within the geographic advertising market of the newspaper. *National advertising* includes ads bought by businesses outside this area. Local advertisements usually carry information about a particular store or service, while national advertising tends to advertise a product or service without indicating a place of purchase. A major subcategory of local advertising is *local retail advertising*, which represents the traditionally strongest area of newspaper advertising demand, often accounting for more than 50 percent of all advertising. This includes department and grocery store advertising, which provide valuable commercial information for consumer decision making.

Local advertising, whether display or classified, need not be run of the paper. The development of printing technology has allowed newspapers not only to design specific news sections of the newspaper for narrow geographic areas but to do the same for advertising. This narrowing of markets is called zoning. *Zoning* often is used to serve the demand of smaller advertisers in suburban areas around large cities. These businesses are not interested in buying advertising read by people on the other side of the metro area and often cannot afford the ROP rates. Businesses pay lower prices for space in the zoned editions designed for readers in their retail trade area.

These *zoned editions* of daily newspapers contain the regular sections of the newspaper that all readers get, plus a specially designed section that is inserted into the regular sections. The success of zoned editions as advertising publications is tied to the ability of the news-editorial content to attract the readers. A section that contains little information of interest to readers will do little to sell the products and services of suburban merchants. Successful zoned sections require a careful identification of geographic areas that are large enough for news coverage to be cost effective, but not so large as to limit the ability of reporters and editors to develop news content of interest to the readers in that area. Too wide an area will result in a collection of stories with only one or two of interest to any one community. Too narrow of a zone will cost more money for coverage than the advertising revenue it produces. A key is letting the information demand rather than distribution needs determine the geographic areas of the zones. If readers are attracted to the zoned editions, advertisers should follow.

Zoning, which has been going on since at least the 1960s,[22] has met with mixed results for metropolitan dailies. It is being adapted by non-metropolitan daily newspapers as a way of better serving readers. For example, in 1988 the *Asbury Park Press* in New Jersey had five zoned editions four days a week for its geographic areas. These were separate, specially designed editions. In addition, the newspaper also published seven weekly zoned editions to allow for more detailed coverage of specific areas within the daily zoned areas. This rather complex setup allows the *Press* to better serve cities and towns in its market with community news. This approach acknowledges the localized demand of readers.

Zoning can also take place on a national level. The *Wall Street Journal* can sell advertising for specific areas of the country where its editions are printed. However, only a few newspapers have national markets. As a result, newspapers have not done well in attracting national advertising during the last 40 years. But the decline in national advertising during that time had several other causes. First, national advertising tends not to be price specific because of regional price variations. Its purpose then is either identity or quality advertising. Both seemed to work better on television where visual and auditory images can be manipulated to impress viewers. Second, newspapers have usually charged more for national advertising than local advertising. This has been used as a selling tool with local advertising, but has lowered demand nationally. Third, until the 1980s no general circulation national newspapers were available.

Fourth, because most newspapers are local commodities, it is difficult to get national coverage for advertising. Network television shows that have a history of attracting large audiences tend to have the advantage for national ads. Fifth, the typography, layouts, and page sizes of newspapers around the country vary so much that it makes placing an ad in several newspapers more costly. Each newspaper might require a different size ad. This expense added to the already high rates.

Despite the disadvantages newspaper companies face for attracting national advertising, changes during the 1980s have raised the possibility of capturing some share of national advertising from television. Fragmentation of television audiences during the 1980s by cable and video cassette recorders means television cannot attract the mass audiences it once did. Earlier, a similar process occurred with magazines, as costs and the development of special interest magazines killed national publications such as *Life*, *Look*, and *Saturday Evening Post*. Television fragmentation, combined with the growth of groups of newspapers, raises the possibility that demand for national newspaper advertising might grow. This growth will be aided by adoption of satellite technology that allows printing of advertising on the same day at various newspapers around the country.

Whether this possibility becomes reality depends upon the other three factors that influence advertising demand: price, income, and the price of advertising in substitute media. Income refers to advertising budgets allocated by businesses. These budgets usually are established on a yearly basis, based on certain assumed prices. Price of advertising in substitute media is related to cross-elasticity of demand among substitutes.

The process of pricing advertising in newspapers has been criticized as being less than optimal and fairly unsystematic.[23] Not only is this often the case, but there is a great deal of freedom given some newspaper advertising representatives for adjusting prices. In reality, few advertisers pay the listed *open line rate*, which represents a standard charge for a unit of space in the newspapers. Variations in price occur because of amount of advertising—the more a business contracts for, the lower the price per inch. The day of the week that an ad runs and the section of the newspaper in which an ad runs can affect pricing as well. Businesses that are frequented by large numbers of consumers, such as large department stores, may also get discounts because their advertising attracts readers.

While the process of pricing varies greatly, the impact of price on demand is fairly consistent. As with most commodities, as prices for newspaper advertising go up, demand goes down, holding all other factors constant. The degree of that relationship is the price elasticity of demand and varies with the categories of advertising.

The role of price is affected by income available for advertising. Since income represents the amount of money a business will spend on advertising during a given time, increases in newspaper advertising prices during that period must come from money spent on other types of advertising or from a decline in total space bought. The same holds for changes in price for advertising in other media.

This interdependency of advertising prices is related to the tendency among most businesses to advertise their product in several different media. If a price increase in newspaper advertising results in a large movement of advertising dollars to radio advertising, the cross-elasticity of demand is elastic. If, however, the price increase results in little change in advertising expenditures, the cross-elasticity of demand is inelastic. The extent of the switch to radio depends on whether radio can do as good a job at advertising the product as newspapers and on the comparative price of radio.

The extent of elasticity is often related to whether the substitute medium is print or broadcast. Print media are usually better substitutes for one another than broadcast is for print. Magazines tend to be better substitutes for newspapers than are radio programs. This doesn't mean that broadcast cannot be a substitute for newspaper advertising. Here the type of business, type of advertisement, and type of advertising message all play roles in determining demand. A grocery store that wants to publish various sale prices will find print a better medium than broadcast. Broadcast takes longer to give the same amount of information and requires more of an effort of memory by the consumer. Print remains available for rereading.

Thus, some businesses and individuals find it hard to transfer advertising when prices increase at newspapers. This includes department stories, groceries and supermarkets, and classified advertisers. The logical alternative is not broadcast but another newspaper or direct mail.

Despite limitations, the fact that newspaper and television remain the media with the largest audiences in local markets means they are substitutes for some advertising. Table 2.3 shows how well they serve as substitutes for various types of advertising. The table examines the substitutability of television advertising for the important types of newspaper advertising. The substitutability is rated either excellent, which means a cross-elasticity greater than one; good, which means a cross-elasticity of demand approximately equal to one; fair, which means cross-elasticity of demand is less than one but significantly better than zero; and poor, which means their cross-elasticity approaches zero. The table also suggests which of the two media has a comparative advantage in various types of advertising.

It has become almost a truism in advertising that certain types of advertising messages do not work well in particular media. Price advertising usually works best in newspapers, while image advertising tends to work best on television. Advertisements concerning awareness and quality, however, show more cross-elasticity of demand. For example,

Table 2.3. How Well Television Substitutes for Newspapers for Various Forms of Advertising

Type of Advertisement	Awareness	Advertisement Function Price	Quality	Identification
National ads	excellent	good	good	excellent
Local retail ads	good	poor	fair	excellent
Classified ads	poor	poor	poor	N/A
Legal ads	poor	N/A	N/A	N/A
Insert ads	good	poor	fair	excellent

Poor means television does not do a very good job fulfilling the particular function for the particular type of ad.
Fair means television is an acceptable alternative, but not a clearly superior substitute in fulfilling the particular function for the particular type of ad.
Good means television has a good, but not overwhelming, advantage in a particular function for a particular type of ad.
Excellent means television is clearly superior at fulfilling a particular function for a particular type of ad.
N/A means not applicable.

efforts to make consumers aware of local retail advertising can work well on television and in newspapers. So, price increases for newspaper local retail or insert advertising could move advertising dollars to television if the predominant purpose of the ads is awareness.

Comparative advantages shown in Table 2-3 are related to various factors that affect advertising demand. Some advantages result from an interaction of advertising message type and the nature of the medium. Others are caused by policy within the industry or individual firms. The reasons mentioned earlier in the chapter for the decline of national advertising in newspapers give television an advantage in quality advertising. This advantage might change if newspaper groups made it easier to place such national ads and equalized their local and national ad rates.

Both advertising and information demand for newspapers are affected by the same types of factors that affect all commodity demand. It is the interaction of the two markets that makes newspapers different from many other commodities. However, the interdependency of demand in the advertising and information markets is not the only aspect of the newspaper industry that makes it different from most other industries. Demand in the intellectual market is extremely important in understanding overall newspaper demand. This will be considered briefly here before we move to the issues of newspapers supplying the demands of their readers.

DEMAND IN THE INTELLECTUAL MARKET

It could be argued that the intellectual market is not a market at all. It need not have geographic boundaries and no money exchanges hands.

Unlike the information and advertising markets, many people remain unaware of their participation in it. Yet this market has been written about for several hundred years. Its existence serves as a basis for the work of those who established the United States government. The commodities exchanged in this market are information, ideas, and opinions. Society benefits from the actions born of these abstract commodities. Ultimately, the survival of United States society as conceived by the founding fathers rests on successful trading in this market.

Despite the historical development of our societal norms through this market, many, if not most, newspaper managers spend little time monitoring demand in this market. This occurs even though it is the operation of this market that justifies the existence of the First Amendment to the U.S. Constitution. Because of this connection between the First Amendment and the intellectual market, the information and advertising markets are inextricably tied to the intellectual market. This was at the heart of the criticism leveled at the press by the Hutchins Commission in 1947.[24]

While the intellectual market is not as clearly defined as the other two markets in which newspapers operate, it remains important. Demand for ideas and opinions is not entirely separate from the demand for information. The content attributes that individuals look for in newspapers flow from both markets. People expect their newspapers to provide the ideas and opinions that will help them answer social and political questions. This is especially true on a local basis, where media organizations that contribute to the intellectual market are fewer in number than at a state or national level. Most cities only have one newspaper. The time limits of local television and radio news mean these papers must provide much of the information about city hall, school boards, county commission courts, and other local governing bodies. If they do not, such information is often missing from the information and intellectual markets.

Research indicates that newspaper readers do indeed demand this type of information. Studies of the relationship between community ties, such as home ownership and a feeling of duty to keep informed, show that civic attitude is related to newspaper subscriptions.[25] Readers' needs for being informed about civic issues and events reflect demand in the intellectual market.

Newspaper firms can meet this demand for civic information through both the news sections and editorial sections of their newspapers. The news sections carry news about civic happenings and analysis of what that news means. The editorial and op ed pages contribute to the intellectual market with editorials, columns, and letters to the editor.

A fairly large quantity of research illustrates the importance of the editorial and op ed pages in servicing readers in the intellectual market. Bogart reported that the typical editorial is read by about the same number of people as the typical news article. He also reported that columnists play an important role in communicating with readers.[26] Editorial stance of newspapers can also have an impact on reader behavior, although the degree of impact varies with the subject and the background of the reader. While evidence indicates editorial endorsement can affect presidential elections to a small degree,[27] the local impact appears to be much greater.[28]

While coverage in news and editorial pages is important, the lack of geographic boundaries for the intellectual market means the definition of what is local will vary. Local need not mean just the city in which a newspaper is located. Perhaps this explains part of the problem of dealing with the intellectual market. The multidimensional aspect of the information market mentioned above also appears applicable to the intellectual market, but with even more complexity.

The intellectual market has economic implications for U.S. newspapers. The core audience from which newspapers get their subscribers appears to value news commodities for their contribution to this market. To ignore this demand is to ignore important attributes that continue to draw readers. To ignore the intellectual market invites others, such as special interest and political groups, to dominate the flow of ideas and information to the United States public. This domination of ideas, opinions, and information by those who profit from governmental power invites problems for society and a lessening need for newspapers.

SUMMARY

Understanding newspaper demand in the information, advertising, and intellectual markets presents an ongoing problem for managers of U.S. newspapers. The complex interaction of these three overlapping markets and the small role of price in two of the three markets limits the applicability of most traditional economic theory. The attitudes and behaviors of newspaper readers that economists would place in the category of "taste" dictate how newspapers must act if they are to be viable businesses. Taste for newspapers, however, is understood on little more than an elemental level. That understanding reflects too often the results of ad hoc surveys unguided by theories of behavior.

The challenge for newspaper owners and managers is to develop an awareness of what they must do to earn the special place in society they have been given, while making an adequate profit. This awareness must center not only on the content that attracts enough readers, but also on the content that will serve the needs of society's intellectual market. These two types of content are not mutually exclusive. Perhaps the approach is one of short-term and long-term responsiveness. The short-term demand for information by readers should not exclude the long-term need of society for the active exchange of ideas.

ENDNOTES

1. George J. Stigler, *The Theory of Price*, Revised Edition (New York: The Macmillan Company, 1952).
2. Strictly defined, elasticity represents the slope of a curve showing the relationship between two variables, circulation and price in this case. This slope is determined by taking the first derivative of the curve. Effectively, however, the elasticity represents the change in circulation with respect to the change in price.

$$\text{price elasticity} = \frac{\text{relative change in quantity}}{\text{relative change in price}}$$

3. George N. Gordon, *Communication and Media: Constructing a Cross-Discipline* (New York: Hastings House, 1975), p. 135.
4. Unlike elasticity of demand, where the demand for a commodity responds to changes in its price, cross-elasticity represents the impact of a change in a substitutes' price. The elasticity is determined by taking the first derivative of change in the quantity of commodity A with respect to the change in the price of commodity B. This assumes the other factors involved are held constant.

$$\text{cross elasticity} = \frac{\text{relative change in the quantity of A}}{\text{relative change in price of B}}$$

5. Classic economic theory assumes every factor constant except price for its elementary analysis. As other factors are allowed to vary, price of substitutes and complements and income can be analyzed. Development of theory related to variations in taste has lagged behind price theory. The theory of monopolistic competition developed by Edward H. Chamberlin during the 1930s has been the most successful theoretical approach in this area. See Edward H. Chamberlin, *The Theory of Monopolistic Competition*, 8th ed. (Cambridge, MA: Harvard University Press, 1962); and Edward H. Chamberlin, "The Product as an Economic Variable," *The Quarterly Journal of Economics*, 67:1-29 (February 1963). Several articles reviewing monopolistic competition were published in *The American Economic Review*, 54:28-57 (May 1964).
6. For a discussion of the history of the uses and gratifications approach see Werner J. Severin with James W. Tankard, Jr. *Communication Theories: Origins, Methods, Uses*, Second Edition (New York: Longman, 1988), Chapter 19. Also see Philip Palmgreen, "Uses and Gratifications: A Theoretical Perspective," *Communication Yearbook 8*, Robert N. ed. Bostrom, (Beverly Hills, CA: Sage Publications, 1984) pp. 20-55.
7. Wilbur Schramm, "The Nature of News," *Journalism Quarterly*, 26:259-269 (Summer 1949).

8. Keith J. Stamm and Lisa Fortini-Campbell, "The Relationship of Community Ties to Newspaper Use," *Journalism Monographs*, No. 84, August 1983.
9. Stephen Lacy, "A Model of Demand for News: Understanding the Impact of Competition on Daily Newspaper Content," *Journalism Quarterly*, 66:40-48, 128 (Spring 1989).
10. Maxwell E. McCombs and James P. Winter, "Defining Local News," *Newspaper Research Journal*, October 1981, pp. 16-21; and James P. Winter, "The Public and Local News," *ANPA News Research Report*, No. 37, October 27, 1982.
11. Kenneth M. Jackson, "Broadening of Reader Interest Seen Through Economic News' Relation to Households," *Newspaper Research Journal*, Winter 1980, pp. 33-41.
12. See Philip Meyer, *The Newspaper Survival Book: An Editor's Guide to Marketing Research* (Bloomington: Indiana University Press, 1985).
13. *1987 Editor & Publisher & Publisher International Year Book* (New York: Editor & Publisher, 1987).
14. *Report of the National Advisory Committee on Civil Disorders* (New York: Bantam Books, 1968).
15. C. David Rambo, "'Alternative' Newspapers Serve an Upscale Crowd," *presstime*, December 1988, pp. 6-9.
16. James N. Rosse, "Economic Limits of Press Responsibility," Discussion paper, Stanford University: Studies in Industry Economics, No. 56, 1975. For more detail see James N. Rosse, "An Economist's Description of the Industry," *Proceedings of the Symposium on Media Concentration*, Vol. 1 (Washington, DC: Bureau of Competition, Federal Trade Commission, Dec. 14-15, 1978).
17. Stephen Lacy and Frederick Fico, "Financial Commitment, Newspaper Quality and Circulation: Testing an Economic Model of Direct Newspaper Competition," Unpublished paper presented to the Association for Education in Journalism and Mass Communication, Washington, DC, August 1989.
18. Mary A. Anderson, "The Health and Wealth of Sunday Newspapers," *presstime*, November 1988, pp. 28-34.
19. William B. Blankenburg, "Newspaper Ownership and Control of Circulation to Increase Profits," *Journalism Quarterly*, 59:390-398 (Autumn 1982).
20. James M. Ferguson, *The Advertising Rate Structure in the Daily Newspaper Industry* (Englewood Cliffs, NJ: Prentice-Hall, 1963).
21. Stephen Lacy, Ardyth B. Sohn, and Lowndes F. Stephens, "Coverage of the Suburbs by Metropolitan and Suburban Newspapers: A Case Study of Two Markets," Paper presented to the Midwest Association for Public Opinion Research, Chicago, November 20-21, 1987.
22. Boyd L. Miller, "More Dailies Zoning for Suburban Readers," *Journalism Quarterly*, 42:460-462 (Summer 1965).
23. Robert G. Picard, "Pricing Behavior of Newspapers," *Press Concentration and Monopoly*, eds. Robert G. Picard, James P. Winter, Maxwell E. McCombs, James P. Winter, and Stephen Lacy, (Norwood, NJ: Ablex, 1988), pp. 55-69.
24. The Commission on Freedom of the Press, *A Free and Responsible Press* (Chicago: The University of Chicago Press, 1947).

25. For examples see Maxwell McCombs, "Newspapers and the Civic Culture," *Newspaper Research Journal*, Summer 1983, pp. 5-9; David Weaver and Virginia Dodge Fielder, "Civic Attitudes and Newspaper Readership in Chicago," *Newspaper Research Journal*, Summer 1983, pp. 11-18; Orjan Olsen, "Measuring Civic Attitudes: Replications and Extensions," *Newspaper Research Journal*, Summer 1983, pp. 19-36; E. F. Einsiedel and Namjung Kang, "Civic Attitudes Among Non-Readers and Non-Subscribers," *Newspaper Research Journal*, Summer 1983, pp. 37-42; R. Warwick Blood, Gerald J. Keir and Namjung Kang, "Newspaper Use and Gratification in Hawaii," *Newspaper Research Journal*, Summer 1983, pp. 43-52.

26. Leo Bogart, *Press and Public*, (Hillsdale, NJ: Lawrence Erlbaum Associates, Inc., 1981).

27. For example, see Robert E. Hurd and Michael W. Singletary, "Newspaper Endorsement Influence on the 1980 Presidential Election," *Journalism Quarterly*, 61:332-338 (Summer 1984); Maxwell McCombs, "Editorial Endorsements: A Study of Influence," *Journalism Quarterly*, 44:545-548 (Autumn 1967); and Tim Counts, "Editorial Influence on GOP Vote in 1948 Presidential Election," *Journalism Quarterly*, 66:177-181 (Spring 1989).

28. Jack Sean McClenghan, "Effect of Endorsements in Texas Local Elections," *Journalism Quarterly*, 50:363-366 (Summer 1973).

3

Newspaper Supply

Traditional economics defines *supply* as the number of units of a product that a firm will sell to consumers at a given price, with all else held constant. These things held constant range from price of substitute goods and raw materials to technology, weather, and disasters. This definition of supply will provide a beginning for this chapter, but only a beginning because of the complexity of the newspaper industry. The first part of the chapter will deal with general concepts of microeconomic theory related to supplying a commodity or product. The second section will concentrate on the application of cost concepts to the three specific markets that newspapers serve. The third section will examine the relationship between supply and demand in these three markets.

ECONOMIC THEORY

The classic theory of the firm, which explains how companies determine the amount of a product they will produce, is somewhat analogous to classic demand theory. As with demand, price plays the key role in determining market behavior, although other factors can have an impact. Demand and supply theory differ in that the theory concerning supply has been developed more extensively. This difference results from the complexity of human behavior addressed by demand theory and from the assumption of classic supply theory that all labor is equivalent. Most microeconomics theories do not address variations in behavior of workers, whereas variation in the behavior of reporters and editors is at the heart of producing a newspaper.

The portion of microeconomics theory that addresses supply starts with firms combining raw materials, labor, technology, and capital—which are called inputs—to create products. The assumed goal of this process is to maximize profits. The relationship of inputs in this process of creating a product is described by the *production function*. This equation describes the proportions of labor and capital (capital here represents cost of technology) used to create the product. Every product has multiple production functions. For example, a car can be produced from a variety of labor and technology combinations. The job of management is to select the production function that will best meet their profit maximization goal.

Two key concepts in determining a production function are costs and productivity. *Costs* concern the prices firms pay for inputs. *Productivity* measures output per unit of input. Production functions that have higher productivity and lower costs are preferable because they contribute to profit maximization. If revenue remains constant, a lower unit cost means a higher unit profit.

Costs are either fixed or variable. *Fixed costs* occur only in the short run and are those costs that would have to be paid even if nothing was produced by the firm because of a temporary closing. This generally means buildings, land, and equipment, but it would also include costs such as insurance, some taxes, and wages for people who would still be employed during a limited closing. High fixed costs create high barriers to entry. Newspapers have high fixed costs, which is why starting a competing daily is so difficult. *Variable costs* are those that change with the volume of production. They have a direct relationship with the level of output and include wages, price of raw materials, and energy costs.

The short run in microeconomic theory has both types of costs because technology is assumed constant—that is, the type of equipment represented in the production function is fixed and only the extent or number of machines used varies. In the *long run*, technology varies and the type of machinery available changes. Also, during the long run more or new land can be bought and new buildings can be built. The introduction of a more efficient machine or the acquisition of new land and buildings in the long run means the formerly fixed cost will become variable. In fact, economists define the *short run* as the period during which technology does not change and no new firms enter the market.

Two other important measures of costs are average cost and marginal cost. *Average cost* is determined by dividing the total cost of producing units by the number of units produced. For example, if the total cost of running a weekly newspaper for a year was $300,000 and 5,000 pages were printed, the average cost per page would be $60 for the year. Average cost is a way of assigning the expenses to the units sold, but it implies that costs are evenly distributed among the units across time. This is not true with newspapers.

Lack of even distribution of costs requires another concept called marginal cost. *Marginal cost* is the extra expense of the last added unit. If a newspaper firm produces 6,000 pages a year at a total cost of $390,000, the marginal cost of page 6,001 is the cost in addition to the $390,000 that is needed to produce that one more page. Because fixed costs exist even if no units are produced, only variable costs affect marginal costs. Marginal cost is extremely difficult to estimate because input units are rarely added one at a time. But it is still a useful theoretical concept.

Average cost is usually applied to both fixed and variable costs as a way of understanding the basis for the expense of producing a newspaper. Because total cost equals fixed plus variable cost, *total average cost* is also an important concept. Table 3.1 shows a simplified imaginary cost schedule for a small newspaper.[1] It presents the variable, fixed and total cost, and then shows the average fixed, average variable and average total costs. Fixed costs in Table 3.1 are $750. This is the cost to gather news, sell ads, and get the paper to the point at which it could be printed. The variable cost represents ink, paper, and expense of delivery. The total cost is a combination of the fixed and variable. The averages for the three types of costs are determined by dividing the types of costs by the units produced. Marginal cost is shown at the right. It is figured by subtracting the total cost for a given unit from the total cost of one unit less.

Several trends from Table 3.1 are important. First, the fixed costs do not change with increases in the number of units. They are constant. The variable costs increase with the number of units because they are tied directly to the production process. The increases in total cost reflect the increases in variable costs because fixed costs do not change.

When average costs are examined, all three types of costs show downward trends, but there is a difference in how quickly the types of costs decline. Because fixed costs are constant and the number of units in the table is small, additional units mean a rapid decline in the average. This is characteristic of all average fixed costs when few units are produced. As the number of units increases, the differences in the average costs gets smaller. The average variable cost declines, but at a much slower rate. This represents the fact that total variable costs increase but the amount added with each increase in number of units is getting smaller. The average total cost declines faster than the average variable cost but

TABLE 3.1. Hypothetical Cost Schedule for a Newspaper

Copies	Total Cost Fixed	Total Cost Variable	Total Cost Total	Average Cost Fixed	Average Cost Variable	Average Cost Total	Marginal Cost
0	750	0	750	---	---	---	170
1	750	170	920	750	170	920	150
2	750	320	1070	370	160	530	130
3	750	450	1200	250	150	400	110
4	750	560	1310	190	140	330	

slower than the average fixed cost, which results from the addition of the two types of costs.

Marginal cost declines in Table 3.1. It cost 170 dollars more to produce one copy than it cost to produce no copy at all. It cost 150 dollars more to produce the second copy. The declining marginal cost results from the declining average variable cost.

The rate of decline in costs is related to the concept of scale. *Scale* means the size of the production process. A large-scale company is one that produces a large number of units. In the long run, as a company increases inputs to produce more units, three types of returns to scale can occur. *Increasing returns to scale* means output increases by a larger proportion than the increase in each input. *Constant returns to scale* means output increases in the same proportion as the increase of each input. *Decreasing returns to scale* means the output increases by a smaller proportion than the increase in each input.

Returns to scale are important because they represent the productivity of the inputs. Some production processes become more efficient as the level of production increases. Some productive processes are not efficient or even available at low levels of production. On the other hand, the difficulty of operating a large scale production can add to the cost because of communication and coordination difficulties. In effect, the returns to scale represent a test of the efficiency and effectiveness of the various production functions.

Returns to scale are associated with costs because increasing productivity means lower unit cost, whereas decreasing productivity means higher unit cost. When a company has declining average and marginal cost, they enjoy *economies of scale*, which means the greater the number of units produced, the lower will be the average unit cost. When the marginal cost and average cost are increasing, the company has *diseconomies of scale*. These two trends in cost represent increasing and decreasing returns to scale.

Perfect competition models predict that companies have U-shaped short-run and long-run average cost curves. The companies enjoy economies of scale for a certain range of production, but then diseconomies come into play. Empirical studies have tended to find declining long-term average cost that eventually become constant.[2] There is little evidence of diseconomies of scale, probably because companies will not produce at levels that result in diseconomies.

Determining Levels of Output

The level of output by a firm is determined by costs and price. According to perfect competition models, in the long run a firm will produce the number of units that will maximize its profits. This means it will sell the number of units demanded at a price, which is determined by the market, that covers its long-run average cost. Included in this cost is a normal profit. Economists define *normal profit* as the amount of profit necessary to insure an entrepreneur will continue to produce the same product under conditions of uncertainty. In practical terms, this means normal profit must be above the rate of return for secure long-term investments. At a profit-maximizing level of production, long-run marginal cost, marginal revenue, long-run average cost, and price are all equal. A company will not produce more at this point because it would mean taking a loss on each additional unit. Marginal revenue would fall below marginal cost and each unit would deduct from profit. A company would not produce less because each unit less could add to profit as long as marginal revenue was greater than marginal cost.

A company need not make a normal profit in the short run. This means a firm may produce units and sell them at a price above average variable cost but below total average cost. In this situation, the price does not cover fixed cost. However, a firm will sell at this rate during the short run to stay in business, but it minimizes its short-run loss. The company plans to return to long-run profitability, but it must stay afloat until that time. This represents the situation in some intensely competitive newspaper markets. A competitive newspaper will invest heavily in its commodity and services, even at a short-run loss, in an effort to be the survivor in what the managers perceive as a battle to the death.

The cost and supply relationships discussed above apply to individual firms. The short-run supply for a market or industry is determined by adding the marginal cost curves of the individual firms. The market supply results from the costs of the firms in that market. In the long run, market supply is determined by the average cost of the combined firms.

Just as demand can be presented on a curve relating price to quantity or quality to quantity, supply can be presented that way as well. These curves represent the various levels of a commodity that will be provided at given prices. Supply curves are positively related to price. As price increases, supply will increase. The overall price paid by consumers is determined by the intersection of the supply and demand curves. This interaction is shown in Figure 3.1, which represents the demand and supply of square inches of advertising space in a newspaper.

Curves S_1 and D_1 represent the starting point for the market. All print firms provide Q_1 square inches of supermarket advertising space at price P_1. This represents an *equilibrium point*, which is a point where suppliers will provide what buyers want. At this point, there is no oversupply or undersupply. Suppose, however, that a new grocery store chain opens two stores in town. The demand for inches of advertising space increases. This

60   THE ECONOMICS & REGULATIONS OF U.S. NEWSPAPERS

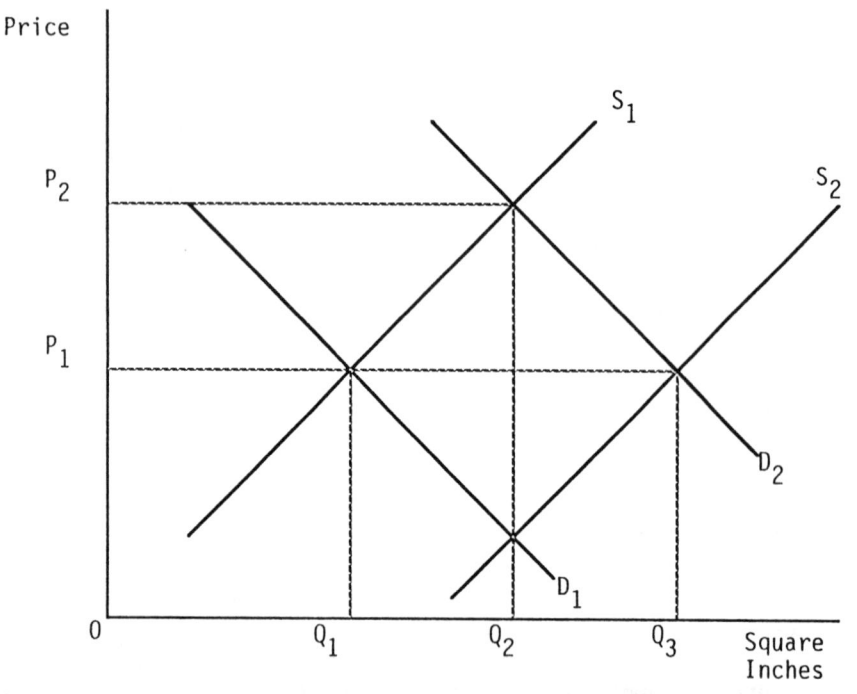

Figure 3.1. Supply and Demand Curves for Advertising Space with Respect to Price

The initial demand (D_1) and supply (S_1) curves in a market are in equilibrium at price P_1 and Q_1 square inches. A new business generates a shift in demand to D_2. The increased price of P_2 is only temporary as the newspaper increases the supply of advertising pages (S_2) to meet the new demand. The new equilibrium will have the original price but with Q_3 inches of advertising and will result in higher profits for the newspaper.

increase is presented by the D_2 curve, which has shifted to the right. At the point where D_2 and S_1 intersect, the price has increased to P_2. This increase represents the fact that the market has not adjusted to the new demand. The higher price is based on the old supply curve. The new grocery stores have increased total demand, which has driven prices up because of limited supply. A newspaper can take advantage of this disequilibrium by lowering its price and offering more ad inches. This means a new supply curve represented by S_2. The lower price might represent volume discounts.

The new demand and supply curves result in a new equilibrium point where S_2 and D_2 intersect. At this point, the print firms are providing Q_3 inches of advertising at the old price of P_1. The new grocery stores are charged the old price, and the newspaper is making more total profit. The price would not stay at the disequilibrium price of P_2 because some firm, such as a direct mail publication, is likely to lower prices to attract more advertising inches. If a newspaper firm were able to charge the price P_2, it would illustrate the presence of monopoly power for the newspaper. Monopoly power means a firm has discretionary power to fix prices and supply independent of market demand. In effect, no ready substitute would be available, so a newspaper could cut supply and raise the price. This is one of the drawbacks of monopoly from society's point of view, which is discussed further in Chapter 7.

Just as demand curves have various slopes that represent their elasticity, so do supply curves. The *price elasticity of supply curves* is the percentage change in the quantity of a product supplied that results from a one percent change in price. Just as with demand, a supply curve can be elastic, inelastic, or have unit elasticity. An *elastic supply curve* has a greater than one percent increase in supply when price increases by one percent. An *inelastic supply curve* has a less than one percent increase when price increases by one percent. A *unit elastic supply curve* has a one percent increase in supply when price increases by one percent. Figure 3.2 shows the three types of supply curves for the information market relating circulation to quality of content. Curve S_1 is inelastic; curve S_2 has unit elasticity; and curve S_3 is elastic. The more inelastic the curve, the more power a firm has in the market.

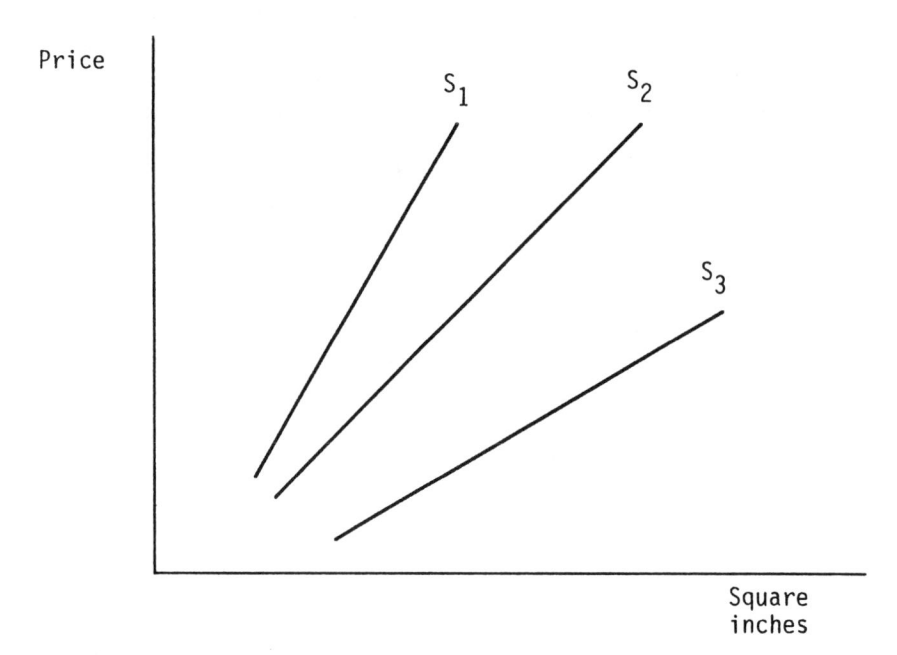

Figure 3.2. Inelastic, Unit Elastic and Elastic Supply Curves for Advertising Space
S_1 represents an inelastic supply of advertising inches with respect to price; S_2 shows unit elasticity; and S_3 represents an elastic supply curve.

The concepts presented here are basic to microeconomic theory when discussing supply. They are, however, not entirely appropriate to newspapers. As mentioned earlier, price does not play as important a role as content in the newspaper information market. This means supply curves based on price alone are not entirely adequate. On the other hand, newspapers do appear to enjoy economies of scale.[3] The next portion of this chapter will adapt some of these concepts, where appropriate, to explain newspaper supply.

NEWSPAPER SUPPLY AND COSTS

Discussion of the supply provided by newspapers to the information, advertising, and intellectual markets will concentrate on the nature of inputs, such as labor and technology, and the impact of these inputs on cost of production. The ties between these three markets are even closer when discussing supply than the ties found with demand. Readers pay attention to the types of information they want. In effect, they can disassemble the newspaper by reading whatever combination of types of news and advertising that suits them. Creating and producing the news and advertising content of a newspaper requires the opposite process. The newspaper firms bring the information for the three markets together in the same process of production. Therefore, it becomes difficult to assign various costs to a particular market. For example, if a manager wants to assign the news-editorial department its share of fixed cost, how should this be done? It is obvious that direct cost of producing news stories and photographs should be assigned to the department, but what about the expense of running the presses and of buying ink and paper? Does the percentage of space in the newspaper or the percentage of revenue determine the appropriate assignment? An assignment of costs is arbitrary to a degree and represents biases of the person assigning the costs.

Cost assignment is the flip side of revenues assignment. How does one assign revenue to a particular market? It is true that at least 70 to 80 percent of the a newspaper's revenue comes from the sale of advertising, but that advertising would not sell without the readers who buy a newspaper for the news and editorial information. Although accurate cost assignment is difficult, an exact assignment is not necessary here. Economics is concerned more with abstraction than with concrete accounting and more with understanding process than justifying behavior.

Before examining the individual markets, defining costs in the newspaper industry can be addressed. The bulk of costs faced by newspapers in all three markets are usually defined as fixed costs. Udell breaks these fixed costs into direct fixed and indirect fixed costs.[4] *Direct fixed costs* are those that occur regardless of volume but are related directly to the daily production of newspaper copies. These include the expenses of creating, producing and distributing the newspaper. The largest proportion of these is labor. *Indirect fixed costs* do not vary with production and are indirectly related to daily operation. These include plant, equipment, debt interest, and certain administrative salaries that incur even if no copies are produced. These costs can vary from year to year but are generally set for a fiscal year, with small variations, by the budget. *Variable costs* vary directly with the number of copies produced. These are ink, newsprint, and inserts.

Information Market

If one were to develop a production function of the news-editorial department of a newspaper, it would overwhelmingly emphasize labor, but this does not mean technology is unimportant. During the past 20 years, computers have had a significant effect on newsrooms by allowing flexibility in writing and editing and by improving graphics, but the bulk of news-editorial expense is still salaries. For example, the news-editorial salaries reported by The Inland Press Association in 1986 ranged from 10.8 percent of total newspaper expenses in the smallest circulation group (3,400 - 5,600) to 8.1 percent of total newspaper expenses in the largest circulation group (233,000 to 446,00).[5] The role of technology will be addressed more thoroughly in Chapter 6. This section is concerned primarily with the role of labor and raw materials, such as paper, as inputs.

The discussion of supply in the information market involves at least three of the six basic processes needed to create a newspaper. It requires the creation of news-editorial information, the reproduction of this information, and its distribution. All of these processes involve costs of various types. Price charged to readers can have an impact on the supply of newspapers that will be made available, but the impact is relatively minor. Cost in the newsroom will be discussed first, followed by a discussion of production and distribution costs.

Newsroom. Labor is the most important direct fixed cost in the information market. Traditional economics has assumed that labor was fairly homogeneous as an input. People in the work force are assumed to be good substitutes when creating a product. This is not the case with the newsroom or with news media organizations in general. The people writing and editing news stories determine the success of that information in meeting the demands of the readers.

Many forces come into play when discussing the performance of the people who produce information. Individual abilities, ethics, and professional orientation help determine what goes into a story. Therefore, quality of information becomes a function of quality of labor.

The concept of quality is an elusive one for newspapers because a generally accepted definition of newspaper quality has not been developed. Economists would argue that quality is represented by the number of people who buy a newspaper. The better the quality, the greater the circulation. This definition, while useful, is not entirely adequate because circulation is also related to many other factors, such as reliability of delivery, personal attitudes, and the nature of competition. An important issue is how to develop a measurement of quality that is reliable and valid from the viewpoints of readers, journalists, and critics.

Studies have found a relationship between quality and circulation, but the studies have varied in the operationalization of quality. Becker and Stone used expert panels to rate the quality of newspapers and found a high positive correlation.[6] Blankenburg used expenditures on news-editorial as a surrogate for quality and found a high correlation with circulation, but he added that the causal relationship was not clear.[7] Lacy and Fico[8] used a survey conducted by Bogart in 1977 of 746 editors from across the United States[9] to develop a quality index and found a relationship between quality in 1984 and circulation in 1985.

The consistent relationship between the various measures of quality and circulation indicates that a quality measure is possible. The exact nature of such a measure is still open to dispute. In addition to content measures, such as in-depth stories, ratio of advertising to news-editorial content and the percentage of stories that are locally oriented, quality is also related to the fairness, balance, and completeness of stories. The overall coverage within a newspaper and the accuracy of information, which plays a role in the credibility of a news organization, also play a part in newspaper quality. A measure encompassing all these dimensions would be difficult to quantify, but it would be useful in understanding the role of newsroom labor in supplying newspapers.

While the exact measure of content quality may be open to debate, the importance of labor in determining content quality is not. Training, intelligence, ethics, and professionalism all play a role. The difficulty of measuring these attributes makes understanding their role even more difficult.

Individual characteristics are important, but they are not the only forces shaping newspaper content. Individuals who work at a newspaper function within organizational and environmental constraints. For example, journalists are socialized into the norms of a news organization.[10] The routinization of news gathering affects what becomes news,[11] and the relationship between a reporter and source affects the news,[12] as does dependence on organizations for story ideas.[13]

The large number of forces that play a role in the creation of information indicate the importance of hiring reporters and editors who are intelligent, creative, and who take a professional approach to their jobs. These types of people will be more likely to resist forces that would push them toward generating information that does not serve the wants and needs of their readers.

In effect, quality journalists produce quality information. But quality journalists can be expensive and demanding. Newspaper firms should pay the salaries that will attract and retain quality journalists, and they should be willing to allow these people the autonomy to pursue quality information. Questions abound about the ability or commitment of newspaper firms to do this. A national study of journalists conducted in 1982-83 found that lack of autonomy and low pay were the prime reasons committed journalists were leaving the field.[14] High public relations salaries provide keen competition for newspapers in attracting people with good communication skills. This competition will continue in the future as more and more journalism majors at universities pursue public relations, magazine and television jobs instead of newspaper work.

As with all economic inputs, the cost of newsroom labor is related to its productivity. If output increases for a given amount of inputs, then unit costs decline. While productivity has traditionally been defined as the units of output per unit of input, the newspaper industry cannot accept such a narrow definition for the newsroom. If this definition were applicable, the best approach would be to hire a number of clerks to simply transcribe press releases. This would show great productivity under the traditional definition, but it would be to the long-term detriment of the newspapers. Readers would soon tire of the obvious bias. Such a reaction would result in loss of credibility, which would lead to a loss of circulation. Quality of information produced by journalists is an important aspect of productivity.

Another aspect of productivity is timeliness. A reporter not only must produce an appropriate number of stories with a particular level of quality, but they must be done on deadline. A journalist who cannot meet deadlines may soon write for an organization that does not have strict time requirements.

Thus, *newspaper productivity* is defined here as the quality and quantity of timely information produced by a journalist for a given amount of effort. Timely refers here not to news values, but to the time allotted for producing the information.

This definition means journalists should be evaluated along at least two dimensions when it comes to their effectiveness in contributing to a successful newspaper commodity. The time constraint is not a dimension, but rather a precondition for being a newspaper journalist. Deadlines must be met. The dimensions of quality and quantity can be somewhat separate in that one reporter may get rather routine stories done quickly and accurately, but he or she may not be a particularly outstanding reporter or writer. Conversely, a journalist may be an excellent reporter and writer who works more slowly at preparing stories. Of course, the most productive journalist is the one who can produce quality work at a quick pace.

As with all inputs in the supply process, journalists should be compensated based on their productivity. This is the key to keeping costs down and profits up, while providing a quality commodity. Productive journalists who are adequately compensated will be more likely to continue with the organization and to provide quality information than those who are not. A basic component of compensation is pay, but it is not the only one. Journalists often seek other rewards from their work, which is another reason classic economic theory fails to explain the role of creative labor in the newspaper industry. These rewards vary greatly but include the autonomy to develop stories and the intrinsic reward of helping others.

Individual journalists are not the only determinants of productivity. All labor works within constraints set up by the organization. One of the most important constraints is the work load. To a degree, quality and quantity are inversely related. The relationship is not perfect because there are some journalists who can reach both goals. However, a reporter with average or slightly above average skills cannot be expected to produce several stories a day and provide the type of context and depth for all the stories that readers often require. Thus, the number of reporters and editors for a given amount of work is an important contributor to individual productivity and to the overall quality of a newspaper.

Although research into the concept of work load and quality of work is not extensive, what is available tends to support the impact of staff size. Danielson and Adams studied the coverage of the 1960 presidential race in a national sample of daily newspapers. They found that completeness of coverage, which meant the number of potential stories covered, increased as staff size increased.[15] Fico studied reporting of the legislatures in two states and found a negative relationship between the number of stories produced and the number of sources used in each story.[16] Another study of 21 large and prestige newspapers found a negative relationship between the total square inches of stories a reporter wrote during a week and the amount of space given different sides in a controversial story.[17] As the work load increased, the balance in space given different sides of a controversy decreased.

Even though the quality and number of journalists at a newspaper contribute most to the nature of the news commodity that sells in the information market, other inputs also play a role. These include the use of graphics, the number of wire services carried, and expenditures on travel, research, and training. All are costs of creating a quality newspaper that will attract readers.

The use of graphics grew during the 1980s. Its development can be attributed to the use of offset printing, which improves quality and reduces costs; the development of *USA Today* as a pioneer in graphics; the competition in major metropolitan markets; the development of television as an alternative news source; and the increasing sophistication of journalists in the use of graphics. Because readers tend to like graphics, this type of expenditure will probably continue.[18]

The importance of wire and press services is second only to the talents of a paper's news staff in determining the quality of information supplied in newspapers. The percentage of all news section space filled with wire service copy averaged 25 percent for papers of less than 100,000 circulation and 21 percent for papers with more than 100,000 circulation in a national study of daily newspapers.[19] Dependence on wire services becomes even greater for foreign news coverage. One study of 114 U. S. dailies found that in November 1984, newspapers averaged 2.5 wire services.[20] This is probably a slight overestimate since the sample was weighted more for larger circulation newspapers. This average was slightly less than the average of 2.8 wire services found in a 1960 study by Danielson and Adams.[21]

The financial difficulties faced by United Press International during the 1980s raised concern about the impact of reduced service from UPI on available news content. However, the growth in the number of supplementary services provided by newspapers and newspaper groups and the increase in papers subscribing to these services suggest that firms will move in to supply the demand for news services if an existing service falters.[22]

While training for journalists is not a direct cost related to supplying newspapers, it is related to the quality of content. This in turn is connected to the quality of supply, which can affect circulation. The need for training journalists to deal better with society's complexity was noted by the Hutchins Commission in 1947. The 1980s saw a growth in the number of reporters and editors taking advantages of training centers, such as the American Press Institute and The Poynter Institute for Media Studies. This development not only increases the skills of journalists, but it contributes to the morale of journalists and can, therefore, affect productivity. The continuing growth in investigative journalism and the use of social science techniques, such as surveys, will necessitate even more training during the 1990s.

Although technology will be dealt with in greater detail in Chapter 6, its primacy as a contributor to increased productivity warrants a brief mention here. The application of computers to writing and editing in the newsroom has been the single most important adaptation of technology to information creation during the past 20 years. Computers have given reporters more flexibility in writing, but the main impact has probably come through the editing process. A 1978 study of copy editors at newspapers in nine states found that editing with computers was slower than pencil editing, but it was also more accurate.[23] A 1986 survey of copy editors who began their careers before the use of computers found that the majority of editors said computer editing was faster and more accurate.[24] These studies imply that adoption has resulted in higher productivity. However, some editors in these studies expressed a concern that computers improved technical editing of grammar, typos, and spelling but allowed less time for working with the reporters' writing.

In addition to writing and editing by staff members, computers have proven useful in receiving and editing wire copy. The ability to combine stories easily from several sources, both wire and staff, is important in providing the best possible article about an event or issue. This is especially true of events occurring at a distance from a newspaper's local market. Finally, computers have greatly improved the quality of newspaper graphics.

The differences in roles for newsroom labor at dailies and weeklies is a matter of degree. The same processes occur at both places. The differences are in timing and amount of space that must be filled. These differences mean a weekly usually has a smaller newsroom staff than a daily because the need to collect and process information under daily deadlines is missing.

One other difference is related to size. Total revenue is very much a function of circulation size, which means large circulation newspapers have more money to allocate to the newsroom. This is why most outstanding newspapers tend to be large circulation dailies, but the correlation between size and quality is not perfect. Quality journalism can still be practiced at smaller newspapers, as demonstrated by weeklies that win journalistic awards for news coverage. Quality at all levels is at least partially a function of the commitment and work ethic of individuals, but because larger newspapers have more people, the probability of having journalists who exhibit this commitment is greater.

The impact of costs on the information market through the newsroom is complicated. Good journalism involves an investment in people, which is difficult to relate to circulation, costs, and profit. However, the inability to correlate does not overshadow the fact that the quality of the information supplied in a newspaper can be improved by developing the skills and creativity of the newsroom staffs or by purchasing quality information from outside the particular newspaper firm.

Circulation and production. Although readers subscribe to newspapers for advertising as well as news-editorial content, the bulk of subscribers still take the paper primarily because of an interest in nonadvertising information. The quality of news is an important determinant of circulation, but it is not the only one. Many studies have found dissatisfaction with delivery service to be the first or second biggest cause of dropped subscriptions. Both the information and advertising markets are dependent upon successful delivery, so the costs of circulating newspapers plays an important role in obtaining the newspaper firm's goals.

The direct fixed costs that are applicable to circulation are the labor, machines, and vehicles that move the newspaper copies from the production department to the distributors and then to the homes, stores, and newspaper racks. The unit cost of labor is much lower in the circulation department than in the newsroom because delivering newspaper copies requires less skill than generating information.

Throughout the years, technology has contributed greatly to productivity in circulation. The development of machines for bundling newspaper copies and trucks for hauling copies contributed to lower unit costs during the beginning of the 20th century. But technology recently has contributed less to the distribution process than it has to the creation and production processes. Because of this, circulation has become an important area for future technological development.

Production is the third source of costs in the information market, although production also contributes to cost in the advertising market. Production involves taking the created information and reproducing it in mass quantities. Historically, the development of printing presses that could produce copies of high technical quality at a fast rate has been a driving force in determining the number of readers a newspaper could supply in a given time. The lowering of costs and increasing of supply that flows from printing technology has contributed greatly to defining types and markets of newspapers today.

Most of the variable costs at a newspaper come from the production process. Newsprint, ink, and Sunday supplements are all costs that increase in direct proportion to the number of copies printed. According to Inland Press Association data, these variable costs can make up from 8 to 25 percent of total newspaper revenue, depending on the size of the newspaper.[25] As circulation increases, the proportion of budget given to these variable costs increases.

Of the variable costs, newsprint receives the most attention, because newspapers currently have no acceptable substitute for delivering information to readers. On top of that, the price for newsprint continues to rise. Between 1985 and early 1988, newsprint went from $535 per ton to $650 per ton. This 21 percent increase in less than three years far exceeded inflation rate for the period.

The main problem contributing to increasing newsprint prices has been the lack of newsprint production capacity. Industry analysts have predicted that this supply problem will decline as capacity increases during the 1990s, but until that time, newspapers will continue to cut newsprint cost by trimming margins and using light weight paper for classified sections.[26]

Another way newspaper firms are dealing with newsprint uncertainty is by buying all or part of paper companies. For example, in 1988 the Tribune Co. of Chicago owned 100 percent of Quebec and Ontario Paper Co. and used about 50 percent of the company's 725,000 metric ton capacity a year.

Production also has extensive direct and indirect fixed costs. The indirect fixed costs are found in the depreciation of the presses and other equipment that help to reproduce copies of the newspaper. Direct fixed costs include labor, raw material, and the cost of maintaining the equipment. Inland Press Association data indicate that fixed production costs equal 5 to 18 percent of total newspaper revenues, depending on circulation size. As circulation size increases, the proportion of budget for fixed production costs declines.

Both circulation and production enjoy economies of scale. These economies come from the high fixed cost necessary to produce and distribute the newspaper copies. Figure 3.3 shows short-run average and marginal cost curves. The cost of producing the first copy is high, which means the average total cost (ATC) curve declines quickly. The shape and slope of the marginal cost curve (MC) are functions of the total variable cost curve. The MC curve will intersect the ATC curve at its minimum point.

Since technology is fixed during the short-run, the ATC curve theoretically will begin to turn up at some point. This represents decreasing returns to scale. Equipment has limits. A truck that can deliver 5,000 copies on time may not be able to deliver 6,000 copies on time. This means buying or leasing another truck, which contributes to increased costs. This problem is illustrated by the upturn in the ATC curve in Figure 3.3. However, as mentioned above, little evidence exists that newspaper firms reach such limits during the long run. Thus, the long-run ATC curve actually tend to be a straight line after a point.

Production economies of scale may come from two sources: the number of copies printed and the number of pages per copy.[27] Theoretically, as the number of copies produced increases, the average cost will fall because of the high fixed cost of printing presses. As newspaper copies grow in number of pages, the cost per page declines. The initial costs of preparing

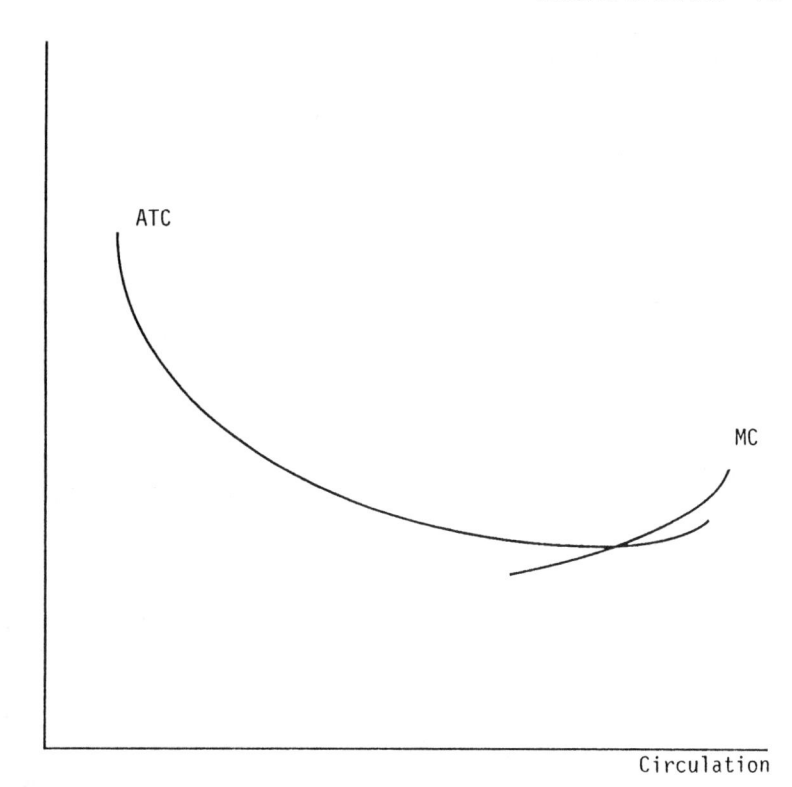

Figure 3.3. Short-run Average Total Cost and Marginal Cost Curves for Circulation
The ATC curve is a short-run average total cost curve. It declines quickly with circulation increases and then turns upward. The MC curve is the short-run marginal cost curve. After an initial decline it eventually increases. The MC curve intersects the ATC curve at its lowest point.

to print a minimal number of pages become dispersed among the additional pages that are printed.

An empirical study of newspaper economies of scale by Blankenburg found economies of scale present in number of pages, but not in circulation.[28] As the number of pages per year increased the average cost of such pages declined. He did not find economies of scale for numbers of copies. The elasticity of mechanical cost with respect to number of copies was 1.08. Thus, for every additional copy, there was an 8 percent increase in average costs. However, it is not clear whether the study included press depreciation as part of the expense. Because high indirect fixed costs create the scale economies, the depreciation, which makes up a greater percentage of expenses at smaller newspapers, should be included in figuring economies of scale.

Even if increased circulation does not have increasing returns to scale, the impact of increased pages is large enough that the overall production process has economies. These economies are especially important for large newspapers because of the need to provide diverse information for a large heterogeneous population. The larger the population that must be served, the more different types of information that are necessary. Adding pages to provide diversity not only can attract more readers but also contribute to economies of scale.

The Blankenburg study was of short-run scale economies. The results may not be applicable to the long-run when technology varies and newspaper firms can adapt to improve efficiency. Litman states that the long-run average reproduction cost curve will be somewhat L-shaped.[29] This is because the scale economies come from the best equipment and specialization of labor. There are no economies in raw materials. Thus, the savings are accrued in the smaller and intermediate levels of circulation and production, but not in the high circulation areas.

Production is not the only area of economies of scale. Circulation can also present savings. The economies of scale for circulation come from the nature of distribution. For example, a truck used to deliver 5,000 copies may hold 5,500 copies. The average and marginal costs for distributing the extra 500 copies is much lower than for the first 5,000. A similar situation exists with labor. A person who is delivering copies has economies of scale to the point of capacity within a given time period. Someone already delivering copies to houses on a particular block can deliver to an additional house on that same block with little added time or effort.

Economies of scale for circulation are not infinite in the short run. At some point, the costs of distribution exhibit decreasing returns to scale. This results from the location of subscribers. Economies result from increasing readers within a geographic area that is being served already, while adding new areas that were not being served may or may not have increasing returns to scale. If those areas are distant from a distribution point, the costs per unit may exceed revenue per unit by a large enough margin that it would take extensive penetration to make circulation in the geographic area profitable. The potential for a high level of penetration is a function of news and advertising content and of reader demand in the geographic market.

Other circulation costs can overcome the economies and make serving an area unprofitable. For example, it is difficult to serve apartment complexes because copies of the newspaper are easily stolen. If a copy is stolen, a second copy must be provided, which increases delivery and production costs. It is also expensive to serve high crime areas because of danger to the carriers. The costs of serving these types of areas can eliminate whatever cost savings are generated by scale economies. As a result, newspapers sometimes eliminate high cost circulation areas from home delivery.

Higher costs are not the only consideration in limiting circulation areas. The relative profitability of an area also comes into play. An area may be serviceable at a reasonable cost, but it may not generate the revenue to cover the cost. With newspapers this means that geographic areas inhabited sparsely or inhabited primarily by low-income people may not be served. Advertisers do not necessarily want the largest number of readers; they want the largest number of readers who are likely to buy their product. In most cases, this means the people who have discretionary income to spend on the advertisers' products. Circulation in low-income areas may not be attractive to many advertisers.

Blankenburg examine this phenomenon in a 1982 study.[30] He found evidence that Gannett newspapers controlled circulation between 1969 and 1979 by eliminating high-cost circulation areas. The study did not go into detail about the reasons behind the high cost.

This tendency to control circulation, and therefore supply, raises issues that are pertinent to the intellectual market. If a democracy's success depends on the give and take within the intellectual market, efforts to control access can affect the optimal functioning of this market. Control of supply means poor and more isolated areas may not be served. The overall impact of this practice is difficult to determine, but controlling circulation in this way indicates that concerns of the advertising and information market can take precedence over concerns of the intellectual market. This practice may hold long-run negative consequences for newspaper firms. Favorable government treatment in regulatory areas, such as antitrust and postal rates, is based on newspapers serving the intellectual market; failure to do this could result in less favorable treatment or even withdrawal of special treatment.

Advertising Market

Because newspapers are a joint commodity, advertising costs include some of the circulation and production costs mentioned above. As mentioned, it is difficult to divide these costs accurately between the two markets. Most newspapers simply create separate accounts for circulation and production.

This section will concentrate on advertising costs that are associated only with the advertising department, since the circulation and production cost were discussed above. As with the newsroom, these costs primarily involve labor. The labor in advertising can be broken down into sales and creative people. The sales force sells the space to advertisers, while the creative people generate the actual advertising information. In reality, much of the creative aspect is done by advertising agencies or in-house departments for larger advertisers. Usually, only small advertisers use creative people at newspapers.

The two areas of advertising labor are not necessarily mutually exclusive. While larger newspapers may have such a division of labor, the advertising workers at smaller papers may do both. At many newspapers, a person with graphics skills may serve both the newsroom and the advertising department.

Just as with the newsroom, the success of the advertising department depends a great deal on the skills of the people involved. These skills differ for the sales and creative forces within the department. Technical skills for the creative function can be learned, but the mental process of creating is not so easily acquired. A similar case can be made for the talents of a sales person.

Labor productivity is the key to controlling advertising department costs. Productivity here is more easily measured than in the newsroom. The number of inches of advertising or the total ad revenue a salesperson generates for a given amount of time are accurate measures of productivity. One could argue that advertisements have a creative dimension, but these ads are usually produced by an agency. Because of this ability to measure, compensation can be connected directly to performance, which is an important difference between the advertising department and the newsroom. The ability to measure productivity means advertising salespeople receive commissions, while newsroom workers do not. This is one reason advertising compensation tends to be higher than newsroom compensation. A reporter may have a higher salary, but the commission advertising sales people receive will make the take home pay much higher for a productive salesperson.

Depending on the system for commissions, advertising sales can yield economies of scale. The increasing returns on inputs for sales people can increase their compensation, while increasing the revenue for the firm.

Intellectual Market

The discussion of newsroom costs is applicable here because information plays a role in the intellectual market. However, if we narrow the discussion to the opinion function of newspapers, some different considerations are necessary. The opinion material comes generally from four sources: staff writers, syndicated columnists, freelance writers, and readers who write letters or guest columns. The combination of these sources in opinion pages depends on the content decisions of the newspaper staff and the costs of using the various types of material. The decisions about content will be dealt with in the next section. Costs of various types of material can be an important issue.

Of the four sources, staff opinion material is usually the most expensive because the firm bears the entire cost of the labor. Syndicated material is less expensive because of scale economies. Hundreds of newspapers buying the same column means a syndicated writer's price is spread among many newspaper firms. The cost of syndicated material is usually based on circulation, although price is negotiable in many cases. Fink reports that the price of syndicated material varies from $4 or $5 a week for small newspapers to $300 a week at large newspapers.[31] While $300 a week may seem expensive, the same large newspapers would pay several times that amount to a staff columnist with a large reader following.

Freelance writers and readers who write letters and columns are the least expensive, but they also contribute to the intellectual market. A university professor or local professional with expertise in an area can provide a more effective analysis of a problem than a staff writer and at a lower cost.

The direct cost of generating opinion information is not the only cost a newspaper has in the intellectual market. When controversial subjects are involved, strong stands by a newspaper in its editorials can offend some readers and advertisers. Some may even drop their newspaper subscription or advertisements in protest. The opinion content need not be offensive in some cases; it may just be inconsistent with the reader's beliefs. These same readers may also buy advertising in the newspaper. An offended business person can have a strong impact on revenues by ceasing to buy advertising space.

A 1980 study by *The Detroit News* of drops in northern suburbs found that 2.7 percent said they stopped taking the newspaper because of editorial content. This is not a large percentage, but it is still a cost that accrues to newspapers. The cost of taking controversial stands tends to be higher in smaller communities. Power is more concentrated, and the population tends to be more homogeneous in its attitudes. The chance of offending a large group of readers and advertisers is, therefore, greater.

This cost illustrates the conflicts that arise in serving the three different markets. Serving the intellectual market means presenting material that is controversial. This in turn means losing some readers. Some newspapers react by serving the intellectual market poorly. This means providing little or no opinion material, providing opinion only on issues that are national and international that would not directly affect the readers, or providing opinion material that is not controversial.

While dealing with controversy in newspaper editorial and op ed pages has a cost, not dealing with such issues may also have a cost. As with limiting circulation in some areas, poor service in the intellectual market has the long-run potential for lowering circulation among readers who expect their newspaper to be active in this market. Newspapers often tend to be conservative in dealing with the intellectual market, offering mostly noncontroversial opinion material. The impact of offended readers and advertisers is easier to measure than is the contribution of strong opinion material to circulation.

NEWSPAPER SUPPLY AND DEMAND

The previous section discussed the costs that newspapers accrue in supplying information for the three markets. Costs play an important role in determining how many copies of a newspaper will be sold and what those copies will contain. However, cost is only one aspect of supply. Costs must be considered in light of revenues, which reflect demand. The subtraction of cost from revenue yields profit, and for better or worse, most newspapers in the United States consider profit in deciding how they will operate, or even if they will operate.

Revenue is simply the units sold multiplied by the price received. Price can be determined in many ways. The simplest is to add the desired profit margin to the cost of supplying newspapers. This system is often used for new products, but this type of pricing for an existing product occurs when firms have a degree of monopoly power. Price of existing products in competitive markets is always subject to the demand of consumers. With newspapers, price is affected by what readers and advertisers will pay.

Actual price is a function of the interaction of supply and demand in the various market places. Across time, this interaction is also influenced by price, but price is not the only important factor in determining how many newspaper copies readers will buy. Quality of the commodity is also important. Which of the two dominates depends on which of the three markets one examines. The following discussion will examine the interaction of supply and demand as it occurs in the information, advertising, and intellectual markets.

Information Market

As mentioned in Chapter 2, quality plays a more important role than price in the interaction of supply and demand in the information market. Newspaper firms often do not cover the variable cost of producing newspaper copies with the price they charge readers. This low price occurs because the newspaper must have readers to attract advertisers at prices that will make an adequate profit. Price in the information market are kept low so as not to eliminate marginal readers. This approach seems to work, with delivery problems and lack of time for reading tending to top the lists of why people don't subscribe to a newspaper. Usually, the percentage of people who drop subscriptions because of price is small. One readership study by a large midwest daily found that only about 5 percent of the readers who dropped the newspaper did so because of price considerations.

Although demand in this market is relatively inelastic with respect to price, content quality is another matter. Different readers subscribe to specific newspapers for different combinations of reasons. These reasons are called content attributes. The more diverse the audience, the more diverse are the groups of content attributes that determine individual's subscription decisions. Newspapers must supply a correspondingly diverse package of information. This diversification of content increases the cost of space and increases the cost of providing specialized information. The increase in costs may or may not lead to increased price. This depends upon the exact elasticity of demand in a given information market.

It is difficult to determine the elasticity of supply with respect to quality of information because there is no adequate measure of quality. However, the supply curve would be downward sloping because as quality declines, circulation declines (see Chapter 2). This downward slope creates a trade-off for newspaper firms. Increased quality means increased costs, which would reduce profit, all else being equal. But increased quality also means increased circulation, which results in greater revenue and increased profit. *The key to optimizing profits is to identify the level of quality that will optimize the trade-off of quality cost and circulation.*

Figure 3.4 represents this trade off. For the sake of illustration, the slope of the supply curve is assumed to equal one. The demand curve, as mentioned in the last chapter, has a kink that represents the minimal level of acceptable value by most readers. To the left of this kink, circulation is elastic with respect to quality because many readers will consider the newspaper too inferior to buy.

Although the elasticity of the supply curve is difficult to identify, the forces that affect it are not. These include the cost of the information quality and the managers perceptions about what level of quality readers demand. The managers work in an uncertain environment. Even with readership studies, the lack of theory to interpret data means guesswork is necessary to meet readers' content demands. Managers who believe readers don't care about quality will create a newspaper with an inelastic supply curve that is close to the origin in Figure 3.4. They believe few readers will respond to changes in information quality, so they spend less on that quality. Managers who think readers will respond to a high quality commodity will produce a newspaper with a more elastic curve further from the origin. They believe better quality papers attract more readers. Price is assumed constant for the analysis.

78 THE ECONOMICS & REGULATIONS OF U.S. NEWSPAPERS

Three quality locations are given in Figure 3.4. Q_1 is a point where the quality demanded exceeds the quality supplied. At this level of quality, supply equals C_2 and demand equals C_4. The market for the newspaper is in disequilibrium. The newspaper has potential for attracting more readers, but this would require a greater investment in the information content than the managers are willing to make. To meet the demand, a new supply curve would be necessary. The elasticity of the demand curve above the equilibrium point means the cost of additional quality would probably exceed the revenue generated by the additional readers attracted by this quality.

Point Q_3 represents quality where the number of copies supplied will exceed the number of copies demanded. At this level, the number of copies that will be supplied equals C_4, but the number of copies demanded equals C_1. The quality is so poor, it costs little to produce, but a significant number of readers will not take the paper at this level.

The equilibrium point for supply and demand is Q_2. At this point the number of copies both demanded and supplied equals C_3. Here the cost of quality is offset by circulation, which will result in adequate advertising sales to reach the desired profit margin.

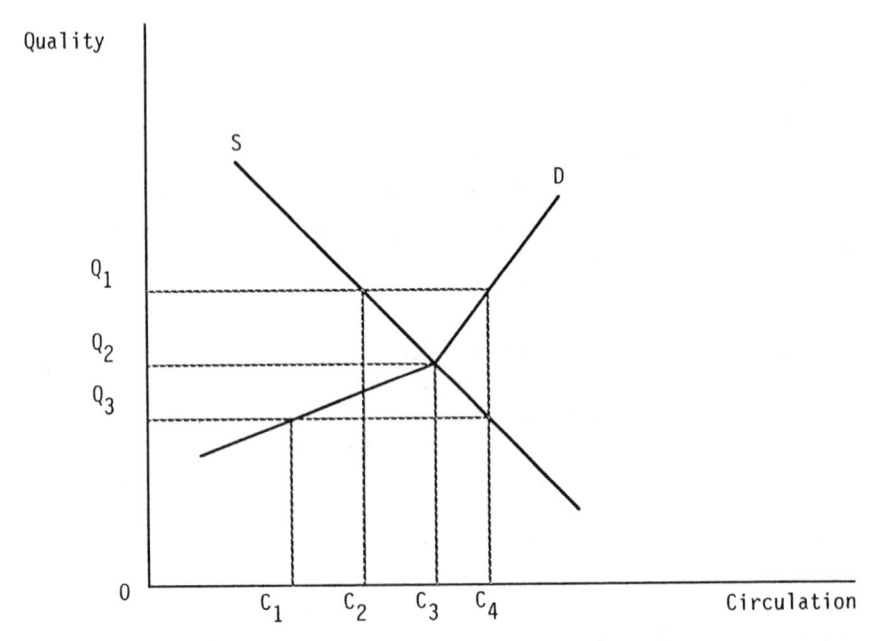

Figure 3.4. Supply and Demand Curves for Circulation with Respect to Quality of Information

The demand for newspapers is in equilibrium at the kinked point where supply (S) and demand (D) curves intersect. Here C_3 newspapers are bought with quality of Q_2. At Q_1 the demand exceeds supply, and at Q_3 the supply exceeds the demand.

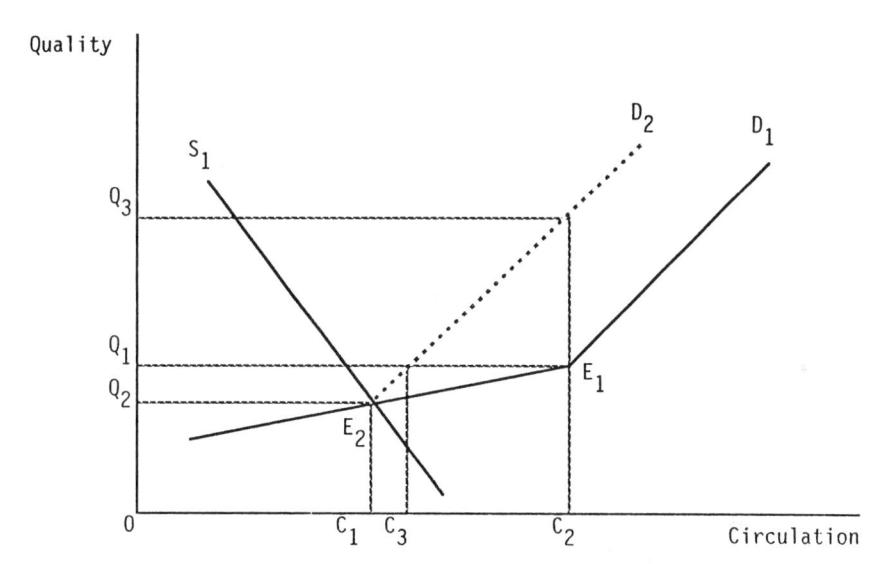

Figure 3.5. The Impact of Low Information Quality on Circulation
The demand curve for newspapers with respect to quality is represented by D_1. The equilibrium point would be E_1 with circulation C_2 and quality Q_1, but the newspaper firm decides to cut back costs to increase short-run profits. The cost reductions are represented by the supply curve S_1. Eventually, readers lower quality expectations and an equilibrium point is set up at E_2. In the short-run the newspaper firms saves the money required to produce a quality of Q_1, but the long-run impact is to reduce circulation and profits. The loss from reduced circulation exceeds the savings from reduced quality because of the elastic nature of the demand curve below the kinked point.

An important element of this supply and demand interaction is the location of the supply curve. The desired short-run profit margin a firm wants will affect the location. The higher the desired profit margin, the closer the curve will be to the origin, assuming demand and other costs are constant during the period being considered. Higher profit margins means lower costs, which means less of an investment in the news-editorial commodity. However, because these desired short-run profit margins do not consider the impact of demand, they can actually result in lower long-run profits. This impact comes from the possibility that demand will adjust to the quality of the newspaper across time.

Figure 3.5 shows how the newspaper supply curve location determined by high short-run profit margin goals can affect demand across time. Supply curve S_1 represents the supply curve that is consistent with the short-run profit margin but not at the equilibrium point E_1 as determined by demand curve D_1. The kink point is normally the equilibrium point, so the D_1 and S_1 curves in Figure 3.5 are in disequilibrium. The less than optimal supply curve with a quality level of Q_2 yields a circulation of C_1, instead of the circulation of C_2 that would exist if the supply curve went through the kink point. Equilibrium at the kink point would have required a quality level of Q_1.

In the short-run, the firm may reach its profit-margin goal with the supply curve S_1, with a savings in cost of Q_1 minus Q_2. However, if this level of quality is offered during the long-run, the readers will adjust to the quality and the demand curve will become D_2. Readers in effect decide that they will lower their quality expectations. A new equilibrium point of E_2 is established. With this shift, the potential for increasing circulation with an increase in quality from Q_2 to Q_1 is lowered from C_2, where it was with the original demand curve (D_1), to C_3 with the new demand curve. To reach the C_2 level of circulation in the long run will require an increase of quality to Q_3, which is considerable higher than the original quality level (Q_1) needed to reach C_2 circulation.

All of this means that short-run cost cutting in the area of quality can hurt the long-run potential for circulation expansion. The demand curve shifts toward the vertical axis because people in the market come to expect a lower quality newspaper. After this perception of lower quality develops, it takes a greater investment in quality to overcome it. This type of analysis represents a newspaper that has a fair amount of discretionary market power and tends to increase profits by cutting news-editorial costs.

Ironically, the effort to increase profits by cutting news-editorial costs can have a boomerang effect by lowering the total profit available for the firm during the short and long run. Had the initial supply curve been at the equilibrium point of E_1, the total profit would have been higher even if the profit margin was lower. In the long run, the cost of getting the C_2 circulation means that the total costs will be higher by Q_3 minus Q_2, thus lowering the total profit across time.[32]

The tendency of newspaper firms to cut quality for profit flows from the uncertainty newspapers face when it comes to understanding demand and the ways of altering newspaper content to meet this demand in the long run. The long-run impact suggests that newspapers that produce short-run high profit margins might be better advised to invest some of those profits in information quality and accept the lower margins that go with this, an argument which can be found regularly in newspaper industry publications.[33]

This theoretical argument has some support in empirical research, but that support is limited by measurement problems. In addition to the four articles mentioned above,[34] Meyer reported that the number of features and the particular features a newspaper carried was correlated with reader retention.[35] As Meyer points out, developing a better understanding of the actual relationship between circulation and content will require more extensive work. This relationship may vary in short-run and long-run impact.

Advertising Market

Although price does not play as large a role as quality in the information market, it is the crucial variable in the advertising market. Here, traditional supply and demand theory is more applicable. However, the advertising market has at least three variations from the classical microeconomic models. First, adding additional units of advertising will almost always produce a lower cost than revenue per unit. Second, the advertising market for newspapers is actually several submarkets. Third, the interdependence of the information and advertising markets defines the nature of the advertising commodity.

Unlike many industries that face severe limits on production, newspapers can add advertising lines and pages almost at will within the production capacity of presses. This ability comes from the economies of scale of page production. The high direct and indirect fixed costs of getting the presses ready to print and to run them account for the scale economies. Adding pages of advertising will almost always add to profit. The main limit is the impact of the additional pages on total production and delivery time and on the perception readers have of the newspaper. Theoretically, the additional pages could reach such a bulk that the increased production time would force later delivery. Increased weight of the newspaper copies also could increase the actual time needed to deliver a route. Practically, however, this is not a serious problem because the increased advertising revenue almost always exceeds increased costs.

Reader perception could be a problem. The increase in advertising gives the impression the newshole is shrinking even if the total amount of news-editorial space remains constant. This can lead to a negative impression of a newspaper firm's commitment to news coverage. The overall impact on perception in a market will depend on many variables, but the potential for lowering the reader's opinion should be considered when significantly changing the advertising-to-news ratio.

The effect of page economies on supply is one of allowing newspapers to offer advertising to many firms without the demand of one advertiser drastically reducing the supply available to other advertisers. This ability to serve an advertiser without taking space from another usually will not lower the quality in the information market, unless the newshole in a newspaper is already small.

As mentioned in Chapter 2, different types of advertising face different degrees of substitutability from other media commodities. Classified advertising and real estate ads, for example, do not have as many substitutes, other than direct mail, as do automobile advertisers. In reality, newspapers do not face one set of supply and demand curves for all advertisers. Rather, there are a series of such curves for the various types of advertising. These sets of curves will vary in their price elasticity. Advertisers who have several alternative media face more elastic supply curves than those who cannot easily find a substitute.

Just as with the information market, costs play a role in determining advertising prices. The costs of composing various types of advertisements are not consistent. Classified ads and insert advertisements take less time and effort to prepare for printing than do display advertisements. The costs of clerical workers and computers are the only expenses of preparing classifieds, while display advertising takes a salesperson to interact with the client, a creative person to develop and design the advertisement, and a computer to set up the advertisement. Usually, newspapers will take their cost and profit expectations as a starting point and then let the market determine pricing and supply.

Perfect competition economic theory assumes that firms are price takers—they supply at the market price, over which they have no control. The market supply and firm supply curves are perfectly elastic. This idea flows from the assumptions that there are many firms and low barriers to entry. Some supply curves for advertising will be perfectly elastic within the short time period between price increases. This depends upon the type of advertising. The point of equilibrium in such a submarket will be where marginal revenue equals marginal cost for that type of advertising. In reality, this means that in some markets, such as classified advertising, this equilibrium point is not reached. This comes from the three characteristics: (a) price is fairly constant within given periods of time; (b) prices are relatively high because of few good substitutes; (c) the average total cost of classified advertising continues to decline over a very large range of demand. Rarely would a newspaper begin to approach its capacity of production and composition. Even if the demand began to stretch the production capacity in the short run, the firm could always add more capacity in the long run.

It is this characteristic of classified advertising and some display advertising that has attracted competition from direct mail and shoppers. These firms enjoy the same production economies of scale as newspapers. They siphon advertising from newspapers by offering targeted markets. Yet newspapers have an advantage over direct marketing publications — the interrelationship of the advertising and information markets. This interrelationship can be examined from two approaches. First, it represents the quality of advertising in newspapers. Second, it has economies of scale for advertisers.

Figure 3.6 shows what can happen during a brief period of time to classified advertising in a market with an inelastic demand curve and one with an elastic demand curve. As mentioned, the low cost of producing classifieds and the stable prices give a perfectly elastic supply curve. In a slightly competitive market with an inelastic demand curve, S_1 is the starting supply curve, which has a price of P_1, classified advertising space

NEWSPAPER SUPPLY 83

INELASTIC DEMAND CURVE

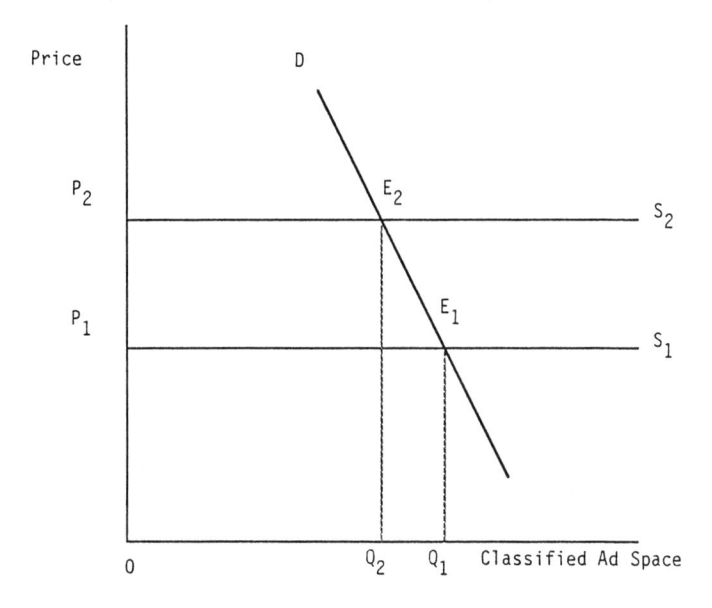

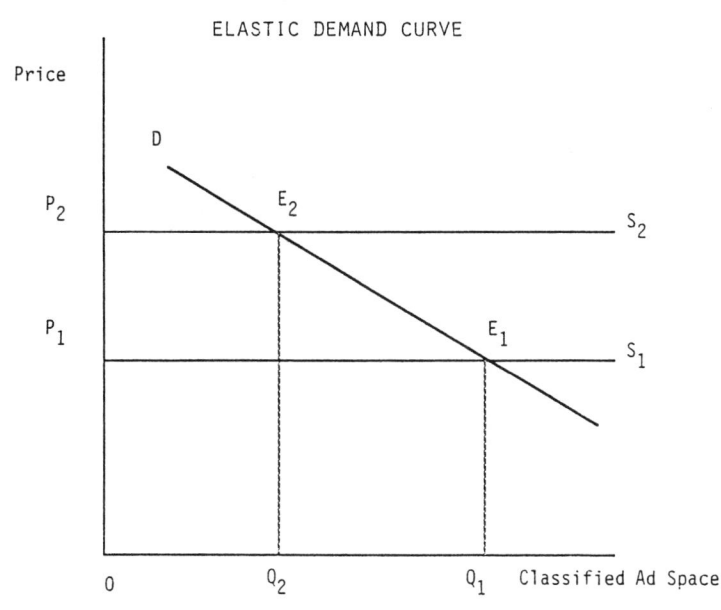

Figure 3.6. The Impact of Price Increases on Classified Advertising Space in Markets with Elastic and Inelastic Demand Curves
The impact on demand for classified advertising that results from a price increase from P_1 to P_2 is much greater in a market with an elastic demand curve. The decline in demand is represented by the difference between Q_1 and Q_2 in both markets.

of Q_1, and an equilibrium point of E_1. Since the market is not very competitive, which means weak direct mail coverage, the newspaper firm can raise the price to P_2 with advertising space equal to Q_2 and an equilibrium of E_2. The resulting profit is represented by $P_2E_2Q_20$, while the original profit is shown by $P_1E_1Q_10$. The new total profit is higher with less advertising space. The more inelastic the demand curve, the higher the price can go with only small decreases in inches of classified advertising.

The elastic demand curve given in Figure 3.6 represents a market where classified advertisers have alternatives. This could be a directly competitive daily market, one with a weekly and daily, or a market with strong total market coverage products. The same price increase in this market from P_1 to P_2 results in a decline in profit with less classified advertising. The new profit would be $P_2E_2Q_20$, compared to the old profit of $P_1E_1Q_10$.

It is easy to see why competition keeps classified ad prices lower, but why does the newspaper with the inelastic demand curve only raise its price to P_2 and not higher? First, classified advertising attracts readers. Too great of a loss of such ads could reduce circulation, which would in turn affect other advertising prices. Second, too high of a price is likely to draw additional competition in the long run to take advantage of the high profits the newspaper is making. Third, too high of a price could result in a downward shift in the demand curve, which would cut inches further and lower profit.

Not all types of newspaper advertising will have a perfectly elastic supply curve. Some types of advertising, such as display ads, have a higher cost of preparation and more competition. Here, firms can influence price by supply, but their ability to set prices at will is limited. These types of advertising submarkets are more likely to have supply curves similar to the ones in Figure 3.2. Higher prices will force some advertisers to go elsewhere, while lower prices will attract advertisers from other media.

Although advertising does not have quality in the same sense as the news-editorial sections of the newspaper, it does have a level of quality from the advertisers' standpoint that is related to the nature of the readers. Advertisers prefer readers who can buy their products, and newspaper readers tend to be from higher socioeconomic classes. This is especially applicable for advertisers who want consumers from a wide geographic range and background. Direct mail has an advantage in that it can target geographic areas with demographic characteristics that fit the advertisers' needs.

In the area of costs, direct mail benefits from being delivered by the U.S. mail service. However, newspapers have the economies of scale of serving two markets with one process. They can receive money for information through the circulation department and turn around and sell those readers to advertisers.

The number of readers and types of readers affects quality even more directly in newspaper competition than in intermedia competition. The effective price of advertising for companies is determined by the price per thousand readers. This milline rate can give the leading circulation newspaper a distinct advantage over a trailing newspaper. The demographic nature of readers can also come into play in this newspaper competition.

Intellectual Market

An important advantage a newspaper has over direct mail publications comes from the intellectual market. Direct mail packages and many shoppers carry little or no opinion content and do not attract readers who seek this content. Of course, the impact of this market on advertising depends heavily on the nature of reader demand for this type of content. If the demand is high and a newspaper meets that demand, the attraction of readers gives newspapers a comparative advantage over direct mail. In other words, the readers will open the newspaper and go through it, whereas a large proportion of readers will toss direct mail material in the waste can.

Whether the activities in the intellectual market can have an effect on the advertising market depends on whether readers want the opinion content and whether newspapers provide material to meet this demand. Evidence exists that readers want newspapers to contribute to the intellectual market. Weaver and Mauro reported that the most common reading pattern for women was evaluation material, which was composed of editorials and columns. This was second for men, behind straight news.[36] Research into the relationship between content and circulation by one of the authors found a .632 correlation between local editorials and circulation in 35 Denver and Detroit suburbs with weeklies and twice-weeklies.[37]

With the obvious demand for opinion material, the newspapers must meet that demand in order to fully take advantage of this market. Stempel studied 25 dailies with more than 100,000 circulation and 75 with under 100,000 circulation in 1978. The large dailies averaged 14 editorials for the five day week examined, while the small papers averaged 9.45. The smaller newspapers had 20 percent local editorials and the large newspapers 19 percent. The larger papers were more likely than smaller to have persuasive local editorials, however.[38] A study of 114 daily newspapers found that the percentage of news and editorial sections given to op ed and editorial material ranged from 8.58 in newspapers with 30,000 to 100,000 circulation to 9.32 in newspapers with circulation more than 100,000. However, only a small proportion of the op-ed and editorial pages were given to editorials about the city in which the newspaper was located. Those under 30,000 circulation allocated 1.42 percent; those between 30,000 and 100,000 gave 2.21 percent; and those over 100,000 allocated 2.65 percent.[39]

A pair of studies by Hynds surveyed editors at more than 180 daily newspapers in 1975 and 1983. Results showed an increase during the eight years in the amount of space given editorials, the number of letters printed and the number of candidate endorsements.[40]

So, newspapers are providing content in an effort to meet the demand in the intellectual market. Whether this supply is adequate is difficult to measure because this market overlaps extensively with the information market and each geographic market will vary as to need and demand. Some critics have argued that newspaper participation in this market generally is inadequate.

Members of the Hutchins Commission said that because of concentration of power in the information and advertising markets, owners and managers of mass media were ignoring their responsibility in the intellectual market.[41] They said the decline of competition and concentration of ownership limits access to the intellectual market, thus reducing the flow of ideas that society needs to adjust to a changing environment. The Commission suggested 13 steps that could widen access to the market.

Most members of the press rejected the analysis and suggestions of the Hutchins Commission.[42] Yet much of what the Commission suggested has been acted upon to some degree since the report was issued. The "social responsibility theory" of the press, which calls on the press to provide a fair, accurate, and complete presentation of news and comment about important events and issues, grew partly from the Commission report.[43] The values expressed by the Commission can be found in various codes of conduct adopted by press organizations.

The Hutchins Commission was not the only organization to accuse the press of failure in the intellectual market. The Kerner Commission issued similar complaints about the way the press treated issues of interest to minorities.[44] The Kerner Commission members said the press had failed minorities in the information and intellectual market and, as a result, had failed society as a whole.

Whether newspaper firms have succeeded at meeting demand in this market is debatable, but managers would be wise to examine their role in this market because it is a market that television, direct marketing, and other substitute media commodities have traditionally neglected. Having this socially mandated role certainly can be a comparative advantage with respect to other media.

Price means very little in this market. As mentioned above, various sources of material for this market have various costs. The effort to supply this market has at least two other costs. First, there is an opportunity cost of taking space from the other sections of the newspaper. Giving space to the editorial and op ed pages can mean losing news, entertainment, and sports space during the short run. However, the opportunity costs of losing news pages may be offset by the benefits of adding opinion material, if the demand in the intellectual market is high. In the long run, of course, more space can be made available.

There is an even more important long-run cost that can come from not supplying this market well. The unique existence of newspapers among other industries in the society is dependent upon the First Amendment, which assumes this market will be served. As the Hutchins Commission warned in 1947, failure in this market could result in society reviewing the informal license granted by the Constitution. Protection from lawsuits in the information market rest on contributions to the intellectual market through information and opinion. Failure to serve this market could also affect special consideration in areas such as antitrust laws. Without the active contribution to the intellectual market, newspapers are no different from any other information or advertising service.

SUMMARY

Supplying demand in the information, advertising, and intellectual markets is a function primarily of costs, price, and quality. The advertising market is the easiest to understand and make decisions about because it conforms closest to perfect competition theories in microeconomics. The information market is difficult to deal with because demand and supply are primarily based on quality of information, even thought this concept is hard to define and measure. The same holds true for the intellectual market. Considerations of supply in the advertising market often dominate considerations of the information and intellectual markets because it is the source of most newspaper revenues. However, neglect of the information market holds the potential for reduced short-run and long-run total profits, and neglect of the intellectual market holds the potential for long-run impact on the special place the newspaper industry has in United States society—a place that has been profitable for U. S. newspapers.

ENDNOTES

1. The authors thank Bill Blankenburg for developing the example in Table 3-1.
2. Walter Nicholson, *Intermediate Economics and Its Application*, 2nd. ed. (Hinsdale, IL: The Dryden Press, 1979), pp. 195-199.

3. William B. Blankenburg, "Newspaper Scale and Newspaper Expenditures," *Newspaper Research Journal*, (Winter 1989), pp. 97-103.
4. *The Inland National Cost and Revenue Study* (Park Ridge, IL: The Inland Daily Press Association, 1987).
5. Jon G. Udell, *The Economics of The American Newspaper*. (New York: Hastings House, 1978), pp. 118-120.
6. Lee Becker, Randy Beam, and John Russial, "Correlates of Daily Newspaper Performance in New England," *Journalism Quarterly*, 55:100-108 (Spring 1978); and Gerald C. Stone, Donna Stone, and Edgar P. Trotter, "Newspaper Quality's Relation to Circulation," *Newspaper Research Journal*, Spring 1981, pp. 16-24.
7. Blankenburg, 1989, *op. cit.*
8. Stephen Lacy and Frederick Fico, "Financial Commitment, Newspaper Quality and Circulation: Testing an Economic Model of Direct Newspaper Competition," Paper presented to the Association for Education in Journalism and Mass Communication, Washington, DC, August 1989.
9. Leo Bogart, *Press and Public*, 1st ed. (Hillsdale, NJ: Lawrence Erlbaum Associates, Inc., 1981).
10. Warren Breed, "Social Control in the Newsroom: A Functional Analysis," *Social Forces*, 33:326-335 (May 1955).
11. Gaye Tuchman, *Making News: A Study in the Construction of Reality* (New York: The Free Press, 1978).
12. Walter Gieber and Walter Johnson, "The City Hall 'Beat': A Study of Reporter Source Roles," *Journalism Quarterly*, 38:289-297 (Summer 1961).
13. Stephen Lacy and David Matustik, "Dependence on Organization and Beat Sources for Story Ideas: A Case Study of Four Newspapers," *Newspaper Research Journal*, Winter 1983, pp. 9-16.
14. David H. Weaver and G. Cleveland Wilhoit, *The American Journalist: A Portrait of U. S. News People and Their Work* (Bloomington, IN: Indiana University Press, 1986).
15. Wayne A. Danielson and John B. Adams, "Completeness of Press Coverage of the 1960 Campaign," *Journalism Quarterly*, 38:441-452 (Autumn 1961).
16. Frederick Fico, "A Comparison of Legislative Sources in Newspaper and Wire Service Stories," *Newspaper Research Journal*, Spring 1984, pp. 35-43; Frederick Fico, "The Replication of Findings on Newspaper and Wire Service Source Use in Two Statehouses," *Newspaper Research Journal*, Fall 1985 pp. 74-80; and Frederick Fico, "Influence of Perceived Editorial Concern and Role Self-Concept on Source Reliance of Reporters in Two Statehouses," *Journalism Quarterly*, 63:332-30 (Summer 1986).
17. Stephen Lacy, Frederick Fico, and Todd Simon, "The Relationship Among Economic, Newsroom and Content Variables: A Path Model," *Journal of Media Economics*, Fall 1989, pp.51-66.
18. Pamela M. Terrell, "Art," *presstime*, February 1989, pp. 20-27.
19. Stephen Lacy and James M. Bernstein, "Daily Newspaper Content's Relationship to Publication Cycle and Circulation Size," *Newspaper Research Journal*, Winter 1988, pp. 49-57.

20. Stephen Lacy, "The Effect of Ownership and Competition on Daily Newspaper Content," Doctoral Dissertation, The University of Texas at Austin, 1986.
21. Danielson and Adams, *op. cit.*
22. Rolf Rykken, "Supplemental Wires Vie for Clients," *presstime*, May 1989, pp. 14-18.
23. Linda J. Shipley and James K. Gentry, "How Electronic Editing Equipment Affects Editing Performance," *Journalism Quarterly*, 58:371-374, 387 (Autumn 1981).
24. William R. Lindley, "From Hot Type to Video Screens: Editors Evaluate New Technology," *Journalism Quarterly*, 65:485-489 (Summer 1988).
25. *Inland National Cost and Revenue Study, op. cit.*
26. Margaret G. Carter, "Newsprint," *presstime*, May 1988, pp. 33-41.
27. For a more detailed discussion of economies and cost curves see Barry Litman, "Microeconomic Foundations," in Robert Picard, James P. Winter, Maxwell E. McCombs, and Stephen Lacy, eds. *Press Concentration and Monopoly* (Norwood, NJ: Ablex, 1988), pp. 3-34.
28. Blankenburg, 1989, *op. cit.*
29. Litman, *op. cit*
30. William B. Blankenburg, "Newspaper Ownership and Control of Circulation to Increase Profits," *Journalism Quarterly*, 59:390-398 (Autumn 1982).
31. Conrad Fink, *Strategic Newspaper Management* (New York: Random House, 1988), p. 168.
32. This analysis is based on the model of newspaper demand developed by Lacy and mentioned in the previous chapter. For more details on the model see Stephen Lacy, "A Model of Demand for News: Impact of Competition on Newspaper Content," *Journalism Quarterly*, 66:40-48, 128 (Spring 1989).
33. For an example of this type of article see Jonathan Kwitny, "The High Cost of High Profits," *Washington Journalism Review*, June 1990, pp. 19-29.
34. See Stone et al.; Becker et al.; Blankenburg; and Lacy and Fico, *op. cit.*
35. Philip Meyer, *The Newspaper Survival Book: An Editor's Guide to Marketing Research* (Bloomington, IN: Indiana University Press, 1985), pp. 76-77.
36. David H. Weaver and John B. Mauro, "Newspaper Readership Patterns," *Journalism Quarterly*, 55:84-91, 134 (Spring 1978).
37. Stephen Lacy and Ardyth Sohn, "Correlations of Newspaper Content with Circulation in the Suburbs," *Journalism Quarterly*, in press.
38. Guido H. Stempel III, "Types and Topics of Editorials in U. S. Dailies," *Newspaper Research Journal*, April 1979, pp. 3-6.
39. Lacy and Bernstein, *op. cit.*
40. See Ernest C. Hynds, "Editorials, Opinion Pages Still Have a Vital Role at Most Newspapers," *Journalism Quarterly*, 61:634-639 (Autumn 1984); and Ernest C. Hynds, "Editorial Pages Are Taking Stands, Providing Forums," *Journalism Quarterly*, 53:532-535 (Autumn 1976).
41. The Commission on Freedom of the Press, *A Free and Responsible Press* (Chicago: The University of Chicago Press, 1947).

42. "The Hutchins Report: A Twenty-Year Review", *Columbia Journalism Review*, Summer 1967, pp. 5-20.
43. William L. Rivers, Wilbur Schramm, and Clifford G. Christians, *Responsibility in Mass Communication*, 3rd. ed. (New York: Harper & Row, 1980).
44. *Report of the National Advisory Commission on Civil Disorders* (New York: Bantam Books, 1968).

4

Competition in the Newspaper Industry

A common conception exists that most daily newspapers in the United States are monopolies. Yet most people working in the newspaper industry will argue that daily newspapers face intense competition from a multitude of sources. In a sense both positions are correct. The vast majority of cities with daily newspapers have only one newspaper firm headquartered within its boundaries. At the same time, those newspapers must compete with radio stations, television stations, magazines, billboards, and direct mail services for a share of the advertising dollar—competition that is rightly viewed as influencing newspaper revenue. In addition to other media, a newspaper may also have larger newspapers from nearby metropolitan areas or national newspapers selling in their markets.

Perhaps the best way to settle this seeming contradiction is the one chosen by Owen. He uses the word monopoly almost interchangeably with the phrase monopoly power. He defines monopoly power as a "worrisome degree of discretionary power, including the power not to maximize profits."[1] It is a rarity to find a newspaper with 100 percent of the circulation or advertising in its market, but management at most dailies can significantly affect much of what happens in their markets, especially in some areas of advertising and news coverage.

Using this definition of monopoly, this chapter will start with a brief review of economic market structure. Next, the various types of competition newspapers face in the information, advertising, and intellectual markets will be reviewed. Finally, the way these types of competition affect performance in these three markets will be examined.

NEWSPAPER MARKET STRUCTURE

All market structure starts with a geographic area. This area is defined by the locations where a newspaper chooses to sell its copies and advertising. Given the geographic market, market structure is determined by two dimensions: the number of firms and the homogeneity of products within the market. A third variable that affects market structure across time is the extent of barriers to entry. Based on these dimensions, markets usually are classified into one of four types: perfect competition, monopolistic competition, oligopoly or monopoly. These categories exist for convenience because in reality individual markets fall on a continuum from perfect competition to monopoly.

First, *perfect competition* markets are those with many sellers, products that are homogeneous, and low barriers to entry. Firms in this type of market have no power to set prices. If a firm raises its price above the market price, consumers with their perfect knowledge will buy elsewhere. Any effort to make above normal profits (defined as profits necessary to continue producing the product at a given level of uncertainty) will bring more firms into the market. These firms will absorb the excess profits.

The second market structure is *monopolistic competition*. This type of market has many sellers, heterogeneous (or differentiated) products, and slightly higher barriers to entry. In monopolistic competition, firms produce commodities or products that are not perfect substitutes. They can be differentiated in several ways, including product characteristics, advertising, and location of the firm's stores. While no two products are perfect substitutes in monopolistic competition, consumers may substitute products for one another depending on the degree of differentiation. The degree of substitutability is a function of how well the two commodities meet the consumers' demands. Barriers to entry would be higher than in perfect competition because of advertising costs and production technology necessary to produce differentiated goods.

The third market structure is *oligopoly*, which means few enough sellers that each firm knows its actions affect the entire market. Oligopolies can have homogeneous or heterogeneous products. The barriers to entry are high. In oligopolies, firms can make decisions with or without taking the other firms' reactions into account. The result of these two options are quite different. If they ignore the possible reactions of other firms, competition tends to create results more similar to monopolistic competition. If the firms anticipate reactions by the other firms, performance tends to be similar to that which you would find in monopoly markets.

The fourth market structure is *monopoly*. A monopoly occurs when only one firm is in the market. Since there is only one firm, the product is neither homogeneous nor heterogeneous compared to products by other firms. Monopolies tend to produce fewer units of a good with higher prices than one would find in a competitive market. This means the firm makes monopoly profits. Monopolies have high barriers to entry, but technologi-

(A) CONTINUUM OF MARKET POWER

Perfect competition	Monopolistic competition	Oligopoly	Monopoly

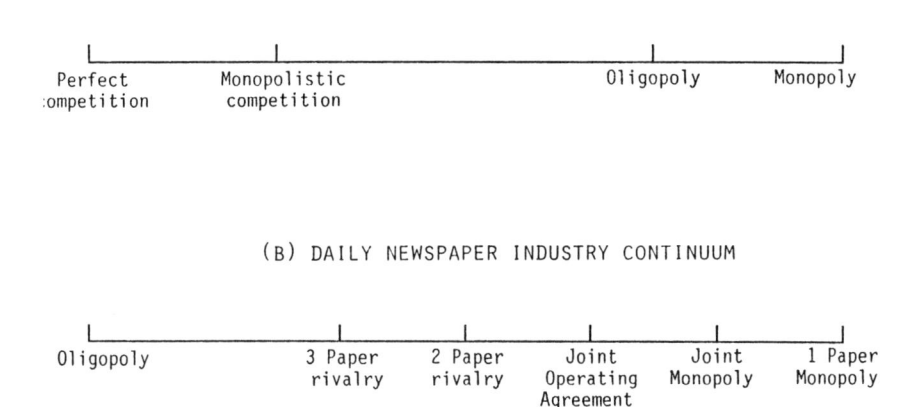

(B) DAILY NEWSPAPER INDUSTRY CONTINUUM

Oligopoly	3 Paper rivalry	2 Paper rivalry	Joint Operating Agreement	Joint Monopoly	1 Paper Monopoly

Figure 4.1. Competition Continuum Based on Number of Firms in the Market
Source: Barry Litman, "Microeconomic Foundations," in Robert G. Picard, James P. Winter, Maxwell E. McCombs, and Stephen Lacy, eds. *Press Concentration and Monopoly* (Norwood, NJ: Ablex, 1988), p. 4.

cal developments can on occasion open the markets. Litman uses a continuum based on number of firms in a market. He puts monopoly on the right end and perfect competition on the left. To the right of perfect competition is monopolistic competition, and to the right of monopolistic competition is oligopoly. He places newspaper markets between oligopolies and monopolies. Litman's continuum for competition in general and for newspapers is shown in Figure 4.1.[2]

One difficulty in applying economic theory to newspapers is defining the number of competitors. This number is reflected in the elasticity of demand for the newspaper commodity. However, this elasticity varies between the advertising and information markets and even within types of advertising. Table 2.3 shows the levels of substitutability of some types of advertising between television and newspapers. Similar tables could be set up for newspapers and radio, newspapers and billboards, newspapers and magazines, and newspapers and direct mail. All this indicates that the markets for some forms of newspaper advertising are likely to have more than a "few" sellers. Thus, the nature of the product becomes as important a variable as the number of firms in understanding competition. Because general circulation newspapers are bundles of information, these submarkets play an important role in whether newspaper firms can meet their goals.

Defining the market structure of the newspaper information market is just as difficult. News commodities are differentiated to attract readers and viewers from other news commodities, but they can also be similar enough to be substitutable because they are trying to draw from the same pool of information users. These countervailing forces of similarity and differentiation exist across time and are important in shaping the nature of news commodities.

The similarities of newspapers show up more in their breaking news than in other types of information. There are certain topics and locations that must be covered for a newspaper to be a general circulation newspaper. These topics reflect a set of shared news values that are part of the organizational structure of newspapers and the socialization process of journalists.[3] Other types of news and information can be used to differentiate newspapers. These other types of information define the categories of newspapers discussed in Chapter 2. The differentiation will help determine how successful these newspapers will be in competitive situations. However, newspapers that become too differentiated move into specialized markets and no longer compete for a general audience.

Monopolistic competition and oligopoly models have been called hybrid models[4] because they fall between perfect and monopoly competition, which were developed earlier in the history of economic analysis. Yet newspapers are not adequately served even by these hybrids. As mentioned in Chapter 1, newspapers are joint commodities. There is little well-developed theory for slightly differentiated joint commodities with demand based on commodity quality as well as price.

Despite the primitive development of economic theory applicable to newspapers, existing theory can be used for understanding a newspaper firm's performance, particularly if one examines specific markets. In these specific cases, the substitutability of commodities in the information and advertising markets can be directly observed. Economic concepts can be modified to help with understanding and predicting in these individual markets.

A second way of using economic theory at a more general level is to take different types of competition, as defined by geography and type of newspaper, and look for patterns of performance. This more general approach will be used here to examine direct, intercity, and intermedia competition.

DIRECT COMPETITION

Direct competition refers to competition between or among newspapers that are headquartered in the same city. This competition can take three forms: competition between separately owned and operated newspapers; competition between newspapers that have a joint operating agreement;

and competition between a morning and evening newspaper owned by the same company. Each of these will be discussed in connection with the three markets in which newspapers operate.

While the nature of ownership is important to competition, so is the publication cycle. As mentioned in Chapter 2, weekly newspapers are not generally good substitutes for daily newspapers; yet they can compete to a small degree in the information market. Weeklies certainly compete against other weeklies in the same market.

Before examining the relationship between competition and newspapers, it would be useful to examine the extent of direct competition in the United States. One of the dominant trends in the country during this century has been the decreasing number of cities with competitive newspapers. Trends since 1920 in the number of cities with competing newspapers can be seen in Table 4.1.

TABLE 4.1. TRENDS IN COMPETITION AMONG GENERAL CIRCULATION DAILY NEWSPAPERS

	1920	1930	1940	1954	1968	1976	1987
Total dailies	2,042	1,942	1,878	1,785	1,749	1,756	1,645
Total daily cities	1,295	1,402	1,426	1,448	1,500	1,550	1,526
One daily cities	716	1,002	1,092	1,188	1,287	1,369	1,416
Percent of total	55.3	71.5	76.7	82.1	85.8	88.4	92.8
One-Combination cities	27	112	149	157	150	122	66
Percent of total	2.1	8.0	10.5	10.8	10.0	8.0	4.4
Joint operating agreement cities[a]	4	16	18	17	19		
Percent of total			>.1	1.1	1.2	1.1	1.2
Cities with two or more separately owned and operated newspapers	552	288	181	87	45	39	25
Percent of total	42.6	20.5	12.7	6.0	3.0	2.5	1.6

Sources: Figures for 1920, 1930, 1940, and 1968 came from Raymond B. Nixon, "Trends in in U.S. Newspaper Ownership: Concentration with Competition," *Gazette*, 14:3:181-193 (1968). Reprinted with permission of Kluwer Academic Publications. Figures for 1954 and 1976 came from Judith Sobel and Edwin Emery, "U.S. Dailies' Competition in Relations to Circulation Size: A Newspaper Data Update," *Journalism Quarterly*, 55:145-149 (Spring 1978). Figure for 1987 were taken from '*88 Facts About Newspapers*, American Newspaper Publishers Association, 1988.

Note: A one-combination city is a city in which the morning and evening newspapers are owned by the same company. Joint operating agreement cities are those in which the two newspapers have signed a joint operating agreement to combine all operations but news-editorial. This type of agreement is legal under the 1970 Newspaper Preservation Act.

[a]Many listings of joint operating agreement newspapers incorrectly list the cities of Bristol, Tennessee and Bristol, Virginia; Madison, Wisconsin; and Lincoln, Nebraska as having joint operating agreement newspapers. This would explain any differences between this table and other published tables.

Of the 1,295 cities with daily newspapers in 1920, 44.7 percent had at least two newspapers available for readers. In 552 cities, these two newspapers were separately owned and operated. By 1987, only 110 cities with dailies had more than one newspaper available and 66 of these were cities where the same company owned both the morning and evening newspapers. Only 25 cities remained in 1987 with separately owned and operated newspapers, and another 19 had joint operating newspapers. In May 1990, the number of cities with separately owned and operated daily newspapers and the number of markets with joint operating papers were equal at 20.

The trend of declining markets with separately owned and operated newspapers was countered for a while, between 1920 and 1954, by the growth of markets with two newspapers owned by the same company. This trend reversed rapidly beginning in the late 1960s. The percentage of cities with combination dailies dropped from about 10 percent in 1968 to less than 5 percent in 1987.

Blankenburg studied this trend in declining two-newspaper combination companies.[5] He found one of the best predictors of the loss of the second newspaper was the difference in circulations. A strong morning newspaper could not support a weak afternoon paper for very long. He also found that large newspaper groups were quicker to close the weaker newspaper in a combination than were independently owned companies.

The number of joint operating agreement newspapers has remained about the same since the Newspaper Preservation Act (NPA) was passed in 1970. At the time of the NPA passage, the Justice Department listed 22 JOA cities. Three of these should not have been listed. The newspapers in Bristol, Virginia, and Bristol, Tennessee, should not have been included because the two papers were not separately owned. The Justice Department ruled in 1987 that the pairs of newspapers in Lincoln, Nebraska, and Madison, Wisconsin, were not JOA newspapers. They are combinations produced by companies that are owned by two different newspaper groups.

Twenty cities had joint operating agreements in 1990. Between 1970 and May 1990, five JOAs were dissolved and six were approved, with one application pending. This indicates that the Newspaper Preservation Act may preserve two separate news-editorial voices in some markets, but it is not the answer to the long-term decline in direct newspaper circulation. About 40 cities have lost competing newspapers since the NPA was passed.

The failure of the NPA to stop the decline in competition comes from its inability to attack a basic cause of the decline—the joint commodity nature of newspapers. While several forces have contributed to the decline of direct newspaper competition, the joint commodity nature, which causes a circulation spiral, is the most powerful. It continues even with a joint agreement.

A circulation spiral develops when a competing newspaper gains an advantage in circulation. When this happens, advertisers move more of their advertising linage to the leading newspaper because they get more readers per dollar. Because readers also buy newspapers for advertising, the leading circulation newspaper picks up more readers with the increase in advertising linage. The increase in circulation means a higher percentage of the market's advertising. This spiral continues as the leading paper gains a higher proportion of advertising linage than of circulation. Since advertising represents 70 to 80 percent of revenues at a newspaper, the newspaper moving down in the spiral edges toward failure and the paper moving up in the spiral becomes more and more profitable and dominant in the market.

Figure 4.2 shows how this circulation spiral is reflected in supply and demand. The two diagrams in Figure 4.2 represent two newspapers with intense competition. Both newspapers have a perfectly elastic supply curve at the same price, P_1. This is a horizontal curve that means the newspapers will supply as many copies as the market wants within press capacity. The ability to do this represents the excess press capacity competitive newspapers have and the need to supply as many copies as they can to attract advertisers. Both papers have the same circulation, C_1. Newspaper One lowers prices to P_2. This lowers the supply curve from S_1 to S_2. The result for Newspaper One is an increase in circulation to C_2. The impact on Newspaper Two is to generate a new demand curve because it has lost some readers to Newspaper One. This is shown by demand curve D_2. The new circulation is C_2. The drop in readers for Newspaper Two is probably not as large as the gain for Newspaper One because some nonreaders who are inclined to take Newspaper One but were not buying copies because of high price are brought into the market. In order to regain readers, Newspaper Two must cut its price. This would result in the new supply curve S_2 for Newspaper Two.

Even if Newspaper Two does reduce its price to P_2, the impact probably will not help it catch up. The movement of readers to Newspaper One by the initial price cut will carry some advertising with the readers. This new revenue can be invested in news-editorial quality, which will create new demand curves for both newspapers. The new curve for Newspaper One is D_2, which increases circulation to C_3. This new demand curve represents three factors: (a) the movement of advertising space from Newspaper Two to One following the increase in circulation, which brings yet more readers, (b) the entry of new readers into the market, (c) the investment of additional profits in the quality of information. The new demand curve for Newspaper Two is D_3, which reduces circulation once again to C_3. The new curve for Newspaper Two represents losses to Newspaper One and the decline in advertising and information quality. Newspaper Two is further hurt by the reduction of revenue that follows the drop in advertising. This

98 THE ECONOMICS & REGULATIONS OF U.S. NEWSPAPERS

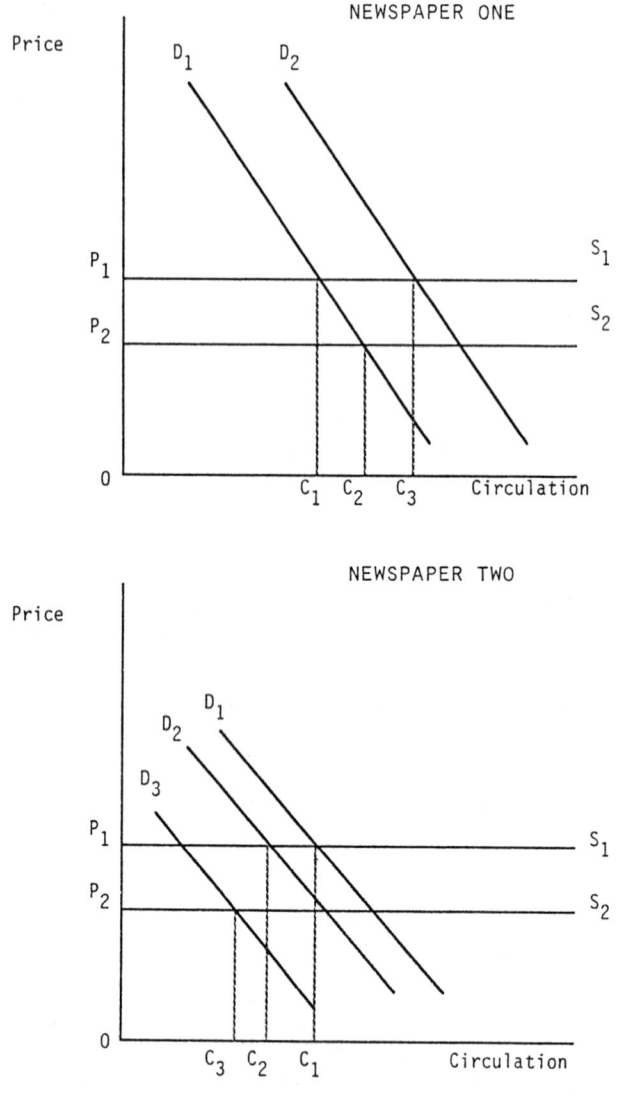

Figure 4.2. Impact of the Circulation Spiral on Directly Competitive Newspapers
A decline in price can contribute to the circulation spiral, assuming equivalent quality of newspapers. A lowering of price from P_1 to P_2 by Newspaper One shifts the supply curve to S_2, which increases circulation from C_1 to C_2. The increase in the circulation for Newspaper One causes the demand for Newspaper Two to shift from D_1 to D_2. The increased advertising and circulation revenues from the circulation growth can be invested in the quality of Newspaper One. This increase in quality will shift the demand curve to D_2 and circulation to C_3. Newspaper Two will see a shift of demand down to D_3. At this point, a price decrease by Newspaper Two to the same level of Newspaper One (P_2) will only limit the decline in circulation.

loss of revenue makes it more difficult to pay for new technology and increase the quality of its newspaper issues. Examples of this price cutting and the corresponding results occurred in Detroit and Little Rock in the late 1980s.

The effects of the circulation spiral shown here occur if the trailing newspaper is unable to reverse the initial trend. This trend may be reversed by increasing information quality, decreasing circulation prices, reducing advertising prices, or a combination of these strategies. The uncertainty about newspaper quality makes investing in quality a difficult option to pursue. As a result, a trailing newspaper tends to cut prices, as well as spending more money on the news-editorial department. This strategy often fails because cutting price means adding to the already accumulating losses, and the trailing newspaper may not have adequate resources to compete with the leading newspaper in the area of quality.

Figure 4.2 starts with a subscription price cut, but this need not be the only way a circulation spiral begins. If one newspaper develops better content quality, it will attract more readers and more advertising. If a newspaper cuts ad rates and attracts more advertisements, it will attract more readers to start the spiral. The important point is that circulation, advertising linage, and information quality are all related.

This spiral is at the heart of the decrease in competition, and it continues in JOA cities, even with reduced ad rates for the second newspaper. JOA newspapers are able to offset some of the spiral's damage by sharing economies of scale that come from production, distribution, and business costs. JOAs simply tend to put off the long-run result of the circulation spiral.

The revenue advantages of being the leading newspaper in a two-newspaper market are further enhanced by the economies of scale a newspaper receives from adding pages to an issue (See Chapter 3). Not only is the leading newspaper getting more advertising pages, which attracts more readers, but the average and marginal costs of the pages decline from economies of scale. The gains in revenue and lowered marginal cost give the leading newspaper a powerful position for continued dominance in its market.

While economies of scale and the effects of the circulation spiral are the most important contributors to declining newspaper competition, they are not the only ones. Rosse mentions several other contributing factors.[6] He said the decline results from newspapers having lost effective market segmentation. Instead of competing for narrow segments of a market, newspapers compete for the same mass audience within a market. This marketwide competition allows the circulation spiral and economies of scale to have their impact. According to Rosse, the factors that have created the failure of market segmentation include a reduced demand for advertising as a result of developing media alternatives, a decline in advertising demand for segmented audiences, a growth of specialized media as alternatives to newspapers, and increases in costs that have put upward pressures on prices.

The impact of available advertising revenue can be an important variable in the impact of the circulation spiral. If a market's economy is growing, the length of time during which two separately owned and operated newspapers can be supported is extended. The Dallas, Houston, and San Antonio markets in Texas during the 1970s, as well as Boston in the mid-1980s, illustrate this point. In situations where the economy pumps more advertising dollars into the market, the revenue may be great enough to keep two papers profitable, even if one is only marginally so. In effect, the pie grows so there are big enough pieces for all. When the economy slows down, advertisers cut back and the pie begins to shrink. Then the spiral takes effect.

Rosse did hold out hope of advancing technology lowering fixed costs of producing newspapers. Lowered costs would allow newspapers to enter markets in an effort to segment the market. This has happened to a degree with suburban newspapers and the weekly specialty newspapers that have developed since the 1960s. The start of a second metro paper in St. Louis, the *Sun*, in 1989 was predicated partly on the savings expected from technological advances. However, the closing of the *Sun* within nine months indicates the savings were inadequate.

Not surprisingly, as direct competition continues to decline, it is the larger markets in the country that manage to retain two or more newspaper firms. New York, Chicago, Boston, and Washington continue to have competition. The newspapers in these cities have national influence because of their circulation size and the quality of their newspapers. Even cities with more regionally oriented newspapers, such as San Francisco, Detroit, Pittsburgh, Dallas, and Houston continue to have some form of competition. The social and economic importance of competitive markets make competition's impact important even as it continues to decline.

Weekly newspapers have faced the same trend in declining competition as daily newspapers, although the impact has not been as great. It is difficult to find estimates of weekly competition in the United States because weekly newspapers are not studied as extensively as dailies. However, some studies are useful in piecing together a picture of competition trends.

A study of rural weekly newspaper editors in 1900 found that about 30 percent of the 147 newspapers from 21 states had a second weekly newspaper in the same city.[7] The percentage was probably much higher for larger cities with their specialized ethnic and foreign language press. Another study found that about 13 percent of the 871 weeklies in four states in 1960 had weekly competition.[8] This study was consistent with a study of suburban newspaper markets that found about 18 percent of 901 suburbs had weekly newspapers, and about 12 percent of these markets had two or more weekly newspapers.[9] These studies suggest that weekly newspaper competition has declined, but not as extensively as daily newspaper competition.

The difference represents the lower barriers to entry for weekly newspapers. Staffs are small and the newspaper firm need not own a press. Specialized newspapers also tend to be published weekly. It may be that market segmentation, which has failed for dailies, is still possible for weeklies.

The Information Market

The effect of direct competition on the information market could occur in many ways. Indeed, research has looked at several dimensions; some have proven fruitful and others have not. Although most newspaper content could fall within the boundaries of the information market, the discussion here deals with nonadvertising and noneditorial content. Advertising content tends to be a function primarily of the advertising market and is addressed in that section. The editorial pages, because they provide a forum for expression and discussion of ideas, is dealt with in the section on the intellectual market. Here the discussion concentrates on news as it is broadly defined to include sports, features, and other information content.

Separately owned and operated newspapers. During the 1940s and 1950s, most research into direct newspaper competition indicated that having more than one newspaper in a city had little impact on content.[10] However, some studies in the 1960s and 1970s found a relationship. Rarick and Hartman studied one market under three different competitive conditions—no competition, slight competition, and intense competition. They found that slight or no competition had little impact on content. However, they concluded that intense competition, which was defined as almost equal shares of market circulation, resulted in a higher proportion of space being given to local news, pictures, columns of opinion, and immediate-reward information.[11]

These researchers found that competitive intensity was the key to better understanding newspaper competition's impact. If the circulation difference is great, the trailing newspaper poses little or no threat to the leading newspaper. A later study compared the impact of competition using a competitive intensity measure and a measure based on presence or absence of competition. Intensity was a better predictor of competition's impact.[12]

Another reason earlier studies failed to find a relationship between competition and content was the measure of content. Unlike earlier research, studies in the 1970s started to examine variables other than content categories based on type of news emphasis and geography. For example, while Weaver and Mullins found few content differences in their study of 46 competitive papers, they did find that the leading newspapers carried more wire services.[13]

Two simultaneous studies of direct newspaper competition that used national samples of newspapers built upon these previous studies and discovered an important relationship between competition and content.[14] As competition intensity increases newspapers tend to spend more money on their news-editorial commodity. This is manifested through more wire services, more reporters for a given newshole, a larger newshole, and more space given to color and photographs on the front page. Litman and Bridges called this the "financial commitment theory."[15] These results were replicated by using number of wire services a newspaper carried as a measure of financial commitment.[16]

Earlier studies had failed to consider the different processes that occur in a news organization. Competition doesn't appear to affect the distribution of news and editorial space, but it does affect the budgeting process. Newspapers with intense competition have larger budgets. A similar phenomenon has been found in local television markets.[17]

This "financial commitment" approach led to the development of a model of how newspaper monopoly power within a city affects the readers.[18] The model contains three axioms with corollaries concerning why and how news consumers use news. The model uses the concept of "consumer surplus"[19] (See Chapter 8) from economic theory to explain how competition influences newspaper content. Figure 4.3 shows the impact of intense competition.

The curve D_m represents a newspaper demand curve for a monopoly relating quality to circulation. The first axiom of the model assumes that circulation is positively related to quality (an assumption that has empirical support).[20] As mentioned in Chapter 2, the demand curve is kinked. There is a point (E_1) below which circulation is fairly elastic with respect to quality. In a monopoly market, circulation would be at C_1 and the level of quality is at Q_1. If the same newspaper had intense direct competition, the demand curve would be D_c, quality would be at Q_3, and circulation would be at C_2.

The increase in quality is necessary for the newspaper to attract readers from its competitor. Newspapers competing for the same readers must match the quality of the competing newspaper in most areas and differentiate themselves in other areas to attract the readers. But the quality also increases for a second reason. Because the city now has two newspapers, the acceptable level of quality to readers, the kinked point, moves further from the origin. Readers expect higher quality because the

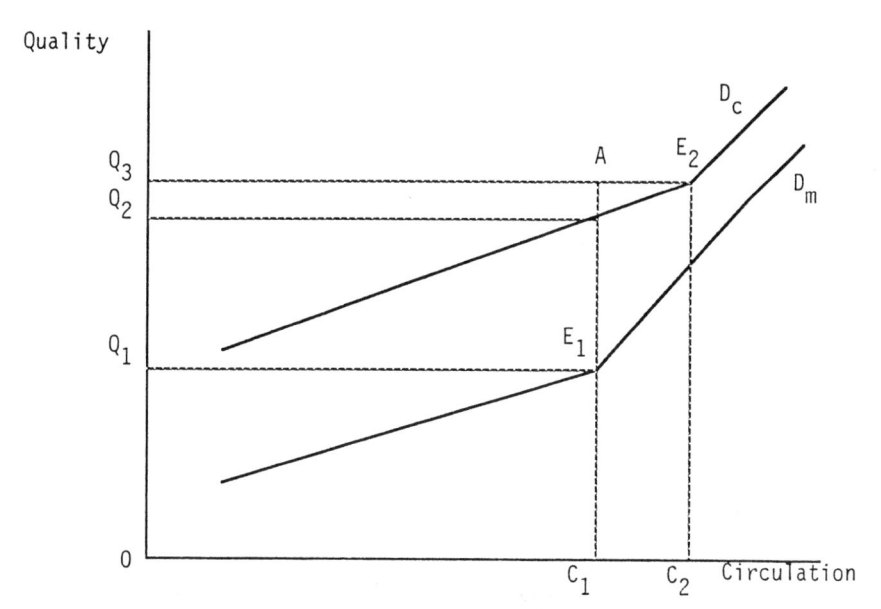

Figure 4.3. Relationship of Circulation to Newspaper Quality in a Directly Competitive Market

The demand curve for a competitive newspaper is shown by D_c, while the demand curve for a monopoly newspaper is shown by D_m. A competitive paper will have greater total circulation represented by the difference between C_1 and C_2. The quality of the competitive paper will be greater than that of the monopoly newspaper by the difference between Q_1 and Q_3.

presence of two substitutable newspapers puts them in a better position to judge quality.

The result of the two forces—greater financial commitment to the news-editorial department and higher reader expectations—is better quality newspapers. The relative impact of these two forces is shown in Figure 4.3. The contribution of financial commitment is the difference between Q_1 and Q_2. The difference between Q_2 and Q_3 is the contribution of greater expectations. The former exceeds the latter. There will also be higher total circulation for the two newspapers because of better quality and the ability of people who do not like one newspaper to take the competitor's newspaper.

While there are few markets that gain daily newspapers any more, markets do lose dailies. The reverse process is that over the long run, cities that lose competition have lower quality newspapers and readers who will accept a lower standard of journalism.

Figure 4.3 does not show the impact on the surviving newspaper of losing competition. The figure is a static comparison of a newspaper under two market conditions. The actual circulation for the survivor will grow, but the market circulation will be lower than it was before the competing newspaper closed. Some people simply don't switch to the surviving newspaper.[21] The impact of this increase in circulation is shown in Figure 4.4, which contains market demand curves. In Figure 4.4, a third demand curve has been added. Curve D_1 is the same as D_m in Figure 4.3. D_1 is a market and firm demand curve because a monopoly firm has the entire market. It represents the circulation of the surviving newspaper that results from the quality of that newspaper. Curve D_2 is the final monopoly demand curve which includes a shift to the right of D_1. The kink point is the same but there is higher demand at any given point because these readers have limited options after the closing of the competing newspaper. The total amount of the shift will vary with the quality of the newspaper and the demands of the audience.

In all this analysis, supply is assumed to match whatever demand there is at a kink point. So, in Figure 4.4, E_2 represents the market equilibrium

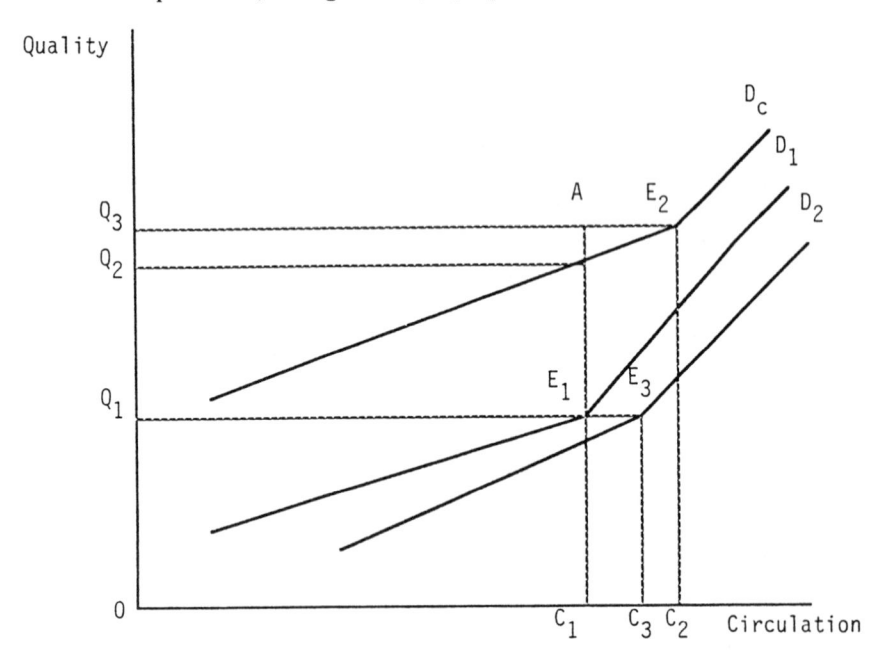

Figure 4.4. The Impact of the Closing of a Daily Newspaper on Circulation in a Directly Competitive Market

The demand curve for a directly competitive market is shown by D_c, with newspaper quality of Q_3 and circulation of C_2 at the equilibrium point E_2. When one of the newspapers closes, the market demand curve becomes the firm demand curve of D_1, which is the curve before the readers have adjusted to the closing. The final equilibrium point is E_3, with a circulation of C_3 and quality of Q_1. At this point, readers of the closed newspaper have decided whether or not they want to buy the surviving newspaper.

with two newspapers; E_1 is a disequilibrium point representing the level of monopoly circulation and quality before reader adjustment; and E_3 is the final equilibrium point after a newspaper closes and readers from the closed newspaper adjust by deciding whether or not to subscribe to the surviving newspaper.

One variable that is not accounted for with this model is ownership objectives. The effects predicted here may not occur if the owners and managers want to continue producing a high quality commodity. An example is *The Philadelphia Inquirer*, which continued to win Pulitzer Prizes after the market became a one-owner combination city instead of a truly competitive market. However, depending on the commitment of the owners is not the same as readers demanding quality journalism before they will subscribe to the newspaper. In effect, a monopoly shifts discretionary power from the reader to the owner.

Although this model has not been tested entirely, some research does support elements of it. It was derived from the "financial commitment" research, but the question is whether increased expenditure means higher quality of journalism. Some evidence indicates that greater expenditure means better journalism, although the correlation is far from perfect.

First, the financial commitment means a greater expenditure on number of reporters for a given amount of news space and on more wire services. A study of the 1960 presidential campaign by Danielson and Adams found a relationship between completeness of coverage, and staff size and number of wire services.[22] Completeness of coverage was determined by examining the events covered by a dozen prestige newspapers from around the United States. A randomly selected list of 42 events from the papers was used to determine completeness. In effect, competitive newspapers would have given more complete coverage of this election.

Second, research using an index of quality based on a survey of more than 700 newspaper editors found a relationship between quality and competition. Intensely competitive newspapers tended to have higher quality ratings for their news sections. The quality rating was based on the ratio of staff written to wire copy, total amount of nonadvertising space, ratio of in-depth to hard news, ratio of illustrated material, number of wire services carried, length of story, ratio of nonadvertising to advertising space, and ratio of staff to space.[23]

Not all studies have supported the relationship between direct competition and quality. One study found that intensity of competition was related to the likelihood of stories only carrying one side of a controversy, but this study was somewhat limited in sample.[24]

Joint operating newspapers. Markets with two separately owned and operated newspapers have received most of the attention in research about competition, but cities with joint operating newspapers and one-owner combinations offer readers more than one news-editorial option. The underlying assumption of the Newspaper Preservation Act is that readers in a market with joined newspapers would be better off than readers in a market with just one newspaper. Yet little systematic research was conducted before or after the law was passed. A study conducted soon after the NPA was passed concluded that JOAs did not appear to keep separate voices in a market.[25] This study suffered from the same problems of the early competitive studies in that it did not look at intensity of competition or the financial commitment of the newspaper companies.

Two studies have supported the assumption of the Newspaper Preservation Act. In a case study of Louisiana, the Shreveport JOA was found to offer distinct newspaper voices.[26] Another study compared 21 JOA papers with 21 competitive newspapers and 21 monopoly newspapers using the financial commitment approach. It also compared JOA papers within four markets. Results showed that joint operating newspapers tend to be more like competitive newspapers than monopoly newspapers in what they spent on the news-editorial commodity. However, they were not quite as committed as newspapers that faced separately operated competition. The comparison of JOA papers in four cities showed these newspapers varied little in allocation of news space, but they had different emphases on the editorial pages.[27]

One-owner combinations. The small amount of research available concerning JOAs seems like a plethora compared to work about the impact of competition between one-owner combination papers on content. Although it has not been tested, it appears that the financial commitment approach would not be applicable to one-owner combinations. There is little incentive to increase expenditure on either of the two newspapers when the money is coming from the same source. Blankenburg's study concerning the closing of one of the two newspapers in such combinations indicates that owners are unwilling to accept the increased expenditure for competition between their morning and evening newspapers.

There is a possible impact, however, that is applicable to these combinations, JOA combinations, and competition between separately owned and operated newspapers. This impact comes from a sociological type of competition among reporters. It appears that having another journalist working the same beat can push a reporter to do a better job. Bird commented on this possible impact almost 50 years ago when he said:

> Lack of competition often means careless and inaccurate reporting, failure to report all newsworthy events and a tendency to "play safe." The reporter need not do his best: he need not even tell the truth. Only the few immediately affected will know the difference. Where there is competition, if a reporter overlooks a story, his rival may get it. If he writes inaccurately, the opposition sets the public right. How gleefully they used to do it! And the reporter who found himself set straight in a rival's story was a long time in making the same error again.[28]

This sociological competition among journalists was found by Hicks and Featherston in their study of three types of ownership.[29] Most journalists who have worked in competitive situations of some sort can recall examples of how this type of competition affects reporting. It is simply a matter of trying to outperform the other reporters. From the point of view of the reader, this type of reporter competition is an important casualty of the decline in competition.

The question of competition and content remains somewhat unanswered, although there is increasing evidence that the decline of newspaper quality follows declining direct competitive intensity.

Impact on circulation price. While the impact of competition on content is an important consideration in the information market, the impact on price is also worth considering. Economic theories of perfect competition would argue that the presence of competition would lower prices. However, newspaper markets are not perfectly competitive. Oligopoly theory suggests that the impact would depend on whether the competitors have de facto collusion, which means they do not lower prices because it will start a price war. Examples of such price wars exist. For example, even though 97 percent of the daily newspapers were charging 25 cents or more for a daily newspaper in 1988, the two Detroit newspapers were charging 15 and 20 cents. This was due to competition. In Little Rock, the *Arkansas Gazette* had lowered its weekly rate to 85 cents in 1988 during the intense competitive battle with the *Arkansas Democrat*.

Despite the anecdotal evidence of competition lowering circulation prices, few systematic studies of the impact of competition on daily newspaper prices exist. The ones that do exist are inconclusive.

Grotta found that readers in cities that changed from competitive to monopoly markets paid higher circulation prices.[30] A case study of Winnipeg, Canada, found similar results.[31] Despite the results, an unpublished report by Picard found no connection between competition and lower circulation prices.[32]

Differences in empirical research may be attributable to differences in operationalization of variables or in controls, but they may also be a result of the joint product nature of newspapers. Because the bulk of revenue comes from advertisers, who buy space on the basis of readership, newspapers often do not price their subscription rates as aggressively as they would if advertising was not so important. Even though newspaper demand is relatively inelastic with respect to price, the exact measure of inelasticity is usually unknown. Aggressive pricing, especially in competitive markets, could cost a newspaper circulation needed for attracting advertisers. Studies of information market pricing should include control of the relative impact of price changes on advertising. This is not a common practice.

Weekly newspapers. Most literature in the area of direct competition deals with daily newspapers. Yet statistics indicate that competition is far more common among weekly newspapers. In the area of content competition, the impact among weeklies will depend upon the nature of the weekly newspaper commodity. If a weekly is a general circulation newspaper, rather than a specialized publication, the information competition will depend upon the degree of substitutability of the newspaper for its competitors. Specialty weeklies will compete to a high degree with general circulation weeklies for advertising rather than for readers.

If two general circulation weeklies faces each other in the same geographic market, there is no reason to think that the effects of competition would be different from those found in daily markets, except that the low fixed cost of weeklies means they can survive on smaller revenue and profit levels. In many cases, the owners and managers of weeklies derive utility other than profit from their operations. They may enjoy the position a journalist holds in a smaller city or town. Owning one's own business may make up for lower profits.

It would be incorrect to assume, however, that weekly newspapers are exempt from the economic realities that face daily newspapers. A weekly competitive market that faces an economic slowdown with its reduced employment and business activity will also see a decline in the amount of advertising funds available. Under these conditions, one of two competing firms may find itself unable to make enough profit to continue operation. Daily and weekly markets differ in that after an economic slowdown has passed it is much easier for someone to start another weekly newspaper if the surviving paper has cut back on quality and increased its prices. These lower barriers to entry have gotten even lower in the 1980s, with computers that produce high quality newspapers with little labor.

Whether competition has an impact on prices for these weeklies may become a moot point as more weeklies move toward voluntary subscription and free circulation. This movement is promoted by the demand for market-wide penetration from advertisers. They want their ads available to as many households as possible. The low fixed costs of weeklies enable them to respond to this demand by giving away their newspaper copies, while keeping their editorial quality stable. It appears the argument that readers will value a commodity they buy more than one they receive free is losing support. Perhaps in reality readers will value newspapers that are useful whether they must pay for them of not.

Advertising Market

Economic theory suggests that newspapers with monopoly power will charge monopoly prices. Although not all research reaches this conclusion, as Owen said, "No economist will be surprised to find that monopolists charge monopoly prices."[33] However, as Owen pointed out, monopolists need not charge monopoly prices if they have a goal that would be served by not doing so.

Some studies have found that monopoly power increases the advertising line rate.[34] Other studies have found that competing newspapers tend to have lower advertising prices per thousand readers.[35] Lago reported that monopoly power did not result in increased daily newspaper advertising rates,[36] but he was looking at the line rate and not the rate per thousand, which is a more appropriate measure.

The most extensive study was conducted by Ferguson in 1983. He found no significant impact of monopoly on the daily advertising rate per thousand, but he did find that competition resulted in higher rates per thousand for Sunday edition advertising.[37] Ferguson used a dummy variable for daily newspaper competition, rather than an intensity measure, which may have affected his results.

Not surprisingly, the little research into the impact of joint operating agreements on advertising prices shows that these newspapers are using the monopoly power they have been given by an exemption to the antitrust acts. One study found that JOA newspapers charged higher advertising rates than competitive newspapers and that JOAs raised their ad rates faster than did monopoly newspapers.[38]

A study of the impact of competition on weekly advertising rates in Wisconsin found no effect.[39] However, the study used line rates and not rate per thousand, and it did not use competition intensity as the independent measure.

Overall, research supports that many monopoly-power newspapers charge monopoly advertising prices, but evidence also exists to the contrary. The contradiction represents different ways of measuring the important variables, but it also represents the complexity of the newspaper industry and the problems of getting accurate data. Competition is one of many factors that affect pricing. The joint product nature of newspapers makes it far more difficult for managers to determine rates that are appropriate in both the information market and the advertising market. Some advertising, especially that from large grocery and department stores, attracts readers. These types of ads might well have lower prices because they add to circulation. Newspapers with monopoly power can charge higher rates, but they also differentiate their rates. Rarely do advertisers pay open line rates. The volume, placement, type of advertising, and impact of the advertising on readership come into play.

Intellectual Market

The essence of the intellectual market is competition. This market exists with the assumption that competition among ideas for acceptance by the public will result in optimal decision making by that public. Every decision may not be optimal. Mistakes occur. But across time, the ideas will emerge that insure the continuation and improvement of the society.

Theoretically, competition in the intellectual market does not require competition in the other markets. Ideally, one media firm could act as a conveyor of ideas, with open access to the intellectual market for all who would contribute. This *common carrier* concept, however, is practically impossible. Newspapers have no common carrier requirement by the law, and the costs of producing space in a newspaper render a common carrier extremely unlikely.[40] Without a carrier to convey ideas to the intellectual market, competition in the information and advertising markets becomes important in providing access to the that market.

The decline of newspaper competition within a geographic area has raised the potential for limiting access to the intellectual market. Before appraising the results of declining competition, an examination of the possible contributions by newspapers to the intellectual market would be useful. Newspapers serve two basic functions in the intellectual market: (a) They are a channel for contributing ideas, and (b) they provide information for evaluating ideas that are in the intellectual market.

Contributing ideas occurs in several ways. Newspapers suggest ideas through their staff editorials and columns. They also provide a channel through which syndicated columnists, guest columnists, and letter writers can place ideas before the public. In addition, they provide advertising space that can also be used for advancing ideas. Even news stories often contain ideas that end up in the intellectual market.

While newspapers contribute to the information market in many of these same ways, the editorial pages carry ideas and information that are meant to influence the acceptance of these ideas in the intellectual market. The same holds true for advertising that is used for access to the intellectual market. A difference supposedly exists between the information in news sections and in the editorial and advertising sections. Most newspaper journalists accept that news should remain as free of bias as possible, while they expect editorial and advertising information to be biased.

Despite the general agreement that news should remain as unbiased as possible, experience demonstrates that the "objectivity" of news remains at best an ideal goal. Some have even criticized objectivity as being inappropriate as a goal.[41] Others have shown that the patterns of news gathering, selection of sources, and dependence on advertising as a source of revenue shape the news.[42] Yet journalism codes of ethics and behavior call for fair and balanced reporting. It seems that most of the bias that occurs in the news sections tends to be unconscious rather than a purposeful effort to mislead the reader.

Some scholars argue that this unconscious bias is not totally benign. They contend that news organizations support the status quo through the way they define which issues and events are important. In other words, newspapers are not agents of change but are agents of the powerful.[43] Generally, ideas and information that question the very basis of our society have limited access to the intellectual market through general circulation newspapers. Empirical evidence exists that newspapers do treat fringe political groups less favorably than more mainstream groups.[44] This has contributed to the development of alternative weeklies.

An underlying assumption of these types of attacks on news media is that they should be agents of rapid and extensive societal change. Certainly, general circulation daily and weekly newspapers are not agents of revolution. Even if they tried to act as such, it would be difficult to accept arguments for extensive social restructuring from an organization that carries advertising for banks, supermarkets, and retail stores. So, here we accept that general circulation newspapers act within a much narrower intellectual market than some other media. The wider intellectual market also is served by various forms of books, magazines, alternative newspapers, radio, film, and television. The narrower intellectual market of general circulation newspapers is one in which ideas usually support the system, and which deals with efforts to adjust rather than restructure the social, economic, and political systems.

Within that narrow market, evidence indicates that newspaper editorial pages continue to be an important element of the newspaper. A survey compared responses of daily editors in 1975 and 1983 concerning their editorial pages. The researcher concluded that editorial pages take organizational stands and provide an exchange of ideas.[45] The question then becomes whether competition affects this vital part of the newspaper.

The section above concerning the information market suggests that direct competition among newspapers would improve the exchange within the intellectual market because it appears that competition improves the quality of information. It might also improve the quantity of information. Two newspapers in a market mean there is more space devoted to news. Even if a majority of the news is somewhat duplicated, having more reporters covering a market increases the possibility of a reporter uncovering information that would be useful in the intellectual market.

A more important area of concern is the editorial and op-ed section of the newspapers. Does competition mean a greater contribution to the intellectual market through the editorial and op-ed pages?

Several early examinations of the impact of competition on editorial pages found some differences between competing newspapers, but the authors generally concluded that the differences were not great enough to argue that competition was important.[46] A study conducted in the 1980s addressed the specific issue of competition and opinion content. The study concluded that economic competition seems to have little impact on newspaper editorial content.[47] However, this study suffered from the measurement problems of earlier studies. It measured competition categorically rather than in terms of intensity. The author added, however, that having two newspapers instead of one might increase the possibility of discovering important stories because of the increased number of competing reporters.

Another national study of dailies found no impact of competition on the distribution of editorial and op ed page space.[48] However, a study of four pairs of JOA newspapers found that papers within the pairs varied in how they allocated space on the editorial and op ed pages.[49]

The weight of empirical research suggests that direct competition has little direct impact on the opinion pages of the newspaper. But this conclusion might be a case of not using the appropriate dependent variable for study, just as happened with earlier studies of news content and competition. Certainly, having two editorial pages increases the amount of total space within a market given to discussion of ideas. The resulting increased space would mean more access for all of the elements of the editorial page. Whether this increased space actually benefits the public by resulting in a greater variety of ideas for the intellectual market remains an unanswered question.

INTERCITY COMPETITION

Intercity, or "umbrella," competition developed primarily following World War II. It resulted from the development of technology for production, distribution, and news gathering and from the movement of people to the suburbs. Population growth and movement created a growing demand for news and information about local issues in these growing suburban towns and cities. Technology allowed these smaller newspapers to reduce production and distribution costs and allowed larger dailies to cover wider areas at cheaper costs.

A conceptual model for this type of competition was first proposed in 1975 by James Rosse.[50] The model hypothesized four layers of newspapers. The first layer is composed of metropolitan dailies that provide a great deal of regional and national coverage. The second layer contains satellite-city daily newspapers that tend to be more local in nature compared to the first layer. These papers still carry a fair amount of nonlocal news. The third layer is made up of suburban dailies, which are almost totally local in nature. Locally oriented weeklies, shoppers, and other specialized nondaily newspapers compose the fourth layer.

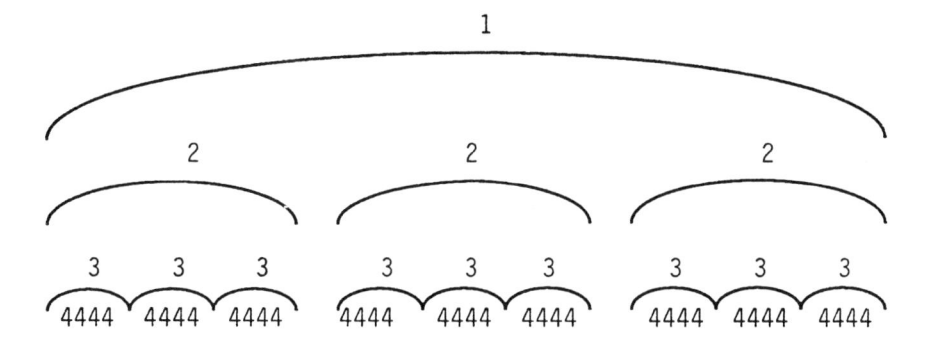

```
                                    1
         _____
        /                                                   \
       /       2                   2                   2     \
      /   _____       _____       _____    \
     /   /           \     /           \     /           \    \
    3   3   3   3       3   3   3       3   3   3
  ⌣⌣⌣ ⌣⌣⌣ ⌣⌣⌣     ⌣⌣⌣ ⌣⌣⌣ ⌣⌣⌣     ⌣⌣⌣ ⌣⌣⌣ ⌣⌣⌣
  4444 4444 4444   4444 4444 4444   4444 4444 4444
```

Key:

Level 1 newspaper in large metropolitan center
Level 2 newspapers in satellite cities
Level 3 local dailies
Level 4 weeklies and other specialized media

Figure 4.5. The Original Umbrella Model of Newspaper Competition
This model proposed by James N. Rosse contains four layers of competition based on geographic coverage.
Source: Bruce M. Owen. *Economics and Freedom of Expression* (Cambridge, MA: Ballinger, 1975), p. 51.

The first published diagram of this model was presented by Owen in 1975.[51] The diagram is reproduced in Figure 4.5 and illustrates the source of the designation of "umbrella" competition. Each layer forms an umbrella over the lower ones. Rosse hypothesized that there would be little competition among the newspapers within each layer. Rather, he said, competition would be among the layers, intensifying as one moved down the model.

Since the original model was proposed, at least two developments indicate that it may not have enough layers. The development of *USA Today* and the national edition of *The New York Times*, plus the continued publication of *The Wall Street Journal* and *Christen Science Monitor*, supports the idea of a layer of national newspapers above the metro daily newspapers. The continued growth of group ownership in suburban areas around large cities also suggests a sixth layer. This layer would be composed of group-owned, nondaily newspapers. The difference between newspapers in this layer and those in the weekly and shopper layer is their ability to attract advertising. An advertisement placed in all papers within a group would reach a much larger audience than an ad placed in an independently owned weekly covering one suburb. This ability to reach a larger audience increases the advertisement's efficiency and makes the group newspapers stronger advertising competitors for the metro and suburban dailies.

114 THE ECONOMICS & REGULATIONS OF U.S. NEWSPAPERS

While the original umbrella diagram provides a good conceptualization of this type of competition, it can also mislead one into miscalculating the competition within a given geographic area. Another way of presenting intercity competition is shown in Figure 4.6. This figure represents umbrella competition within selected cities in Michigan. It demonstrates how the number of layers will vary from one area to another.

The diagram assumes six layers—the original four, plus the national daily and group-owned nondaily layers. Detroit, for example, has national papers, metropolitan dailies, and weeklies circulating within its boundaries. Residents of Mt. Clemens, which is north of Detroit in the same standard metropolitan statistical area, can buy the national dailies, the two Detroit metro dailies, a suburban daily and a group-owned nondaily. In Plymouth, a suburb to the west of Detroit, a reader can purchase a national daily, the Detroit metro dailies, an independent weekly, and a

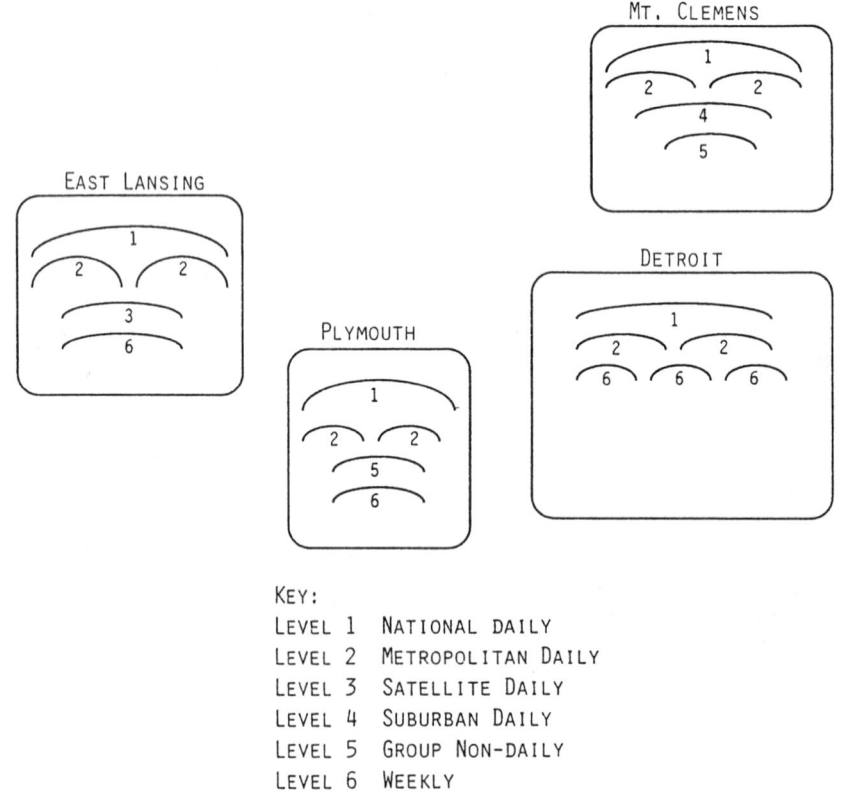

KEY:
LEVEL 1 NATIONAL DAILY
LEVEL 2 METROPOLITAN DAILY
LEVEL 3 SATELLITE DAILY
LEVEL 4 SUBURBAN DAILY
LEVEL 5 GROUP NON-DAILY
LEVEL 6 WEEKLY

Figure 4.6. The Modified Model of Umbrella Competition
This umbrella model proposes six layers of competition based on geographic coverage and group affiliation.

group-owned twice-weekly. In East Lansing, which is about 80 miles west of Detroit, a reader can select from among national dailies, the metro Detroit dailies, a satellite-city daily, and a group-owned weekly.

Thus, the actual configuration of the umbrella competition will vary with location. Within a particular location, the extent and nature of the competition in the information and advertising markets will vary as well. Because of the relative newness of umbrella competition, research is limited. Some studies, however, do address issues facing newspapers in the three types of markets.

The Information Market

Competition among layers will vary based on several variables, including managerial decisions, market structure, and even geographic conditions. Each market has its own peculiarities. However, some generalities can be drawn about this umbrella competition.

An early research effort used a survey to test some of Rosse's hypotheses and found little competition for news among metro dailies, suburban dailies, and weeklies.[52] Editors in higher layers perceived competition for news to be greater among layers than did editors in lower layers. Most of the suburban daily newspaper managers showed little concern about intercity competition for news. Few of the weekly publishers and editors felt metro dailies were competing with them for news.

Later studies used content analysis to examine this news competition. A 1987 article looked at the relationship between intercity competition among dailies and news content and found a strong relationship between the penetration in a given county by a daily newspaper that was headquartered elsewhere and the content of the hometown daily.[53] As the penetration increased, the percentage of the news section used for news and the percentage of the news section given local news increased. It appears that local dailies protect themselves from outside competition by providing more coverage of their hometown, which is difficult and expensive for an outside paper to do. This could explain the earlier survey results. Editors in small cities and towns may feel their local coverage protects them from the news competition of metro dailies.

This same study looked at Rosse's hypothesis that as one moves down the layers, the newspapers become more local in nature. The suburban dailies carried more news about their hometown than did the metro and satellite dailies, which showed no significant difference in hometown coverage. However, the satellite dailies did carry more news than the metro dailies about their home county. Suburban dailies carried more county news than did the satellite and metro dailies. Whether the dailies become more local as you move down the layers appears to depend on how one defines "local." If city and county coverage are combined, Rosse's hypothesis was supported.

Another study examined suburban coverage by metro dailies and hometown nondailies in Detroit and Denver and found that the two types of papers are not good substitutes for news.[54] The metro dailies only averaged about 50 square inches of news per suburb for the constructed week. Advertising content of the metro dailies was more important in attracting suburban readers than news content about suburbs.

These results are supported by a case study of circulation in southern California.[55] The author found that local coverage helped the lower-layer dailies protect their franchise despite intense competition for circulation throughout the crowded region. A similar study of Boston found little circulation competition among the umbrella layers, but it was based on aggregate data rather than data for individual submarkets within the Boston area.[56]

A problem with protecting a newspaper franchise by increasing local coverage is that the definition of what constitutes local coverage can vary from market to market. This is especially true with suburban areas, where people may live in one town, work in another, and shop in still another. Managers have difficulty understanding just what their readers consider local.[57] The study of Detroit and Denver suburban newspapers showed that nondailies in the two metro areas had almost equal penetration, even though the average percentage of content devoted to the hometown differed greatly. The Detroit suburban papers had more news about towns surrounding them than did the Denver newspapers. This probably reflects more connections with these suburbs through work and shopping.

Although news content may be of limited substitutability with umbrella competition because of differing definitions of local coverage, the competition for circulation in suburban areas appears to be intense. The survey mentioned above found that circulation managers at suburban dailies perceive intense circulation competition from the metro dailies. The weekly publishers perceived competition from metro dailies for circulation, but of less intensity than that felt by the suburban daily managers. The perceptions of the suburban daily executives probably reflect the price of subscribing to two daily newspapers. Some readers do not think taking both a metro and suburban daily is worth the expense, and so they take one or the other. Many weeklies have eliminated their circulation competition with other newspapers by providing free distribution. Even paid subscription weeklies cost considerably less per year than dailies. The weeklies become complements to, rather than substitutes for, dailies. At the same time, the full-market coverage of free weeklies places them in a good position for attracting local advertising.

In summary, it appears the information market is affected by intercity competition. However, the competition is limited by publication cycle. Dailies are better substitutes for each other than they are for weeklies. A second limit is the inherent advantage newspapers have in covering their own territory. The advantage is commodity differentiation through local coverage. From a reader's view, this is as it should be. A newspaper that cannot cover its hometown better than an intruding daily probably does not deserve to survive. It may be possible for metro dailies to battle these hometown dailies by providing extensive local coverage of the hometowns. Zoning provides a way of doing this, but its success depends on how good a substitute zoning makes the larger dailies for local hometown news. The costs of high quality coverage can be expensive.

The Advertising Market

Although news competition in the information market is limited by topic area, the advertising market appears to be limited only by geography. Satellite-city newspapers do not compete extensively with metro dailies for advertising because their readers shop in distinctly different geographic areas. This is not the case with suburban dailies, suburban weeklies, and metro dailies. Papers in these layers battle with each other, as well as with other media, for the limited advertising funds in a geographic area. The main battleground is the suburbs, where the affluent consumers are concentrated.

Competition among the layers in a metropolitan area is probably greatest for advertising.[58] The metro dailies want the suburban reader, but a good suburban daily can often survive by achieving adequate circulation in its hometown with its local news coverage. The metro daily counters with its advantage of scale economies for chain-store advertisers. The metro daily can give relatively cheaper rates per thousand for a wider area. This advantage may disappear if suburban newspapers form cooperatives or are group-owned.

Advertising cannot be ignored as content. The Detroit and Denver study of suburban coverage found that advertising coverage of a particular suburb in metro dailies was a good predictor of penetration in that suburb. This indicates that suburban readers use the metro dailies' advertising for information.

Suburban advertising competition has contributed to the development of zoned editions by dailies. Zoned editions focus on narrow geographic areas with sections inserted into the daily newspaper. While most zoned editions are used for suburban coverage by metro dailies, there is a trend toward satellite dailies using zoned editions to move into other newspapers' territories. Daily newspapers publish the zoned sections as often as they can justify with revenues, with zoned sections usually appearing once or twice a week.

Zoned editions vary in the size of area covered and serve three purposes. First, they increase the ability of larger dailies to cover news in smaller cities. In so doing, the large dailies become better substitutes for the smaller dailies or weeklies. Second, the zoned editions allow large dailies to charge lower rates for the advertisers who need to cover a limited geographic area. Often, the small independent store owner cannot afford to pay for readers outside his market. Third, they help attract the upscale readers advertisers want. If done well, the zoned sections can help a newspaper make inroads into the local newspaper's advertising market.

Success of a zoned edition depends on two factors. The coverage area must be small enough that it can be adequately covered by the news department. An area that is too large limits the space per city available for local coverage. This reduces the substitutability of the zoned edition for the hometown paper. Second, the news resources must be adequate to cover the area. The success of the edition is based on its attraction of advertising, which is based on its attraction of readers. Inadequate and incomplete coverage will not lure readers away from the dailies and weeklies already published in the city.

Because of these factors, results of zoning efforts by metro dailies are mixed. In some cases, the metro dailies simply do not spend the money to increase readership because the benefits will not cover the expense. This often occurs because the suburbs contain few dailies and, therefore, metro daily circulation is already high.

The Intellectual Market

Because umbrella competition tends to result in greater local coverage by the lower-layer newspapers, the intellectual market is enhanced. Ideas are important, but so is this information needed to buttress them. Increased local coverage provides this additional information. However, as yet, there is no evidence concerning the quality of the increased local coverage. Umbrella competition, unlike direct competition, appears to be unrelated to financial commitment.

Research has shown little direct relationship of umbrella competition to the intellectual market through the editorial and op ed pages. Suburban and satellite dailies do not carry any more local editorials than do metro dailies. Intercity competition seems not to be an important factor in determining what issues newspaper manager and owners address in their opinion pages.

INTERMEDIA COMPETITION

Defining intermedia competition is difficult. As pointed out in Chapter 2, the substitutability of various media is limited in some of the three markets but not in others. Depending on the story and the news programs watched, television can be used to get information that is also found in newspapers. This would be more likely to occur with national and international news because of the number of television news organizations in the United States covering this type of news. At a local level, the substitutability may be quite different. When it comes to the advertising markets, there is more substitutability, but the degree depends on the type and geographic emphasis of advertising.

The idea of substitutability involves short-run rational comparison and decisions by individuals and organizations. A more long-run approach was taken by McCombs with his "Relative Constancy Hypothesis."[59] This hypothesis was first suggested by Charles E. Scripps and researched by Kinter.[60] It proposes that the percentage of Gross National Product spent on mass media by consumers remains about the same across time. This limited-resource concept implies that new media must take resources from existing media. This seems intuitively appealing, but the hypothesis has some problems.

First, support for the concept results primarily from the nature of percentages. When a figure that exceeds a trillion dollars, such as the U.S. gross national product, is reduced to percentages, changes of billions of dollars become fractions of percentages. For example, the figures used by McCombs showed a decline of GNP spent on mass media from 4.15 percent in 1967 to 4.02 percent in 1968. Although this appears to be a slight decline in funds available for media, the total dollars spent on mass media increased from $32.9 billion to $34.77 billion. As the base figure increases, larger and larger changes in actual dollars are necessary to create what appear to be large fluctuations in percentages.

Second, empirical results have not supported the hypothesis. Wood reexamined the data McCombs used and concluded that new media would not necessarily hurt existing media.[61] This conclusion was consistent with studies of mass media history. Two studies found very little long-lasting impact of radio's development on the newspaper industry.[62] Other studies found that television affected newspaper advertising dollars, but again it did not significantly change the long-term profitability of newspapers because television took advertising money from other media as well, and even generated new advertising dollars.[63]

Despite the shortcomings of the "relative constancy hypothesis," the idea that across generations members of society may switch from reading the newspaper to watching television news may well be valid. The problem in examining this possibility is the lack of adequate demand theory for media use. A smaller percentage of the U.S. population subscribes to newspapers now than 30 years ago, and more people watch television news than 30 years ago. The link, if it exists, is not clear-cut. Thus, the analysis here will be limited to more short-run considerations in the three markets that newspapers serve.

The Information Market

Little evidence indicates that television news is a good substitute for newspapers for local and state news. The 1975 Bogart study cited above found that television news viewing was not proportionately greater in cities where newspapers were losing circulation. A summary by Stone of studies concerning newspapers concluded that television is not a substitute for newspapers. People who tend to read newspapers also tend to watch television news.[64] Studies of cable television impact have found that people who subscribe to cable are more likely to read newspapers.[65] Similar findings, mentioned above, were reported about radio when it was a leading source of information before television developed. It appears that for those who seek news broadcast and print news may be complements.

Other print media, such as magazines and books, fail to compete extensively with newspapers for information for two reasons. First, the publication cycle is such that they are not good substitutes. Even a weekly newspaper cannot compete consistently with daily newspapers for breaking news. Second, most cities with daily newspapers do not have local news magazines. Timeliness and proximity work in newspapers' favor. The lack of substitutability is a short-term phenomenon. Over time, the changes in news-acquiring habits may well involve indirect substitutions among various media. Such a possibility is crucial to understanding historical trends in circulation.

If other media are not good substitutes, will they have a direct effect on content of newspapers? Evidence indicates they will not. A study that examined the relationship between competition from radio, cable, and broadcast television and newspaper content found no impact on the financial commitment of newspapers to the news commodity.[66]

While intermedia competition does not appear to affect content, lack of competition does. Stempel's work concerning cross-ownership of media firms within the same market shows that the newspaper in a market with cross-ownership carried fewer local stories than newspapers in comparable cities with no cross-ownership.[67] A larger sample study by Gromley found results consistent with Stempel's.[68] He reported that cross-ownership resulted in newspaper and television news staffs sharing carbons of news stories on a regular basis, that cross-ownership increased the probability a television station would hire a reporter from the newspaper, and that cross-ownership increased the likelihood that the newspaper and television station would be located in the same building. The overall impact was a homogenizing effect of the news.

The Advertising Market

Discovering the impact of intermedia competition on advertising rates and revenue is extremely difficult. First, as pointed out in Chapter 2, some types of advertising lend themselves to one media more readily than to another. Second, advertising pricing often involves discounts for quantity and long-term commitment. Newspaper rate-card prices are at best a point from which bargaining begins. Third, geography affects the degree of competition. Newspapers face a great deal more competition for national advertising than for local advertising.

Perhaps even more confusing is the question of defining advertising rates. Rates are usually for amounts of space, but advertisers are also concerned about the number of readers. This is usually reflected in the rate per thousand readers, or milline rate. The confusion is enhanced further when competition is between print and broadcast. It is difficult to compare rates for space with rates for time.

The difficulties of studying advertising and competition are reflected in the mixed empirical results found in the literature. An early study by Owen found that joint ownership of a newspaper and television station resulted in higher advertising prices.[69] The study was replicated by Lago with no such results.[70] He concluded the difference was because he controlled for circulation. A study of Canadian media replicated and supported the Owen study.[71] A follow-up study of Canada used the milline rate and supported the earlier Canadian study and Owen.[72] It appears that the impact joint-ownership is related to milline rate rather than absolute rate.

Like these early results, later studies continued to disagree on the relationship between intermedia competition and advertising rates. Ferguson used data from 815 newspapers and concluded that increasing numbers of radio and television stations in a market were associated with lower national and run-of-the-paper advertising rates.[73] Busterna, however, studied the elasticity of demand for national newspaper advertising with respect to prices of other media from 1971 to 1981 and found no relationship.[74] Unlike Ferguson, he did not use the milline rate.

Ferguson also examined the impact of cross-ownership of newspapers and television and radio stations in the same market. He found no relationship between cross-ownership of radio and newspapers and newspaper milline rates. However, cross-ownership of television and newspapers lowered the milline rate for newspapers. Despite mixed results, it appears that intermedia competition keeps milline rates lower, even if the actual rates are not affected.

An area of intermedia competition that has yet to develop may be the most important issue of the 1990s for newspapers. The regional bell operating companies (RBOCs), sometimes called the seven "baby bells," want to enter the electronic information business as information producers, rather than just conduits. Newspaper organizations oppose such a move. The RBOCs argue that the current regulation that prohibits them from producing information violates their First Amendment rights. The newspaper companies argue that the monopoly the RBOCs have over transmission lines will give the seven regional companies unfair competitive advantages.[75]

In 1987 U.S. District Judge Harold H. Greene decided that the RBOCs could deliver but not create electronic information. A 3-member appellate panel, however, ruled in April 1990 that Green had applied the wrong standard.[76] The outcome of the battle will rest either with the courts or Congress, but it may have a long-run impact on the competitive environment faced by newspapers as they move into the specialty medium called electronic information. This medium could become an important profit center for newspapers, which already have large amounts of information available.

The impact of policy in this area could affect both the information and the advertising markets because telephone companies already compete to a small degree with newspapers through the Yellow Pages.

The Intellectual Market

Data about the impact of other media outlets on the editorial functions of a newspaper are primarily related to cross-ownership. Stempel's study, cited earlier in the chapter, found that the cross-ownership newspaper ran about half the editorials that the two control newspapers ran. The editorials were less likely to be about local issues. This study did not examine the impact of cross-ownership on television editorials because the stations did not run any.

Deregulation of television since the Stempel study has aimed at encouraging television's participation in controversial issues because the requirement of the "Fairness Doctrine" has been eased. While there is little data about the corresponding impact of cross-ownership on television editorials, research implies there is little likelihood that conflicting editorials would occur with cross-ownership. It would seem the homogeniety of news found by Gromley would apply to editorials from the same owner through different news outlets.

If deregulation results in a more active opinion function by television news, one would assume that different ownership would increase the probability of differing editorial opinions being offered. This increased access to the intellectual market is at least part of the justification for deregulating television news. Despite the potential of deregulation, the limited research about television news departments and editorials indicates that television is not active in the intellectual market. One study found that 14 stations in Oregon and Michigan averaged only about 1.5 editorials per week during a two week period.[77]

SUMMARY

The impact of competition on the information and advertising markets results from the substitutability of the commodities. The more alike the commodities, the more likely readers and advertisers can move among them to meet their demand. The impact on the intellectual market is one of access. Society benefits from having as many media outlets as possible that present ideas and opinions.

The impact in all three markets relates to geography. Local orientation defines newspaper economic markets in the United States. Similarly, the intellectual market can have geographic limits as well. Media firms choose which intellectual markets they will enter, whether they be local, state, regional, national or international. Contributing to the local intellectual market can have business advantages and disadvantages. Readers and advertisers may appreciate or become angry at the discussion of local issues in the editorial and op-ed pages. Anger can be reflected in loss of readers and advertising. Appreciation can be reflected in increased readership. Which reaction occurs depends on the nature of readers and advertisers in a market, as well as the nature of the issues being presented.

Because substitutability plays such an important role, direct competition has the greatest impact on the advertising and information markets. Intense direct newspaper competition results in a greater financial commitment to the news department and lower advertising prices. Obviously, it insures two voices in the information and the intellectual markets, although there is no guarantee the voices will always differ.

Umbrella competition affects the information and advertising markets in some ways based on geographic emphasis and the publication cycles of the competing newspapers. Dailies that compete intensely through intercity competition tend to have large newsholes and more local news in an effort to differentiate themselves and become less substitutable. But little competition occurs between weeklies and dailies in the information market. They are more likely to be complements than substitutes.

Umbrella advertising competition tends to be more intense than competition in the information market because of limited advertising funds in any geographic market. However, newspapers in the various layers of umbrella competition are far from perfect substitutes. Large metro dailies have the advantage of larger geographic coverage and may attract advertisers who have several outlets in these wider areas. Suburban newspapers have the advantage of lower prices because of their narrower area, and, therefore, may attract more local, independent advertisers who don't need or want to advertise all over a larger area.

The impact of intermedia competition is difficult to determine in all three markets. The natural differences in media make them imperfect substitutes. Research shows little or no impact in the information market and mixed effects in the advertising market. The exception is cross-ownership, which results in less diverse information and intellectual markets.

Overall, competition serves a useful purpose from the reader's perspective because it provides options. The ability to substitute information and advertising commodities makes newspaper firms more responsive to readers' needs and wants. From the newspaper manager's perspective, competition increases cost and uncertainty.

The historical assumption underlying the role of the intellectual market in society is that the more information outlets the better. More outlets mean more ideas and opinions have access to the intellectual market. This assumption seems sound despite anecdotal evidence to the contrary. The assumption holds in the long run, although short-term variations will always be present.

Of course, a problem facing society is that the most effective type of competition— direct newspaper competition—continues to decline. If the current trend continues, fewer than a dozen cities will have two or more separately owned and operated newspapers by the end of the twentieth century, with 20 or so cities possibly having joint operating agreement newspapers. This prediction assumes current technology will continue being used and regulation will not change drastically.

As direct daily competition disappears, readers and advertisers must rely upon the development of umbrella competition, alternative weeklies, and other media to offer them options in the information, advertising, and intellectual markets. Whether these alternatives can provide the impact of direct competition will have an important bearing on local democratic governance during the next century.

ENDNOTES

1. Bruce Owen, *Economics and Freedom of Expression* (Cambridge, MA: Ballinger Publishing, 1975), p. 4.
2. Barry Litman, "Microeconomics Foundations," in Robert Picard, James P. Winter, Maxwell E. McCombs, and Stephen Lacy, eds. *Press Concentration and Monopoly* (Norwood, NJ: Ablex, 1988), pp. 3-34.
3. For more information about the impact of socialization and structure see Warren Breed, "Social Control in the News Room: A Functional Analysis," *Social Forces*, 33:326-335 (May 1955); Mark Fishman, *Manufacturing the News* (Austin, TX: University of Texas Press, 1980); and Gaye Tuchman, *Making News: A Study in the Construction of Reality* (New York: The Free Press, 1978).
4. Litman, *op. cit.*
5. William B. Blankenburg, "Consolidation in Two-Newspaper Firms," *Journalism Quarterly*, 62:474-481 (Autumn 1985).
6. James N Rosse, "The Decline of Direct Newspaper Competition," *Journal of Communication*, 30:65-71 (Spring 1980).
7. Jean Folkerts and Stephen Lacy, "Weekly Editors in 1900: A Quantitative Study of Demographic Characteristics," *Journalism Quarterly*, 64:429-433 (Summer-Autumn 1987).
8. Eugenia Zerbinos, "Analysis of the Increase in Weekly Circulation, 1960-80," *Journalism Quarterly*, 59:467-471 (Autumn 1982).
9. Walter E. Niebauer Jr., Stephen Lacy, James M. Bernstein and Tuen-yu Lau, "Central City Market Structure's Impact on Suburban Newspaper Circulation," *Journalism Quarterly*, 65:726-732 (Fall 1988).
10. For examples of these studies see: Stanley K. Bigman, "Rivals in Conformity: A Study of Two Competing Dailies," *Journalism Quarterly*, 25:127-131 (Spring 1948); Wesley F. Willoughby, "Are Two Competing Dailies Better Than One?" *Journalism Quarterly*, 32:197-204 (Spring 1955); and Raymond B. Nixon and Robert L. Jones, "The Content of Competitive vs. Noncompetitive Newspapers," *Journalism Quarterly*, 33:299-314 (Summer 1956).
11. Galen Rarick and Barrie Hartman, "The Effects of Competition on One Daily Newspaper's Content," *Journalism Quarterly*, 43:459-463 (Autumn 1966).
12. Stephen Lacy, "The Effects of Intracity Competition on Daily Newspaper Content," *Journalism Quarterly*, 64:281-290 (Summer-Autumn 1987).
13. David H. Weaver and L. E. Mullins, "Content and Format Characteristics of Competing Daily Newspapers," *Journalism Quarterly*, 52:257-264 (Summer 1975).
14. Barry R. Litman and Janet Bridges, "An Economic Analysis of Daily Newspaper Performance," *Newspaper Research Journal*, Spring 1986, pp. 9-26; and Lacy, 1987, *op. cit.*
15. Bridges and Litman, *Ibid.*

16. Stephen Lacy, "Newspaper Competition and Number of Press Services Carried: A Replication," *Journalism Quarterly*, in press.
17. John Busterna, "Ownership, CATV and Expenditures for Local Television News," *Journalism Quarterly*, 57:287-291; and Stephen Lacy, Tony Atwater, and Xinmin Qin, "Competition and the Allocation of Resources for Local Television News," *Journal of Media Economics*, Spring 1989, pp. 3-14.
18. Stephen Lacy, "A Model of Demand for News: Understanding the Impact of Competition on Daily Newspaper Content," *Journalism Quarterly*, 66:40-48, 128 (Spring 1989).
19. Consumer surplus refers to the added value consumers derive from perfect competition. Since firms in perfectly competitive markets cannot charge different prices to different consumers and the markets set the prices, consumers benefit from low prices. When a monopoly replaces competition, the monopolist sets prices and can even charge different prices to different buyers in some circumstances. Some of the value that the consumers were receiving before the monopoly is then transferred to the monopolists and some is lost altogether. The result is a higher price and less value for the consumers.

    While some economists have attacked the "consumer surplus" as being a misuse of demand curves and resulting in only a small misallocation of resources, the concept is still a useful starting point for examining the impact of competition on newspaper quality.
20. Gerald C. Stone, Donna B. Stone, and Edgar P. Trotter, "Newspaper's Quality's Relation to Circulation," *Newspaper Research Journal*, Spring 1981, pp. 16-24; and Lee B. Becker, Randy Beam and John Russial, "Correlates of Daily Newspaper Performance in New England," *Journalism Quarterly*, 55:100-108 (Spring 1978).
21. Walter E. Niebauer Jr., "Trends of Circulation and Penetration Following Failure of Metropolitan Daily Newspapers," Unpublished paper presented to the Association for Education in Journalism and Mass Communication, San Antonio, Texas, August 1987.
22. Wayne A. Danielson and John B. Adams, "Completeness of Press Coverage of the 1960 Presidential Campaign," *Journalism Quarterly*, 38:441-452 (Autumn 1961).
23. Stephen Lacy and Frederick Fico, "Financial Commitment, Newspaper Quality and Circulation: Testing an Economic Model of Direct Newspaper Competition," Unpublished paper presented to the Association for Education in Journalism and Mass Communication, Washington, DC, August 1989.
24. Stephen Lacy, Frederick Fico, and Todd Simon, "The Relationship Among Economic, Newsroom and Content Variables: A Path Model," *Journal of Media Economics*, Fall 1989, pp. 51-66.
25. Birthney Ardoin, "A Comparison of Newspapers Under Joint Printing Contracts," *Journalism Quarterly*, 50:340-347 (Summer 1973).
26. Ronald G. Hicks and James S. Featherston, "Duplicating Content in Contrasting Ownership Situations," *Journalism Quarterly*, 55:549-553 (Autumn 1978).

27. Stephen Lacy, "Content of Joint Operation Newspapers," in Robert G. Picard, James P. Winter, Maxwell E. McCombs, and Stephen Lacy, eds. *Press Concentration and Monopoly* (Norwood, NJ: Ablex, 1988), pp. 147-160.
28. George L. Bird, "Newspaper Monopoly and Political Independence," *Journalism Quarterly*, 17:210 (September 1940).
29. Hicks and Featherston, *op. cit.*
30. Gerald L. Grotta, "Consolidation of Newspapers: What Happens to the Consumer?" *Journalism Quarterly*, 48:245-250 (Summer 1971).
31. Dores A. Candussi and James. P. Winter, "Monopoly and Content in Winnipeg," in Robert G. Picard, James P. Winter, Maxwell E. McCombs, and Stephen Lacy, eds. *Press Concentration and Monopoly* (Norwood, NJ: Ablex, 1988), pp. 139-145.
32. The results of the report are mentioned in Robert G. Picard, "Pricing Behavior of Newspapers," in Robert G. Picard, James P. Winter, Maxwell E. McCombs, and Stephen Lacy, eds., *Press Concentration and Monopoly* (Norwood, NJ: Ablex, 1988), p. 65.
33. Bruce M. Owen, "Empirical Results of the Price Effects of Joint Ownership in Mass Media," Research Memorandum No. 93, Research Center in Economic growth, Stanford University, November 1969, p. 16.
34. G. F. Mathewson, "A Note on the Price Effect of Market Power in the Canadian Newspaper Industry, *The Canadian Journal of Economics*, 5:298-301 (May 1972); Owen, *Ibid.*; and Grotta, 1971, *op. cit.*
35. Robert G. Picard, "Pricing in Competing and Monopoly Newspapers, 1972-1982," *LSU School of Journalism Research Bulletin* (1986); and Robert R. Kerton, "Price Effects of Market Power in the Canadian Newspaper Industry," *The Canadian Journal of Economics*, 6:602-606 (November 1973).
36. Armando Lago, "The Price Effects of Joint Mass Communication Media Ownership," *The Antitrust Bulletin*, 16:789-813 (1971).
37. James M. Ferguson, "Daily Newspaper Advertising Rates, Local Media Cross-Ownership, Newspaper Chains, and Media Competition," *Journal of Law and Economics*, 24:635-654 (October 1983).
38. Robert G. Picard, "Pricing Behavior in Monopoly Newspapers: Ad and Circulation Differences in Joint Operating and Single Newspaper Monopolies,1972-1982" *LSU School of Journalism Research Bulletin* (1985); and Robert G. Picard and Gary D. Fackler, "Price Changes in Competing and Joint Operating Newspapers: Advertising and Circulation Differences," *LSU School of Journalism Research Bulletin* (1985).
39. William B. Blankenburg, "Determinants of Pricing of Advertising in Weeklies," *Journalism Quarterly*, 57:663-666 (Winter 1980).
40. The Supreme Court ruled in *Miami Herald Publishing Co. v. Tornillo*, 418 U.S. 241 (1974) that newspapers could not be required by law to print replies to editorials criticisms of political candidates.
41. For example see: John C. Merrill and S. Jack Odell, *Philosophy and Journalism* (New York: Longman, 1983).
42. For a good review of literature concerning constraints on newsgathering see Pamela Shoemaker with Elizabeth Kay Mayfield, "Building a Theory of

News Content: A Synthesis of Current Approaches," *Journalism Monograph*, No. 103, June 1987.
43. For example, see J. Herbert Altschull, *Agents of Power: The Role of News Media in Human Affairs* (New York: Longman, 1984).
44. Pamela J. Shoemaker, "Media Treatment of Deviant Political Groups," *Journalism Quarterly*, 61:66-75, 82 (Spring 1984).
45. Ernest C. Hynds, "Editorials, Opinion Pages Still Have Vital Roles at Most Newspapers," *Journalism Quarterly*, 61:634-639 (Autumn 1984).
46. See Gerard H. Borstel, "Ownership, Competition and Comment in 20 Small Dailies," *Journalism Quarterly*, 33:220-222 (Spring 1956); Bigman, *op.cit.*; and Willoughby, *op. cit.*
47. Robert M. Entman, "Newspaper Competition and First Amendment Ideals: Does Monopoly Matter?" *Journal of Communication*, Summer 1985, pp. 147-165.
48. Lacy, 1987, *op. cit.*
49. Lacy, 1988, *op. cit.*
50. James N. Rosse, "Economic Limits of Press Responsibility," Discussion paper, Stanford University: Studies in Industry Economics, No. 56, 1975.
51. Owen, *Economics and Freedom of Expression: Media Structure and the First Amendment*, *op. cit.*, p. 51.
52. Stephen Lacy, "Competition Among Metropolitan Daily, Small Daily and Weekly Newspapers," *Journalism Quarterly*, 61:640-644, 742 (Autumn 1984).
53. Stephen Lacy, "The Impact of Intercity Competition on Daily Newspaper Content," *Journalism Quarterly*, 65:399-406 (Summer 1988).
54. Stephen Lacy, Ardyth B. Sohn, and Lowndes F. Stephens, "A Content Analysis of Metropolitan and Suburban Newspapers in Denver and Detroit," *Newspaper Research Journal*, Spring 1989, pp.39-50.
55. Diana Stover Tillinghast, "Limits of Competition," in *Press Concentration and Monopoly: New Perspectives on Newspaper Ownership and Operation*, in Robert G. Picard, James P. Winter, Maxwell E. McCombs, and Stephen Lacy, eds. (Norwood, NJ: Ablex, 1988), pp.71-87.
56. Susan M. Devey, "Umbrella Competition for Newspaper Circulation in the Boston Metro Area," *Journal of Media Economics*, Spring 1989, pp. 31-40.
57. Lacy, 1984, *op. cit.*
58. For examples see: Clarice N. Olien, George A. Donohue and Phillip J. Tichenor, "Metropolitan Dominance and Media Use," *ANPA News Research Report*, No. 36 (September 1982); Maxwell E. McCombs and James P. Winter, "Defining Local News," *Newspaper Research Journal*, October 1981, pp. 16-21; Kenneth M. Jackson, "Local Orientation of Suburban News Subscribers," *Newspaper Research Journal*, April 1982, pp. 52-59; and Kenneth Jackson, "Broadening of Reader Interest Seen Through News' Relation to Households," *Newspaper Research Journal*, Fall 1980, pp. 33-42.
59. Maxwell McCombs, "Mass Media and the Marketplace," *Journalism Monographs*, No. 24, August 1972.
60. Charles V. Kinter, "How Much Income Is Available to Support Communication?" *Journalism Quarterly*, 25:38-42 (March 1948).

61. William C. Wood, "Consumer Spending on the Mass Media: the Principle of Relative Constancy Considered," *Journal of Communication*, Spring 1986, pp. 39-51.
62. Harvey J. Levin, "Competition Among Mass Media and The Public Interest," *Public Opinion Quarterly*, Spring 1954, pp. 62-79; and Stephen Lacy, "The Effect of Growth of Radio on Newspaper Competition, 1929-1948," *Journalism Quarterly*, 64:775-781 (Winter 1987).
63. Leo Bogart, "How the Challenge of Television news Affects the Prosperity of Daily Newspapers," *Journalism Quarterly*, 52:403-410 (Autumn 1975); Roger G. Noll, Merton J. Peck, and John J. McGowan, *Economic Aspects of Television Regulation* (Washington, DC: The Brookings Institute, 1973); and Hugh S. Fullerton, "Technology Collides with Relative Constancy: The Pattern of Adoption for a New Medium," *Journal of Media Economics*, Fall 1988, pp. 75-84.
64. Gerald Stone, *Examining Newspapers: What Research Reveals About America's Newspapers* (Newbury Park, CA: Sage, 1987), pp. 108-126.
65. Stephen Lacy, "Effect of Intermedia Competition on Daily Newspaper Content," *Journalism Quarterly*, 65:95-99 (Spring 1988).
66. Gerald L. Grotta and Doug Newsom, "How Does Cable Television in the Home Relate to Other Media Use," *Journalism Quarterly*, 59:588-591, 609 (Winter 1982); and Joey Reagan, "Effects of Cable Television on News Use," *Journalism Quarterly*, 61:317-324 (Summer 1984).
67. Guido H. Stempel III, "Effects of a Cross-Media Monopoly," *Journalism Monographs*, No. 29, June 1973.
68. William T. Gromley Jr. *The Effects of Newspaper-Television Cross-Ownership on News Homogeniety* (Chapel Hill, NC: University of North Carolina, 1976).
69. Owen, 1969, *op. cit.*
70. Lago, *op. cit.*
71. Mathewson, *op. cit.*
72. Kerton, *op. cit.*
73. Ferguson, *op. cit.*
74. John C. Busterna, "The Cross-Elasticity of Demand for National Newspaper Advertising," *Journalism Quarterly*, 64:346-351 (Summer-Autumn 1987).
75. Larry Kahaner, "'Baby Bells Grow Into Giants," *presstime*, February 1990, pp. 18-27.
76. "Court orders reconsideration of RBOC leash; ANPA looks to Judge Greene to retain it," *presstime*, May 1990, p.64
77. James M. Bernstein and Stephen Lacy, "In-depth Coverage and Commentary in Local Television News," unpublished paper presented to the Association for Education in Journalism and Mass Communication, Minneapolis, MN, August 1990.

5

Newspaper Ownership

Ownership rivals competition for amount of attention from newspaper scholars and critics during the 20th century. Even though the two are inextricably related, growth in the size of groups appears to have generated more concern about ownership's impact than exists about the effects of declining competition. This emphasis probably reflects both societal and historiographic traditions in the United States.

U. S. society always has valued the idea of independence and entrepreneurship. The image of the committed journalist struggling to print the truth despite economic problems and government interference has become part of social lore. Although the history of newspapers during the 19th century holds many examples of people starting newspapers and rising to social and political prominence, James Gordon Bennett and Horace Greeley for example, evidence indicates that editors at large newspapers during the last century were not unlike people who ran other large industries.[1] Today, many newspapers, usually weeklies, continue to be owned and operated by individuals and families, but the underlying assumption that this results in better newspapers is not necessarily accurate. This issue lies at the heart of the concern about ownership and will be discussed in light of research later in this chapter.

A second reason ownership has received so much attention involves the nature of journalism history. A quick glance through scholarly journals reveals the tendency of journalism historians to view history as a series of actions by individuals, mostly men. While there has been a recent movement away from this "great man" approach, the bulk of journalism history during the 20th century falls into this category.[2] This approach deals with the flow of events as a result of individual decision making rather than as the result of economic, political, and social forces within society. The "great man" approach has contributed to the emphasis on ownership because of the assumption that individual decisions by owners are the most important factors in newspaper development.

The growing emphasis on ownership also is related to the decline of competition discussed in Chapter 4. Competition moves power from the owner to the consumer. A newspaper with monopoly power need not respond to the readers' demands during the short run because during this period no other firms can enter the market. Thus, if a newspaper firm reduces quality by cutting expenditures in the news-editorial department, readers in a one-newspaper city have little choice if they want to continue subscribing to a local newspaper. If two newspapers exist in a local market, both have to continue to invest in the editorial commodity or lose circulation.

The growing ownership concentration across markets and the declining competition within markets have created the potential for negative effects on society. These two trends were a basis for concern expressed by the Hutchins Commission in 1947, and they are the basis for the discussion within this chapter. The first section will deal briefly with ownership trends, followed by a discussion of ownership goals. The final section will review research about the impact of various types of ownership in the three newspaper markets.

TRENDS IN NEWSPAPER OWNERSHIP

Four ownership trends stand out as important: (a) the growth of group ownership of newspapers, (b) the growth of multimedia ownership, (c) the growth of publicly owned groups, and (d) the growth of conglomerates with media and nonmedia companies. The first one extends backward to 1909-1910, when 13 groups owned 2.9 percent of the dailies in the United States.[3] The trend has intensified greatly since then, as can be seen in Table 5.1. In 1920, 31 groups owned 7.5 percent of all dailies with an average of 4.9 dailies per group. By 1960, 109 groups owned 31.8 percent of all dailies, with an average of 5.1 newspapers per group. In 1986, the percentage of dailies owned by the 127 groups reached 69.1 percent. In the

TABLE 5.1. Trends in Ownership of Daily Newspapers

	1920	1940	1960	1986
Circulation (000)	27,791	41,132	58,881	62,453
Total Cities	2,042	1,878	1,763	1,657
Total Daily Cities	1,295	1,426	1,461	1,513
Newspaper Groups	31	60	109	127
Group Newspapers	153	319	560	1,158
Average Dailies per Group	4.9	5.3	5.1	9.1
Group Newspapers Percentage of Total	7.5	17.0	31.8	69.9
Newspaper Owners	1,920	1,619	1,312	626

Source: John Busterna, "Trends in Daily Newspaper Ownership," *Journalism Quarterly*, 65:831-838 (Winter 1988).

years between 1920 and 1986, the number of owners dropped from 1,920 to 626. By 1986, the 12 largest groups, topped by Gannett with 90 dailies, accounted for more than 47 percent of all daily circulation in the United States.[4]

National data concerning the growth of group ownership among nondaily newspapers are difficult to find. The impression one gets from reading the newspaper trade press is that the same trend among dailies exists among nondailies. Research concerning Minnesota is available that supports this impression. Olien, Tichenor and Donohue found that only four nondailies in a sample of 60 were group-owned in 1965. This figure rose to 30 out of 59 20 years later.[5] There is no reason to think that Minnesota differs greatly from other states.

- The growth of publicly held groups has been parallel to the growth of all groups. Public and private groups differ in that public-group stock is available for purchase by the general public. A fairly high correlation can be found between public ownership and the number of newspapers in a group because the public offering of stock generates money to purchase more newspapers. Of the 20 largest newspaper groups in 1987, nine were publicly owned. Four of the five largest were publicly held.[6] In 1986, the 13 publicly owned newspaper groups and newspapers accounted for about 38 percent of the total daily circulation and 16 percent of the 1,657 dailies in the United States.[7]

- Large newspaper groups have not been satisfied with being just newspaper organizations. They have diversified into other media, including television and radio stations, cable systems, magazines and book companies. In 1986, the 15 largest newspaper groups in the United States, based on daily circulation, also owned 173 nondaily newspapers, 71 television stations, 67 radio stations, more than 295 cable systems, more than 133 magazines, and 16 book companies.[8]

- In addition to these three newspaper industry trends, a fourth trend in mass media ownership also has emerged. This involves the acquisition of media organizations by nonmedia corporations. Examples of this trend include General Tire & Rubber Co. buying into the film industry, Gulf + Western entering the book industry, and Scott and Fetzer entering the book industry.[9] While this trend had not drastically affected the newspaper industry by the end of the 1980s, the high profits and cash flow from newspapers and the public ownership of newspapers make such a trend a strong possibility during the 1990s.

Reasons Behind Group Growth

The rapid growth of groups resulted from incentives for both buyers and sellers. Compaine listed five reasons groups continue to buy existing newspapers.[10] First, newspapers are profitable investments. During 1980, the median profit margin for publicly held newspapers after taxes was 8.5 percent of sales, which was almost twice that for all industries.[11] In 1986, newspapers had a 27 percent return on assets, which was highest for all media industries, and newspaper firms showed a 5 percentage point increase in profit margins during the previous five years, which was second only to the record industry among media.[12] Groups see other newspapers as one of their most profitable investments. The growth of revenue for newspaper firms during the early 1990s is expected to be only slightly behind that of television.[13]

- Second, not only do newspapers make money, but they also are a scarce commodity. High barriers to entry from high fixed cost make buying a daily newspaper cheaper than starting one. Only two major metropolitan dailies were started during the 1980s: *The Washington Times*, which remains unprofitable, and The St. Louis *Sun*, which opened in 1989 and closed 211 issues later in April 1990.

- Compaine's third reason for the growth of groups is that professional management used by a group usually can turn a profitable newspaper into an even more profitable one. This process includes using technology and financial services that might not be available to an independent newspaper. However, others have argued that this increased profitability simply represents cutting of costs that are important to the newspaper.[14]

- Fourth, tax laws have allowed the generation of large amounts of cash through the amortization and depreciation of goodwill. Tax laws also allow accumulated undistributed profits to be used to acquire additional newspapers and, in this way, to be exempt from tax on excess accumulated profits.

- Finally, Compaine states that the high volume of cash generated by newspapers attracts buyers. Large cash flow provides flexibility in business dealings.

On the seller's side, Compaine mentioned five conditions that have contributed to the growth of groups. First, weak management has caused some independent newspapers to become victims of rising costs. The increasing costs of newsprint and technology necessary to remain competitive require expertise that independent papers may not be able to afford.

- Second, family squabbles concerning goals and management can lead to selling a newspaper. A good example of this situation is the sale of *The Courier-Journal* in Louisville to Gannett in 1986. Arguments within the Bingham family led not only to the sale of the paper but to a segment on 60 Minutes about the family in-fighting.

- Third, inheritance taxes must be paid on privately owned newspapers when the owner dies. If the estate does not have much cash, the newspaper must be sold to pay those taxes. The tendency of second and third generations to lose interest in journalism means efforts to save a newspaper's independence under such circumstances are half-hearted at best.

- Fourth, capital gains tax rates traditionally have been lower than income tax rates. This has encouraged the selling of newspapers to get the lower tax rate. Even though the difference in rates changed with tax reform in 1988, efforts to lower capital gains tax rates continued into the 1990s.
- Fifth, the prices offered by groups for newspaper firms often are so high that owners feel compelled to sell the newspaper. For example, *The Courier-Journal* sold for $300 million and the *Houston Chronicle* sold for $400 million in 1987.

The trend toward public ownership also rests on tax laws, but public ownership has other advantages as well. Publicly traded stock raises money for investment in technology and other properties. It also allows employees to be rewarded through stock sharing plans.[15] The trend of going public, however, has created problems for some groups that wish to retain control of their newspapers. The takeover mania that seemed to dominate business in the last half of the 1980s became a problem for Media General, Inc. and the *St. Petersburg Times*. Both companies were fighting unfriendly takeover efforts as the decade came to a close. Newspaper companies have responded in several ways to the potential for unfriendly takeovers. These include setting up two-tier stock structures that maintain control by the families that run the newspapers and even include going private again, as the Harte-Hanks group did.

Development of multimedia groups reflects a reaction to a changing environment. As a new medium develops and evolves, newspaper groups have protected themselves against loss of profits by buying into the new medium. If they lose advertising revenues in the newspaper industry, they can pick them up through the new medium.

The move toward diversity and the high profits of media firms also have contributed to the development of conglomerate corporations that own media firms and companies in other industries. The potential negative impact on the information and intellectual markets is that a media company may not publish information that would embarrass or hurt the financial standing of another company in the same conglomerate.[16]

Although newspaper companies have not succumb as much to this trend as book and movie companies, newspapers are not immune. For example, the *Anchorage Times* was sold to Veco International Inc. in late 1989. Veco contracts with oil companies, and the management of the competing daily in Anchorage raised the issue of whether the *Times* can cover the oil industry objectively.[17] Whatever the performance of the *Times*, the potential for a conflict remains, as it does for all newspaper firms owned by another type of company.

Because the impact of owners on a newspaper's performance results primarily from the goals of the owners, these trends are important. Different types of ownership may have different goals. Before examining research concerning the effects of ownership on the information, advertising, and intellectual markets, an evaluation of various types of business goals would be useful.

OWNERSHIP GOALS

Newspaper firms, like any company, can pursue whatever goals the owners and managers desire. A newspaper could produce copies composed entirely of news, opinion, or advertising as long as management is willing to accept the consequences of those actions in the marketplace. The history of the United States contains many examples of newspapers that were subsidized in order to pursue something other than a financial goal. Partisan newspapers published during the early decades of the United States were created to promote party politics more than make money. Few of these papers survived for long.

Despite examples of papers with nonfinancial goals, most newspapers have tried to weld the desire to affect society with the aim of financial survival. This dual effort explains why newspapers serve three markets. One can argue about their success, but the decision to try to supply more than one market does not necessarily mean all newspaper owners accept the same goals. Even managers within a newspaper may vary their goals across time.

Economic and management theory can aid in understanding the nature of goals and the potential impact of various types of goals on newspaper performance. Greer mentioned five theories of organizational behavior associated with various organizational goals.[18] These theories also suggest possible patterns of behavior for achieving the goals.

Traditional microeconomic theory assumes that firms maximize profits. In a competitive market, a firm maximizes profits when it produces at a level where marginal costs equals marginal revenues. Profit maximizing is called marginal behavior. This assumed goal of the firm has been attacked as being simple and unrealistic because managers cannot accurately measure their marginal costs and revenues.[19] The maximization assumption appears to be based on the use of calculus by economists for qualitative analysis. However, the unrealistic nature of profit maximization need not prevent it from being a useful predictive tool in competitive markets. Firms often perform as if they are maximizing profit even if this is not their goal. The goal of theory is to explain and predict, rather than present a replica of reality.

Whatever the arguments for and against profit maximization for most companies, one can see why alternative goals would be pursued by a newspaper firm. First, most nonmedia firms do not have the public information function that is part of the newspaper industry. The protection afforded newspapers by the First Amendment adds a socially mandated goal to the profit objective of newspaper organizations. One point made by the Hutchins Commission was that, if newspapers do not fulfill their social function, society has the right to withdraw the protection of the First Amendment.

Second, newspapers do not exist in markets that are even close to perfectly competitive. Machlup explained that the lack of competitive pressure may allow managerial discretion in organizational goals, although he remained unconvinced that the profit maximization motive should be abandoned in economic analysis.[20] As pointed out above, a competitive newspaper market usually means the newspapers are struggling for survival. Under such conditions, maximizing profits would become a long-run goal with short-run goals aimed at survival.

If newspapers do not pursue profit maximization, what other goals would they have? At least four other theories offer possible answers to this question. These will be explained briefly and their applicability to newspapers examined.

Williamson said managers maximize their own utility because the separation of management from ownership means strict profit maximizing need not be observed.[21] The manager can pursue profit maximizing or choose some other goal, which means managers keep some profits to enhance their utility. The discretionary profit, which is above a minimal acceptable profit to the owners, may be spent on staff, expense accounts, office suites, executive services, and other perks. The staff helps to reduce insecurity and expand power, while the perks enhance status and prestige.

Williamson conducted case studies of three firms in adverse conditions and found that they reacted in ways consistent with his theory. Using existing data, he found that high managerial representation on the board of directors resulted in high earning retention rates.

Baumol offered another alternative theory.[22] He said some firms would maximize sales revenue with a minimum profit level. His theory was developed for oligopoly markets. Sales revenue is a main concern in these markets because declining sales have numerous disadvantages. They can make banks less likely to loan money, cause distributors to go to other firms, and result in consumers buying substitutes because of a perceived decrease in popularity. Baumol presented evidence based on his experience with business.

A problem with sales revenue maximization is that a company concerned only with maximizing sales revenue could do so by selling at less than cost and ultimately run itself out of business. So, Baumol hypothesized that a goal of sales revenue maximizing would require a minimal level of profit. This level is determined in the short-run by the need to make the company's securities attractive in the capital markets.

In his revised editions, Baumol noted that some critics contend the sales revenue maximizing model is consistent with long-run profit maximizing. In effect, the firm expands sales to maximize long-run profits. Baumol expressed his skepticism about the existence of long-run goals. He doubted an organization's ability to carry out long-run goals, which would extend beyond any particular manager's tenure. He said such goals would have to be directed by a corporate unconsciousness, and he rejected the idea that such an unconsciousness exists.

A third alternative was presented by Marris when he said firms work to maximize the present value of the firm's future stream of sales revenue.[23] This would maximize the growth of the firm because a dollar's worth of sales this year is more valuable than a dollar's worth of sales next year. The value of money decreases with time. Greer said that under such a model a given present value of future sales can be achieved by a high current sales revenue combined with low future revenues, by low current sales revenue combined with high future sales revenue, or by a combination between these extremes.[24] The objective of the firm is to maximize growth by deciding on the appropriate combination of current sales and allocation of resources to meet future sales demand.

This model also rests on a distance between owners and managers. Just as with Baumol, Marris' model requires a minimal profit level for the owners. He also stresses the need for profit to grow. The profit margin for a particular good depends upon its stage of development and the overall allocation of resources needed to maximize growth.

Cyert and March developed a behavioral theory of the firm after rejecting the assumptions of profit maximizing and of single-mindedness of the firm.[25] They criticized profit maximizing because people pursue many goals and because managers tend to seek satisfactory profits rather than maximum profits. They also added that firms do not have perfect knowledge, which is a traditional assumption for rational action by managers.

Cyert and March rejected single-mindedness of the firm because individuals and not collections of individuals have goals. They also said traditional microeconomic theories ignore the decision process in organizations. Their theory is based on the interactive process among competing power centers in the organization.

In place of the traditional theories of maximization, Cyert and March postulate a coalition theory of behavior based on three areas of behavior inside the firm—goals, expectations, and choice. They developed these areas of interaction through a set of exhaustive variable categories and a set of relational concepts. Variables affecting *organizational goals* are the importance of goals and aspiration levels individuals have toward the goals. *Organizational expectations* are inferred from available information. *Choice* involves the responses to problems by identifying alternatives consistent with goals. The four relational concepts that are applied to these areas of behavior are (a) quasiresolution of conflict, (b) uncertainty avoidance, (c) problematic search, and (d) organizational learning. These concepts determine how the firm establishes expectations, defines goals, and chooses between alternatives of achieving goals.

These four alternative theories and the goal of profit maximization concern goals set by owners or managers. They can be divided broadly into two categories: maximizing and behavioral. Maximizing theories assume that some goal is maximized, although the goal varies with the theory. The behavioral approach rejects the assumption of maximization and replaces it with an assumption of "satisficing" goals, which are objectives that require less than maximizing behavior. Evidence supports all the various theories. Disagreement about the "correct" goal comes from the differing assumptions about the role of theory in economics and business. For example, Friedman rejected realism as a test of a theory.[26] He said the ultimate test is the ability of a theory to predict.

In effect, traditional microeconomic theory assumes that organizational goals do not vary. The theorists who do not assume profit maximization argue that the goal of the firm is a variable which helps to explain and predict changes in observed prices or output.

Although the five theories assume various goals, firms that have different goals may be similar in their behavior. After surveying empirical results, Greer concluded that behaviorism and maximizing sales revenue are consistent with profit maximizing.[27] However, John Williamson developed a model that predicted sales and profit maximizers would act differently.[28] Marby found that under some conditions sales and profit maximizing are consistent in results.[29] Baumol pointed out this consistency, but he also mentioned the differences between the assumptions of microeconomic theory, which assumes constant goals, and industrial organizational theory, which does not.[30]

Which goals best fit the three types of newspaper ownership? Privately held group newspapers probably come closest to profit maximizing. Management is closely connected to ownership, with the manager answering directly to the owner. Managements of private groups have a reputation for cutting costs to improve profit margins when they take over a newspaper.[31]

Privately owned newspapers are in a position to pursue whatever goals the owners please because of the close proximity between ownership and management, which are often the same. Most of these newspapers are run by individuals or small groups, who can pursue behavioral goals.

An independent owner can seek outstanding journalism and take editorial stands without fearing the wrath of owners from afar. If any of the three ownership types are inclined to pursue a goal other than profit maximizing, it probably would be this type. However, independent newspaper owners just as easily may select profit maximizing as a goal.

Publicly held newspapers could resemble privately held group newspapers or independent newspapers in their organizational goals. The distance between ownership and management that comes with public ownership would allow the pursuit of some goal other than maximization, perhaps Williamson's manager utility model. For example, one could argue that the creation of *USA Today* was not an act that represents short-run profit maximization as a goal. While this newspaper was only marginally profitable at the end of the 1980s, it serves many other purposes. Because Gannett employees from around the country work on *USA Today*, it serves as a training site where employees learn the organization's philosophy. Working in the Washington area for a few months also can serve as a reward for Gannett employees from other newspapers.

Evidence is mixed as to whether nonmaximizing models are an accurate portrayal of publicly held group newspapers. Some public groups tend to cut costs drastically when they acquire a newspaper. On the other hand, some of the most prestigious newspapers, such as *The Washington Post*, *The New York Times*, and *The Los Angeles Times*, are owned by public corporations. The latitude that managers of publicly held newspapers have for spending money on staff and other services may depend on whether large portions of the stock are held in a few hands.[32]

Perhaps it is impossible to generalize about the goals that any type of ownership will pursue. Just as independent owners vary greatly on the goals they pursue, group managers' goals often vary. A crucial aspect of understanding ownership's impact is whether the individuals who make the important decisions in a firm believe that high journalistic standards and performance are good for business in the long run. This belief is a function of individual background and corporate culture.

The goals pursued by a given management can be influenced greatly by the environment in which they operate. For example, two newspapers in an intensely competitive market will tend to maximize circulation and not profits. This comes from the effort to avoid the circulation spiral discussed in Chapter 4. This circulation maximizing behavior will occur even if it means short-run losses. This happened in Detroit and Little Rock during the last half of the 1980s.

The difficulty of generalizing about the goals of an organization may or may not be present when one discusses the behavior of various types of ownership. An extensive literature, both anecdotal and quantitative, exists concerning the impact of ownership on the three newspaper markets. The following section will review these studies and articles.

THE IMPACT OF OWNERSHIP ON NEWSPAPER MARKETS

The rapid growth of groups has caused concerns among scholars and critics about the potential abuse of local newspapers by owners. This potential for abuse exists in the information, advertising, and intellectual markets and has resulted in numerous suggestions on how to limit power. While the potential is a result of the quasimonopoly nature of most newspaper markets, much of the concern comes from ownership being located outside the community in which the newspaper is located. This concern received support in research concerning Minnesota dailies. Donohue, Olien and Tichenor found that out-of-state group-owned newspapers tended to have less conflict reporting than did independent papers and newspapers with in-state group ownership.[33]

While the growth of groups is a fact, not everyone sees the acquisition of newspapers by groups as a threat to effective and efficient performance in the three markets. Loevinger argued in 1979 that the concentration of power from the growth of groups is not extensive.[34] He reported that about one-third of the newspaper groups owned only two newspapers, and the average number of newspapers owned by a group is slightly more than six. He also argued that existence of intermedia and umbrella competition lessen whatever power these groups have.

Compaine reached a similar conclusion about group ownership. He also said concentration of ownership is not great; there are some economic benefits from group ownership; and there is little empirical evidence that groups affect content.[35] A study by Nixon and Hahn supports Compaine's position that concentration is slight in the United States.[36] Their index ranked the United States as the country with the lowest press concentration of the 32 countries studied.

Research seems the best way to settle disagreements about the impact of group ownership, although research seems just as contradictory as the arguments in this area. These contradictions are related to variations in the degree of impact in the three markets served by newspapers and to differences in the nature of the research. The following sections review and discuss the research that relates to ownership and its impact.

The Information Market

The concern about the negative impact of group ownership results primarily from two types of behavior. First, there is concern that groups will be more likely than independent newspapers to pursue a profit maximizing goal at the expense of the news-editorial department budget. Second, there is concern that a group will not have the local commitment and understanding to provide extensive and adequate local coverage.

Literature concerning effects of groups falls into two categories: anecdotal and quantitative. Anecdotal material involves descriptions of individual cases, while quantitative research uses statistical methods to analyze samples or to generalize beyond a sample. Conclusions drawn from anecdotal literature often depend on the author's purpose. Cases exist where group acquisition of newspapers improved and lowered performance in the information market. A researcher need only seek a case to support a position and such a case can be found.

An excellent example of the conflicting results of anecdotal studies is Ghiglione's collection of articles about 10 newspapers which were bought by groups.[37] The only generalization that can be made from these articles is that the impact of group ownership on newspapers depends upon the nature of the newspaper when it was bought and on the particular group that buys the newspaper. The book presents cases in which groups improved quality, as defined by the individual authors, and cases in which groups lowered quality.

Bagdikian said a group buying a newspaper usually means the paper is no better or worse than before.[38] However, he added that groups improve the profitability of newspapers and use the money to buy other newspapers, not to improve editorial quality. The danger from group ownership, he concluded, is that the loss of independent newspapers will create a permanent standard of mediocrity for newspapers.

A recurring and unfortunate impact of some group ownership is interference with local autonomy. The Panax group is a classic example discussed by Compaine. This group owned eight dailies and forty weeklies in 1977. John P. McGoff, president of the group, fired two editors who refused to print articles the group's headquarters wanted on the front page. The fired editors said the articles contained "half truths" and "innuendoes." The articles claimed President Carter condoned promiscuity among his staff and was grooming his wife for the vice presidency. Compaine concluded:

> It is this type of domination which can undo the positive roles of many of the chains and may even outweigh the lack of overall empirical evidence of systematic malevolence by chain owners.[39]

Ghiglione and others conducted an extensive and systematic examination of the New England press in 1973, but they did not use statistical analysis.[40] The conclusion, again, was that group ownership's impact varied. Some of the New England editors interviewed for the study said groups had provided more money for the editorial department. However, the investigators also found editors who reported staff cuts, dropped news services, and the use of canned editorials when groups took over. The researchers repeated the fear that group newspapers might be less responsive to community needs because the people who run them may not be as committed to the community as people who run independent newspapers.

Statistical research allows efficient summary of large amounts of data and generalization based on random selection of samples. One of the problems with the existing statistical studies is the inconsistency of content measures. While some studies overlap, they often look at different areas of content. There is also a tendency to use samples of convenience and to differ in the operational definition of group ownership. The following review will take a chronological approach to these studies in an effort to find recurring and systematic effects of group ownership.

Some quantitative studies suggest groups have little or no effect on the quality of newspapers. For example, Grotta discovered little difference in content between a sample of group newspapers and a control group.[41] The analysis examined change in number of editorial employees, change in size of newshole, change in proportion of local news to total news, change in size of editorial page newshole, and change in proportion of local to total editorial content. However, a problem arises in drawing conclusions about groups from this study. The author examined the hypothesis that group ownership would improve newspapers. He compared newspapers that were group newspapers between 1950 and 1960 and that remained group papers in 1968 with a control group composed of independent and group newspapers that did not change ownership during the period. His conclusion that groups did not improve newspapers was justified, but the application of the research to the groups versus independents controversy is confounded by the makeup of the control groups.

Becker, Beam, and Russial used the data gathered in the New England newspaper study to examine factors that may affect quality of newspapers.[42] Using the evaluations, coders rated the the newspapers on a five-point scale for quality in four areas of news coverage and presentation. The study found that newspapers owned by large corporations were generally better than smaller independent newspapers. The newspapers were coded as single corporation newspaper, small group, and large group.

The results reported in this study suffer from two problems. First, the ownership variable is really a measure of the number of newspapers owned by a company and not the difference between group and nongroup newspapers. Second, quality is often related to financial resources. The relationship found here may represent the fact that the larger groups have more resources and own larger newspapers. The New England results probably can be more accurately interpreted as showing quality is related to economic power that comes with being a large company. The findings reveal little about differences between large independents versus large group newspapers, or between small group newspapers versus small independent newspapers.

Drew and Wilhoit studied newshole allocation of 149 newspapers by surveying managing editors.[43] The sample was based on a 46 percent response rate from a national stratified random sample of editors. The editors estimated various newshole allocations by their newspapers. No significant differences were found between group and independent newspapers in newshole size, proportion of newspaper devoted to news, and types of news in the newshole.

One statistical case study examined coverage of the 1982 Knoxville World's Fair before and after a newspaper was bought by a group.[44] The authors coded stories and assertions about the World's Fair before and after the purchase of the *Knoxville Journal* by Gannett. Similar stories were coded in the *Knoxville News-Sentinel*, which has been owned by Scripps-Howard since 1958. They concluded the change of ownership made no difference in fair coverage. However, one of the two tables showed a statistically significant change in the leaning of *Journal* assertions about the fair. The *Journal* became more positive following the purchase by Gannett. At the same time, the *News-Sentinel* became more neutral in its assertions.

Hale studied the attitude of readers toward group ownership. He surveyed readers in Waco, Texas, two and a half years after Cox bought a formerly independent newspaper. Despite an expressed preference for independently owned newspapers, readers evaluated the Cox newspaper as about equal in quality to the independent newspaper that preceded it.[45]

A case study by Soloski found that the publisher of a group newspaper is evaluated on the basis of economic goals that may be achieved at the expense of news coverage.[46] This occurs despite efforts to insulate managers from the direct influence of the group. He also pointed out that group managers often have no vested interest in the local community. News content can also be affected by use of the group news service, accounting procedures and management techniques.

In a study related to Soloski's, Parsons, Finnegan and Benham expressed concern about the possible effects of group ownership, but their approach was sociological rather than economic.[47] Their model states that organizational, community, and professional roles all affect journalists.

These roles may or may not be in conflict. They hypothesized that group managers have different goals and potential for movement within the organization than do independent newspaper managers. These differences can create conflict among roles with the result being more of a commitment by group editors to the organization than to the community. The authors conducted a pilot study of editors and concluded that groups diminish the likelihood of an editor's maintaining longstanding ties to a particular community even though group editors said they value such ties.

Although this model has a sociological base, it is consistent with an economic approach to group ownership. Since a group grows primarily for business reasons, the goals and structure of the organization are determined by these purposes. It may be that a group manager hoping for promotion would set short-run goals inconsistent with the long-run interest of a newspaper and community, whereas an independent owner committed to a community might have short-run goals that are more consistent with the long-run interests of the local readers.

A survey by Demers and Wackman sought to examine the motives of group versus independent managers.[48] Their results are somewhat consistent with those of Soloski and of Parsons, Finnegan, and Benham. They found that group managers, both editorial and noneditorial, were more likely to list profit as an important motive of their organization. This occurred after controlling for other influences. The authors warn, however, that the low response rate (11 percent) leaves the conclusions open to question.

Results by Demers and Wackman were inconsistent with a survey of Minnesota editors conducted earlier.[49] In this survey of 60 weekly and 18 daily newspapers managers, the mention of profit as a basis of satisfaction was negatively correlated with corporate ownership. In this study, corporate ownership was operationalized with four levels: independent, group headquartered in the town where the newspaper is published, group headquartered somewhere else in Minnesota, and group headquartered outside of Minnesota. There was a positive correlation between group ownership and the significance of business stories and the percent of newshole given to nonlocal business stories. This study showed a relationship between group ownership, attitudes, and news values, but the relationships were not necessarily negative ones from the readers' viewpoints.

A national study using existing data found weak negative relationships between the size of group to which a paper belonged and the size of full-time staff, the number of wire services carried, and the weekday lines of news carried.[50] The study did not control for circulation, which is a measure of financial resources available to the newspaper.

A content analysis of 114 randomly selected dailies from throughout the

United States found that five of 22 content categories were related to group ownership. Three of these were editorial-opinion categories and will be discussed in the section on the intellectual market. The only differences found in the news sections were a negative correlation between group ownership and the total percentage of newspaper given news-editorial content and a negative correlation between group ownership and the square inches of copy per staff reporter.[51]

In a smaller study, 21 prestige and large circulation newspapers were examined for their fairness and balance in reporting. The group newspapers were less likely to have both sides of a controversy represented in an article, but they were more likely to have a light work load for their reporters. Since this study found a negative relationship between work load and balance, as measured by square inches about different sides of a controversy, group membership was associated with more balanced stories.[52] The work load results are consistent with the national content analysis.

A study of 42 weekly and small daily newspaper managers from Minnesota found that managers who owned their papers were less concerned about profit maximizing than were managers who did not own part of their newspapers.[53] This study runs counter to the theories that suggest distance between owners and managers will result in goals other than profit maximizing. It is consistent with the idea that independent owners will produce quality newspapers. The limitation of the study is that it dealt with attitudes and not actual behavior.

Glasser, Allen and Blanks examined the impact of group ownership on the news play given a controversial story generated by a newspaper within the group.[54] They concluded that the greater play given the Gary Hart story by Knight-Ridder newspapers, compared to non-Knight-Ridder newspapers, represented a subtle influence on individual editor's decisions. The influence they found was similar to that found by Soloski.

As mentioned in the discussion of ownership goals, the performance of publicly held group newspapers may differ from that of privately owned groups newspapers. Meyer and Wearden studied ways in which people in the newspaper industry evaluate newspapers.[55] They surveyed newspaper financial analysts, publishers, editors, and newspaper staff members. The latter three were divided into those who worked for privately owned newspaper companies and those who worked for publicly held newspaper corporations. However, there appeared to be no breakdown of private companies into group and nongroup companies. The researchers found that newspaper financial analysts evaluated newspapers along financial standards, while publishers, editors, and staff tended to evaluate papers along standards of journalistic quality. There was no significant difference between the workers at publicly held and privately owned newspapers in the way they evaluated newspapers.

The Meyer and Wearden study was one of attitudes. The results might well represent a "halo effect." Respondents who work in journalism might be more likely to give high rankings to qualitative content standards rather than financial standards because of professional norms. The results may not reflect actual performance standards at the newspapers. However, a study that examined content found few difference between publicly owned and privately owned groups in news and editorial content.[56]

What, then, does the research reveal about the impact of group ownership on the information market? Two things stand out. First, while studies have found an impact in some areas of content, the impact will not be found in all groups in all areas. There appear to be few, if any, systematic effects due to group ownership. Second, the few effects found are not all negative. It appears that groups tend to have larger staffs for the amount of work that needs to be done, even if the space for content is less than in nongroup newspapers.

The most consistent evidence of group impact deals with the commitment of editors to a particular community. Group publishers and editors are more likely to move from one city to another, but the negative effect of this tendency rest on two assumptions. First, it is assumed that community commitment and organizational commitment produce conflict. Second, it is assumed that community commitment will mean a better newspaper. Neither assumption is necessarily true.

If good journalism is good business, a strong community commitment, even if it will not last for a lifetime, makes sense for movement up the organization. The idea that community commitment means a better newspaper depends on how one defines community. Many editors have argued with the president of the local Chamber of Commerce about whether "negative" news is good for the community. Community commitment may mean commitment to the readers for some publishers and commitment to the established community leaders for others. In some situations, readers might benefit from an editor who will not spend his or her entire life at a newspaper.

Perhaps the best summary of group ownership effects is to say that some groups perform well by journalistic standards and some do not, just as some independent newspapers perform well and others do not. This statement implies research should concentrate on identifying those newspapers and newspaper groups that have high or low journalistic standards. If, as mentioned in Chapter 2, readers adjust to mediocrity and lower their expectations, these people would be served by having information with which to evaluate the quasimonopoly local newspaper. A preliminary effort has been taken in this direction. One study used a survey of editors conducted by Bogart to develop a quality index.[57] The index was applied to newspapers owned by groups and a group of independent papers. As expected, some groups scored high, and others scored low. The average for the 26 independent newspapers fell right in the middle of the group scores.

The economic impact of ownership on the information market primarily occurs through the financial commitment to the news-editorial commodity. The relationship is shown in Figure 5.1 with supply curves. Curve S_1 represents the supply curve of an independent newspaper with respect to news-editorial quality. The market is in equilibrium at the kink point in the demand curve. After selling to a group, one of three things happen: (a) the supply curve remains basically the same, (b) the financial commitment increases with a shift to curve S_2, (c) and the financial commitment declines with a shift to curve S_3. With demand D_1, the result of the increase in financial commitment is an increase in circulation from C_1 to C_2. The result of a decrease in financial commitment is a decrease in circulation from C_1 to C_3. The increase in circulation is not as great as the decrease because of the difference in the elasticity of the demand curve on either side of the kink point. Although it may seem unlikely that a newspaper would cut circulation, with monopoly power a circulation drop does not mean a decrease in advertising rates or linage, as long as the drop in circulation is not great. The savings from the cut in news-editorial budget, shown by the drop in quality from Q_1 to Q_3, can combine with the continued revenue levels to increase profit.

The extent of the circulation increase or decrease depends on the nature of the demand curve in the market and on the elasticity of supply. As discussed in Chapter 3, any point above or below the kinked point is in disequilibrium. Across time the kink in the demand curve will tend to move to the intersection of the supply and demand curves. This occurs because of changes in the expectation of readers toward quality. If all other factors are equal, it is foolish for a firm to have a supply curve that intersects at any point other than the kink. If it is below, small changes in quality will bring large changes in circulation. If it is above, the cost of providing the higher level of quality may not be paid for by increased revenues at this point. However, all things are rarely equal. The factors mentioned above, as well as variations in individual organizational goals, may result in an increased or decreased financial commitment after a newspaper is bought by a group.

Just which direction the supply curve will move, or whether it will move at all, depends on the particular group that buys the newspaper. The relationship shown in Figure 5.1 implies that any increase in quality through financial commitment would be small because of the elasticity of the demand curve past the kinked point. This suggests that any increases

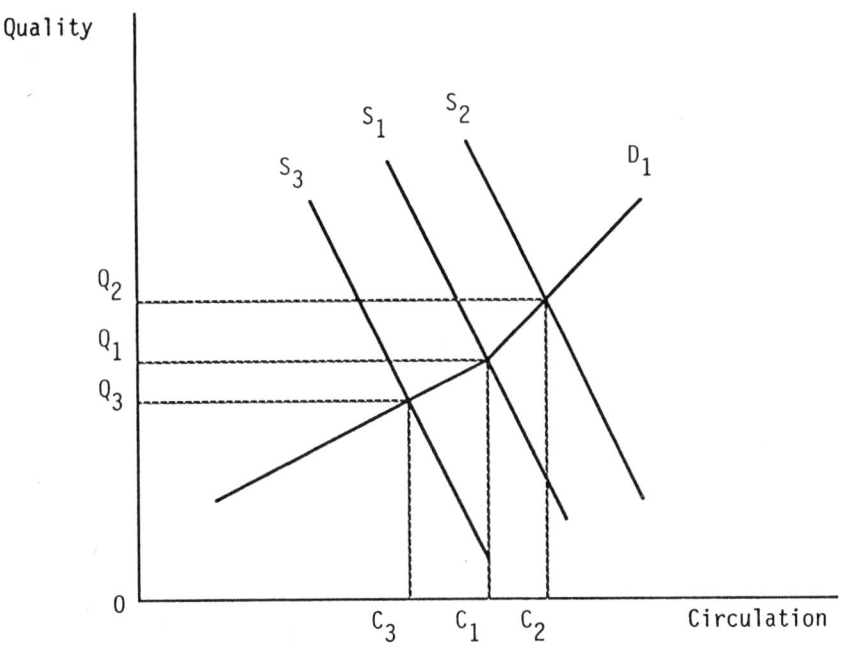

Figure 5.1. Three Possible Effects of Group Ownership on Newspaper Quality and Circulation

The three supply curves represent three types of commitment by group owners to newspaper quality. The corresponding levels of circulation and quality are determined by interaction with the demand curve (D_1). Curve S_1 is the supply curve of an independent newspaper in equilibrium. After a group buys the newspaper, it faces three choices: (a) retain the same commitment to quality, which would be the same supply curve; (b) increase the commitment to quality, shown by the S_2 curve; (c) decrease the commitment to quality, shown by S_3.

in quality by new ownership will be gradual. Such increases may reflect an effort to retain readers after an ownership change as much as an effort to attract new readers. Reader perception of decreased community commitment by the new owners could result in a new demand curve that would be to the left of the one in Figure 5.1. Greater financial commitment would be needed to overcome the perception of the readers.

While the impact of group ownership through newspaper management has been examined extensively, another area of potential impact has not received as much notice. This problem is grouped under the heading of "interlocking directorates." This occurs when the boards of directors of large newspaper groups overlap with the boards of other types of industries. This interrelationship can lead to news censorship either through subtle suggestions or downright manipulation.

The potential impact of interlocking directorates has been examined, although the number of studies is small. Two studies go into detail about the various overlapping board members for the large newspaper corporations in the United States.[58] These studies contain numerous stories of how conflicts of interest between the interlocking board members and news departments of media have led to manipulation of information. They also indicate that the managers of these large newspaper groups see no problem with the overlap of directors.

One research article examined possible causes for having interlocking directorates.[59] The author found that as dependency on major advertisers increased, the percentage of board members from major advertisers increased; as the extent of external financial obligation increased, the percentage of board members who are chief executives of financial firms increased; and as the companies diversified, the number of lawyers and competitor's proxies on the board increased. This research indicates a purposeful creation of interlocking directorate, which could imply purposeful interference in the information market.

Despite these preliminary examinations of interlocking directorates, little evidence exists that this phenomenon leads to daily changes in newspaper content. The fact that the stories of interference become known indicates that the problem is not yet as serious as it could become. Yet little research exists about the potential subtle impact of this situation. Such research could become more important as the industry moves toward more concentration.

The Advertising Market

Although the impact of groups on information depends upon the group and its goals, research indicates a more systematic relationship between group ownership and advertising prices. Most evidence suggests that group ownership means increased advertising rates.

Hale studied 200 daily newspapers that dominated their county markets.[60] Dominance meant the paper was the only daily published in a county in which out-of-county papers reached fewer than 11 percent of the households. The 113 group newspapers charged more for advertising and subscriptions than did independent newspapers.

The Hale study confirmed earlier results by Blankenburg, who studied 54 Gannett newspapers and an equivalent number of newspapers not owned by Gannett.[61] He found the Gannett newspapers charged significantly higher rates in 11 out of 12 categories. The conclusion was that at least one group's management charges higher advertising prices than do independent newspaper managers.

Owen studied the effects of ownership on prices and found that groups increased advertising prices.[62] His study of 156 newspapers showed advertising prices were about 7 percent higher for group newspapers. Grotta examined whether advertisers received any benefits from group ownership of newspapers.[63] He compared newspapers that changed from independent to group papers with newspapers that did not change and found prices increased after group ownership.

Although these studies indicate groups either charge higher advertising rates or fail to pass on any cost advantages from economies of scale to consumers, conflicting studies exist. Lago disagreed with Owen's model because Owen excluded circulation as an independent variable in his regression equation.[64] Lago found no significant effect of chain ownership on advertising prices in his sample of 357 daily newspapers. Blankenburg criticized Owen, Lago, and other earlier studies because: (a) they depended on national rates, instead of local rates; (b) they used open rates, which are usually changed when advertising is actually sold; (c) they did not control for variance in column width; and (d) they did not use the rate per 1,000 circulation.[65]

In the largest study in this area, Ferguson examined 815 daily newspapers for effects of various variables on local retail and national run-of-paper advertising rates.[66] He found that small group ownership was associated with higher daily national and retail milline advertising rates. He also found that large group ownership was associated with higher Sunday national and retail milline advertising rates. Large groups were those with at least three newspapers in different cities with circulations above 10,000.

Since the preponderance of evidence indicates that groups charge more for advertising, one is left with the question: Why? At least three factors are evident. First, group managers tend to be evaluated on their short-run profit performance. This standard would result in more aggressive pricing than with independent papers. Second, groups often have better access to research and experience in other markets. This would provide a better estimate of advertising price elasticity with respect to other media. The tendency of some managers not to price aggressively represents an effort not to run off advertisers because price elasticity is difficult to estimate. Third, the fact that most newspapers, and therefore most group newspapers, have some monopoly power allows group managers to take advantage of the aggressive pricing strategy and better research.

Whatever reason underlies the increase in advertising prices, the difference between group and nongroup newspapers can be demonstrated with supply curves for advertising. In Figure 5.2, supply curve S_1 represents the amount of ad space the newspaper will sell at a given rate as an independent. When a group buys the newspaper, it increases prices.

This increase is represented by supply curve S_2. Given the demand curve D_1, the increase in price from P_1 to P_2 will result in advertisers buying fewer lines of advertising than they did when the newspaper was independent. The overall profit will be higher, however. The revenue of the group paper is represented by the space in the rectangle $P_2E_2A_2 0$, which is greater than the old revenue represented by the space under the rectangle $P_1E_1A_1 0$. The revenue is greater because of the inelastic nature of the demand and supply curves, which is due to the monopoly power most newspapers have. Because revenues increase with the price increase and costs decline because of fewer lines, the result is increased profit. The ability to charge higher prices will vary with the type of advertising. Some types have more inelastic demand and supply curves than others (see Chapter 3).

While research is relatively consistent with regard to group ownership and daily newspaper advertising prices, the little research into weekly price behavior is less so. Blankenburg found no relationship between group ownership and advertising prices at Wisconsin weeklies.[67] However, a longitudinal study of 15 weeklies compared the newspapers before and after they were owned by a public corporation.[68] Circulation, number of pages, advertising volume, and advertising rates increased with group ownership. Profits increased for the majority of the newspapers. However, extraneous variables were not controlled for, so the advertising rate increase could have been due to factors other than ownership.

The Intellectual Market

Of the three markets served by newspapers, the intellectual market dominates the concerns about group ownership's impact. It is the opinion function of newspapers, with its contribution toward public policy, that warrants the special treatment of the newspaper business. Yet, this dependence works two ways. Just as democracy depends on the way newspapers supply the intellectual market, so newspapers depend on their performance within this market to survive in their present form.

The crucial relationship between democracy and newspapers is a traditional one, but it has taken on more importance during the 20th century because of two trends. First, the decline of direct competition among newspapers has affected access to the local intellectual market. The declining competition has probably not affected the national intellectual market drastically because magazines, television, and public radio offer opinion-oriented articles and programs that concern national issues. The real danger is that the local intellectual markets are facing less access and dissemination of ideas. This danger comes from the second trend. On a local level, the development of alternative media outlets, such as

Price

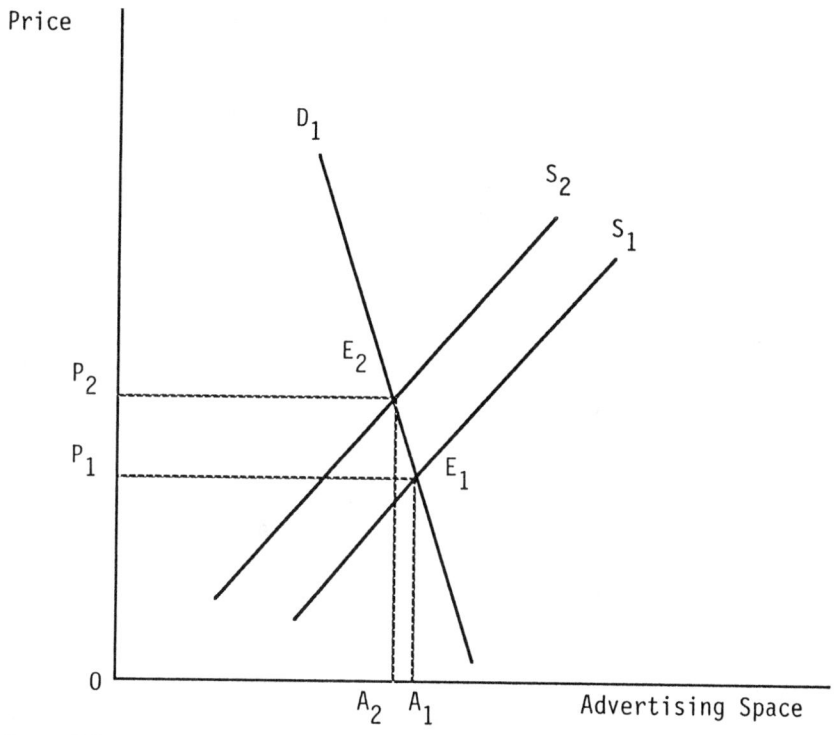

Figure 5.2. The Possible Impact of Group Acquisition on Advertising Prices and Space

A group facing an inelastic demand curve for advertising could increase advertising prices after acquiring a newspapers and increase profits at the same time. The initial equilibrium at E_1 with price P_1 and amount of advertising space A_1 changes when a newspaper firm increases the price of advertising to P_2. Given the demand curve D_1, the advertisers will demand only A_2 at this price. The newspaper responds by shifting its supply curve to S_2 and a new equilibrium point E_2 results. At this point, prices and profits are higher and advertising space is slightly lower than those at the initial equilibrium.

television and radio, has not provided extensive alternative access to the intellectual market. Much of this can be attributed to regulation and the lack of full First Amendment protection for broadcast media. Research indicates that participation by television news departments in the local intellectual market through in-depth reporting has increased in some large markets, but participation through editorials by television station management remains low.[69]

Some efforts have been undertaken to open the intellectual market through alternative and ethnic press. The lowering of production costs by computer technology has resulted in an increase in the number of alternative nondaily newspapers, but these exist in only a fraction of the cities that have daily newspapers and even fewer cities served solely by weeklies.

It is the lack of competition in the intellectual market that concerns many critics of the newspaper industry. Roach expressed two main concerns about possible effects on the marketplace of ideas. She said concentration of ownership could decrease the diversity and independence of media voices. She also mentioned a possible conflict of interest between newspaper management and the goals of corporations that own enterprises other than newspapers.[70]

Bagdikian said the concentration of ownership in groups will result in an overemphasis on the bottom line.[71] This means owners would respond more to the needs and demands of advertisers than to the needs of the readers in the intellectual market. The likelihood that a media firm will respond to those who finance the firm is the basis for a theory of news content developed by Shoemaker.[72]

The tendency to respond to financial sources need not be bad for the intellectual market if there are a variety of firms and types of financing. Shoemaker's theory takes four patterns of financial backing from Altshcull.[73] These are: the *official* pattern, which means government backing; the *commercial* pattern, which involves advertisers and commercial allies; the *interest* pattern, which means a special interest group, such as a political party, provides financing; and the *informal* pattern, which involves backing by relatives, friends, or anyone who supplies money other than the groups mentioned previously. Economic theory concerns firms that seek a profit. Therefore, the decline in the number of such firms need not be a worry if organizations with other forms of financial backing replace them. But so far, such alternative forms are limited.

Even if participation by noncommercial types of organizations is not forthcoming, the damage to the intellectual market from limited number of newspaper firms can be limited if the firms take a common carrier role. This role was suggested by the Hutchins Commission but has not been embraced by mass media organizations. As a common carrier, newspapers would provide space for a variety of voices without exercising editorial control. The reluctance to pursue the role of common carrier stems from the close relationship between the three newspaper markets and from the tendency of readers and advertisers to view a newspaper as a monolith. People unfamiliar with the internal workings of a newspaper, which includes most Americans, often do not recognize the difference between the news pages and the editorial pages or between news and advertising. This means newspapers that give up control of editorial and op ed content could face negative repercussions on circulation or advertising sales.

Just as with the information and advertising markets, increasing concentration provides owners more discretion to affect the intellectual market. The question of whether this discretion is being used in a way that promotes or limits access to the intellectual market and the exchange of ideas therein is one that can be examined with research.

A small body of empirical literature exists concerning editorial content of newspapers. Borstel evaluated 20 dailies in communities of less than 25,000 population in the northern United States.[74] He found little difference in editorial content between group and nongroup newspapers. Since he was also studying competition, only 6 of the 20 newspapers were group owned. This combines with the lack of randomness in selection and the small population of the cities studied to limit the generalizability of the study.

Wackman, Gillmor, Gaziano, and Dennis examined the endorsement of presidential candidates by group and nongroup newspapers for the 1960, 1964, 1968, and 1972 elections.[75] The nongroup newspapers were less likely to endorse a candidate and group newspapers tended to be consistent in the candidates they endorsed. The authors said this homogeneity of endorsement was caused not by formal controls but by hiring practices, management procedures, and peer pressure.

This study received partial support in a later study that surveyed editorial page editors at newspapers with circulation greater than 50,000.[76] The presidential endorsement during the 1984 election was more likely to reflect the politics of the publisher at a group-owned newspaper than at an independent newspaper. Because group-owned publishers were more consistently Republican, Reagan dominated the endorsements by group newspapers. The cause reflects the informal impact of the organization mentioned by Wackman et al.

However, a replication of the Wackman study for the 1976, 1980, and 1984 elections did not support the original study.[77] Part of this failure may be a result of different measurements of homogeneity of endorsements in the two studies.

One study found group ownership tended to lower the vigor of editorial pages.[78] The author examined 16 group-owned newspapers and a control group of 8 nongroup newspapers, all located on the west coast. The group newspapers had been bought by a group between 1960 and 1975. The control group was independently owned in 1960 and in 1975. A constructed three-week period from six months before and a constructed three-week period from six months after ownership changes were examined. Newspaper editorials became less controversial and less likely to be about local issues after newspapers were bought by groups, compared with the control group.

A follow-up before-and-after study of 28 newspapers that were purchased by groups did not support the above results.[79] Hale found only one of 16 measures of editorial page content differed after group acquisition.

He suggested that group owners may not tamper with editorial page traditions because change would be too obvious to readers.

Some studies have even shown positive effects of group ownership on the opinion function of newspapers. A survey of 410 daily editors showed that group-owned newspapers between 25,000 and 100,000 were more likely than independent newspapers to use opinion surveys.[80] A content analysis of 68 dailies found that group-owned newspapers published more letters to the editor, more editorials and more local editorials than did independent dailies.[81] These results were supported by a content analysis of 114 dailies that found group-owned dailies devoted more of their editorial page to editorials about their home city, more of their total news and editorial space to editorial and op-ed material, and more of their editorial space to cartoons.[82]

Results of research in the area of ownership and the intellectual market fall into three types. First, evidence indicates that groups do not reduce the overall editorial-op ed space and space for local editorials. Two national content analyses suggest that they actually increase space in these areas. Second, there is mixed evidence that when it comes to presidential endorsements; group newspapers may be more uniform in their support. The third area deals with vigor. Here the evidence is mixed as to whether groups reduce the aggressiveness of editorials about controversial subjects.

Again, just as with the information market, it appears that the impact of group ownership depends on which group owns the newspaper.

SUMMARY

The continuing expansion of groups makes ownership an issue that will remain important for years to come. The importance is enhanced by the monopoly power that most dailies and weeklies have in their geographic markets. The important issue is how particular groups and groups in general are exercising the discretionary power these quasimonopolies provide them.

Just how groups perform for the public depends upon their goals. In understanding the impact, it is important to recognize that stated goals may not be the goals manifested in behavior.

The evidence supports the position that groups use their market power in advertising markets. Groups charge more for most, but not all, advertising. The degree to which this occurs depends on the available substitutes in the particular markets.

Research is mixed in the information and intellectual markets, but these markets are more important to society because of the responsibilities given newspapers by the First Amendment. Where groups do exercise their discretionary power, they tend to do so in two ways for both the information and intellectual markets. In the information market, they can cut the news-editorial department budget. This may reduce the quality of information. Second, some groups have interfered with local autonomy of news values.

In the intellectual market, some groups have influenced editorial positions on presidential endorsements. This influence tends to be more through informal than formal methods and varies across time. Second, it appears that newspapers owned by some groups are less likely to pursue controversial issues than independent and other group newspapers.

The fact that not all groups use their discretionary power in all cases does not lessen that power. As long as competition is limited, groups need monitoring so the public will know how the power is being use by the individual groups. Two relatively new issues are the impact of conglomerate ownership and the interlocking directorates that often come from this type of ownership. The possibility of stock performance affecting public group newspapers also remains an important consideration for future research.

ENDNOTES

1. Jack R. Hart, "Horatio Alger in the Newsroom: Social Origins of American Editors," *Journalism Quarterly*, 53:14-20 (Spring 1976).
2. For a discussion of the different approaches to journalism history, see John D. Stevens and Hazel Dicken Garcia, *Communication History* (Beverly Hills, CA.: Sage, 1980).
3. Raymond B. Nixon, "Trends in U. S. Newspaper Ownership: Concentration with Competition," *Gazette*, 14:3:181-193 (1968).
4. John Busterna, "Trends in Daily Newspaper Ownership," *Journalism Quarterly*, 65:831-838 (Winter 1988).
5. C. N. Olien, P. J. Tichenor and G. A. Donohue, "Relation Between Corporate Ownership and Editor Attitudes about Business," *Journalism Quarterly*, 65:259-266 (Summer 1988).
6. *88 Facts About Newspapers*," (Washington, DC: American Newspaper Publishers Association, 1988).
7. These figures were taken from Busterna, *op. cit.* and from *88 Facts About Newspapers, ibid.*
8. "Holdings of 15 Largest Newspaper Companies," *presstime*, January 1987, p. 29.
9. For a discussion of this trend see Ben H. Bagdikian, *The Media Monopoly* (Boston: Beacon Press, 1983) and Benjamin M. Compaine, ed., *Who Owns the Media?* 2nd. ed. (White Plains, NY: Knowledge Industry Publications, 1984).
10. Compaine, *Ibid.*

11. Compaine, *Ibid.*
12. *Veronis, Suhler & Associates 5th Annual Communication Industry Report* (New York: Veronis, Suhler & Associates, 1987).
13. *Veronis, Suhler & Associates 2nd Annual Five-Year Communications Industry Forecast* (New York: Veronis, Suhler & Associates, 1988).
14. For example, see Denby Fawcett, "What Happens When a Chain Arrives," *Columbia Journalism Review*, November/December 1982, pp. 29-30.
15. Philip Meyer and Stanley T. Wearden, "The Effects of Public Ownership on Newspaper Companies: A Preliminary Inquiry," *Public Opinion Quarterly*, 48:564-577 (1984).
16. Bagdikian, 1983, *op. cit.*
17. See M.L. Stein, "Anchorage Times Sold to Oil Company," *Editor & Publisher* December 2, 1989, pp. 34, 36.
18. Douglas F. Greer, *Industrial Organization and Public Policy* (New York: Macmillan, 1980).
19. See Walter Nicholson, *Intermediate Microeconomics and Its Application*, 2nd. ed. (Hinsdale, IL: The Dryden Press, 1979), pp. 228-230.
20. Fritz Machlup, "Theories of the Firm: Marginalist, Behavioral, Managerial," *American Economic Review*, 47:1-33 (March 1967).
21. Oliver E. Williamson, *The Economics of Discretionary Behavior: Managerial Objectives in a Theory of the Firm* (Englewood Cliffs: Prentice-Hall, 1964).
22. William J. Baumol, *Business Behavior, Value and Growth*, 2nd. ed. (New York: Harcourt, Brace & World, 1967).
23. Robin Marris, *The Economic Theory of "Marginal" Capitalism* (New York: The Free Press of Glencoe, 1964).
24. Greer, *op. cit.*
25. Richard M. Cyert and James G. March, *A Behavioral Theory of the Firm* (Englewood Cliffs: Prentice-Hall, 1963).
26. Milton Friedman, "The Methodology of Positive Economics," *Essays in Positive Economics* (Chicago: University of Chicago Press, 1953).
27. Greer, *op. cit.*
28. John Williamson, "Profit, Growth and Sales Maximization," *Economica*, 33:1-16 (February 1966).
29. Bevars D. Marby, "Sales Maximization Versus Profit Maximization: Are They Inconsistent?" *Western Economic Journal*, 6:154-160 (March 1968).
30. Baumol, *op. cit.*
31. See Loren Ghiglione, ed. *The Buying and Selling of America's Newspapers* (Indianapolis: R. J. Berg, 1984) and Benjamin M. Compaine, "The Daily Newspaper Industry in the United States: An Analysis of the Trends in Production Technology, Competition and Ownership, Economic Structure, Circulation, Advertising, Newsprint and Labor," Ph.D. dissertation, Temple University, 1978.
32. See Jonathan Kwitny, "The High Cost of High Profits," *Washington Journalism Review*, June 1990, pp. 19-29.
33. George A. Donohue, Clarice N. Olien and Phillip J. Tichenor, "Reporting Conflict by Pluralism, Newspaper Type and Ownership," *Journalism Quarterly*, 62:489-499, 507 (Autumn 1985).

34. Lee Loevinger, "Media Concentration: Myth and Reality," *The Antitrust Bulletin*, 24:479-498 (1979).
35. Compaine, 1984, *op. cit.*
36. Raymond B. Nixon and Tae-youl Hahn, "Concentration of Press Ownership: A Comparison of 32 Countries," *Journalism Quarterly*, 48:5-16 (Spring 1971).
37. Ghiglione, *op. cit.*
38. Ben H. Bagdikian, "The Myth of Newspaper Poverty," *Columbia Journalism Review*, March/April 1973, pp. 19-25.
39. Compaine, 1978, *op. cit.*, p. 538.
40. Loren Ghiglione, ed., *Evaluating the Press: The New England Daily Newspaper Survey* (Southbridge, Mass.: by the Editor, 1973).
41. Gerald L. Grotta, "Consolidation of Newspapers: What Happens to the Consumer?" *Journalism Quarterly*, 48:245-250 (Summer 1971).
42. Lee Becker, Randy Beam and John Russial, "Correlates of Daily Newspaper Performance in New England," *Journalism Quarterly*, 55:100-108 (Spring 1978).
43. Dan G. Drew and G. Cleveland Wilhoit, "Newshole Allocation Policies of American Newspapers," *Journalism Quarterly*, 53:434-440 (Autumn 1976).
44. Ned Browning, Don Garrison and Herbert H. Howard, "Effects of Conglomerate Takeover on a Newspaper's Coverage of the Knoxville World's Fair: A Case Study," *Newspaper Research Journal*, Fall 1984, pp. 30-38.
45. Dennis F. Hale, "What Subscribers Think of Group Ownership of Newspapers," *Journalism Quarterly*, 57:314-316 (Summer 1980).
46. John Soloski, "Economics and Management: The Real Influence of Newspaper Groups," *Newspaper Research Journal*, November 1979, pp. 19-28.
47. Patrick Parsons, John Finnegan, Jr., and William Benham, "Editors and Their Roles," in Robert G. Picard, *et al.* eds. *Press Concentration and Monopoly* (Norwood, NJ: Ablex, 1988), pp. 91-103.
48. David Pearce Demers and Daniel B. Wackman, "Effect of Chain Ownership on Newspaper Management Goals," *Newspaper Research Journal*, Winter 1988, pp. 59-68.
49. Olien, Tichenor and Donohue, 1988, *op. cit.*
50. Barry R. Litman and Janet Bridges, "An Economic Analysis of Daily Newspaper Performance," *Newspaper Research Journal*, Spring 1986, pp. 9-26.
51. Stephen Lacy, "The Effects of Group Ownership on Daily Newspaper Content," Unpublished paper presented to the Midwest Association for Public Opinion Research, Chicago, November 1986.
52. Stephen Lacy, Frederick Fico and Todd Simon, "The Relationships Among Economic, Newsroom and Content Variables: A Path Model," *Journal of Media Economics*, Fall 1989, pp. 51-66.
53. John C. Busterna, "How Managerial Ownership Affects Profit Maximization in Newspaper Firms," *Journalism Quarterly*, 66:302-307, 358 (Summer 1989).
54. Theodore L. Glasser, David S. Allen and S. Elizabeth Blanks, "The Influence of Chain Ownership on News Play: A Case Study," *Journalism Quarterly*, 66:607-615 (Autumn 1989).

55. Meyer and Wearden, *op. cit.*
56. Stephen Lacy, "The Effects of Ownership and Competition on Daily Newspaper Content," Ph.D. dissertation, University of Texas at Austin, 1986.
57. The rating of the groups was presented in Stephen Lacy and Frederick Fico, "Newspaper Quality and Ownership: Rating the Groups," Unpublished paper presented to the Midwest Association for Public Opinion Research, Chicago, November 1988. The index included the total amount of non-advertising space in the news sections, the ratio of non-advertising to advertising space in the news section, the length of all news stories, the ratio of in-depth coverage to hard news, the ratio of staff written to wire copy, the percentage of news space given graphics and photographs, the number of wire services carried, and the number of square inches of copy per full-time reporter. Seven of the eight measures came from a survey of 746 editors conducted in 1977 by Leo Bogart. The survey results are reported in Leo Bogart, *Press and Public: Who Reads What, When, Where and Why in American Newspapers*, 1st ed. (Hillsdale, NJ: Lawrence Erlbaum Associates, 1981), pp. 195-201.
58. See Peter Drier and Steve Weinberg, "Interlocking Directorates," *Columbia Journalism Reviews*, November/December, 1979, pp. 51-68; and Ben H. Bagdikian, *The Media Monopoly, op. cit.*
59. Kyun-Tae Han, "Composition of Boards of Directors of Major Media Corporations," *Journal of Media Economics*, Fall 1988, pp. 85-100.
60. Dennis F. Hale, "Chains Versus Independents: Newspaper and Market Characteristics," Unpublished paper presented to the Association for Education in Journalism and Mass Communication, Gainesville, FL., August 1984.
61. William B. Blankenburg, "A Newspaper Chain's Pricing Behavior," *Journalism Quarterly*, 60:275-280 (Summer 1983).
62. Bruce M. Owen, "Empirical Results of the Price Effects of Joint Ownership in Mass Media," Research Memorandum No. 93, Research Center in Economic Growth, Stanford University, November 1969.
63. Grotta, *op. cit.*
64. Armando M. Lago, "The Price Effects of Joint Mass Communication Media Ownership," *The Antitrust Bulletin*, 16:789-813 (1971).
65. Blankenburg, 1983, *op. cit.*
66. James M. Ferguson, "Daily Newspaper Advertising Rates, Local Media Cross-Ownership, Newspaper Chains, and Media Competition," *Journal of Law and Economics*, 28:635-654 (1983).
67. William B. Blankenburg, "Determinants of Pricing of Advertising in Weeklies," *Journalism Quarterly*, 57:663-666 (Winter 1980).
68. Cathy Shook Huck, "Newspapers Inc.: The Impact of Corporate Ownership on Its Community Newspapers," Unpublished master's thesis, Murray State University, 1972.
69. James M. Bernstein and Stephen Lacy, "In-depth Coverage and Commentary in Local Television News," Unpublished paper presented to the Association for Education in Journalism and Mass Communication, Minneapolis, Minnesota, August 1990.

70. Catherine B. Roach, "Media Conglomerates, Antitrust Law, and the Marketplace of Ideas," *Memphis State Law Review*, 9:257-280 (1979).
71. Ben H. Bagdikian, "The U.S. Media: Supermarket or Assembly Line?" *Journal of Communication*, Summer 1985, pp. 97-109.
72. Pamela J. Shoemaker, with Elizabeth Mayfield, "Building a Theory of News Content," *Journalism Monographs*, No. 103, June 1987.
73. J. Herbert Altshcull, *Agents of Power* (New York: Longman, 1984).
74. Gerard H. Borstel, "Ownership, Competition and Comment in 20 Small Dailies," *Journalism Quarterly*, 33:220-222 (Spring 1956).
75. Daniel B. Wackman, Donald M. Gillmor, Cecilie Gaziano and Everette E. Dennis, "Chain Newspaper Autonomy as Reflected in Presidential Campaign Endorsements," *Journalism Quarterly*, 52:411-420 (Autumn 1975).
76. Byron St. Dizier, "Editorial Page Editors and Endorsements: Chain-owned Versus Independent Newspapers," *Newspaper Research Journal*, Fall 1986, pp. 63-68.
77. John C. Busterna and Kathleen A. Hansen, "Presidential Endorsement Patterns within Daily Newspaper Chains," Unpublished paper presented to the Association for Education in Journalism and Mass Communication, Washington, DC, August 1989.
78. Ralph R. Thrift, "How Chain Ownership Affects Editorial Vigor of Newspapers," *Journalism Quarterly*, 54:327-331 (Summer 1977).
79. F. Dennis Hale, "Editorial Diversity and Concentration," in Robert G. Picard, *et al.* eds. *Press Concentration and Monopoly* (Norwood, NJ: Ablex, 1988), pp. 161-176.
80. David Pearce Demers, "Opinion Polling Practices of Chain and Independent Papers," *Journalism Quarterly*, 65:500-503 (Summer 1988).
81. David Bruce Daugherty, "Group-owned Newspapers vs. Independently Owned Newspapers: An Analysis of the Differences and Similarities," Ph.D. dissertation, University of Texas, 1983.
82. Lacy, 1986, *op. cit.*

6

Newspapers and Technology

Technology plays an essential role in all industries. Historically, new methods of producing goods and services have directed much of the social and economic development of the United States. For example, United States participation in the Industrial Revolution made it a world power. Just as technology defined the Industrial Revolution, it also defines the information and service economy in which the United States finds itself today.[1]

No information industry has been more dependent upon technology than newspapers. Without the printing press, newspapers would not exist. The news would be passed by word of mouth or handwritten newsletters. Without satellite printing plants and trucks for delivery, the geographic reach of newspapers would be limited drastically. Technology makes newspapers a mass medium. It defines the geographic market; it determines timing for news presentation; it affects presentation of the news; it influences the work conditions in the newsroom; and it increases productivity. The impact of technology occurs on an industry-wide level, on an individual employee level, and on all organizational levels between.

This chapter examines the economic consequences of technology and briefly reviews some of the technological changes that have affected newspapers during the history of the industry. Some of the effects have been intended, while others have been unanticipated. Some have improved the industry, and some have created problems for the industry.

TECHNOLOGY AND THE NEWSPAPER INDUSTRY

Technology is a long-run variable in economic analysis. Short-run economic analysis holds constant both technology and the number of firms in a market. The ability to enter a market and the use of technology can be related. For example, the development of cheaper printing processes that use computers have lowered the cost of starting a newspaper. These cost savings have combined with the high profits of the industry to attract alternative weeklies into larger markets. Whether the cost savings will be large enough to make the growing number of alternatives a national trend remains to be seen.

However, just as technology can lower barriers to entry, it can also raise barriers to entry. A contributing factor to declining direct competition among daily newspapers is the high fixed cost that comes with owning large production facilities. A daily newspaper must be able to produce a large number of issues with many pages in a short amount of time, which requires fast presses with several units. Such a production facility, while efficient, is expensive. The cost of setting up such a facility means few companies will enter daily markets with a new newspaper.

The industry-wide impact of technology results across time from the adoption of new technology by individual firms. *Companies usually adopt technology to reduce costs, increase revenue, or a combination of both.* In all three cases, the result can be increased profit. The speed with which a new technology spreads through the industry depends on how extensively the technology reduces costs or increases revenues. Cold-type technology, for example, was adopted fairly quickly. This printing process has a photochemical base, rather than the hot-metal base of linotype machines, for forming the printing plates. It reduced the costs of preparing newspaper content for printing and of the printing process itself. Cold type also allows better reproduction and use of color. Improved quality of reproduction and graphics helps make the commodity more attractive to readers and is more likely to gain and retain readers.

Although generating revenue and cutting costs are important factors of technology adoption, they are not the only ones. The cost of existing technology affects the timing of technology adoption. A company that recently invested in a particular technology usually will delay adopting another technology until its investment is returned. For example, newspaper firms that bought a letterpress right before the development of offset printing were among the last to buy offset, even though offset presses produce a better looking newspaper and cut production costs. The timing of the transition is based on comparative cost of the old technology versus the new.

Existing investment in equipment is not the only factor that affects the diffusion of technology in the newspaper industry. Internal organization characteristics, such as managerial skills at planning and knowledge of the technical aspects of the industry, also influence the timing of innovation adoption. The expense of training and the possible repercussions of new technology on the employees are also costs to be considered.

A company's market affects adoption as well. Competition plays an important role in the decision to adopt technology. In a competitive environment, controlling costs and generating additional revenue are crucial for survival. One would expect a more rapid adoption of technology in markets that have intense direct and intercity newspaper competition.[2] Most markets do not have high degrees of these types of competition, so it is understandable that many newspaper move slowly in adopting some newer technologies.

Just as monopoly power gives management discretion as to the content it supplies to readers, monopoly power also provides a degree of discretion in technology adoption. Old equipment can be used longer because readers have few substitutes. Lack of competition lowers the incentive to spend money on equipment even if it will produce a better-quality product. But just as readers may tire of poor information quality, they may also tire of poor reproduction quality. As other media, such as television and magazines, improve format quality, even quasimonopoly newspapers must move to newer and better technology.

Another factor that can affect adoption of new technology is group ownership. Groups usually have better information about technology and get lower prices from buying multiple units. A technological change that works well at a few newspapers in a group will spread rapidly throughout the organization. The successful use of computers to produce graphics at USA Today rapidly became a trademark of all Gannett newspapers in the 1980s. Groups also can enjoy price reductions for buying in large quantities. A company purchasing 200 computer terminals will pay a lower unit price than one buying 25.

A new technology that becomes an industry standard tends to follow a consistent pattern of adoption, which is S shaped. Figure 6.1 shows this adoption curve.[3] The vertical axis is the percentage of firms adopting a technology, while the horizontal axis represents time. The S curve shows a slow start for adoption and then accelerates. Finally, it levels off short of 100 percent. This shape represents the tendency of most firms to avoid the risk of adoption and the higher cost of technology in earlier stages of development. Once the technology has proven successful at the early-adoption firms and the price drops due to increased production, other companies move quickly into the adoption process.

The exact slope and spread of the adoption curve can vary. Curve I_1 is a slower adoption process, compared to I_2. The speed of adoption is related to the factors mentioned above and will change with time. For example, the adoption of rapid printing presses in the 1830s by the "penny press" resulted from a combination of intense competition and unmet reader and advertiser demand. In other words, the technology reduced unit costs and helped generate more revenue. The timing was right, and a restructuring of the industry resulted. The adoption of offset printing was slower because of the lack of competition, investment in existing printing

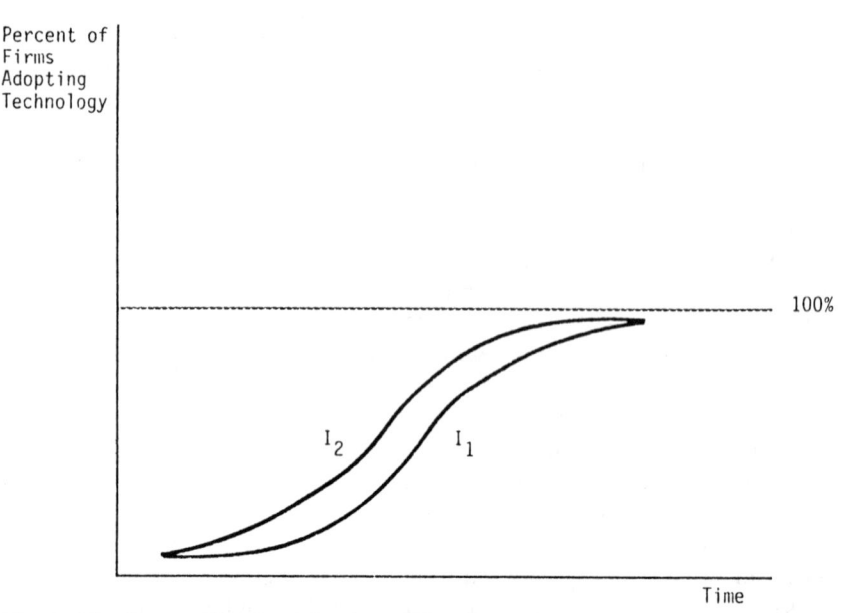

Figure 6.1. Curves Showing Adoption of New Technology
Technology adoption usually follows an s-shaped curve. The speed of adoption varies. I_1 represents a slower adoption process than I_2.

technology, and limited impact on demand. While offset has altered content, it has not reshaped the industry.

TECHNOLOGY'S IMPACT ON NEWSPAPER MARKETS

Although technological change has a tremendous impact on the newspaper industry, the adoption of technology is a decision made at the firm level. Not all new technologies become the industry norm. For example, the optical character reader (OCR) used in the 1970s were a temporary step for some newspapers between typewriters and video display terminals. Many newspapers skipped OCRs entirely. The following section will deal with the impact of technology change on supply and demand. Then a review will follow about past and current technological effects in the three markets newspapers serve.

Technology and the Firm

At the level of the firm, the impact of technology on costs occurs through the production function. Technology changes the production function by increasing the proportion of capital inputs to labor inputs in the production process (See Chapter 3). Cost reductions come from the new technology costing less per input unit than labor. The resulting output with fewer workers at a lower cost means increased productivity per worker.

Figure 6.2 shows a long-run average cost curve (LRAC) for circulation at a newspaper firm. The curve reflects Litman's analysis. As he points out, the actual cost curve facing a newspaper includes both circulation and issue size decisions, which he combines for a three-dimensional long-run average cost surface. For heuristic reasons, this discussion will assume issue size constant and discuss only the impact of technology change on circulation costs.[4]

Curve $LRAC_1$ is the old cost curve. Economies of scale accrue until point Q_1 is reached. This is where the long-run average costs start to increase. The adoption of cost saving technology would result in a shift of the LRAC downward. The new technology's cost curve is $LRAC_2$. Average long-run costs would be lower at every level of production. This shift, shown by the movement from C_1 to C_2, means lower costs and higher profits.

In Figure 6.2, Q_1 is the circulation level at which economies of scale for the new long-run average cost curve cease. It is located at the same

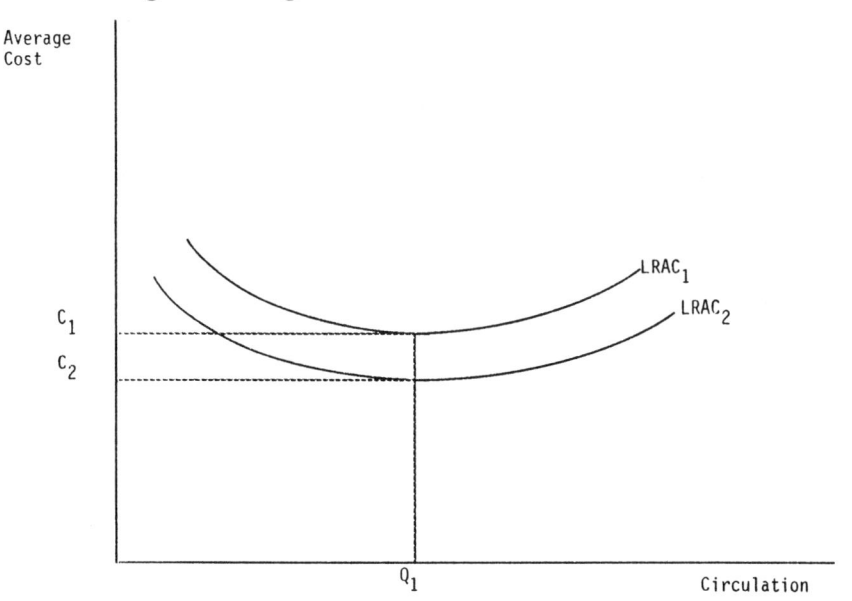

Figure 6.2. The Impact of Technology Change on a Firm's Long-run Average Cost Curve
A new technology will lower the long-run average cost curve from $LRAC_1$ to $LRAC_2$ and lower the average cost for a firm across a wide range of circulation. A new long-run average cost curve will not necessary reduce costs equally throughout the entire range of average cost.

circulation level as the old long-run average cost curve. This need not be true of all changes in the LRAC curve. If the new technology reduces the circulation level where economies begin or extends the point where they stop, the firm would enjoy the scale economies over a wider range of circulation. This would mean additional savings and would increase the incentive to adopt the technology. It is also possible that the new technology would lower long-run average cost, but raise the circulation level at which economies of scale begin. In this case, the impact of lost economies at lower levels of circulation would have to be weighed against the overall reduction in average costs to decide if the technology should be adopted.

As long-run average costs decline from more efficient production and distribution systems, one would expect more firms to enter the various markets. This expectation runs counter to the reality of the newspaper industry. Many industries with high barriers in the short run do open up to more competition with technological changes, but these industries are not joint commodities. The connection between the information market and the advertising market creates the circulation spiral that discourages entry into a geographic market with an existing daily. Cost savings may keep a second newspaper alive longer, but the barriers remain high because of declining revenues and not because of costs. Overall, gains in circulation are more important in surviving direct competition than reductions in costs, although both are helpful.

In general, the lower the barriers to entry before technological change, the more likely this change will help increase the number of firms. This is why technology is more likely to increase the number of weeklies than the number of dailies.

The lowering of long-run costs can have a short-run impact on the information and advertising markets, since the new technology defines the next short-run period after its adoption. The exact impact depends on how management decides to use the cost savings. Lower costs generate higher profits that can be distributed to owners, transferred to readers and advertisers in the form of lower prices, or reinvested in the newspaper in some form. Distribution of increased savings as profits will result in little market impact.

Figure 6.3 shows the possible impact of a technology change on the advertising market when cost savings are transferred to the advertiser. The initial demand for square inches of advertising is D_1, while the supply is S_1. This gives an equilibrium point of E_1 with price P_1.

Suppose the newspaper adopts new technology that makes the creation and reproduction of advertising cheaper. This could result from use of computers to compose ads and from sending proofs of advertisements over telephone wires for approval by advertisers. As a result of the new

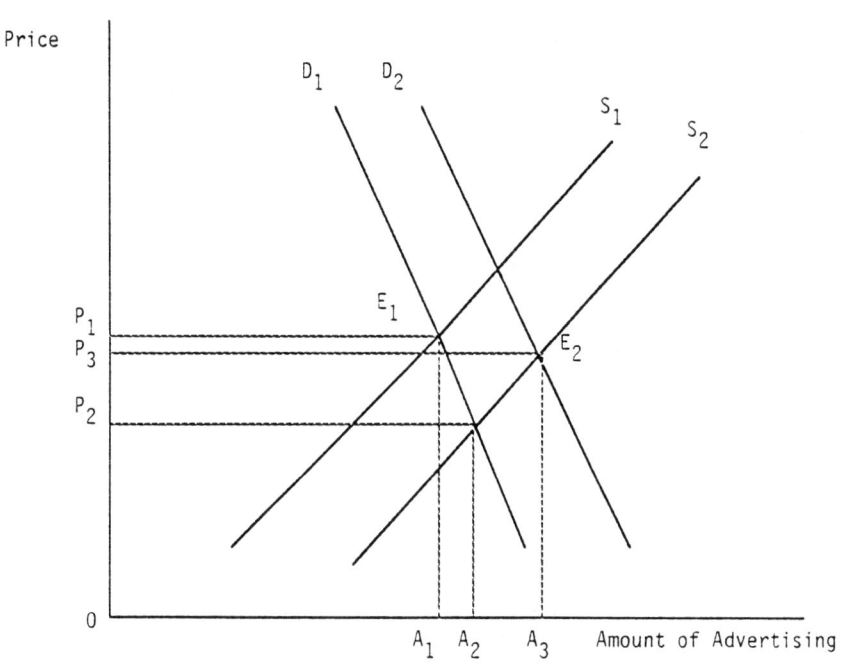

Figure 6.3. The Impact of Technological Change on the Advertising Market
The cost savings of new technology can result in higher profits if the savings are passed to advertisers through price cuts. The initial demand (D_1) and supply (S_1) curves give an equilibrium of E_1. If technologically based cost savings sift the supply curve to S_2, which means more ad space is supplied at the same price, demand adjusts to D_2. The new equilibrium (E_2) results in a lower price (P_3) with more advertising space (A_3) and a higher profit. The extent of these changes is determined by the elasticity of the supply and demand curves.

technology, costs decline. The newspaper passes the savings to advertisers in the form of a new supply curve, S_2. This represents a willingness to supply more advertising space to advertisers over a range of prices. A lower price, P_2, results at the point where the new supply and old demand curves intersect. This is not an equilibrium point, however, because the lower prices also bring new advertising dollars into the market. These dollars can come from money spent by the current advertisers on other media or from new advertisers. This influx of money results in a new demand curve, D_2. The interaction of the new supply and demand curves give a new equilibrium point E_2 and price of P_3. The new equilibrium price is below the initial price of P_1, so the advertisers still benefit from the cost savings, but it also provides a greater amount of profit, shown by the rectangle $P_3E_2A_30$, than the original price, shown by the rectangle $P_1E_1A_10$.

Whether increased profits and lower prices from technological savings actually occur depends on several variables. This result is likely to take place in markets with elastic demand curves. The elasticity is related to the number and degree of substitutes in the geographic markets. You might see this type of result with technology that increases the productivity of distributing insert advertising, since direct mail is very competitive for inserts. Yet, it may not occur with classified advertising because few good substitutes exist. If the cost savings are not passed on to advertisers, the supply curve remains the same. The savings simply become part of profit or are invested elsewhere in the firm.

Technology changes can affect the information market as well. A change that increases the productivity of the newsroom staff can improve the quality of the newspaper. An example is the telephone. The appearance of the telephone during the late 1800s contributed greatly to the efficiency of reporters. In effect, the productivity of hours spent on reporting increased. A similar possibility exists with databases and computers. If one assumes quality of reporting is related to amount of information possessed by journalists, databases hold potential for improving reporting. Indeed, "big stories" are emerging from the increased use of computers to filter through large quantities of information.[5] Reporting is not the only area of improving newspaper quality. Computer graphics also can meet reader demand for quickly understandable information.[6]

Technology may have an indirect impact on the information market. If a newspaper experiences cost savings in other departments due to new technology, it can use that money for long-run investment in the quality of the news-editorial content. The results basically would be the same as if the savings from technology applied directly to the creation of content.

Whichever way the costs savings occur, the impact of technology on reader demand can be seen in Figure 6.4. The demand curve D_1 and the supply curve S_1 are in equilibrium at E_1, where circulation is C_1 at quality Q_1. Technological innovations that increase quality move the supply curve to S_2. The result is increased circulation to C_2 at quality Q_2. If this investment is temporary, that is, the organization decides to use the technological efficiencies to increase profit by firing some news-editorial staff, the supply curve will shift back toward the origin. If the resulting equilibrium is lower than E_2, a drop in circulation results, as shown by Figure 3.5 in Chapter 3. If the investment is permanent, the readers becomes accustomed to the new quality and the kinked point of the demand curve moves to the new intersection of the demand and supply curve. This forms a new equilibrium, E_2, and the lower part of the kinked demand curve moves up creating the new demand curve D_2.

The long-run impact of technology on journalistic quality depends on what the firm wants to do with the savings from increased productivity. If

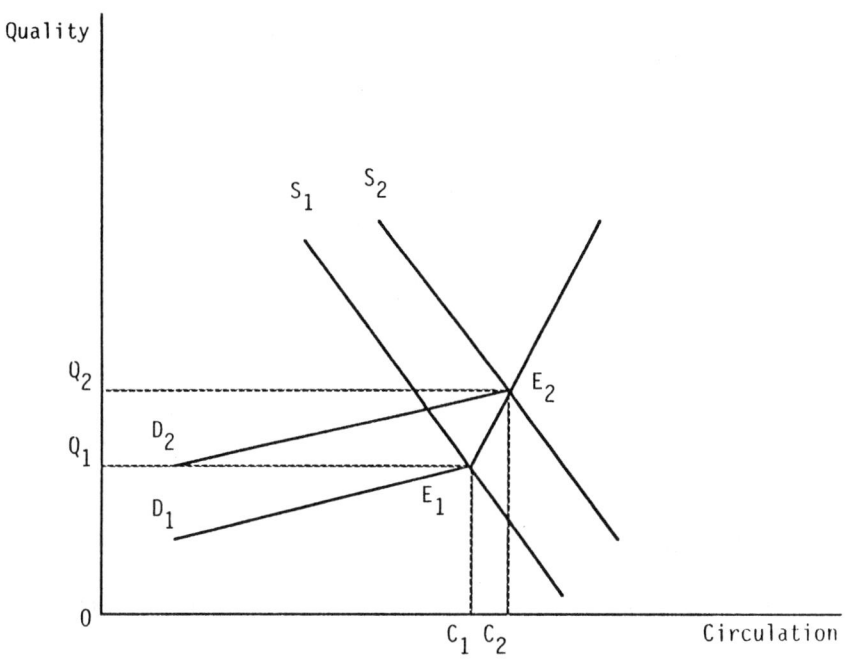

Figure 6.4. The Impact of Technological Change on Newspaper Quality and Circulation

Technology adoption that increases the quality of newspapers can increase circulation. Initial demand (D_1) and supply (S_1) curves are in equilibrium at E_1. Technology that contributes to increased quality, either directly or indirectly through the reinvestment of cost savings, moves the supply curve to S_2, which represents higher quality supplied at all levels of circulation. Across time, readers expect the higher quality, and their demand curve shifts to D_2. The new equilibrium at E_2 has higher quality and circulation when compared to the equilibrium before the technology adoption.

it goes into profit, circulation can remain the same or drop. If it is invested in better quality, circulation increases and readers begin to expect the higher level of quality. Just where the cost savings go will depend on organizational goals, levels of competition, and the existing quality of the newspaper.

Technological change affects processes other than advertising and news creation, but not necessarily in the same fashion. The adoption of new technology by the circulation department usually has little impact on the price of newspapers. The cost savings are either directed into profits or are invested elsewhere in the newspapers. Subscription prices tend to be inelastic downward. They can go up, but rarely do they come down. The tendency of newspapers not to pass on circulation cost savings to readers results from the lack of competition that would force them to do so.

On the other hand, intensely competitive newspapers are likely to adopt new technology and pass on savings as lower prices or higher quality. Often technological changes help competitive newspapers differentiate their commodity in an effort to get the edge in the circulation battle for survival. One study found that dailies in intensely competitive markets were more likely to use color and graphics on the front page than newspapers in monopoly or slightly competitive markets.[7]

The various effects shown in Figures 6.3 and 6.4 may or may not occur with the adoption of technology. Factors that affect the outcome of technological change include competition, ownership goals and policies, the nature of the particular technology involved, and the speed of adoption. The following sections will deal with the specific technologies that have been adopted for the information, advertising, and intellectual markets. These technologies have not been cost free. Some hidden costs have been discovered only after adoption.

The Information Market

Technological innovation in the information market affects three processes: creation, production, and distribution. The impact on creation occurs through the reporting, writing, and editing of information in the newsroom. Visual communication can be affected as well. The impact on production and distribution is applicable to the advertising and intellectual markets as well, but it will be considered in the information market because of the important role circulation plays in the information market.

Newsroom. The news sections have been affected greatly by new technology throughout history. The invention of the steamship, the telegraph, the telephone, and computers all had an impact. The steamship and telegraph increased the speed of acquiring news from far away places during the early 1800s. The vulnerability of telegraph wires during the Civil War is credited with developing the inverted pyramid style of writing. The telephone greatly increased news-gathering productivity. Computers can increase writing quality and speed, and databases have increased the productivity of analyzing existing information. A survey found that reporters and newspaper librarians believe database research improves their news coverage and poses few dangers to quality of journalism.[8]

Despite the usefulness of technology, adoption does not guarantee easy adaptation by journalists to the new equipment. Since newspapers are currently in the middle of the computer revolution and that revolution is being documented well by researchers, it provides an excellent example of dysfunctions that can occur.

Databases, for example, are not always used because they can intimidate reporters and they require new skills. Ward, Hansen, and McLeod studied a large metro daily that adopted an electronic library. Before adoption, almost all journalists used the clip files. After the electronic library was adopted, 16 percent said they did not use it.[9] This indicates a potential drop in information quality because of less extensive background searches for stories.

An in-depth study of the impact of technology on three Texas dailies by Sylvie and Danielson found that adoption of technology for economic reasons did not result in the ready acceptance of the technology by the staff.[10] The ease of adaptation depended on the nature of the technology and the managers of the newspapers. Some types of technology were learned more easily than others. Technology tended to change the nature of management, calling for better skills at motivation during periods of adoption and training. They concluded that the interaction of technology and the social environment is a concern that management needs to consider in adopting technology. These results were consistent with earlier studies in this area.[11]

The problems and issues addressed by Sylvie and Danielson resulted more from managerial concerns than from economic conditions, but the impact of resistance to technological change is a short-run economic problem because it reduces potential productivity. The long-run average cost curve summarizes a series of short-run average cost curves. Initial lowering of costs might be less than anticipated because of the hidden costs of overcoming resistance and the explicit costs of training. However, if the technology truly improves productivity, over time the long-run average cost curve will reflect the maximum cost savings. Older journalists either adapt to the technology or are replaced through attrition by younger journalists who are less resistant to the technology.

But some unexpected costs of technology are not easily taken care of by time and training. Extensive use of computer terminals may hold health hazards for journalists and other newspaper workers. Early health concerns concentrated on the possible effects of VDT radiation on workers.[12] Despite mixed research results, the first stringent law governing VDT use was passed in Suffolk County, New York, in 1988.[13]

Radiation is not the only potential health problem of VDT use. During the mid-1980s, journalists at several newspapers began developing repetitive strain injuries, which is a skeleto-muscular problem that affects the arms, wrist, upper backs, and shoulders of people who use VDT terminals extensively. Although the exact cause is not known, the number of cases grew quickly during the late 1980s, and managers had begun taking measures to reduce the incidents of this painful injury.[14]

Social, managerial, and physical problems are not the only concerns that arise from use of new technology. Ethical issues are involved as well. For example, the potential cost and time savings of electronic photography make it highly attractive to the newspaper industry.[15] Instead of taking photographs on silver-based film and processing the film chemically, a photographer captures the image on a diskette and sends the image over telephone lines to a computer where an editor makes color corrections. The editor then sends the photograph to the pagination terminal where it is integrated into the newspaper. This technology means photographs taken within minutes of deadline can be used. It also poses the potential for abuse. A person can use the computer to manipulate the photograph and create an image that was not what the photographer shot.[16]

Problems concerning ethical use of technology have a way of becoming business problems. Lying with photographs can have the same effect as lying in written copy. Both affect a newspaper's credibility with readers once the ethical violations are revealed. Doubtful information is of little use to readers, and demand may decline if readers become too doubtful of accuracy in a newspaper's content.

Use of computers for information analysis and photography is a recent phenomenon at most newspapers. A better example of technology adoption in newsrooms is electronic writing and editing, which began in the 1970s. Research in this area reveals what happens during the process of adaptation by journalists to new technology.

A 1978 study examined the impact of electronic editing on speed and accuracy of editing by 137 editors at 42 newspapers.[17] Although differences between pencil and electronic editing were not great, the authors concluded that editing with computers was slower but more accurate for editors who had used VDTs for more than two years. These findings were confirmed in a case study conducted a few years later at the *Milwaukee Journal*.[18] In 1987, Lindley surveyed editors at 127 newspapers with circulation of more than 50,000.[19] His results showed that editors who began their careers during the era before the use of VDTs felt electronic editing was faster and produced fewer mistakes than pencil editing. Of the editors, 83 percent agreed with the statement that VDTs made editing cleaner, while 64 percent said VDT editing was faster. These result show an adaptation by those who were most likely to resist technological change.

As with all technology, electronic editing raises the issue of unanticipated dysfunctions in journalism. One study of the use of computers to send press releases found that electronic releases resulted in less editing than did press releases sent through the mail.[20] This occurred with releases of lesser news value. This research implies that electronic mail could shift control of newspaper content from journalists to sources in some cases. These particular results could be limited to the two newspapers studied in this research, or they may represent the difficulty of understanding text on a VDT terminal, as the researchers suggest. Whatever the cause of the findings, the research illustrates a hidden cost that may occur with developing uses of new technology.

Production. The long-term impact of computer technology on newspaper content will not be known for several years. Most staffs are still adapting to new ways of using technology. However, the cost savings from this technology and related cold-type printing have become obvious. Ultimately, the backshop will be eliminated at most newspapers. *Backshop* is the term applied to getting information into a finished form that can be turned into a plate for printing. Eliminating the backshop means a significant savings in labor costs and a shifting of some backshop responsibilities to the newsroom. In effect, the production function has shifted away from labor and toward a greater emphasis on capital in the form of computers.

The overall cost savings to individual firms from the transition to computers for typesetting were established by Wright and Lavine using Inland Press Association data.[21] They found drastically declining costs of composition between 1959 and 1980 for the typical 20,000 circulation newspaper. After adjusting expenses for inflation, they reported that mechanical department expenses dropped from about 46 percent of the entire newspaper payroll expense in 1959 to about 24 percent in 1980. This was reflected in the decline from an average of 40 full-time employees to 22 full-time employees during this period.

The adoption of computer technology for composing was important particularly because other departments within the newspaper saw significant increases in labor expenses during this period. Overall newspaper labor expenses dropped by slightly more than 6 percent between 1959 and 1980.

As with other uses of computers, the elimination of the backshop holds potential hidden costs that could affect the newsroom. Proofreaders, who were once the last line of defense against spelling and grammatical errors, have disappeared from almost all daily newspapers. The previously mentioned Lindley study found that almost 46 percent of editors who started editing before the adoption of VDTs said they prefer having proofreaders. However, the need for a return to this system is doubted by some.[22] The question is whether editors with their added responsibilities can perform adequately the job once done by the proofreaders. The answer may lie in yet more technology as computer programs to check spelling and other mechanical aspects of writing continue to develop. These programs could provide editors with more time to work on writing style and structure by handling the mechanical problems of writing.

Circulation. Technological impact on the production function is well established, and the effects of new technology on the creation of information are now being studied. An area that has not been as dramatically affected by technology development in recent years is the circulation process. While jobs such as billing and stuffing insert ads use computers, getting a newspaper copy from the press to the reader is done basically the same today as it was 60 years ago. Newspapers sell as single copies through newsracks and at stores or as multiple copies delivered to a reader's home or office. Getting the copy to its destination still involves putting it on a truck and physically moving it to a geographic location.

The Wright and Lavine study of the typical 20,000-circulation newspaper illustrates the lack of technological impact on circulation. Circulation and distribution labor costs represented slightly under 10 percent of the total labor budget in 1959, but by 1980 they accounted for more than 12 percent. This increase occurred despite a 17 percent drop in real wages for the average circulation employee. The increased labor costs reflected the doubling of part-time employees, while the number of full-time employees remained constant from 1959 to 1980. Contrary to developments in the production process, the distribution process became more labor intensive.

This trend illuminates a comparative advantage of television and radio technology. Average distribution costs are relatively low because stations distribute across cable or through the air. Once a program is distributed, an additional viewer adds no cost. This advantage led newspaper groups to pursue the idea of an electronic information service during the 1980s. Knight-Ridder began a service known as Viewtron in Miami in 1983. It closed in 1986 after losing more than $50 million. The system was not a newspaper in the traditional sense; it was an interactive information system that allowed users to access large amounts of information and to bank and shop from their homes. Times-Mirror started a similar system in Orange County, California, in 1984. It closed in 1986. Time, Inc. tried a similar type of system, which closed in 1983 after losing about $25 million.

These electronic information distribution systems failed for several reasons. First, the general public was unwilling to invest in the equipment necessary to use the services. Second, visual quality of some services paled compared to television. Third, use often meant the telephone and computer were tied up and could not be used for other purposes. Fourth, videotext systems do not allow individuals in a household to divide up the information and read different sections simultaneously. Splitting a video screen at the breakfast table so one person can read about business and the other about sports is difficult. Fifth, such systems require the reader to exercise news judgment as to which stories are important. Newspaper layout allows readers to rely upon editors' expertise because location is an indicator of importance.

It would be fairly easy to come up with more reasons why electronic information services have not been used by more consumers. However, videotext has become useful for more specialized information needs. The investment in video information distribution underlines two important points about adopting technology for newspapers. First, supply does not generate demand. The fact that printed information can be sent over telephone wires or on the electromagnetic spectrum does not mean that large numbers of readers want to receive it that way. All of the factors that affect demand—price, price of substitutes and complements, income, and taste—play a role in whether a new type of distribution technology will prove successful.

The second point is that newspaper firms have to make such investments even if they will lose money on many of them. Despite potential losses, competitive and cost advantages gained from being first in the adoption of new technology warrant experimentation. Failure is just part of that experimentation. The continued interest by the newspaper industry in electronic information delivery illustrates this point.[23]

Newspaper companies are not the only firms interested in electronic information delivery. As the 1990s began, the newspaper industry was battling the Regional Bell Operating Companies (RBOCs), created by the breakup of AT&T in the early 1980s, over who should produce the information sent over telephone lines.[24] Cable companies and broadcasting firms have also entered the fray, which centers around the future wiring of United States homes with fiber optics. The capacity of the fiber optics will allow a greatly enhanced delivery of information by the telephone companies' delivery system. The one system could handle telephone, television, fax machines, computer-aided information retrieval, and more.

The newspaper companies are not as concerned about the delivery of information as they are the creation of information by the RBOCs. Arguments advanced by the newspaper industry contend that allowing the RBOCs to create information could lead to information monopolies and that the fragmentation of information markets would reduce the role of newspapers in unifying readers socially and politically with common information. On the other hand, the RBOCs argue that to prevent them from creating information violates their right to free speech and that newspaper companies are already in the field of videotext with little competition.

The outcome of the conflict will most likely be decided in the federal courts and Congress. Such a resolution may well affect the way people in the United States will receive their information during the 21st century.

Missing from much of the discussion about electronic information delivery is the role of demand. Perhaps the absence of this discussion and the initial failure of videotext experiments illustrate the lack of and need for demand theory in the area of mass media. As mentioned earlier, classic economic demand theory is inadequate for the study of mass media because content is assumed constant and homogeneous. Even monopolistic competition theory, which recognizes the role of product differentiation, does not have adequate demand theory. Since the alteration of a newspaper commodity can affect demand, a better understanding of the nature of demand would reduce the risk of technological investment.

Overall, technology has and will continue to shape the content of newspapers, the way they are produced and, to some degree, the way they are delivered. Historical trends have been inconsistent in these areas. The greatest impact has come in production, followed by the creation of information in the newsroom, and then by circulation. As the backshops disappear from newspapers, the advantages of technology in production probably will rest with better and faster presses, which will have a marginal impact on costs compared to other recent trends. However, the greatest potential change is in the circulation process. Developing printers that could reproduce large amounts of information in a household quickly with good quality while the reader sleeps would revolutionize the distribution process. Such a possibility remains remote, but it would allow newspaper firms the great cost savings that television now has by combining the production and distribution systems.

Advertising Market

Because newspapers are a joint commodity, the advertising market is affected by the same production and distribution technologies as the information market. However, the advertising creation process can improve with the adoption of technology that cuts costs and increases quality. Cost savings come in the actual creation of advertising content and in the process of having advertisements checked by the advertiser. Increased quality comes from better printing and from the growing flexibility of computers to generate attractive and effective advertising content.

Savings in the creation of display advertisements come, as with other technological processes, from shifting the emphasis of the production function away from labor. The adoption of display advertising computer systems started in the early 1970s. By the end of the 1980s, they were affordable for almost all medium and large newspapers. Although earlier generations of the computer systems were crude, the more recent systems are having dramatic impact on staffing. *The Home News* in New Brunswick, New Jersey, a 58,000 circulation daily, cut nine positions after adopting such a system; the 56,000-circulation daily in Hollywood, Florida, eliminated six composing room positions after getting such a system; and the composing room supervisor at the *Toronto Star* estimated that their staffing needs have been cut in half.[25]

The systems not only cut labor costs, but they allow advertising departments to create more attractive and effective ads. Part of this advantage comes from the increased sophistication of the software, but another contributor is the time that is saved. Artists can now experiment with design. If the experiment does not turn out as hoped, then another approach can be taken in the same amount of time it formerly took to produce relatively simple art work.

Display advertising is not the only type of advertising that benefits from technology. Remote entry of classified advertising holds potential benefits. Remote entry allows an advertiser to enter a classified ad directly into the computer system. This lowers newspaper-generated errors, improves copy flow, eliminates messenger problems, and allows better control of copy.[26] The first system was adopted in 1985, but the use of such systems still was concentrated at larger newspapers at the end of the decade.

The combination of electronic advertising creation and satellite transmission promises even greater savings and services. This process allows newspapers to receive advertisements from remote locations, whether the senders are advertisers or other newspapers in a group. As television faces increasing segmentation and newspaper groups grow in size, the opportunity to attract national advertising will expand. A technical drawback of this possibility is distributing the advertisements quickly. However, a demonstration in May 1989 showed that advertisements could be produced on a personal computer, sent to a newspaper by satellite, and published within a few hours.[27]

The satellite transmission process also may help the industry take advantage of the marketing trend to regionalize national sales. The increasingly sophisticated tools of marketing are allowing national firms to identify and cater to more localized areas of consumer demand. The ability to send and modify advertising with computers provides a possibility for newspaper firms and groups to respond to this advertising demand.[28]

As with all new technology, adoption for the advertising process has not always been smooth. Problems arose with satellite transmission and reception equipment.[29] However, the advertising market does not seem to face the level of resistance to technology found in the information market.

The Intellectual Market

The two reasons for adopting technology, decreasing costs, or increasing revenue are difficult to apply to the intellectual market. Cost and revenue are economic considerations at the level of the firm, while the intellectual market is concerned with larger social, political, economic, and cultural issues. However, if one accepts the proposition that readers expect newspapers to contribute to the intellectual market as a matter of course, then demand in this market can have an overall impact on decisions in other markets.

The potential impact of technology on the intellectual market through the editorial and opinion content of newspapers takes three forms. First, the use of computer technology for research can increase the quality of opinion material. Second, the savings from other markets can be used to increase space devoted to the intellectual market. Third, technological advances that lower costs may allow more voices to enter a market or more existing voices to survive.

The possible improvement in the quality of reporting mentioned above is applicable to the intellectual market. Editorials and columns can contribute to the intellectual market in several ways, but basically they try to persuade or to provide information and ideas. Since newspaper readers tend to be educated people and educated people tend not to be persuaded by one-sided arguments, use of computers to access information and opinions about an issue should allow more persuasive two-sided arguments in newspaper editorials. Certainly, access to many ideas and large amounts of information can improve editorials and columns. The minimal requirement of accuracy, which holds true for all newspaper material, warrants the use of the advanced searching abilities of computers.

Although databases have potential for improving editorial and op-ed material, evidence indicates that databases are not being used by editorial page writers. A survey of 40 such writers at 27 newspapers was conducted by Kerr and Niebauer in 1985.[30] Even though 73 percent said the biggest problem facing editorial writers was lack of time for adequate research, 68 percent said they seldom or never used databases in their work. Personal biases, budget considerations, and lack of training were the main reasons given for not using these resources.

A second area of impact is the allocation of more space to the opinion function as a result of cost savings in other markets. Although this possibility exists, establishing such a connection is difficult. Despite evidence that newspapers have increased resources given to the editorial-opinion function over the years, no evidence exists that technological costs savings are the source of this allocation. This type of a commitment to opinion material occurs on a firm-by-firm basis and depends on the goals of individual managers and owners.

The third impact of technology in the intellectual market is the creation or continued existence of newspaper voices. A *voice* is a separately owned and operated editorial department. The argument about lowering costs and, therefore, barriers to entry was made in Chapter 4.

This effect is more likely to occur for weeklies than for dailies. However, printing technology has lower barriers to entry for smaller dailies through central printing, which means several newspapers print at the same plant.

Bowers discussed this impact in 1969.[31] He said central printing lowered barriers to entry for smaller newspapers because central printing distributes the economies of scale among several papers. This sharing of some first copy costs allows newspapers to lower the short-run average cost curve and capture some of the savings that would not be available if they owned a printing press for their relatively small number of daily copies. Almost all large metropolitan areas now have groups of nondailies that use central printing.

While central printing technology has helped smaller newspapers, computer and printing technology have also helped larger metropolitan dailies. Zoned editions that developed in the 1960s began to increase competition in suburbs and in counties outside of metropolitan areas that have dailies.[32] Although there is little evidence that such competition has led to increased activity in editorial content about local markets,[33] the mere existence of zoned coverage of such areas holds the potential for more local voices.

THE FUTURE OF NEWSPAPER TECHNOLOGY

The problem with discussing the future of technology in any industry is the rapidity with which technology can change. Yet technology defines the nature of an industry, and newspapers are no exception. Just as the history of the newspaper industry can be viewed in terms of technological change, so its future will be determined by its capital investment in the creation, production and distribution processes. Speculation about future technology is essential to long-term planning.

In the information market, newspaper firms will continue to use computers to retrieve, generate, and analyze information. The time that is saved in handling large amounts of data can be reinvested in news quality or translated into profit. Which one of these occurs depends a great deal on the farsightedness of the managers and owners of the papers.

More specifically, newspapers will continue a recent trend to generate more of their own information. The use of surveys, content analyses, and analysis of existing data can help them move toward a sociological approach to news and help them become less dependent on official sources for news and interpretation. Using computers to analyze data can provide context for events and issues that would benefit readers and society. Creating such information will not cut costs, but it may help increase revenues. Although newspapers are tapping new revenue centers by selling their content through databases, the real economic benefits to the newspaper firms will come through a better commodity that will attract readers, regardless of delivery systems.

The use of graphics will continue to grow. The next step is to harness and understand the potential of this communication device. Current use sometimes misinforms as much as informs. Confusion over the best use of technology is common in earlier stages of adoption.[34]

Newspapers will see the disappearance of chemical-based photography in the near future. Electronic photography holds much promise for increasing timeliness of photographs and for saving time and money. The cost savings, however, will accrue for most newspapers only after more extensive adoption in the industry.

In the area of production, pagination will continue its spread. Pagination allows the newspaper to be designed and composed entirely on computer. But the speed of adoption has not met expectations because the process is a complex one that has faced resistance. Speed of adoption and adaptation will depend on the speed with which all departments move toward computerization.

– Continued improvements in desktop publishing will result in more alternative nondailies, but the actual extent will depend on the willingness of advertisers and readers to support such publications. The increasing possibility that television will move toward direct payment for programming would contribute to the spread of such publications. If television charges viewers, newspapers would become more attractive to advertisers, who may shift a portion of their advertising budgets to more specialized publications.

The circulation process will involve increasing use of technology for monitoring the delivery of newspaper copies, but the drastic change to an entirely new system of delivery appears to be at least a couple of decades away. Satellite printing plants may help distribution problems if efficient smaller presses can be developed. This more localized printing would improve delivery and increase the timeliness of news, but it also would reduce existing economies of scale.

Advertising departments will continue to follow the movement of newsrooms toward more computer technology, just as satellite transmission of the ads will grow. This movement is important not only for reducing costs but also for establishing the preconditions of pagination.

The complete computerization of all departments will result in cost savings that can be used in any number of ways. They may help keep newspapers more price competitive; they may help newspapers produce a better commodity; or they may help newspaper organizations make higher profits. The first two will be better than the third for the long-run financial well-being of newspapers.

The future impact of technology on the intellectual market probably will be marginal. The connection of this market to the financial well-being of the newspaper is too diffused to convince many managers of its relevance to business concerns. One possible trend does pose possibilities in this area. The increasing development of newspaper information as databases and videotext content means the information and opinions in newspapers can be accessed in an additional way. Thus, newspapers that have a limited geographic market will be available to wider areas via computers. Often the ideas expressed in editorials and columns are less parochial than information in the news sections. The telephone lines may become a more personalized way of getting the ideas into the market place.

SUMMARY

The modern newspaper industry, born of technological change, has seen a long parade of new processes and equipment shape its commodity. The most obvious technological effects have come in cost savings because such changes are more easily measured. But cost savings do not preclude variations in the information and advertising content. Technology has made today's newspapers more appealing than at any time in history. The use of the technology was necessary because today's readers are more sophisticated than ever and they can select from the greatest variety of information sources in history.

Technology, however, is not adopted in a vacuum. Its adoption always carries problems that delay the full return expected when management decides to acquire the new technology. Just as technology defines the long run for newspaper economics, its use requires long-run planning by owners and managers. This means anticipating dysfunctions on the supply side that can decrease productivity and variations on the demand side that will limit the advantages of new technology.

Technology should serve not dictate. The benefits should be somewhat balanced among the three markets. It is the balance that makes newspapers important, and it is is the balance that will insure survival of newspapers as something other than just information services.

ENDNOTES

1. For a discussion of the development of the information economy see Fritz Machlup, *The Production and Distribution of Knowledge in the United*

States (Princeton, NJ: Princeton University Press, 1962), and Marc U. Porat, *The Information Economy*, Vols. 1 through 8 (Washington, DC: U. S. Department of Commerce/Office of Telecommunication, 1977).
2. Edwin Mansfield, *Principles of Microeconomics*, 4th ed. (New York: W. W. Norton, 1983).
3. Walter Nicholson, *Intermediate Economics and Its Application*, 2nd. ed. (Hinsdale, IL: The Dryden Press, 1979), pp. 166-167.
4. For an extensive discussion of newspaper cost curves, see Barry Litman, "Microeconomic Foundations," in Robert G. Picard, James P. Winter, Maxwell E. McCombs, and Stephen Lacy, eds. *Press Concentration and Monopoly* (Norwood, NJ: Ablex, 1988), pp. 3-34.
5. Tom McNichol, "Databases: Reeling in Scoops with High Tech," *Washington Journalism Review*, July/August 1987, pp. 27-29.
6. James K. Gentry and Barbara Zang, "Newspapers' New Face: The Graphics Editor Takes Charge," *Washington Journalism Review*, January/February 1989, pp. 24-28.
7. Keith Kenney and Stephen Lacy, "Economic Forces Behind Newspapers' Increasing Use of Color and Graphics," *Newspaper Research Journal*, Spring 1987, pp. 33-41.
8. Thomas L. Jacobson and John Ullman, "Commercial Databases and Reporting: Opinions of Newspaper Journalists and Librarians," *Newspaper Research Journal*, Winter 1989, pp. 15-25.
9. Jean A. Ward, Kathleen A. Hansen, and Douglas M. McLeod, "Effects of the Electronic Library on News Reporting Protocols," *Journalism Quarterly*, 65:845-852 (Winter 1988).
10. George Sylvie and Wayne Danielson, "Editor and Hardware: Three Case Studies in Technology and Newspaper Management," Department of Journalism, The University of Texas at Austin, May 1989.
11. Bruce Garrison, "Electronic Editing Systems and Their Impact on News Decision Making," *Newspaper Research Journal*, January 1982, pp. 43-53, and John M. Shipman, "Computerization and Job Satisfaction in the Newsroom: Four Factors to Consider," *Newspaper Research Journal*, Fall 1986, pp. 69-78.
12. See Louis Slesin, "VDT Radiation: What's Known, What Isn't," *Columbia Journalism Review*, November/December 1984, pp. 40-41; and Loren Stein and Diana Hembree, "VDT Regulation: The Publishers Counterattack," *Columbia Journalism Review*, November/December 1984, pp. 42-44.
13. "Impact of VDT Law Studied," *presstime*, July 1988, p. 70.
14. See Diana Hembree and Sarah Henry, "A Newsroom Hazard Called RSI," *Columbia Journalism Review*, January/February 1987, pp. 19-24; and Rolf Rykken, "Repetitive Strain Injury," *presstime*, June 1989, pp. 6-8.
15. Rosalind C. Truitt, "Electronic Photography," *presstime*, October 1988, pp. 30-37.
16. Howard Bossen, "Zone V: Photojournalism, Ethics and the Electronic Age," *Studies in Visual Communications*, Vol. 2, No. 3.
17. Linda J. Shipley and James K. Gentry, "How Electronic Editing Equipment

Affects Editing Performance," *Journalism Quarterly*, 58:371-374, 387 (Autumn 1981).
18. Bruce Garrison, "The Electronic Gatekeeper: Editing on the Copy Desk of a Metropolitan Newspaper," *Newspaper Research Journal*, May 1980, pp. 7-17.
19. William R. Lindley, "From Hot Type to Video Screens: Editors Evaluate New Technology," *Journalism Quarterly*, 65:485-489 (Summer 1988).
20. Kurt Neuwirth, Carol M. Liebler, Sharon Dunwoody and Jennifer Riddle, "The Effects of 'Electronic' News Sources on Selection and Editing of News," *Journalism Quarterly*, 65:85-94 (Spring 1988).
21. B. E. Wright and John M. Lavine, "The Constant Dollar Newspaper: An Economic Analysis Covering the Last Two Decades," Unpublished report, Inland Daily Press Association, February 1982.
22. Rolf Rykken, "Proofreaders: Cold-Type Printing Rendered Them Obsolete—Or Did It?" *presstime*, March 1989, pp. 36-37.
23. For example, see Robert M. Johnson, "Electronic Publishing," *presstime*, February 1988, pp. 10, 12.
24. For a discussion of the debate concerning fiber optics and the future of home information delivery see Jerome Aumente, "Battling the Telecos," *Washington Journalism Review*, May 1990, pp. 21-25.
25. Rosalind C. Truitt, "Display Ad Systems," *presstime*, September 1988, pp. 24-25.
26. "New ANCAM Standards Give Boost to Remote Entry of Classifieds," *presstime*, October 1988, pp. 62-63.
27. "PC Allows Quick Handling of Display Ad," *presstime*, June 1989, p. 79.
28. Craig C. Standen, "Regionalization Gives Newspapers New National Ad Opportunities," *presstime*, April 1989, p. 50.
29. "AD/SAT: Not All Sweetness at the Speed of Light," *presstime*, July 1987, p. 45.
30. John Kerr and Walter E. Niebauer Jr. "Use of Full Text Database Retrieval Systems by Editorial Page Writers," *Newspaper Research Journal*, Spring 1987, pp. 21-32.
31. David R. Bowers, "The Impact of Centralized Printing on the Community Press," *Journalism Quarterly*, 46:43-46, 52 (Spring 1969).
32. See Boyd L. Miller, "More Dailies Zoning for Suburban Readers," *Journalism Quarterly*, 42:460-462 (Summer 1965); Keith Roberts, "Antitrust Problems in the Newspaper Industry," *Harvard Law Review*, 82:2:319-366 (1968); John Morton, "Hitting the Target," *Washington Journalism Review*, July/August 1983, p. 15; and John Morton, "Renaissance of the Regionals," *Washington Journalism Review*, March 1983, p. 16.
33. For example, see Stephen Lacy, "The Impact of Intercity Competition on Daily Newspaper Content," *Journalism Quarterly*, 65:399-406, (Summer 1988); and Stephen Lacy, Ardyth B. Sohn, and Lowndes F. Stephens, "Suburban News Coverage: A Content Analysis of Metropolitan & Suburban Papers in Denver & Detroit," *Newspaper Research Journal*, Spring 1989, pp. 39-50.

34. For discussions of this problem see James W. Tankard Jr., "Quantitative Graphics in Newspapers," *Journalism Quarterly*, 64:406-415 (Summer-Autumn 1987); and James W. Tankard Jr., "Effects of Chartoons and Three-Dimensional Graphics on Interest and Information Gain," *Newspaper Research Journal*, Spring 1989, pp. 91-103.

7

Antitrust and Market Regulation of Newspapers

The only opportunity for direct government intervention into the economics of the newspaper industry stems from the operation of laws concerning competition, primarily federal antitrust law, although other statutory and administrative provisions, both federal and state, may be brought to play against newspaper companies.

Even though enforcement of such laws results in the only direct regulatory effects upon newspapers, it is critical to note that antitrust and similar laws do not address newspapers specifically. Furthermore, they are not regulatory in the usual sense; that is, antitrust laws are not enabling statutes interpreted by a regulatory agency over a specific industry or subject area, such as the Communications Act of 1934.

Antitrust laws are general statutes designed to affect all businesses engaged in interstate commerce. Only the Newspaper Preservation Act,[1] which is an *exception* to antitrust law, specifically addresses newspapers. Newspaper antitrust, then, is but a very small part of the overall antitrust picture.

It is an unusual and especially interesting part, however. The uniqueness of the newspaper industry has made application of antitrust laws an uncertain and therefore risky matter for those choosing to enforce the public policy assumptions underlying the statutes. Several characteristics of the industry combine to make it unique and antitrust enforcement therefore problematic. A primary characteristic is the role of the press in society. The press is the only industry singled out for special protection in the U.S. Constitution.[2] Although no newspaper antitrust case to date has hinged on the First Amendment status of the press, that status is always lurking in the background of cases. Newspapers are the prototypical provider in the intellectual market. A second characteristic of the industry that makes antitrust fit uneasily is the joint commodity nature of newspapers. News content and advertising act as separate but related commodities. A third characteristic concerns the arena of competition. The vast majority of newspapers are marketed locally, but contain news and advertising of both a local and non-local nature. The local newspaper, in turn, is more likely than ever before to be owned by a nationwide company.

The result is that many newspaper antitrust cases are decided on basic issues—the nature of the product and the definition of the market—seldom contested in antitrust actions involving other types of businesses. This chapter briefly reviews the background of federal antitrust laws, then assesses how they have been applied to the newspaper industry. Effects of other provisions aimed at market regulation of either newspapers or the marketplace of ideas are also discussed.

BACKGROUND OF FEDERAL ANTITRUST LAW

Federal antitrust statutes that may affect newspapers include the Sherman Act of 1890, the Clayton Act of 1914, the Federal Trade Commission Act of 1914, the Robinson-Patman Act of 1936, and the Celler-Kefauver Antimerger Act of 1950. As a practical matter, only the Sherman and Clayton acts present significant potential for enforcement against newspapers. The Celler-Kefauver Act became part of the Clayton Act.

The other acts mentioned have not played a major role in market regulation of the newspaper industry. The Federal Trade Commission Act of 1914[3] gives the Federal Trade Commission (FTC) broad authority to regulate unfair methods of competition or unfair or deceptive practices,[4] but the FTC also has the authority to promulgate guidelines relating to advertising[5] under the Robinson-Patman Act. Although that act was codified as an amendment to the Clayton Act, its primary focus is on pricing and promotional plans in general rather than on actions of competitors as such.[6] Because the interpretation of unfairness is quite difficult, and also due to limited statutory scope, the Clayton Act has not been a major area of newspaper antitrust activity.

The Sherman Act[7] is the most significant antitrust law since it is the broadest and therefore most-used. The act was passed during a period of rapid concentration in American industry. Between 1887 and 1904, a wave of mergers resulted in giant companies, such as Standard Oil and U.S. Steel, with the power to manipulate their markets.[8] The process of creating these large corporations sometimes included behavior that ran counter to socially accepted business practices. The resulting statute declared illegal contracts, "combinations," and trusts in restraint of trade. Monopolization or attempts to monopolize, singly or with co-conspirators, were also declared illegal. Enforcement of the statute has been aimed largely at unilateral exclusionary practices,[9] although collusive practices such as price fixing may also be the basis for a Sherman Act case. The primary way of accomplishing the goals of the statute was apparently government enforcement; the first three sections of the act make violations a criminal offense. The punishment is severe, with fines up to one million dollars for corporations and prison sentences possible for individuals. Private suits by parties suffering business injury may also be brought. The private plaintiff may claim treble damages and attorney fees if successful.

The enforcement and damage provisions foreshadow recent history. The U.S. Department of Justice may choose or not choose to bring actions. Just as in other areas of business activity, enforcement has been scarce in the Reagan and Bush administrations. On damages, provision for treble damages for private plaintiffs is evidence that Congress expected that successful actions would be rare, and that allowing extra damages would punish the occasional losing defendant and serve to warn others who might engage in anticompetitive practices.

The provisions of the Sherman Act do not contain definitions. Key terms such as "restraint of trade" and "attempt to monopolize" were left for litigants and courts to interpret. Although judges and lawyers who administer and interpret the act were sometimes reluctant to admit it, the consensus of legal opinion is that antitrust laws are based on social assumptions of appropriate economic behavior, and are hence economic in character. The test in an economic antitrust case is whether particular economic behavior tends to be anticompetitive within the meaning and/or intent of the statute.[10]

Champions of competition in the early 1900s were soon convinced that the Sherman Act was inadequate at stopping industrial concentration. The FTC Act and the Clayton Act were both passed in 1914 as a result. One key provision allowed private plaintiffs to bring civil actions.[11] The Clayton Act differs from the Sherman Act in several ways. It is aimed at consensual collusive behavior in the form of mergers resulting in anticompetitive effects, while the Sherman Act primarily focused on actions of individual firms. The Clayton Act's wording is broader, too. It declares that no corporation may merge with another where the effect is "substantially to lessen competition or to tend to create a monopoly."[12] The act also prohibits price discrimination and tying arrangements. Congressional intent behind the Clayton Act was also clearer, and any doubt about the act's purpose as a preventive statute was laid to rest with the 1950 amendments.[13] The "tend to lessen competition" test was not limited to cases involving direct competitors so long as a merger had the undesirable effect within a "relevant" market. The act was again amended in the Hart-Scott-Rodino Antitrust Improvements Act of 1976,[14] which requires advance notice to the Justice Department and the FTC of impending mergers and acquisitions of smaller companies by large ones.

The two laws are products of their times. One effect of that is the failure to specify. But the intent of the legislators is clear: antitrust laws are designed to correct abuses in the economic system. Their motivation may have been as much moral indignation as economic equity, but modern analysts agree that inefficient allocation of resources is the evil to be prevented. Sociopolitical justifications for antitrust law have also been posed. These may include moral notions, concerns over consumer welfare, or even preservation of small businesses. These justifications are examined in Chapter 8 as part of evaluation and recommendation concerning antitrust law and the press. Some scholars argue that the true goal of antitrust law is the promotion of efficiency and competition.[15] But the means chosen is negative, not affirmative, preventive rather than promotive. If antitrust law encourages efficiency or competition, it does so in an extremely indirect fashion. The only 'encouragement' is in the treble damages provision (or perhaps the criminal penalties), apparent recognition of the difficulty of filing and ultimately prevailing in an antitrust case.[16] From an operational point of view, the goal is narrower—prevention of inefficiency and anticompetitive behaviors when they can be found and proved. The promotion through prohibition approach of the antitrust laws encourages desirable behaviors only by specifying undesirable ones. That is typical of U.S. laws. The stiff penalties have, ironically, apparently resulted in government either not filing actions or choosing to pursue civil rather than criminal remedies.

Newspapers more than most companies seem unlikely targets for a criminal antitrust charge. Newspapers are primarily local products, and it is unlikely the government would seek to file charges unless a case had very widespread impact. Private civil suits are the norm in the industry. But the rationale for applying antitrust to newspapers at all must be assessed first.

NEWSPAPERS, ANTITRUST, AND THE FIRST AMENDMENT

Application of antitrust law to newspapers is relatively recent compared to other industries. The exact reasons for this comparative delay are perhaps known only to long-past U.S. Department of Justice antitrust lawyers. But two reasons seem likely. First, the newspaper industry had traditionally been highly competitive, especially the daily newspaper segment in the first part of the twentieth century. Second, many argued that the First Amendment itself should protect newspapers from antitrust.

The competition argument had largely disappeared by the time of the first major journalism antitrust case in 1945. Between 1920 and 1945, direct competition disappeared in 435 cities.[17] The First Amendment argument had been undermined by a 1937 Supreme Court decision upholding application of federal labor law to newspapers, despite a First Amendment challenge.[18] The initial attempt of the government to apply antitrust was against the Associated Press, however, rather than against a newspaper. In *Associated Press v. United States*,[19] the Court rejected AP's attempt to use the First Amendment as a defense against regulation.

The government had sought an injunction against AP for violating two aspects of the Sherman Act, the conspiracy in restraint of trade section, and the attempt to monopolize section. AP's bylaws, which prohibited members from selling news to non-members and which allowed members to block their competitors from becoming members, were claimed to violate the act. Non-competing non-members were routinely admitted to the cooperative association, however. The bylaws had strict enforcement provisions. On antitrust grounds, the Court's decision was easy to reach. It said the restrictions in the bylaws were reastraints of trade on their face. Indeed, the Court thought the Sherman Act especially applied to AP because the act was specifically aimed at preventing separate businesses from acting in association to restrain trade.

On the First Amendment issue, the Court devoted only a paragraph, albeit a long one, to dismissing AP's claim. In an often-quoted passage, Justice Black's opinion said:

> Surely a command that the government itself shall not impede the free flow of ideas does not afford non-governmental combinations a refuge if they impose restraints upon that constitutionally guaranteed freedom. Freedom to publish is guaranteed by the Constitution, but freedom to combine to keep others from publishing is not.[20]

The Court had addressed AP's contention that news organizations should be specially protected from summary judgment procedures earlier in the opinion. AP raised the argument that actions for injunctions by government could interfere with the traditional autonomy of the press. This is an argument which, in slightly different form, has been persuasive with the Court in recent years (see Chapter 9). In a telling passage, the Court rejected the contention that the press was different and deserved special procedural protection:

> Our legal system has not established different measures of proof for the trial of cases in which equally intelligent defendants are charged with violating the same statutes. Member publishers of AP are engaged in business for profit exactly as are other business men who sell food, steel, aluminum, or anything else people need or want.

This passage requiring uniform application of general laws against the press as against other businesses reflects an interpretation the Court has consistently adhered to. As in the First Amendment holding, the opinion was long on strong rhetoric, but short on constitutional and economic analysis.

The Court's equating newspapers with other products simply ignores the long history of summary procedures as a governmental method of stifling the news content of the press. It also denies the existence of organizational and economic differences. The Court similarly did not address the meaning of the press clause of the First Amendment in its decision, other than to say that the amendment "rests on the assumption that the widest possible dissemination of information from diverse and antagonistic sources is essential..." But the traditional, and then only, means to prevent government interference with a free press were the rules against prior restraints on publication and against punitive taxes.[21]

While the *AP* decision is considered the foundation of newspaper antitrust law, it is important to see that decision in context. Decades of familiarity have lent the majority opinion an air of authority it originally lacked. Of the eight justices involved in deciding the case, only five clearly decided against AP. Justices Douglas and Frankfurter wrote concurring opinions designed to narrow the scope of the decision. Douglas focused on the fact that the bylaws had the inescapable effect of restraining trade, while Frankfurter saw the restraint of trade in news as implicating the First Amendment interests of newspaper readers. To Douglas, then, the First Amendment argument was beside the point, while to Frankfurter enforcement of the Sherman Act aided the goals of the First Amendment. Three justices would have sent the case back to the trial court for trial. Justice Roberts wrote a separate opinion that attacked the logic of the majority: "It is a tedious task to separate the generalities thus mingled in this opinion..." Roberts criticized the majority for having turned AP, for all purposes, into a public utility, and also for judicial improvisation in interpreting the act. Justice Murphy was upset with the cursory dismissal of the First Amendment claim:

> [I]t is clear that they are engaged in collecting and distributing news and information rather than in manufacturing automobiles, aluminum or gasoline. We cannot avoid that fact. Nor can we escape the fact that governmental action aimed directly at the methods or conditions of such collection or distribution *is* an interference with the press, however differing in degree it may be from governmental restraints on written or spoken utterances themselves.[22]

More than forty years later, it is easy to forget that the justices themselves were split on whether or not antitrust was applicable to the press, and that they were also split on how it was to be applied to the press. Black's majority opinion, which stressed uniform application of antitrust to newspapers as to other businesses, set the stage for future cases.

OVERVIEW OF NEWSPAPER ANTITRUST CASES

Based on history, newspaper managers have little reason to fear finding themselves on the defending end of an antitrust suit. Remarkably few cases are filed against newspapers. Actions brought by government are particularly scarce. As a practical matter, a newspaper will usually be defending against a private competitor if defending at all. The track record indicates that defendants prevail in most cases. An analysis of 45 newspaper antitrust cases from 1980-1986 showed that out of 80 overall claims of antitrust violations (cases often featured multiple claims), defendants prevailed on the merits on 23 claims and prevailed through dismissal on 31 claims, with plaintiffs prevailing on the merits on only six claims. The result on remaining claims was not yet known.[23]

Despite the record of plaintiffs losing, there are strong inducements for filing suit. Treble damages is one; they may make a less-than-sure case worth the risk. The provision for attorney fees for plaintiffs is another. Yet another is more strategic. Antitrust suits are complicated and expensive to defend. A plaintiff may seek compromise, not victory, a consent decree or a settlement rather than judgment.[24]

Plaintiffs face an uphill battle. The preconditions supporting application of antitrust law must be established prior to offering proof of any particular anticompetitive actions. The preconditions include proof of impact on interstate commerce—essentially a non-issue in modern cases[25] —and proof that the parties were competitors in the market.

Defining the Relevant Market

The first element of any antitrust case, then, is defining the relevant market. In general, relevant market refers to the "area of effective competition."[26] Therefore, the relevant market defines the spheres in which anticompetitive conduct could occur. The market itself has two aspects, the geographic market and the product market. The *geographic market* is the physical area within which two (or more) firms may exert influence on the market behavior of others. No strict rule governs the delineation of a geographic market. It is sufficient to show that the area of overlapping competition represents a practical and proper market.[27]

The *product market* is made up of all products that are reasonably interchangeable.[28] Product market therefore concerns cross-elasticity of demand for products. For two products to be in the same market, they must be good substitutes for each other. And the product market in turn must include all interchangeable goods within the same overall relevant market.[29]

The plaintiff bears the burden of proving the relevant market, both geographic and product, and a court is free to ignore a plaintiff's evidence in light of extrinsic evidence of commercial realities.[30] The existence of submarkets may also be critical, especially in newspaper cases. For example, whether the market is defined as the total display advertising market or as the newspaper display market may make or break a plaintiff's case.[31]

Cases on geographic market. The geographic market appears superficially as the easiest for a plaintiff to show. At its simplest, it reflects the area in which buyers can purchase the product. Mere product availability, however, is never sufficient. The defendant must do a significant volume of business in the geographic market. The *Associated Pres* opinion perhaps presents the broadest view of geographic market in a press case—it obviously took the market to be the entire country, although discussion of the restrictive effect of AP's bylaws in local markets appears to have swayed the Court most.

United States v. Times Mirror Co.[32] is the leading case on proof of both markets. In the *Times Mirror* case, the government claimed that the purchase of the Sun Company, publisher of the San Bernardino *Sun*, by the parent company of the *Los Angeles Times* violated the Sherman Act as an unlawful combination restraining commerce, and the Clayton Act since the merger would substantially lessen competition. The *Sun*, the largest independent daily newspaper in southern California at the time, circulated almost entirely in San Bernardino County, while the *Times* circulated over many counties. The government claimed that San Bernardino County was the relevant geographic market since there was no significant overlap between the two newspapers elsewhere. The *Times* argued that the geographic market should be even smaller, since the *Times* primarily circulated in the western parts of the county and the *Sun* the eastern. Relying upon earlier non-newspaper cases, the *Times* asserted that the market should not begin until a point at which 80 to 85 percent of the two papers' total circulation was reached. Since the *Times* and other newspapers recognized the county as a separate market for planning and circulation, the *Times* was held to its position. The court rejected a formula approach, asserting instead that percentages of trade were useful, not necessary, in delineating the market.[33]

The *Times Mirror* case is often cited for the argument that antitrust law may be applied to umbrella newspaper competition.[34] But the case predates the umbrella concept, and the court does not appear to have considered the case as one involving anything but head-to-head competition. The umbrella concept likely requires analysis of the behavior of all or most competitors in a market. The *Times* court's focus was on industry concentration as evidence showing anticompetitive effects of the acquisition.[35] But in so doing, the court examined the industry throughout southern California, apparently laying the groundwork for an umbrella approach. The court considered concentration both in terms of ownership and in terms of circulation in determining that the acquisition would have an anticompetitive effect. Ironically, the *Sun* was ultimately sold to Gannett.

The determination of the geographic market in newspaper cases since *Times Mirror* shows a combination of factors. The parties' definition of the market remains the most important. In *Woodbury Daily Times v. Los Angeles Times-Washington Post News Service*,[36] the smaller newspaper, published in Gloucester County, New Jersey, claimed that exclusive territorial subscriptions granted by the defendant to the Philadelphia *Inquirer* constituted an unreasonable restraint of trade. The plaintiff argued that Gloucester County, southeast of Philadelphia, should not be considered the relevant market; this reverse twist on the usual proof was required to establish that exclusivity served no purpose other than to restrain trade. The defendant claimed that the eight-county metropolitan area used by the Audit Bureau of Circulation was the relevant market. The court determined that either market was a relevant market, since both included Gloucester County, and the *Inquirer* was engaged in significant competition with the *Daily Times* in the county. The court was influenced by an average rate of market penetration of 21 percent by the *Inquirer* in Gloucester County. And the Sunday *Inquirer* rate of 37.5 percent was only five percent below that of the local paper's Sunday rate.

The *Woodbury* court appeared to endorse a formula while announcing that it was not. It relied in part on a consent decree involving an exclusivity contract between a news service and the Boston *Globe*.[37] The decree stipulated that the *Globe* could not claim exclusivity in any county where its circulation was less than 5,000 copies and less then 20 percent of households. To buttress its conclusion that the two newspapers were substantial competitors, the court noted that the *Inquirer* makes a particular effort to cover southern New Jersey news, including special New Jersey zoned editions, but there was no discussion indicating that any of that coverage was of Gloucester County.

The *Daily Times* case is troubling on several counts, including its discussion of the alleged anticompetitive conduct, to be discussed later. But the court's approach to the geographic market issue hopelessly mixes up the notions of geographic and product markets. The court appears to have taken the *Inquirer*'s reporting in New Jersey as proof of competition in the product market—but never said so. The high Sunday penetration rate, blended with weekdays to yield an overall rate, is given determinative status by formula without the court questioning why a metro Sunday edition might sell so well in the suburbs. The obvious answer is that the two papers, at least on Sunday, are very different sorts of products. The court even asserts that commuters from the county who buy the *Inquirer* during their Philadelphia workday should be considered as a 'boost' to the *Inquirer's* county penetration rate. Under the *Times Mirror* approach, including Gloucester County within the geographic market is probably justifiable, and even the assumption that a significant amount of competition is needed seems necessary. The formula used, however, if widely adopted by other courts, could prevent application of antitrust in many umbrella-type situations where penetration is less then 20 percent.

In most cases, though, the relevant geographic market is simply not an issue, either because the area is small and well-defined and therefore assumed,[38] or is defined by explicit or implicit agreement of the parties.[39]

Cases on product market. Given the dual commodity nature of newspapers, it should not be surprising to find that proof of the relevant product market can get relatively complicated. Confusion over the substitutability of other media in the advertising and information markets only adds to the complexity. Early cases tended to define the product market broadly. In the *Associated Press* case, the product market was clearly that for 'news,' however defined.

The lack of definition continued in *Lorain Journal Co. v. United States*.[40] In that case the government had brought a civil action against the newspaper for its practice of refusing to sell space to advertisers who had bought air time on the only local radio station. The Supreme Court agreed that the practice constituted an attempt to monopolize within the meaning of the Sherman Act. By so holding, the Court necessarily must have concluded that the relevant product market was for advertising. It should be noted, though, that the opinion does not directly address the product market issue. Any reliance on the case as precedent for considering all media advertising the product market must be based on inference only.

Two years later in *Times-Picayune Publishing Co. v. United States*[41] the Court held that the Sherman Act was not violated when the morning *Times-Picayune* and the afternoon *States*, both owned by the same company, required advertisers to buy space in both to advertise in the morning paper. The government had argued that the tying arrangement was an attempt to run a competing afternoon paper, the *Item*, out of business. The *Item* led the *States* in afternoon circulation. Tying is considered violative of antitrust when a company that is dominant in the market uses that market power to coerce customers into buying a second, possibly unwanted, product along with the product wanted.[42] The Court held that the two companies were selling exactly the same product, newspaper advertising space. But the Court also concluded that the newspaper advertising market was not distinctive enough to be treated separately as a submarket. As a result, all media advertising was apparently considered the product market. The Court was also influenced by the fact that the *Item* had increased ad linage in the five years before the lawsuit, finding the increase mitigated against any inference of a deleterious effect on competition. Five years later in 1958 the *Item* and the *States* marged. Both are now owned by the Times-Picayune Co.

The opinion rests on two incorrect interpretations of the economics of the newspaper industry. First, by considering all advertising media in the product market, the Court ignored the inelasticity of demand between newspapers and other media, especially broadcast media. Perhaps the majority was influenced by the example of cross-media competition in the small community of Lorain, Ohio two years earlier. Second, linage increases at the *Item* were taken as showing that newspaper competition was intense and healthy. But the *Item* was already in financial trouble. Furthermore, the government had argued that the *States* was being operated at a loss for the sole purpose of putting the *Item* out of business; that the *Item* was the afternoon leader was irrelevant if the total newspaper market is considered, the government argued. The second argument places too much emphasis on short-run changes and ignores the long-run impact of the circulation spiral.

One case using a broad product market properly was *Kansas City Star Co. v. United States*.[43] The company owned the morning *Star* and the afternoon *Times*, which reached 96 percent of all homes in the city. The company also owned the only television station in town and a leading radio station. The government filed both criminal and civil antitrust charges. The practices of requiring subscribers to purchase both papers, plus the Sunday *Star*, of requiring advertisers to purchase ads in both papers, and also of tying broadcast ad sales to newspaper ad sales were said to violate the act. The only competing newspaper, the *Journal-Post*, had already gone out of business. The Kansas City Star Company controlled about 85 percent of all media revenues in Kansas City. Given those facts, using the total media advertising market makes sense. The company and its advertising manager were found guilty on the criminal charges. The civil charges were dropped upon acceptance of a consent decree which required divestment of the broadcast properties. Probably no company ever has or ever will again match the market domination proved in this case.

The tendency to consider the entire advertising market as the relevant market has been rejected in later cases, although it should be noted that the Supreme Court has not directly addressed the issue in a newspaper antitrust case. Two cases in the 1960s helped establish a rule that the daily newspaper market is the relevant market. One of the cases is the *Times-Mirror* case, in which the district court considered the daily newspaper market as consisting of morning, evening, and Sunday papers. The defendant's claim that metro dailies and suburban dailies were each unique and non-interchangeable products was rejected because, even if true, the Clayton Act does not require that products be identical to be in the same product market.[44] The court analyzed competition between newspapers for advertising, but did not signal that the newspaper advertising market was itself a separate product market. The court seemed to consider it a part of the overall daily newspaper market. While the case has been relied upon extensively for the rule that only newspapers, not all media, should be in the product market,[45] the opinion nonetheless fails to delineate the dual commodity nature of newspapers in the antitrust context, and therefore its usefulness is limited.

A second case, *Citizen Publishing Co. v. United States*,[46] upheld a district court decision that Citizens, owner of the Tucson *Daily Citizen*, and Star Publishing, owner of the Arizona *Daily Star*, had violated the Sherman Act by price fixing, profit pooling, and directly restraining competition under a joint operating agreement. The Supreme Court accepted the trial judge's determination that daily newspaper publishing was the relevant product market.

In many later cases, the courts have been forced to deviate from the analysis of these cases. When shoppers, usually circulated on a weekly basis, assert that a local daily or weekly newspaper with a total market publication is engaging in anticompetitive behavior, only advertising is appropriately considered in determining product market. But the question of what advertising to consider is much more difficult to determine.

In *Drinkwine v. Federated Publications, Inc.*,[47] the plaintiff in a four-claim antitrust suit had been in the business of preparing shopper-style advertising publications that were inserted in the only local daily newspaper, the Idaho *Statesman*. The plaintiff also had distributed the materials in local weekly papers. When the daily started competing with him for the insert ads, and made it harder for plaintiff to do business with the *Statesman*, plaintiff sued. He argued that the product market was local display advertising distributed in a daily newspaper. Since advertising customers had indicated that direct mail, weekly papers, and even door-to-door delivery of materials were realistic substitutes, the attempt to narrowly define the product market failed.

Depending on the nature of the parties and the specific areas of competition, the product market should be tailored to fit the case. Busterna refers to a case in which the product market was defined as that for "news, advertising, and editorial comment in paid circulation and free distribution newspapers and shopping guides..."[48] Any newspaper facing the prospect of a suit should anticipate defending on the basis of an extremely narrow market, however. For example, in *Advantage Publications v. Daily Press*,[49] the plaintiff published a number of weekly newspapers distributed by mail. Although featuring more advertising than most newspapers, they were not shoppers. The court used the plaintiff's designation of the product market as "direct mail newspaper advertising" in considering a claim for a preliminary injunction against the defendant, which was accused of using predatory tactics to run Advantage out of business. Interestingly, the geographic market was also defined narrowly. While the plaintiff urged that the entire Tidewater area of southeast Virginia be considered, the court analyzed competition between the two parties as it spread from zip code to zip code.[50]

While narrow market definitions are now the rule, an occasional exception may surprise litigants. Surely the plaintiff was surprised in *Sales and Advertising Promotion v. Donrey*[51] when the judge said that newsprint display advertising was not the relevant product market in a case between a free-circulation shopper and the local daily newspaper's newly-launched weekly equivalent. The judge said that the definition was "inappropriate" under the Sherman Act, but did not explain further. Instead the judge said that the product market probably included newspaper, radio, billboard, and direct mail, since they are "reasonably interchangeable." The plaintiff's claim of predatory practices could not possibly be proved with the market so enlarged.

ANTITRUST CLAIMS AGAINST NEWSPAPERS

Claims brought against newspapers are perhaps most easily classified as within the two types of anticompetitive practices generally divided by Posner into collusive practices and exclsuionary practices.[52] Collusive practices refer to anticompetitive behaviors between or among firms in a market. Examples of collusive practices would include behavior such as two firms agreeing to set prices so low that other firms are precluded from making a profit, or perhaps precluded from entering the market. Exclusive agreements represent another form of collusive behavior. For example, in the *Lorain Journal* case, the exclusive advertising agreements between the newspaper and its advertisers not only restrained competition from the radio station, but effectively coerced the advertisers themselves. An exclusive supply contract, as when a firm gains exclusive rights to a product by offering a kickback or other business favor, would be another form of collusive behavior.

Exclusionary practices are usually unilateral, single-firm matters. Any practice designed to dominate a market or to exclude others from a market other than for competitive reasons is likely to be exclusionary. It should be apparent, then, that legitimate business actions aimed at competing rather than at stifling competition will be defenses against an antitrust claim. This has happened with some frequency in newspaper cases. Exclusionary practices account for the largest number of anitrust claims filed, including those against newspapers. The most-frequent exclusionary practice claimed is predatory pricing, with price discrimination and tying arrangements trailing far behind in number.[53] It is unclear whether an antitrust action against a merger, typically based on the Clayton Act, represents exclusionary or collusive action. It is exclusionary to the extent that it keeps would-be competitors out of the market, but collusive inasmuch as it requires joint behavior by two businesses.

Whatever the type of claim, newspapers apparently have little to fear from the government, which brought only one case in the 1980s,[54] a result consistent with a dearth of federal antitrust enforcement generally. Unless there is a major policy or political change in Washington, threats of antitrust suits are most likely to come from competitors and would-be competitors. In general, defendants hold most of the cards. The complexities of proof in these cases make it difficult for plaintiffs to build a case, much less win one. Both sides will normally need expert witnesses to establish the economics underlying the claim or defense.

Predatory Pricing

Predatory pricing is simply pricing a product or service below cost, usually to run another firm out of business, with the plan of making up the losses later through higher prices.[55] Determining the existence of predatory pricing is nowhere near as simple as this basic definition might imply, however. Even in a simple, single-product industry such as the widget business so beloved by business schools and law professors, determining true cost or actual marginal cost requires a thorough review of the business overall. When a newspaper, with its dual-commodity nature, is involved, that determination is more difficult, largely because the true costs of editorial content and advertising are not as distinct as with other products. Although the determination is less tricky than nuclear physics, it is complex and, more importantly, virtually ignored by most newspaper managers.[56] In the absence of evidence that a market had barriers to entry, proof of predatory, below cost, pricing is the first essential element.

An example of the difficulties of proof occurred when a shopper entered a market in which a monopoly newspaper controlled the print advertising market. The newspaper published a shopper which was circulated in addition to the regular newspaper. Its rates, as a monopolist, were above its marginal costs. When faced with competition, it lowered its rates. But, the court said, the rates remained above cost, therefore precluding plaintiff's predatory pricing claim.[57] The rates were close to those of the plaintiff. The court was convinced that the lowering of rates occurred to meet competition, not to squelch it—precisely the result desired under the antitrust laws. In the meantime, however, the plaintiff went out of business. All else indicates that the defendant had the necessary intent, the second element of predatory pricing, but absent this first prong a case, as this one, will be dismissed.

Occasionally a plaintiff will benefit from the accounting practices of a defendant. In the *Advantage* case, the plaintiff was able to get a preliminary injunction in part because the defendant had not added labor costs in its accounting for the unprofitability of its shoppers, created to compete with a new shopper in its market. The $1,000 per week loss estimated by the defendant appeared nominal. But by considering only the costs of materials, the court determined, the defendant was ignoring labor costs as an element of loss. The defendant claimed that the labor cost would have accrued in any event out of its other newspaper operations, and therefore had not apportioned it.[58]

The second element of predatory pricing requires proof of intent to run a competitor out of business, or to coerce a competitor into raising prices. The second might itself be an anticompetitive collusive practice if there is contact or 'negotiation' between the firms. A leading case is *Buffalo Courier-Express v. Buffalo Evening News*.[59] When a new owner took over the six-day-a-week *News*, added a Sunday edition, and promoted circulation via a no-charge subscription that was the same as the old six-day price, the *Courier-Express* claimed predatory pricing. The give-away was to run five weeks. A federal district judge granted an injunction limiting it to two weeks. The judge also placed restrictions on purchase price changes by the *News*. The new Sunday edition, planned to sell for 30 cents, was ordered to be priced at 50 cents, same as the *Courier-Express*. The *News*' former 'fat' Saturday edition had sold for 30 cents. On appeal, the court could find neither evidence of below-cost pricing nor of predatory intent. The appeals court scolded the trial judge for issuing the injunction on the basis of proof of irreparable injury to the *Courier-Express*. At the time, the plaintiff had the Sunday market to itself; the *News* was the overall daily circulation leader, by a margin of about two-to-one. An injunction would have been proper if the plaintiff was likely to go out of business before a trial could be held. The court relied on the history of competition in the Buffalo market and on the *News*' owner's assertions that he was only interested in competing. The court found corroboration of pro-competitive intent in the ratio of the *News* purchase price to gross revenues, a ratio far below what would be expected to buy a paper which had or was about to achieve a monopoly. It was also noted that giveaways were a standard method of introducing a newspaper. The *News* eventually became the only newspaper in town.

Overt actions by the defendant—often by advertising representatives—provide strong evidence of an intent to run another firm out of business. In the *Advantage* case, agents of the defendants had, among other things, told advertisers that the plaintiff was about to go out of business, given advertisers rebates on past paid advertising, and had orally offered a rate (never proved with documents) laughably below that of plaintiff. The judge noted that a pattern of conduct may be sufficient to establish the intent. Just what conduct, or how extensive the pattern, must be assessed on a case-by-case basis, however.

Variation among cases is to be expected, but one case stands out as anomalous. It is the *Donrey* case, discussed and criticized earlier for including all advertising in the product market. A pattern of conduct that included memos, meetings, and creation of a "combat" plan were all not enough to establish intent in the eyes of the trial court judge. Not even a written note explaining that its planned competition with the shopper plaintiff would cost $50,000 the first year sufficed. Nor did a pick-up rate of $1.00 per column inch for multiple-run advertisements prove intent. That the defendant could produce no documentation to substantiate its rationale for the pick-up rate also failed. The court would only say that the pattern appeared predatory, not that it was predatory.[60]

A third requirement in predatory pricing cases is that there must be evidence proving that the attempt to monopolize is likely to work, or close enough to create a "dangerous probability of success."[61] Mere danger that a competitor is likely to fail is not enough—that may be attributable to healthy competitive behavior rather than to predatory behavior. Rather, a plaintiff must show that impending financial doom is traceable to the predatory actions of the defendant. Note that this requirement demands proof of causation, and is paralleled in other antitrust claims. The company that is merely foundering for reasons unrelated to predation, but which may sink faster due to defendant's actions, cannot claim the sort of direct causation intended by this requirement.[62]

In civil actions brought by private parties, the statutes require a fourth element, that the claim be based on damages. It is difficult to imagine, however, that a suit would be filed without a claim for damages.

Plaintiffs nearly always lose newspaper predatory pricing cases. The reasons should be obvious. The protypical case involves a monopoly or dominant newspaper that suddenly has competition for advertising. The dominant firm responds by lowering its already-high rates, but will seldom drop below cost due to its scale advantages. Similarly, the dominant firm may offer prospective advertisers deals previously not offered. That is a classic response to competition. Some have argued that predation is therefore best dropped as an antitrust ground, since it transfers the competition to a legal battleground where costs are measured in attorney fees and inconvenience. Given the record of dismissals, it is reasonable to suggest that many of the suits are nuisance suits. But, with or without predation, the result seems the same: monopoly or dominant firms eliminate competitors. It is a result consistent with judicial interpretation of antitrust law, but one at odds with the goals underlying antitrust law.

Price Discrimination

Charges of price discrimination may be brought under the Robinson-Patman Act or under either the Clayton or Sherman acts. Price discrimination is also barred by statute in many states.[63] Price discrimination occurs when buyers are charged different prices for the same product. A typical price discrimination claim in newspaper antitrust would be a charge that some advertisers were offered volume discounts or rebates while others were not. A claim of violation, however, requires more. In general, a showing that the acts charged lessen competition, tend to create a monopoly, or were designed to injure or destroy competition is needed.[64] One of the claims of the *Courier-Express* in the Buffalo case was essentially a price discrimination claim: that the *News* was selling low to injure or destroy competition. Given that newspaper subscription prices bear little relation to cost or value, it should be little surprise that lower prices in an otherwise-underpriced industry would be allowed.

In practice, most likely cases would involve advertisers, and probably only major advertisers at that. Competitors are only indirect victims of price discrimination, if at all. No other parties would be able to make a credibly large damages claim. Busterna found no cases in his seven-year review in which plaintiffs prevailed, although one received nominal damages of a dollar. That should be little surprise; differential pricing that is aimed at meeting competition will always be defensible.

The company-distributor relationship has been subject to competitive analysis, however. In a recent non-newspaper case, the Supreme Court said that pressures on distributors to keep prices low were not an antitrust violation when the prices were well above predatory levels.[65] Congress is expected to pass price fixing legislation that would limit violations to those that set minimum prices.[66]

Refusals to Deal

Refusal to deal claims have mainly been of two types. In the type most frequently brought, a newspaper decided to transform its circulation from an independent dealer to a company-operated system. Often that change results in former independent dealers being offered employment, but it almost always means that the independent businesses close. The independent dealers then sue on restraint of trade/monopolization grounds. A leading case on the issue is *Paschall v. Kansas City Star Co.*[67] In this case, the newspaper company terminated its contracts with all independent carriers and started its own delivery system. The change for the first time also assured uniformity of pricing to subscribers. Although the court found that the vertical integration by the *Star* created anticompetitive effects, it also found that those effects were more than offset by the economic and social welfare effects of uniform pricing, more consistent delivery, and stability in newspaper revenues. The court relied extensively on economic analyses urging that lower prices and greater efficiency might result if there is an elasticity in demand for the product. That reliance is puzzling inasmuch as the court did not additionally address the question of substitutibility for a monopoly daily newspaper.

In any event, the *Paschall* case is consistent with a large number of other vertical integration cases involving distribution. A recent case, *Alpert's Newspaper Delivery, Inc. v. New York Times Co.*,[68] reaches the same conclusion, although for slightly different reasons. The plaintiffs were unable to show that the *Times* had monopoly power in the multi-newspaper southern Connecticut market. Had proof of monopoly been made, the plaintiffs would likely have suffered the fate of *Pascahll* anyway. A later case, *Kowalski v. Chicago Tribune Co.*,[69] relied on the relationship between advertising and circulation revenues in determining that keeping newspapers cheap was an abiding concern of the industry. The plaintiff distributors must have been chagrined to find Professor (now Judge) Richard Posner writing the majority opinion. If a newspaper imposes fixed prices on independent dealers, despite the unilateral nature of the imposition, the fix may constitute a 'collusive' restraint of trade between the paper and the dealers.[70]

A second type of case involves exclusionary actions relating to content. The most notorious case is *Home Placement Service, Inc. v. Providence Journal Co.*,[71] in which the *Journal* was found to have violated the Sherman Act by its refusal to run advertisements from a rental referral company. The court found that the newspaper and the plaintiff were competitors in the rental housing referral and advertising business. That narrow definition of the product market virtually assured that plaintiff would prevail. No other case requiring a newspaper to carry advertising it preferred not to—excepting a line of cases in which newspapers had violated a pre-existing contract[72]—has apparently been decided on antitrust or other grounds.

More typically, a competitor complains of an exclusive service contract, as the Woodbury *Daily Times* did when it was unable to subscribe to the Los Angeles *Times*-Washington *Post* news service.[73] In the *Woodbury* case, the district court assessed the reasonableness of the exclusive subscription. The judge found that exclusivity was critical to the competitive value of intellectual property in general, and to the newspaper industry in particular. Without exclusivity, the value of almost all syndicated materials would be diminished. The plaintiff's argument that *this* service was unique was rejected. First, the restriction did not impede the flow of news. The *Daily Times* remained free to generate its own news stories, or for that matter, to subscribe to a large number of other available alternative news services. The court indicated that exclusivity serves the marketplace of ideas—the intellectual market—by forcing even more coverage from various sources. Given the rapid increase in supplemental news services in recent years, the court's argument is likely to gain strength.[74]

Despite a track record of plaintiffs' failing in exclusive subscription or syndication cases, a record detailed in the *Daily Times* case, competitors continue to pursue this type of claim.[75]

Tying Arrangements

Tying arrangements were discussed earlier. The leading case is the 1957 *Kansas City* case analyzed in the material on market definition. Few claims either of tying or of price discrimination succeed, in large part because of the difficulty of proof under the Sherman Act. Although these practices are also prohibited under the Clayton Act, its provisions apply only when commodities are involved. There is some difference of opinion as to whether newspapers are a commodity or a service. Conflicting federal district court cases have determined that newspaper advertising is not a commodity[76] but that newspapers overall are a commodity.[77] Busterna argues that the "essence" of a newspaper is intangible and therefore a service: information and advertising attention.[78] This tangible versus intangible analysis, although required to apply the statutes, misses a critical economic fact. That a newspaper is delivered in tangible form (ink and paper) elevates form over function. Anything scarce and measurable, such as newshole or ad space, should be regarded as a commodity. Classic services, such as those provided by accountants or lawyers, are not capable of objective measurement or valuation, and hence are properly considered services. The statutory distinction between commodities and services is based at least in part on the traditional assumption that services are more evanescent, an assumption which is itself questionable (see Chapter 9). A plaintiff should not be relegated to a stricter proof solely because of the label used.

Merger and Collusion

Although these two claims are brought under separate portions of the Clayton and Sherman acts respectively, they have one major point in common. Each requires the participation of two or more firms. Merger allegations fall under Section 7 of the Clayton Act. The *Times-Mirror* case is the leading case. The statute prohibits mergers which substantially lessen competition or tend to create a monopoly in a market. And since market is defined locally, the anti-merger provision has not been applied in the context of chain acquisitions of newspapers in different communities. Since there is usually no competition among dailies in the market, there can be no lessening of competition.

If there is to be activity in merger claims, it is likely to be in situations such as where a daily newspaper begins to buy weekly newspapers and shoppers within its geographic market. If the product market overlaps, as it should for advertising, this type of horizontal merger may be actionable, although exceptionally hard to prove.[79] A merger need not be with a direct competitor to give rise to a complaint. Merger of printing or other facilities by a dominant newspaper firm with an intent to wipe out a specific competitor, although indirect, may arguably fall within the ambit of antitrust. So far that argument seems to have failed.[80]

Collusion implies conspiracy between at least two firms. In many cases, a collusion claim accompanies another charge. For example, in many cases a pattern of arguably predatory pricing will also appear to be a result of concerted action. It makes sense to piggy-back the claims.[81] Predation concerns the *effects* of allegedly anticompetitive behavior, while collusion concerns the *intenion* of stifling competition. But the same body of evidence may serve to prove both.

The Tucson litigation is the most well-known example of collusion in newspaper antitrust. The government charged that the joint operating agreement between the Tucson *Daily Citizen* and the Arizona *Daily Star* violated both the Sherman and Clayton acts. The agreement dates to 1940, and was extended in 1953 to run until 1990. It was later extended again, to 2015. A jointly owned company, Tucson Newspapers, Inc., was established. Advertising, production, and circulation were all jointly controlled. Profits were pooled. And principals with either newspaper were forbidden from starting competing businesses. In *United States v. Citizen Publishing Co.*,[82] the Supreme Court upheld a trial decision finding against the defendants on all charges.

The defense was based on the failing company doctrine, which holds that merger cannot be anticompetitive if the acquired company was doomed to go out of business.[83] It was argued that the *Citizen* was the failing newspaper. But there was no evidence that, as the Court put it, the joint agreement was the "last straw" for the *Citizen*. Even if the joint agreement had been the last straw, approval under the failing company doctrine seems inappropriate. Here a company was created, not taken over by another.

As a result of the case, the 19 joint operating agreements then in existence became technically illegal. This situation was short-lived. Congress passed the Newspaper Preservation Act the very next year.

THE NEWSPAPER PRESERVATION ACT

So much has been written about joint operating agreements and the Newspaper Preservation Act[84] since the statute's passage in 1970[85] that this analysis will be brief, focusing on the statute itself. The NPA was passed because Congress accepted the argument that newspapers in most cities are natural monopolies. The continued pattern since 1970 of newspapers closing in large cities, despite the NPA, is proof of the argument and also telling evidence that the NPA has not preserved many newspapers. On June 10, 1990, the Knoxville *News-Sentinel* and the Knoxville *Journal* announced dissolution of their recent JOA, which left 19 JOAs.

The act provides a limited exemption from antitrust—in other words, legalized collusion in the form of price fixing, profit pooling, and market allocation. A proposed joint operating agreement must be approved by the U.S. Attorney General. The practice has been for administrative hearings to be held prior to actual decision by the Attorney General. Approval of a joint operating agreement preserves the presence of two newspapers but by allowing a joint monopoly effectively precludes future competitors in a market. Congress weighed the pros and cons and opted for the surer thing, keeping two newspapers. Congress' stated concern was to aid the intellectual market.

The basic approach of the act was to modify how a firm qualifies for exemption. A paper need not be failing, but only in "probable danger of financial failure,"[86] to qualify for the antitrust exemption. The other partner newspaper was assumed to be financially healthy by the act.

Only two key legal issues have emerged. The first was the constitutionality of the NPA. It was challenged in two cases.[87]

Both federal district court cases upheld the act against a claim that it violates the freedom of the press guaranteed in the First Amendment. Both lower court cases, however, predate the creation by the Supreme Court of a rule holding than differential treatment of the press is presumptively unconstitutional as a violation of freedom of the press (see Chapter 9).[88] If the rule against differential treatment is applied strictly, the NPA obviously comes within its scope.

The second key legal issue has concerned what is needed to show that a newspaper is in probable danger of financial failure.

In *Committee for an Independent P-I v. Hearst Corp.*,[89] opponents of a proposed JOA between the Seattle *Post-Intelligencer* and the Seattle *Times* contended that the *Post-Intelligencer* was not in probable danger of failure because there was a possibility that it could become profitable again. The court said it was sufficient to show that a paper was suffering losses which were more than likely irreversible. To decide otherwise would require waiting until the newspaper had lost the viability to even enter into a JOA. The court also refused to require the newspaper to show that it was unable to find an outside buyer. In addition, the case clearly established that the financial assessment is to be based on the two specific newspapers in the market, not on the financial condition of any parent companies. Otherwise, profitable chain papers in other markets would be forced to subsidize the unprofitable.

The issue was renewed when the Detroit *Free Press* and Detroit *News* filed for a joint operating agreement in 1986. In previous JOA applications, the failing newspaper was readily detectible—via lower circulation and lower advertising revenues. In Detroit, by contrast, the *Free Press*, the paper claimed to be failing, was only slightly behind the *News* in circulation, but considerably behind in advertising revenues. Following hearings, both an administrative law judge and the Antitrust Division of the Department of Justice were on record opposing the JOA. The administrative law judge had concluded that the *Free Press* was not a failing newspaper. He further concluded that both papers, each of which was suffering losses, could become profitable simply by ending their bitter, competitive practices, most notably the lowest metro daily cover prices in the nation. In August 1988, then Attorney General Edwin Meese nonetheless approved. He said that the *Free Press* had entered the "zone" of probability and that losses were not reversible by any unilateral means, and made it clear that he preferred interpreting the act in favor of merger.

Challenged in federal district court, Meese's decision was upheld.[90] On appeal, the decision was again upheld.[91] The appeals court majority emphasized the narrow scope of review. Since the Attorney General was expressly given the authority to interpret the NPA, under the Administrative Procedure Act his decision could not be overturned unless it could be proved the decision was arbitrary, capricious, or an abuse of discretion. In plain words, those challenging the Detroit JOA were required to show that Meese had no good, rational basis for his decision.

The court determined that Meese was well within his authority under the NPA to decide that a newspaper on the "brink" of the circulation spiral was a failing newspaper. Meese agreed with the Seattle rule that it was sufficient to show a return to profitability was unlikely; but he added his own twist concerning an inability to reverse losses through unilateral action, thus recognizing that the Detroit newspaper war itself could be resolved only through the death of one paper or creation of a JOA. Critics of the JOA pointed to the immediate return to profits possible by raising the prices of both papers; but critics generally overlooked the effects of raising prices. The *Free Press* had raised Sunday prices before the *News* did, and had taken a circulation beating. It was unlikely to risk another.

On May 1, 1989, the Supreme Court agreed to hear the case, stunning all observers. The Court had declined the chance to review earlier JOA cases. Since the Court does not disclose its reasons for hearing a case, it was hard to speculate. Parties in the case prepared their briefs by focusing on the administrative law issues of the interpretive authority of the Attorney General. But the appeals court approach to those issues was consistent with a long line of administrative law cases. On the other hand, it seemed unlikely that the Court anticipated addressing constitutional issues, since those had not been raised in earlier proceedings. But it could be argued that the constitutional issues should have been raised because of new First Amendment interpretations.

The long build-up was for nought. The Court technically affirmed the court of appeals in November 1989 when it divided 4-4; Justice Byron White did not participate.[92] The *News* and *Free Press* joined operations before the month ended. The tie vote is evidence that the vitality of the Newspaper Preservation Act itself is a close matter, and students of the act should consider what the effects of its demise might be.[93] The Detroit JOA, just as the Seattle JOA, was delayed by legal battles. By contrast, the partial merger of the *Dispatch* and *Daily Record* in York, Pennsylvania, took place one day less than a year after the application was filed with the Attorney General.[94] A citizens group in York chose to seek repeal of the act rather than to continue legal challenges.

While the legal, economic, and journalistic issues raised by the NPA continue to fascinate observers of the newspaper scene, the importance of those issues dwindles as the number of competing daily newspapers dwindles (see Chapter 4).[95] In part as a result of the intensity of debate over the Detroit situation, Congress held oversight hearings in summer 1989 to consider amending the NPA. Legislation to repeal the Newspaper Preservation Act was introduced by a Michigan congressman.[96]

ENDNOTES

1. 15 U.S.C. secs. 1801-1804.
2. U.S. CONST. amend. I.: "Congress shall make no law...abridging the freedom of speech, or of the press..."

3. 15 U.S.C. sec. 41 et seq.
4. Charles R. McManis, *The Law of Unfair Trade Practices* (St. Paul, MN.: West Publishing Co., 1983).
5. See, for example, "FTC urged to keep co-op rules," *presstime*, August 1989, p. 38.
6. S. Chesterfield Oppenheim, Glen E. Weston, Peter B. Maggs and Roger E. Schechter, *Unfair Trade Practices and Consumer Protection: Cases and Comments* 4th ed. (St. Paul, MN.: West Publishing Co., 1983), pp. 758-769.
7. 15 U.S.C. sec. 1 et seq.
8. Edwin Mansfield, *Principles of Microeconomics* 4th ed. (New York: W.W. Norton & Co., 1983), p. 261.
9. Richard A. Posner, *Antitrust Law: An Economic Perspective* (Chicago: The University of Chicago Press, 1976), pp. 29-30.
10. Contintental T.V., Inc. v. GTE Sylvania, Inc., 433 U.S. 36 (1977).
11. 15 U.S.C. sec. 15.
12. 15 U.S.C. sec. 18.
13. Brown Shoe Co. v. United States, 370 U.S. 294 (1962).
14. 15 U.S.C sec 18a.
15. Posner, *op cit.*, p. 236.
16. There are many analogous punitive provisions in statutes addressing violations that are difficult to apprehend or prove. Tony Atwater, Todd F. Simon & Laurie Thomas, "Satellite News Feeds: Protecting a Transient Interest," paper presented to the Mass Communication and Society Division, Association for Education in Journalism and Mass Communication convention, San Antonio, Texas, August 1987, pp. 24-28.
17. Raymond B. Nixon, "Trends in U.S. Newspaper Ownership: Concentration With Competition," *Gazette*, 14:3:181-93 (1968).
18. Associated Press v. National Labor Relations Board, 301 U.S. 103 (1937).
19. 326 U.S. 1 (1945).
20. *Ibid.* at 20.
21. Grosjean v. American Press, 297 U.S. 233 (1936).
22. 326 U.S. at 32.
23. John C. Busterna, "Antitrust in the 1980s: An Analysis of 45 Newspaper Actions," *Newspaper Research Journal*, Winter 1988, pp. 25-36.
24. Donald M. Gillmor, Jerome A. Barron, Todd F. Simon & Herbert A. Terry, *Mass Communication Law: Cases and Comment* 5th ed (St. Paul, MN.: West Publishing Co., 1990), p. 544.
25. *Tiftarea Shopper v. Georgia Shopper*, 786 F.2d 1115 (11th Cir. 1986).
26. *Standard Oil Co. v. United States*, 337 U.S. 293, 299 n. 5 (1949).
27. *United States v. Philadelphia National Bank*, 374 U.S. 321 (1963); see also, *Brown Shoe Co. v. United States*, 370 U.S. 294 (1962).
28. *United States v. E.I. DuPont de Nemours & Co.*, 351 U.S. 377 (1956).
29. *Telex Corp. v. IBM Corp.*, 510 F.2d 894 (10th Cir. 1975).
30. *JBL Enterprises, Inc. v. Jhirmack Enterprises, Inc.*, 698 F.2d 1011 (9th Cir. 1983).
31. *Sales and Advertising Promotion v. Donrey*, 598 F.Supp. 538 (N.D. Okla. 1984).

ANTITRUST AND MARKET REGULATION 211

32. 274 F.Supp. 606 (C.D.Cal. 1967), aff'd per curiam, 390 U.S. 712 (1968).
33. 274 F.Supp. at 289.
34. Gillmor et al, *op cit.*, p. 551.
35. 274 F. Supp. at 290-292.
36. 616 F.Supp. 502 (D.N.J. 1985), aff'd, 791 F.2d 924 (3d Cir. 1986).
37. *United States v. Chicago Tribune-New York News Syndicate, Inc.*, 1975 Trade Cas. [CCH] par. 60,185 (S.D.N.Y. 1975).
38. *Main Street Publishers v. Landmark Communications*, 16 Med. L. Rep. 1402 (N.D. Miss. 1988).
39. *People's Press v. Yazoo Publishing Co.*, 12 Med. L. Rep. 1249 (S.D. Miss. 1985).
40. 342 U.S. 143 (1951).
41. 345 U.S. 594 (1953).
42. *Ibid.* at 614.
43. 240 F.2d 643 (8th Cir.), *cert. den.*, 354 U.S. 923 (1957).
44. 274 F.Supp. at 618.
45. John C. Busterna, "Daily Newspaper Chains and the Antitrust Laws," *Journalism Monographs* No. 110 (March 1989), pp. 6-8.
46. 394 U.S. 131 (1969).
47. 780 F.2d 735 (9th Cir. 1985).
48. Busterna, "Antitrust in the 1980s: An Analysis of 45 Newspaper Actions," *op cit.*, p. 36.
49. 9 Med. L. Rep. 1761 (E.D.Va. 1983).
50. *Ibid.* at 1763-1766.
51. 598 F.Supp. 538 (N.D. Okla. 1984).
52. Posner, *op cit.*, pp. 28-29.
53. Busterna, "Antitrust in the 1980s: An Analysis of 45 Newspaper Actions," *op cit.*, p. 28.
54. *Ibid.*
55. *International Air Industries, Inc. v. American Excelsior Co.*, 517 F.2d 71 (5th Cir. 1975).
56. Robert G. Picard, "The Relationship Between Newspaper Costs and Predation Lawsuits," *Newspaper Research Journal*, Winter 1990, pp. 12-25.
57. *Main Street Publishers, Inc. v. Landmark Communications, Inc.*, 16 Med. L. Rep. 1402 (N.D.Miss. 1988).
58. 9 Med. L. Rep. at 1767-1768.
59. 601 F.2d 48 (2d Cir. 1979).
60. 11 Med. L. Rep. at 1206.
61. *Walker Process Equipment v. Food Machinery*, 382 U.S. 172 (1965).
62. *Drinkwine v. Federated Publications, Inc.*, 780 F.2d 735 (9th Cir. 1985).
63. Oppenheim et al., *op cit.*, pp. 947-952.
64. *FTC v. Anheuser-Busch, Inc.*, 363 U.S. 536 (1960).
65. "Supreme Court eases pricing policy restrictions," *presstime*, April 1990, p. 58.
66. *Ibi.*
67. 727 F.2d 692 (8th Cir. 1984).
68. 876 F.2d 266 (2d Cir. 1989).

212 THE ECONOMICS & REGULATIONS OF U.S. NEWSPAPERS

69. 15 Med. L. Rep. 2451 (7th Cir. 1988).
70. *Newberry v. Washington Post Co.*, 438 F.Supp. 470 (D.D.C. 1977).
71. 682 F.2d 274 (1st Cir. 1982).
72. Gillmor et al, op cit., pp. 540-541.
73. *Woodbury Daily Times v. Los Angeles Times-Washington Post News Service*, 616 F.Supp. 502 (D.N.J. 1985).
74. Rolf Rykken, "Supplemental Wires Vie for Clients," *presstime*, May 1989, pp. 14-18.
75. *Oakland Tribune, Inc. v. The Chronicle Publishing Co.*, 762 F.2d 1374 (9th Cir. 1985); see also, "Dallas feud starts anew in court over transfer of features," *presstime*, September 1989, p. 47.
76. *National Tire Wholesale, Inc. v. Washington Post Co.*, 441 F.Supp. 81 (D.D.C. 1977).
77. *Sun Communications, Inc. v. Waters Publications, Inc.*, 466 F.Supp. 387 (W.D.Mo. 1979).
78. Busterna, "Antitrust in the 1980s: An Analysis of 45 Newspaper Actions," op cit., p. 31.
79. *Sun Newspapers, Inc. v. Omaha World-Herald Co.*, No. CV82-6-627, slip op. (D.Neb.), aff'd, 1983-2 Trade Cas. [CCH], par. 65,538 (8th Cir. 1983); *United States v. Tribune Co. and Sentinel Star Co.*, No. 82-260 (M.D.Fla. 1982).
80. *Sun Newspapers*, op cit.
81. *Tiftarea Shopper v. Georgia Shopper*, 786 F.2d 1115 (11th Cir. 1986).
82. 394 U.S. 131 (1969).
83. *International Shoe Co. v. FTC*, 280 U.S. 291 (1930).
84. 15 U.S.C. secs. 1802-1804.
85. For a critique from a journalism perspective, see, John C. Busterna, "Improving Editorial and Economic Competition with a Modified Newspaper Preservation Act," *Newspaper Research Journal* (Summer 1987), p. 71; for a critique from a legal perspective, see, John P. Patkus, "The Newspaper Preservation Act: Why It Fails to Preserve Newspapers," *Akron Law Review*, 11: 435 (1984).
86. 15 U.S.C. sec. 1802 (5).
87. *City and County of Honolulu v. Honolulu Newspaper Agency, Inc.*, 7 Med. L. Rep. 2495 (D.Haw. 1981); *Bay Guardian Co. v. Chronicle Publishing Co.*, 344 F.Supp. 1155 (N.D.Cal. 1972).
88. *Minneapolis Star and Tribune Co. v. Minnesota Commissioner of Revenue*, 460 U.S. 575 (1983).
89. 704 F.2d 467 (9th Cir. 1983).
90. *Michigan Citizens for an Independent Press v. Attorney General*, 695 F.Supp. 1216 (D.D.C. 1988).
91. *Michigan Citizens for an Independent Press v. Thornburgh*, 868 F.2d 1285 (D.C.Cir. 1989).
92. *Michigan Citizens for an Independent Press v. Thornburgh*, No. 110 S. Ct. 398 (1989).
93. Stephen Lacy, "Impact of Repealing the Newspaper Preservation Act," *Newspaper Research Journal*, Winter 1990, pp. 2-11.

94. "After York approval, JOA focus moves west," *presstime*, April 1990, p. 50.
95. Mary A. Anderson, "JOA Law May Be At a Turning Point," *presstime*, October 1989, pp. 6-9.
96. Bryan Gruley, "Pursell plans challenge of JOA law," *Detroit News*, June 1, 1990, p. 1E, col. 2.

8

Newspaper Economics and Antitrust

In the simple world of perfect competition, individual firms cannot cut production to increases profits; nor can they set prices that gouge consumers or keep other firms from entering a market. Such a world is a useful model for understanding economic behavior, but in reality, it rarely exists. Instead, most companies face markets with few firms. Some markets get this way because of the nature of the product involved or because of technological efficiency. Other markets get this way because some firms don't play within the rules set forward by models of competition. As a result of this latter type of behavior, the United States has a set of antitrust laws designed to reduce the negative effects of unacceptable business practices.

Antitrust laws are designed to correct abuses in the economic system that produce inefficient allocation of resources. Antitrust laws are economic in nature and are based on social assumptions of appropriate economic behavior. The test in an economic case is whether particular economic behavior tends to be anticompetitive.[1]

This chapter briefly reviews the economic basis of antitrust laws and how they have been applied to the newspaper industry. Then the problems of applying antitrust will be examined, with suggestions for the future.

THE ECONOMICS OF ANTITRUST LAWS

The basic justifications for antitrust are economic, although Posner lists three sociopolitical arguments for antitrust law.[2] Busterna listed two general justifications for antitrust.[3] The first is the maximization of consumer welfare, or the value of society's wealth. The second is the maximization of some combination of several elements that include consumer's welfare, producers welfare, the preservation of small businesses and other considerations. Busterna's second justification includes some of Posner's sociopolitical reasons.

Which of the justifications is appropriate depends upon the assumptions concerning economic behavior and the role of government in economic and social behavior. Here it is assumed that all industries need not be treated the same. Indeed, it is the assumption of this book and the First Amendment that the newspaper industry plays a role in society that most industries do not. Before evaluating the impact of this unusual position on antitrust, it would be helpful to review the general justifications for antitrust law. Such a review must start with the concept of consumer surplus.

Economic Justification for Antitrust Laws

Basic to antitrust law is the economic analysis of the impact of monopoly on consumers. This is the *consumer's surplus* argument. This analysis attempts to demonstrate the overall impact of monopoly market power on consumer utility.[4] According to economic theory of perfect competition, firms cannot charge different prices to different buyers. If they did, another company would charge a lesser price and attract the buyers of the product. As a result, all firms sell at one competitively set price. This price means that firms can only make normal profits, rather than the surplus profits that charging different prices to different consumers would generate.

The value of this nonnormal profit would accrue to the consumer in the absence of monopoly power and is called consumer's surplus. In Figure 8.1, the total value of the product in a market is shown by the area $0P_2BEC_1$. This area is defined by the point where supply equals demand (at point E). This is also the point at which marginal costs, represented by the supply curve (P_1E), equals marginal revenue, represented by the demand curve (DE). With a large number of firms, the marginal cost to any firm is a straight line parallel with the horizontal axis. No one firm can charge more than the price (P_1) determined by the intersection of the supply and demand curve. If a firm did charge more, consumers could substitute the cheaper product of another firm. No firm would charge less than this price because, if it did, it would lose money.

The individual firm's demand curve in the market is represented by the line P_1E, which is also the industry supply curve. This horizontal demand curve for the firm represents the fact that no one firm can affect prices. Each firm then has the price equal to marginal revenue. The market demand curve is DE.

As a result of this interaction of supply and demand, firms produce a quantity equal to C_1 at a price of P_1. The consumers pay the equivalent of $P_1 0 C_1 E$ and get a value of $0P_2BEC_1$. The difference in the area (DP_1E) is the consumer surplus.

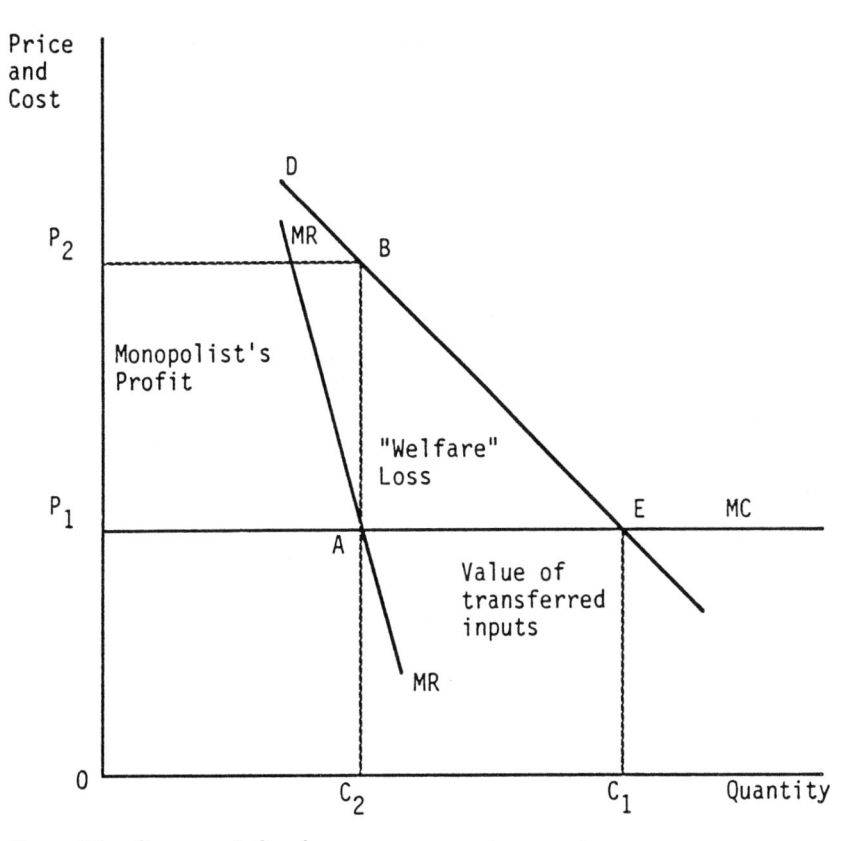

Figure 8.1. Consumer's Surplus
This analysis illustrates the economic impact of monopoly power. In a perfectly competitive market, the quantity produced of a good would equal C_1 at price P_1. When a monopoly forms, the seller can sets prices. The result is production of quantity C_2 at price P_2. The value shown the rectangle AEC_1C_2 is transferred from the consumers to the monopolist when a monopoly forms, and the value represented by the triangle AEB is simply lost.

When a firm becomes a monopoly in the market, the firm demand curve becomes the same as the market demand curve (DE). With a negatively sloping firm demand curve, the marginal revenue curve is always below the demand curve. Since companies maximize profits at the point where marginal revenue equals marginal cost, the new level of output will be C_2, instead of C_1 as in a competitive market. A lower output means a higher price, which is P_2. The value of the output is redistributed as a result. The value represented by the area under C_1EAC_2 is transferred to other goods and the amount equal to P_1P_2BA is transferred to the firm as monopoly profit. The area under ABE is not transferred to anyone and becomes a deadweight loss. Thus, little remains of the surplus value (the amount under DP_1E) that flowed to the consumer under a competitive market.

The negative impact of monopoly, then, is that it creates overpricing and underproduction. This transfers utility or value from the consumer to the producer and results in some being lost altogether. Not all economists accept this consumer surplus argument. Some argue that the consumer surplus concept is an inappropriate use of the demand curve.[5] Others argue that the impact of monopoly is slight. Harberger estimated a misallocation of only .1 percent.[6] However, in answer to Harberger, Posner said the misallocation found represented the costs of monopoly assuming the existence of antitrust laws, which would make this figure a measure of the failure of the laws.[7]

As mentioned in Chapter 4, a shortcoming of this traditional analysis is its dependence on price as the important determinant of output. The analysis presented in that chapter shows that newspaper monopoly power can reduce newspaper quality as well as increase price.

The economic effects of monopoly are not the only justifications for the existence of antitrust. Posner list three sociopolitical reasons monopoly power should be regulated. First, some have argued that monopoly power redistributes wealth from the poor to the rich. Second, the concentration of monopoly power results in efforts to manipulate the political process to protect those with monopoly power. Third, the development of monopolies prevents smaller business from surviving, which runs counter to the notion in our society that the promotion of small business is a desired goal. Posner, however, rejects the sociopolitical arguments and maintains that antitrust should be based on the economic implications.

Busterna deals with basically the same types of arguments.[8] The consumer welfare approach deals with whether a particular case will result in a net loss, a gain, or no impact on consumer welfare. His second approach calls for courts to judge cases by some broad set of values and standards that may or may not be consistent with the impact on consumer welfare. Busterna holds that either approach could be used to justify the application of antitrust to newspapers.

It should be noted that the sociopolitical arguments raised by Posner and advocated by others[9] have always been popular. After all, who wants to redistribute wealth to the wealthy, or concentrate manipulative power, or hurt small business? The problem with the arguments of those who advocate affirmative action in the competitive sphere is that the antitrust laws just are not written that way. The are designed and have been interpreted to prevent abuses, thereby limiting the negative effects of anticompetitive behavior. If antitrust accomplishes actual good, it does so indirectly, perhaps even inadvertently.

As a matter of economics, rejection of sociopolitical arguments by Posner rests on several assumptions. First, the justification for antitrust activities must be generalizable to all industries. Second, economic and sociopolitical activities and consequences can be easily separated for analysis. Third, the basis for applying antitrust law must be consistent with the economic knowledge and theory that was available at the time the antitrust laws were passed. These assumptions will be examined more thoroughly below.

Natural Monopolies

Antitrust laws may not be applicable to all monopoly or oligopoly markets. The behavior that is collusive or exclusive in one market may not be in another. Illegal behavior depends on the intent of the firm and the nature of the industry.

For example, a firm may be the only one in a market not because of predatory behavior but because it is a a natural monopoly. *Natural monopolies*, such as local telephone companies, usually develop because of economies of scale. Such industries have economies that are so efficient that only one firm will survive. These types of industries are usually directly regulated in an effort to limit their accumulation of monopoly profits.

A similar situation arises in oligopolies, where noncollusive managerial decisions can have the same result on prices as collusion. An example is a market with two firms that produce widgets. They are similar, but one produces blue widgets and one produces red widgets. In year one, they both charged a dollar for a widget. The blue-widget firm raised its price to $1.05 at the beginning of year two. If the red-widget firm thinks its widgets are good substitutes for blue widgets, it may hold its price at the first-year level. This would allow it to gain some of the other firm's business. If, however, blue and red widgets are not good substitutes, the red-widget firm may decide to increase its price as well. The second scenario means both increase prices. The increases did not involve collusion, but the result would be the same.

Antitrust laws cannot prevent natural newspaper monopoly power. Such monopoly power develops over time for reasons discussed in Chapter 4. However, there can be unnatural monopoly power even in a market that would become a single-newspaper town in the long run. *Unnatural monopoly power* comes from a premature natural monopoly. It results from practices that are illegal under antitrust laws even in markets that are destined to lose all but one daily newspaper.

The negative impact of unnatural monopoly power would be similar to that of an illegal monopoly established in any market. The economic difference between unnatural and another form of illegal monopoly power is that the cumulative impact across time would be less for unnatural monopoly power. The cumulative impact of an illegal monopoly starts with the establishment of the monopoly and last until something happens to remove the monopoly. The cumulative impact of the unnatural monopoly is the utility lost from the time the unnatural monopoly starts until the time that the natural monopoly would have developed. Although there is no way to actually pinpoint this time period, the inability to quantify does not alleviate the negative impact of illegal practices.

IMPACT OF NEWSPAPER MONOPOLY POWER

The unusual nature of the newspaper industry makes it a difficult and confusing area for the application of antitrust law. This difficulty comes from several factors. First, the newspaper industry has a socially and politically sanctioned function within United States society. Newspapers' role of serving the intellectual market stems from the First Amendment and the assumptions underlying it. Second, newspapers are joint commodities. As such, classical economic theory underlying antitrust laws is inadequate for dealing with the industry. This section will discuss the impact of newspaper monopoly power on the three markets and the current arguments concerning the application of antitrust to newspapers. Finally, a discussion of possible future directions concerning newspaper and antitrust will be addressed.

Because newspapers are joint commodities that have a mandated social function, the application of antitrust is not as easy as with other industries. An individual can buy a shoe and nothing else, but a person who buys a general circulation newspaper must buy the advertising with the news-editorial and vice versa. The person cannot be forced to read the advertising, but the purchase is made jointly. This joint commodity nature unites the advertising and information market. The role of the news-editorial pages, and sometimes advertisements, in the intellectual market further clouds the economic and, therefore, antitrust pictures. Although these markets are connected, they will be dealt with separately for analytical reasons.

Information Market and Monopoly Power

The consumer surplus argument does apply to the information market. As pointed out in Chapter 4, monopolies do charge higher circulation rates for copies of their newspapers. So, part of the value that the lower competitive price presented to consumers is transferred to the newspaper firm. The actual impact on an individual reader is relatively small. The difference in price may range from 5 to 15 cents per copy. However, the cumulative impact in a market becomes much greater.

Suppose the closing of a daily within a market resulted in a nickel increase in daily home delivery price. Over a year, each reader is paying $18.25 more for the newspaper. When this price increase is multiplied by the number of subscribers, the total loss of value becomes much greater. If the surviving newspaper has a circulation of 100,000 after the competitor closed, this is a transfer of $1.8 million in value from readers to the newspaper firm. This value would continue to be transferred as long as the monopoly power exists.

This example is conservative in its estimates. Most price increases due to monopoly power will be greater than a nickel. In larger markets, the accumulated value to the newspaper firm will be greater.

While the loss due to consumer surplus in the information market is worth considering, its impact is probably not as great as it could be because newspaper firms traditionally are less aggressive in pricing than are firms in other industries. This stems from the importance of circulation in selling advertising. A more significant impact may occur in terms of quality. The "quality consumer surplus" argument presented in Chapter 4 is applicable here.

Intense competition results in more financial commitment. Newspapers with intense competition tend to have larger newsholes, more reporters for a given amount of space, and a larger number of wire services. The result of this increased financial commitment is increased quality.[10] The exact loss of value is difficult to determine because quality is not as easily measurable as price and the actual value lost from decreased quality will vary from market to market. Yet, the loss is real.

Although the loss of quality is difficult to measure from a reader's point of view, the gain for the newspaper firm is not. The savings from a smaller newshole, fewer reporters, and fewer news services can be measured. It is again a reason the newspaper firms profit from monopoly power.

The financial gain for the newspaper firm is only a partial measure of utility lost by readers. It is impossible to measure the impact on readers due to a loss of information. However, it is not difficult to see the impact of a relatively small investment of time, money, and personnel in a story. The Watergate story, for example, did not tie up a great deal of resources at *The Washington Post*, although it did involve great risk. So, while the financial gains to a firm are not a good measure of lost reader utility, they may represent a minimal measure of lost utility. A greater loss, but one that is difficult to measure, would be the issues and events not covered by a newspaper with monopoly power because of reduced financial commitment.

222   THE ECONOMICS & REGULATIONS OF U.S. NEWSPAPERS

The combined loss of value from price increases and decline of quality argues against the desirability of newspaper monopoly power from a reader's viewpoint. There is also an impact on the advertising market.

Advertising Market and Monopoly

The loss of value in the advertising market is analogous to the loss from consumer surplus, but the analysis is slightly different because the initial market was an oligopoly rather than a competitive market. The impact is shown in Figure 8.2, which represents the market supply and demand curves.

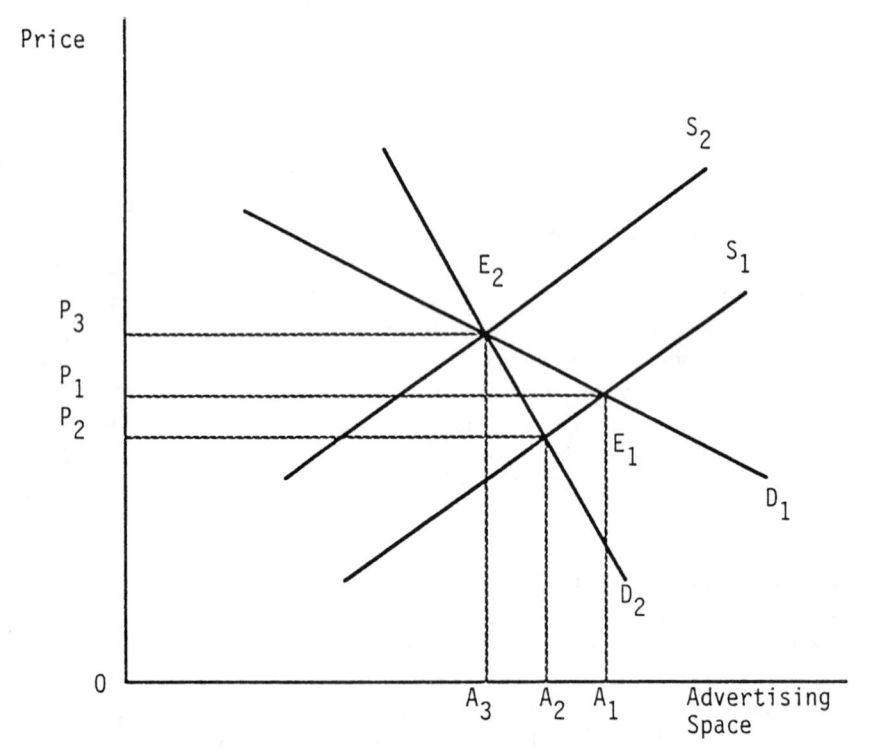

Figure 8.2. The Impact of Monopoly on Advertising Space and Price
The market supply (S_1) and demand (D_1) curves before a monopoly are in equilibrium at point E_1 with price P_1 and amount of advertising space of A_1. After one newspaper closes, demand decreases and the demand curve becomes more steep, changing to D_2, because demand becomes more inelastic with fewer good substitutes. The surviving newspaper would provide less advertising space at a lower price if it retained its initial supply curve. The result is a shift in supply curve to S_2, where the newspaper provides less space (A_3) for a higher price (P_3) at the equilibrium point E_2. The newspaper firm also enjoys higher profits at E_2.

The initial market supply and demand curves are represented by curves S_1 and D_1. These curves are elastic with respect to price because of the presence of two newspapers. The equilibrium point at E_1 results in a market price of P_1 and a total supply of advertising space of A_1. Suppose one of the two newspaper ceases production. The result is a drop in demand from D_1 to D_2. This drop results from the overlapping advertising that occurred during competition. For example, larger department stores will often advertise in both newspapers in order to reach the entire market.

Not only does the demand drop, but the elasticity of the demand curve changes as well. With two newspapers, the elasticity is greater. If one paper increases prices greatly, there is an easily substitutable alternative. With the second paper closed, such an option ceases to exist. There is less of a reaction to price changes with one newspaper than with two.

If the surviving newspaper firm makes no adjustment in its supply, the result would be a lower price at P_2 and reduced space at A_2. However, since the new monopolist has more power to control price and available space, the firm will reduce its supply by moving the supply curve to S_2. This will cause a new equilibrium point at E_2. At this point, the new amount of advertising space available is A_3 at a price of P_3. This space is less and the price is greater than with competition.

The overall loss of value is determined by subtracting the area within $OP_3E_2A_3$, which represents total value after the monopoly is established, from the area under $P_1E_1A_1O$, which represents total value before the monopoly. Part of this value accrues to the newspaper firm in the form of increased profit, and part is a loss to both advertisers and the newspaper firm.

For example, a competitive newspaper charging $1 a column inch for display advertising and selling 1,000 inches would have display ad revenue of $1,000. Once the competing newspaper closes, the same newspaper might charge $1.25 an inch. This means the paper could sell only 800 inches and still make revenues of $1,000, or it could sell 1,000 inches and have revenues of $1,250. In the former case, profits would increase because costs would decline from having to produce less ad space. In the latter case, profits would increase from having greater revenues.

As with the information market, it is easy to see that monopoly power has a negative impact on the advertising market. Advertisers pay more money for less space. The exact impact will depend on the slopes of the new demand and supply curves and the ultimate price of advertising. The slopes depend on the prices and quality of substitutes.

As discussed in Chapter 2, some types of newspaper advertising have low cross-elasticity with other forms of advertising media. Advertisers priced out of the newspaper advertising tend to move toward less-desirable substitutes, such as shoppers and direct mail.

One might argue that advertisers get an advantage from monopoly because the cost per 1,000 will be reduced by having more readers at a single newspaper. This could happen, but it would result only if the monopoly newspaper decided not to price its advertising as high as the market would allow, an unlikely situation in the long run. Evidence presented earlier indicates that newspaper monopolists do tend to change monopoly prices.

Intellectual Market and Monopoly

The measurement problems found in the information market are many times greater in the intellectual market. The impact of a particular idea or bit of information on the well-being of society is impossible to accurately quantify. However, the notion of ideas or bits of information in the intellectual market represents the basic units in the marketplace of ideas. The assumption of the First Amendment is that society is best served by the largest and broadest supply of ideas and bits of information regardless of source.[11] The importance of ideas and information to the evolution and survival of communities and societies is not erased by measurement problems. Nor do measurement problems negate the important role that newspapers play in the way society adjusts to problems.

Despite the measurement problems, a graphic illustration of the impact of monopoly on the intellectual market is possible. Figure 8.3 presents such an illustration. One underlying assumption is that the utility a community receives is positively correlated with the number of ideas and bits of information available. A second assumption is that the number of ideas and bits of information is negatively related to cost. As the cost of developing ideas and information increases, the number of ideas and bits of information will decrease.

The curves presented in Figure 8.3 are, in effect, supply and demand curves. No assumptions are made concerning the actual slopes of the curves because such an analysis is beyond the scope of this book and because such assumptions are unnecessary for this illustration. D_1 represents the utility that the community gets from the increase in ideas and bits of information with a competitive newspaper market. As the number increases, the utility increases. S_1 represents the supply of ideas and information available in relationship to cost in a market with competitive newspapers. As cost increases, ideas and information decrease. E_1 is the equilibrium of demand for ideas and supply available from all sources with newspaper competition. At E_1, there are I_1 ideas and bits of information available with a community utility of U_1.

If one newspaper closes, the supply will decline because the amount of information and opinion material produced by a surviving newspaper is

Community
Utility/
Cost

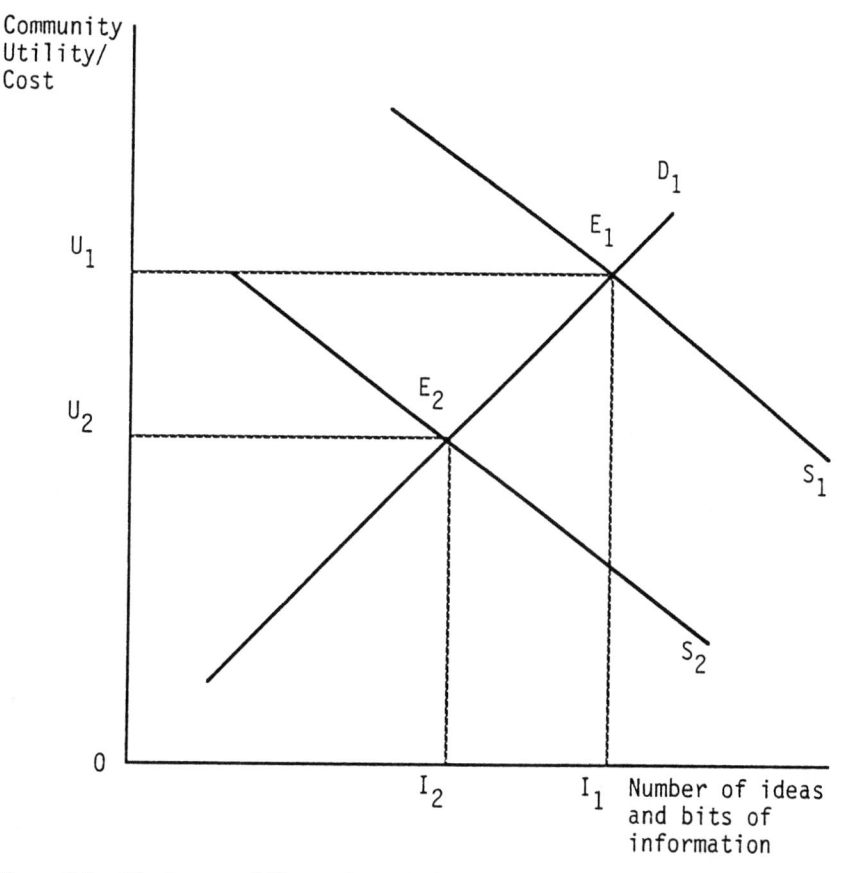

Figure 8.3. The Impact of Monopoly on the Intellectual Market
The demand for ideas and information is D_1, which shows that community utility increases as the number of ideas and bits of information increase. The initial supply of ideas is shown by S_1, which yields an equilibrium of E_1. When access to the intellectual market is limited by monopoly power, the supply curve shifts toward the origin, because access decreases, and gives a new equilibrium at E_2. This new equilibrium has lower costs for information and ideas, but it also provides less utility for the community.

less than that provided by two competitive newspapers.[12] The result is a new supply curve S_2. With the new supply curve, the equilibrium becomes E_2. At this point, the supply of information and ideas is I_2 and the community utility is U_2, both of which are lower than with competition. The utility lost is measured by subtracting the area under $U_2E_2I_2O$ from the area under $U_1E_1I_1O$.

The exact difference in these two areas is a function of many other variables. The loss would depend on how extensively the closing newspaper participated in the intellectual market and whether other media or interpersonal communication would step in to provide the information and ideas that would no longer be provided by the closed newspaper. Even if other media eventually developed into perfect substitutes—a most unlikely event—the community would temporarily and irrevocably lose utility.

Even though the effects are difficulty to quantify, the creation of a newspaper monopoly would have some degree of negative impact on the intellectual market. Fear of decreased newspaper competition causing fewer ideas to disseminate was the underlying value expressed by the Supreme Court in the *Associated Press* and other cases.[13]

Justifications for Applying Antitrust to Newspapers

Some scholars have questioned the applicability of antitrust to newspaper competition. Owen, for example, argues that direct competition is a disequilibrium condition and that any application of antitrust to this competition is doomed to failure.[14] He does suggest that antitrust would be helpful in dealing with umbrella competition. However, the tendency of most newspaper markets to develop natural monopoly power is no reason to declare open season on competition. The argument that being a natural monopoly should preclude enforcing antitrust is comparable to saying that the inevitability of death makes suicide and murder acceptable.

As mentioned above, some markets can become unnatural monopolies. The use of illegal means to force a monopoly earlier than would take place naturally has two negative results. First, it takes away a certain number of years in which the readers, advertisers, and community would enjoy the benefits of competition.

Second, an illegally created monopoly removes the ability of readers to decide which of the competing newspapers deserves to survive. In a closely contested market, the readers select which newspaper will survive because the advertising will usually follow the circulation. In effect, readers vote with their purchases over a period of years for the newspaper they would prefer to have after the market becomes a monopoly. This vote is made somewhat on the basis of price, but since there is a tendency of newspapers to match a competitor's price, the vote is made primarily on the basis of content. Anticompetitive behavior, such as predatory pricing, short-circuits this voting process.

If one accepts that antitrust enforcement is appropriate to the newspaper industry, the question of what standards to use for judging negative effects must be answered. As mentioned above, Posner argues that all antitrust should be applied only on the basis of economic analysis. These arguments are not accepted here, given his definition of economics.

As discussed previously, the limitation of antitrust to traditional economic analysis rest on three assumptions. First, it is assumed that the justifications for antitrust application should be consistent for all industries. This assumption ignores the special place in society of mass media in general and newspapers in particular. This special place was mentioned in *United States v. Times Mirror Co.* The court said, "It (the newspaper industry) has sufficient peculiar characteristics and uses which make it distinguishable from all other products."[15]

A second traditional assumption is that economic and sociopolitical aspects of the newspaper industry can be easily separated for analysis. While a separation can be made, such separation is arbitrary and ignores the reasons behind the First Amendment. Newspapers enjoy constitutional protection not because they sell information in the information market and advertising in the advertising market, but because they contribute significantly to the intellectual market.[16] This recognition was at the heart of the Supreme Court's ruling in the *Associated Press* case and has been applied in many later cases concerning economic effects on the press. The sociopolitical marketplace of ideas argument was a major reason the Court applied antitrust to newspapers in the first place. To ignore that is to elevate economic effects above content effects.

The final traditional assumption is that the basis for enforcing antitrust must be consistent with economic theory accepted when antitrust laws became law. The economic evaluation of monopoly is based on the tradeoff of loss due to the consumer surplus effect with increased production efficiencies that can be gained from monopolies.[17] In addition to this balancing act, externalities should also be considered.[18] These two approaches are applicable to the impacts discussed above on the information, advertising and intellectual markets. What is missing from this application is the impact on information quality. This absence is due to antitrust analysis being based on perfect competition models. The assumptions of these models are inappropriate for newspaper demand, as discussed in Chapter 2. Work on monopolistic competition and imperfect competition was not pursued to a high degree until the 1930s, after the basic antitrust laws were passed.[19] Economists know more now about nonperfect competition than they did in 1914. Such knowledge should not be ignored in applying antitrust laws. The "original intent" argument is weak in any event because there is little evidence that Congress relied on economic models.

Future Application of Antitrust to Newspapers

Despite the recent dearth of antitrust application to newspapers,[20] the impact outlined above argues for the appropriateness of its use. Three types of competition are worth examination: direct, umbrella, and intermedia. All three present different problems, but all three are important areas for consideration. In addition, the possibility of applying antitrust to group ownership will be discussed.

Direct competition. Generally, any form of illegal activities under existing antitrust law should be considered harmful to this market. Although there are few such daily markets left, those that continue to survive often contain some of the country's most important newspapers. These markets should continue to be scrutinized for efforts to force unnatural monopoly power. The geographic market for such cases would be the metropolitan area, which would include at least all counties contiguous to the city of publication. In applying antitrust, the impact in all three commodity markets should be considered. The product market for information and most advertising should be limited to newspapers. It is in these markets that newspapers are most distinct and acceptable substitutability of other media is weakest. But considering the intellectual market, all news media that provide opinion and information material about the geographic market should be included.

While daily direct competition has been dying, weekly competition continues in many areas. A tendency exists not to pursue antitrust violations in these markets for three reasons. First, most small newspapers do not have the resources to pursue antitrust actions. This means they usually sell to the competitor when faced with illegal practices that have put them at a disadvantage. Second, the U.S. Justice Department lacks resources. Third, there has been an overall decline at the federal level in the pursuit of antitrust cases.

Umbrella competition. As mentioned earlier, precedent exists in the form of *United States v. Times-Mirror* for applying antitrust law to umbrella competition. Research shows that such competition among dailies will increase the newshole and increase the percentage of newshole given local coverage.[21] Both of these generally benefit the readers. Yet markets exist, such as Dallas, Chicago, and Knoxville, where the same company owns metropolitan dailies and suburban dailies or weeklies. The growth of groups is also resulting in the joint ownership of metro dailies and nearby satellite dailies. The potential for harm is obvious and present.

The application of antitrust within umbrella competition should be guided by existing research. For example, metro dailies and suburban weeklies tend to be substitutes for some advertising and complements for most readers. Research suggests the following guidelines.

First, substitutability of newspapers within the information market tends to be limited by publication cycle. Dailies are substitutable for dailies and weeklies for weeklies, but it is unusual for a weekly to be a good substitute for a daily. Thus, a main area of concern is the relationship among national, metro, satellite, and suburban dailies.

These relationships represent the relevant product market. The relevant geographic market will vary with location and with ownership of newspapers. For example, the *Grand Rapids Press* (Michigan) in 1986 had a daily penetration of 29 percent in neighboring Ottawa County and less than 1 percent penetration in neighboring Muskegon County. This may be related to the fact that Booth Newspapers, which owns the *Grand Rapids Press*, owns a newspaper in Muskegon County but not in Ottawa County. The *Grand Rapids Press* competes in one county where its parent company does not own a newspaper, but it is absent in the other county where the company already has a daily. This example illustrates the variation in geographic market when it comes to umbrella competition.[22]

The foregoing suggests two ways of defining the geographic market. The first is simple and involves the actual area in which newspapers circulate. The second would be based on the potential market, whether or not this market actually is being served. This potential market would be an area in which one would reasonably expect competition if it were not for ownership restraints. In such a situation, the purchase of a daily by another daily in a bordering county would be anticompetitive.

Second, substitutability among umbrella layers in the advertising market is not limited by publication cycle. It is not unusual for weeklies and dailies to compete for advertising. In such situations, the geographic market takes precedence over the product market in defining potential anticompetitive impact.

The product market is all newspapers. The geographic market is those areas where both newspapers sell and distribute advertising. There is a problem in deciding market share in such a situation. For example, when a metro daily competes with a suburban weekly, the geographic market should be the smaller area, which means the area in which the suburban weekly circulates. It would be inappropriate to make the market the entire geographic area in which the daily distributes because the weekly cannot service such a large area and does not compete there.

Third, almost all mergers of newspapers within a given circulation area will lessen the number of ideas contributed to the intellectual market, except when a joint agreement is approved. The degree will vary, of course, but the amount of information and number of ideas available will almost always be reduced when one newspaper goes out of business. The extent of the negative impact will depend upon the number and activities of other media firms in that geographic market and on the extent of activity by the newspaper being acquired in the intellectual market.

The impact stems from the tendency of newspapers to cut costs in order to improve profits. These cost savings come from a reduced number of news-editorial pages and number of reporters. The impact of cutting pages is obvious, but the impact of reducing reporters is not as obvious because it is difficult to measure things that did not happen. Mark Fishman reported the impact of too few reporters at a newspaper.[23] The enterprise and investigative stories have to be done on the reporter's own time. This means many of these stories do not get written.

In summary, antitrust application to behavior in umbrella competition should be and could be pursued more actively. Roberts predicted that such competition may follow direct competition down the same one-firm path.[24] Even if this prediction is accurate, such an eventuality does not mean illegal behavior should be tolerated. Any purchase of a newspaper, whatever its publication cycle, by another nearby company deserves examination. The potential impact in all three commodity markets should be examined for anticompetitive impact. Since newspapers do enjoy special legal advantages, the antitrust laws should be interpreted broadly under umbrella situations and not be based just on financial impact. The role of newspapers in the intellectual market, the role of the intellectual market in politics, and the role of politics in economics combine to make any effect on the intellectual market an economic effect. The traditional approach makes newspaper antitrust analysis nothing more than clever accounting.

Intermedia competition. The competitive relationship among media varies greatly with the market. For example, ownership of a radio station by a newspaper in Los Angeles would have little impact on any of the three commodity markets because of the large number of media firms. However, cross-ownership between a newspaper and radio station in Big Spring, Texas could have negative effects in all three markets because there are only two radio stations and one newspaper in the city.

There is little evidence that television and radio are good substitutes for newspapers in the information market. The substitutability in the advertising market depends on the type of advertising involved. The effects on the intellectual market of cross-ownership tend to be negative in smaller cities.[25]

Probably the best approach to cross-ownership within a market is that taken by the Federal Communication Commission.[26] A media company is not allowed to own both a newspaper and an over-the-air broadcast company in the same market. The rule explicitly assumes that cross-ownership harms the intellectual market, and implicitly assumes harm to the other markets. The authority of a state to prevent cross-ownership of a newspaper and cable television system in the same market has also been upheld.[27] Cross-ownership should continue to be prohibited. The ability of market dominance via cross-ownership to result in severe abuse was shown in *Kansas City Star Co. v. United States* (see Chapter 7).[28] Cross-ownership among other media would depend upon market shares and substitutability of the product or services within the geographic market. Geographic market for cross-media antitrust analysis should be defined, as in umbrella newspaper competition, as the smaller space served by competing firms. One area of potential cross-media competition is especially noticeable. Many newspapers have implemented or are considering cable-disseminated database text services. Ironically, the newspaper industry has avidly lobbied against allowing regional Bell companies from entering that market.[29]

Ownership. The growth of newspaper groups has led some critics to warn of the negative impact of such large groups (see Chapter 5). Antitrust laws are not applicable to group ownership per se because antitrust requires specification of product and geographic markets. As long as a group does not buy a second newspaper in the same city, or in close proximity thereof, antitrust laws have little jurisdiction. However, some researchers argue that antitrust laws could be applied to prevent the further growth of groups. This section reviews some of those arguments.

Coulson said that while antitrust cannot be applied to group expansion on the basis of local geographic markets, it might be applicable if the entire nation was defined as the market.[30] While such an application may hold possibilities, there are some problems. First, no legal precedent exists for such an application. This means at the very least that new standards would have to be developed, which would require new antitrust laws, or dramatic reinterpretation and judicial broadening of existing laws. To achieve a judicial broadening, litigants would need to prove clearly the actual harms or potential harms from further growth, and also be able to show at what level the harms occur. This may be possible, but it has yet to be done. A legislative approach, statutory amendment, would require less rigorous proof, since Congress needs only a rational basis to pass legislation based on the commerce clause of the Constitution. But even Congress must be convinced, and the lack of evidence would still be a problem. In addition, there is a formidable newspaper lobby to contend with in a legislative initiative.

A second problem with expanding antitrust to cover ownership itself is that the current antitrust limits are a reflection of existing economic theory. To apply laws, the cross-elasticity of demand for distant newspaper market would have to be established. Litigants could attempt to convince the courts that cross-elasticity is irrelevant when a national market is considered, but that would amount to admitting that direct competition is irrelevant. Either proving cross-elasticity or urging its unimportance seems less than hopeful.

A third problem is that it is difficult to establish what level of concentration on a national scale is harmful. While many observers have decried concentration of ownership, no formula likely to persuade the courts has been suggested. Congress need not adopt a formula in the event of legislation. It could simply adopt a flat numerical standard. But convincing Congress of the harmful effects of concentrated ownership in distant markets will be difficult at best.

Perhaps a better application would be on a regional basis, using the concept of umbrella competition. Legal precedent exists for application to umbrella competition, but research needs to be conducted on a wider scale to understand the impact of such competition on a region.

Busterna provides an extensive examination of using antitrust laws to limit group ownership.[31] He argues that the nation may be the appropriate geographic market for national newspaper advertising and that control of a large percentage of dailies by a few firms could lead to collusion. The first argument may indeed be appropriate in some cases, but the definition of national advertising needs to be clarified. Some advertising sold at a national level does not cover the entire nation. In fact, one of the advantages of newspapers and other print media is the ability to target regional markets for national advertisers. The fact that collusion could occur is not enough in itself to dictate how many newspapers a group can own. As mentioned above, oligopolies can behave as if colluding, even when they are not.

Busterna also argues that newspapers are not natural monopolies. He repeats an argument made by Owen[32] that the vertical integration of news gathering, production, and distribution creates the economies of scale that produce the natural monopoly. They argue that competition could continue by separating some of the six processes required to create a newspaper. This would redefine the industry, but the argument ignores the role of the joint commodity nature of newspapers in creating natural monopoly power. Besides, economies of scale can be enjoyed by a firm even if it does not own a printing press. The economies are passed on by the contract printer as discounts for large amounts of business. Divesting newspapers of their presses would not prevent the movement toward monopoly cities.

In several situations, Busterna argues for the use of precedent in other industries to limit group growth. Some of these arguments have merit, but they all ignore the unique nature of the newspaper industry, which has already been acknowledged in antitrust cases. The problem with trying to stretch existing law to cover potential negative effects is that the stretching could snap the First Amendment. Just as the First Amendment should not allow private interest to dominate debate on public policy issues, neither should fear of private domination be lightly accepted as justification for government intervention. The proposed justifications for ownership restrictions are, after all, content based, and it is when content is at issue that the amendment restricts government the most.[33] And the federal government's track record on content regulation is less than inspiring in any event.[34] To regulate the ownership of newspapers so that content will be better will require compelling proof that the regulation will in fact lead to better content.

While the application of antitrust to controlling group ownership may have potential, there are other methods of promoting diversity of ownership. A system of tax laws to promote independent ownership could be developed;[35] given the effect of tax laws in encouraging group growth, such inducement would be equitable. Such legislation would need to apply to all types of businesses and not only to newspapers to avoid First Amendment conflicts. The continued development of technology also offers possible solutions. Concentration in newspaper ownership is a problem only if other voices are not available. Printing, cable, and broadcast technology may well open up the information, advertising, and intellectual markets in ways that will make newspaper group ownership potentially less harmful. Indeed, in times of rapid technological development, one would expect that innovation will concentrate on areas that yield high profits. The profits enjoyed by newspapers may well result in technological developments that will help to solve the access problems. As illustrated by the long-distance telephone industry, monopoly may not be forever.

SUMMARY

Increasing concentration and declining competition in the newspaper industry are important public concerns. Arguments that newspaper monopoly power has little negative impact run counter to research and anecdotal evidence. Antitrust law has proven ineffective at preventing the decline of direct newspaper competition. This results from monopolies within cities occurring naturally and from the lack of diligence in applying law to intercity competition.

Application of such laws can help preserve umbrella competition because such competition involves commodities that have a lesser degree of substitutability than newspapers in directly competitive markets. However, unenforced laws serve little purpose, and the Justice Department has not shown much desire to pursue newspaper antitrust. This leaves the individual companies to pursue antitrust cases in court—a costly and lengthy process that lies beyond the reach of most smaller newspaper companies. For most smaller competitors, the private antitrust lawsuit appears to be a strategic decision. Few litigants can actually expect to win, judging from past cases. The strategic market and nuisance value are therefore the main gains sought—a hope that the dominant firm will choose to appease rather than crush.

Antitrust law has no direct role in controlling group concentration on a national level under existing precedent. Some arguments for extending antitrust laws to include group ownership have merit, but would not be easy to pursue on a practical basis. Pursuing such a course holds potential for irreparable damage to the First Amendment. The potential dilemma of choosing between control by big business and big government is not appealing, but it need not be the only choice. Growth of communication technology has already increased access to the information, advertising and intellectual markets. Entrepreneurs are needed to develop and adopt new technologies in ways that serve the public and reduce the power of companies that control a large segment of the newspaper industry.

ENDNOTES

1. *Continental T.V., Inc. v. GTE Sylvania, Inc.*, 433 U.S. 36 (1977).
2. Richard A. Posner, *Antitrust Law: An Economic Perspective* (Chicago: The University of Chicago Press, 1976).
3. John C. Busterna, "Daily Newspaper Chains and the Antitrust Laws," *Journalism Monographs*, No. 110, March 1989.
4. This analysis can be found in most beginning and advanced microeconomic texts. For example, see David Laidler, *Introduction to Microeconomics* (New York: Basic Books, 1974), pp. 149-163; and Walter Nicholson, *Intermediate Microeconomics and Its Application*, 2nd. ed. (Hinsdale, IL: The Dryden Press, 1979). For an early treatment of consumer's surplus, see Alfred Marshall, *Principles of Economics* (London: Macmillan and Co., 1890), pp. 465-72.
5. See Edward H. Chamberlin, *The Theory of Monopolistic Competition*, 8th ed. (Cambridge, MA: Harvard University Press, 1962), p.27.
6. Arnold C. Harberger, "Monopoly and Resource Allocation," *American Economic Review* (1954), reprinted in *Microeconomics: Selected Readings*, 3rd. ed., Edwin Mansfield, ed. (New York: W.W. Norton, 1979), pp. 206-217.
7. Posner, *op. cit.*, pp. 14-15.
8. Busterna, *op. cit.*
9. David C. Coulson, "Antitrust Law and Newspapers," in Robert G. Picard, James P. Winter, Maxwell E. McCombs, and Stephen Lacy, eds. *Press Concentration and Monopoly* (Norwood, NJ: Ablex Publishing Co., 1988), pp. 179-195; Robert G. Picard, "Evidence of a 'Failing Newspaper' Under the Newspaper Preservation Act," *Newspaper Research Journal*, Fall 1988, pp.73-82.
10. Stephen Lacy and Frederick Fico, "Financial Commitment, Newspaper Quality and Circulation: Testing an Economic Model for Direct Newspaper Competition," Paper presented to the Association for Education in Journalism and Mass Communication, Washington, DC, August 1989.
11. *Whitney v. California*, 274 U.S. 357 (1927) (Brandeis, J., concurring).

12. For example, see Maxwell McCombs, "Effect of Monopoly in Cleveland on Diversity of Newspaper Content," *Journalism Quarterly*, 64:740-744, 792 (Winter 1987).
13. *Associated Press v. United States*, 326 U.S. 1 (1945).
14. Bruce M. Owen, *Economics and Freedom of Expression: Media Structure and the First Amendment* (Cambridge, MA: Ballinger Publishing, 1975), p. 52.
15. *United States v. Times Mirror Co.*, 274 F. Supp. 606 (C.D. Cal. 1967), aff'd per curiam, 390 U.S. 712 (1968). For a further discussion of this point see Coulson, *op. cit.*
16. *Minneapolis Star & Tribune Co. v. Minnesota Commissioner of Revenue*, 460 U.S. 575 (1983).
17. Busterna, *op. cit.*
18. The externality impact argument is presented in John Busterna, "Welfare Economics and Media Performance," *Journal of Media Economics*, Spring 1988, pp. 75-88.
19. Classics in the area of nonperfect competition are Edward H. Chamberlin, *The Theory of Monopolistic Competition* (Cambridge, MA: Harvard University Press, 1933) and Joan Robinson, *The Economics of Imperfect Competition* (New York: Macmillan, 1933).
20. John C. Busterna, "Antitrust in the 1980s: An Analysis of 45 Newspaper Actions," *Newspaper Research Journal*, Winter 1988, pp. 25-36.
21. Stephen Lacy, "The Impact of Intercity Competition on Daily Newspaper Content," *Journalism Quarterly*, 65:399-406 (Summer 1988).
22. *Newsaper Circulation Analysis: Newspaper Rates and Data, Part II*, 1987/88, Vol. 69, No. 11 (Wilmette, IL: Standard Rate & Data Service, Inc., 1987).
23. Mark Fishman. *Manufacturing the News* (Austin, TX: University of Texas Press, 1980).
24. Keith Roberts, "Antitrust Problems in the Newspaper Industry," *Harvard Law Review*, 82:2:319-66 (1968).
25. Guido H. Stempel III, "Effects on Performance of Cross-Media Monopoly," *Journalism Monographs*, No. 29, June 1973; and William T. Gromley, *The Effects of Newspaper-Television Cross-Ownership on News Homogeneity* (Chapel Hill: University of North Carolina, 1976).
26. Donald M. Gillmor, Jerome A. Barron, Todd F. Simon, and Herbert A. Terry, *Mass Communication Law: Cases and Comment*, 5th ed. (St. Paul, MN: West Publishing Co., 1990), pp. 863-874.
27. *Times Mirror Co. v. Division of Public Utility Control*, 9 Med. L. Rep. 1270 (Conn. Super. Ct. 1983).
28. 240 F.2d 643 (8th Cir.), *cert. den.*, 354 U.S. 923 (1957).
29. "ANPA asks Congress to keep lid on BOC electronic publishing," *presstime*, September 1989, p. 46; and "Court orders reconsideration of RBOC leash; ANPA looks to Judge Greene to retain it," *presstime*, May 1990, p. 64.
30. David C. Coulson, *op. cit.*
31. Busterna, " Daily Newspaper Chains and the Antitrust Laws," *op. cit.*

32. Owen, *op. cit.*
33. *Consolidated Edison Co. v. Public Service Commission*, 447 U.S. 530 (1980).
34. *Syracuse Peace Council v. FCC*, 867 F.2d 654 (D.C. Cir. 1989).
35. Robert G. Picard, James P. Winter, Maxwell E. McCombs, and Stephen Lacy, eds."Policy Implications," *Press Concentration and Monopoly* (Norwood, NJ: Ablex, 1988), pp. 204-205.

9

Business Regulation of Newspapers

Newspapers are not subject to various types of direct regulation of content, unlike the way other media, such as broadcasters licensed by the Federal Communications Commission or cable systems franchised by local governments, are. The courts have consistently said that attempted direct government regulation of the news content of newspapers is unconstitutional.[1] Even indirect regulatory attempts, such as trying to 'license' by requiring journalists covering state government to file financial reports, are declared unconstitutional if it appears that the regulation is aimed at affecting news content.[2]

But the newspaper industry is subject to regulatory agencies just as non-media businesses are. The U.S. Supreme Court for more than 50 years has repeated that laws of "general application" do not violate the First Amendment when applied to newspapers or other news media. In *Associated Press v. NLRB*,[3] the press argued that the First Amendment was violated by enforcement of the National Labor Relations Act against news organizations. The argument was rejected. As a result, most types of regulatory activity affecting newspapers have never been a subject of dispute, at least unless there is evidence that a regulation masked an intent to inhibit content. Laws regulating worker safety, standards for pensions, building inspections, and the like, have therefore not been contested on the ground that they pose special problems to the press.

Several areas of regulatory activity, however, do have particular impact on the press. These include taxation, labor law, postal law, distribution and licensing regulations, and advertising regulation. All have three major characteristics of particular concern for newspapers in common. First, each tends to be of "general application" on its face. Second, each area of regulation is capable of having a dual effect, both on the finances of newspapers and on the content of newspapers. Third, each must in some way be industry-specific to be effective. While the broad provisions of an enabling statute may be capable of general application, administration of regulations typically requires a narrow focus on the context of specific disputes rather than a general focus. FCC licensing standards, for example, are stated in general, but a licensing proceeding is concerned with a specific context.[4] Industry-specific regulation allows newspapers to argue that the regulation affects *both* the economic and intellectual markets, raising First Amendment issues. But at the same time, health regulation aimed at effects of materials such as ink used heavily by newspapers cannot support a First Amendment argument.

The areas of regulation referred to above may be further divided into two types: those that are of general application on their face, and those that apply specifically to the press. Tax and labor laws apply facially to all enterprises; the focus here, then, is on their specific application to newspapers. But postal law and regulation of distribution apply in certain respects only to newspapers or print media. In addition, special statutory provisions often exist to favor newspapers or other media.

This chapter will review the first four major areas of statutory and regulatory activity. The review is confined to discussion of ways in which newspapers are especially affected. No attempt to quantify either the economic or content effects of regulation is attempted, although examples of both are drawn from specific disputes. Advertising law, it should be noted, is an area of regulation that has entire books devoted to it,[5] mainly on the matter of content regulation. Indirect regulation of advertising occurs through operation of contract law or of laws regarding official or public notice advertising, and is limited to non-content related regulation. Since the bulk of advertising regulation is outside the scope of this book, it is not addressed here.

TAX LAWS AND NEWSPAPERS

Tax statutes would appear to be the classic example of laws of general application. That is especially true of general income tax laws, corporate or individual, state or federal. But even in income tax, only the rates tend to be truly general. The formulae for determining taxable income are typically extremely complex and, in many instances, industry or context-specific.[6] There is no distinctive issue for newspaper managers when tax law applies generally; familiarity with current administrative and statutory standards relating to accounting, depreciation, valuation of inventory, and the like, is needed just as in any business.[7] It is assumed that managers will act rationally and attempt to keep tax liability to a minimum. Newspapers naturally have depreciation, valuation, and even accounting issues specific to the industry, but that does not change the general nature of tax rules applied to these issues.[8]

When tax law operates to differentiate between newspapers and other taxable entities, however, the rules change. In most situations, tax officials may classify industries as they please, and the courts will not second-guess the decision. Taxes that apply specifically to the press require special justification.

Discriminatory Taxation

In 1983, the U.S. Supreme Court declared that a tax that singles out the press from other taxpayers is presumptively unconstitutional as a violation of the First Amendment. In *Minneapolis Star and Tribune Co. v. Minnesota Commissioner of Revenue*,[9] the newspaper challenged the application of a "use" tax to purchases of ink and newsprint. Like most states, Minnesota exempted consumer purchases of newspapers from the state sales tax.[10] There are two rationales behind such exemptions. First, legislatures say that the exemption will encourage purchase of newspapers, leading to a better-informed public. Second, it is difficult to collect sales tax on such small purchases—and almost impossible on newsrack sales. Neither rationale is persuasive. It is hard to believe that the penny or two tax—four or five cents on Sunday—will significantly affect sales of a product with a cover price so low in relation to product cost. The second rationale is disingenuous, since the seller normally has the burden of remitting sales tax to the state, not the buyer. A newspaper could either raise its price to cover increased taxes or could choose to absorb it within its present price structure.

The Minnesota state legislature sought to raise revenue by imposing an alternative use tax. Ordinarily a use tax is a compensating tax applied to purchases made outside the borders of the taxing state, essentially a device to prevent sales tax avoidance. The amounts that would be owed by a newspaper under the Minnesota ink and paper use tax would have been considerably less than amounts owed under the general sales tax. The paper challenged the statute nonetheless. It also challenged an exemption for the first $100,000 spent on ink and paper as a discrimination against large newspapers. In its first year of operation, only 14 of 388 newspapers in the state incurred any use tax liability because of the exemption.

Since the Court declared the use tax unconstitutional in its entirety, the issue of discrimination between newspapers based on their size was not addressed at length, but the Court did note that preferential treatment by statute of some members of the press was also presumptively unconstitutional. Writing for a seven-member majority, Justice O'Connor reviewed First Amendment history and concluded that a primary purpose of the amendment was to prevent government from using taxes to punish or control the press. She said that a strict rule was necessary:

> [D]ifferential treatment, unless justified by some special characteristic of the press, suggests that the goal of the regulation is not unrelated to suppression of expression, and such a goal is presumptively unconstitutional..... Differential taxation of the press places such a burden...that we cannot countenance such treatment unless the state asserts a counterbalancing interest of compelling importance that it cannot achieve without differential taxation.[11]

Merely raising tax revenues for the state was not considered compelling. It is important to note that the compelling interest test is the same test as used for direct content regulation.[12] The *Minneapolis Star* case raises almost as many questions as it answers. What special characteristics of the press will suffice to allow differential taxation? What state interests will be considered compelling? In other First Amendment cases, compelling interests have typically been interests of constitutional magnitude themselves.[13] Perhaps the biggest unanswered question is, what will be considered differential? Perhaps the biggest concern arising from the case is the concern that the broad rule, if applied strictly, would threaten any statutory or administrative preferences for newspapers.

One ironic result of the case is that application of the regular sales tax would be constitutional since that statute did not single out the press. Justice Rehnquist, the lone dissenter, calculated that in the 1975 tax year the sales tax would have cost the paper almost $1.2 million more.

The Court hinted a willingness to reconsider the breadth of the *Minneapolis Star* principle in a 1991 case, *Leathers v. Medlock*.[14] In *Leathers*, Arkansas applied its general sales tax to purchases of cable television services, but specifically exempted newspapers by statute. Cable companies challenged the distinction as unconstitutional discrimination. The Court upheld the statute because there was no attempt nor suspicion it was intended to interfere with content.

The *Minneapolis Star* decision expanded previous press protection against inhibiting taxation established in *Grosjean v. American Press*.[15] In that case, the evidence showed that a tax on newspaper advertising had been passed with the intention of inhibiting news coverage. Ever since, the rule has been that discriminatory intent violates the First Amendment. In *Minneapolis Star*, though, there was no impermissible intent.

The principle that statutes which "single out" the press are presumptively unconstitutional is capable of broad application. The opinion does not limit its presumption of First Amendment violation to laws that have a negative effect on the press. Presumably such beneficial statutes as journalists' shield laws or even the Newspaper Preservation Act might be scrutinized closely since they single out the press. In the years since the

Minneapolis Star decision, the principle has been invoked dozens of times to challenge tax laws and other laws.

One immediate effect of the case was reconsideration of newspaper sales tax exemption in many state legislatures.[16] Most states have retained the exemption, but the temptation to raise revenues is great. In Missouri, the state supreme court judicially removed the agency-created newspaper exemption from sales tax in the wake of *Star*.[17] The Missouri court also said that the revocation was retroactive. Whether reluctance in most states to extend the tax is due to press lobbying or to legislative concern for keeping newspapers affordable is unclear. That the exemption for newspapers has been a traditional exception has also influenced legislators. Since the Court did not define "the press" in *Minneapolis Star*, it would appear plausible that magazine or book publishers not entitled to a similar exemption could challenge the special sales tax status of newspapers.

The challenges since 1983 have arisen primarily in sales and use tax cases, although challenges have also been brought against business license taxes and even amusement taxes. The operation of those taxes must be examined as a backdrop to the challenges.

Sales and Use Taxes

In most states, a flat rate sales tax is applied to the purchase of tangible goods. Only a handful of states apply a sales tax to the purchase of services. Sales of services have traditionally been exempted from most states' sales tax statutes, and since the sale of newspaper advertising space has traditionally been deemed a sale of a service by the courts, sales tax has usually not been applied to those sales. Florida's attempt to enlarge its sales tax to include advertising sales produced a brouhaha in the press, along with threats of litigation challenging the tax on First Amendment grounds.[18] Since the tax applied to services generally, it must be presumed that it was constitutional on its face. To the extent that it applies specifically to advertising, it applied to all advertising media, and was again apparently valid. In any event, sales of advertising space and/or time would appear to be just the sort of "special characteristic" of the press intended by the Court in *Minneapolis Star*. The Florida service sales tax was rescinded by the legislature, but not before the state supreme court had upheld its constitutionality. A sales tax on advertising that applies specifically to one medium but not all is likely invalid. A city sales tax on advertising media only was declared unconstitutional because it would have the effect of restraining the press.[19] Had the statute applied generally, it apparently would have been upheld despite the fact that the press would be affected more than other taxpayers. When the city of Denver amended its sales tax law to remove the newspaper exemption, newspaper firms argued that application of the tax violated the First Amendment. But since the tax was general, it was upheld.[20] Oklahoma's sales tax which exempted sales of publications when the transaction falls below 75 cents only was declared unconstitutional because of the facial differential treatment.[21]

Despite its dual commodity nature, production of the actual newspaper, as opposed to sales of advertising within the newspaper prior to printing, has always been considered manufacturing of a tangible product for sales tax purposes.[22] That status allows newspaper companies to benefit doubly under sales tax laws. Most states' laws provide that purchases by a company of articles that are "used" or "consumed" in the manufacture of a tangible product for eventual sale are themselves exempt from sales tax. Newsprint, ink, and even presses are so used or consumed. And since most states exempt the eventual sale of the newspaper itself, the press may escape sales tax liability at both ends of the production process.

Newspapers understandably vie for broad interpretations of what is used or consumed in manufacturing. The broadest interpretation allowed a newspaper to escape tax on purchases of materials such as desks, pens, flashbulbs, and reporter's notebooks.[23] More typically, the exemption will apply only to purchases of materials that become a component part of the manufactured product. Application of such an exemption will tend to reduce a newspaper's variable costs at a relatively predictable rate (see Chapter 3).

One area of dispute concerning this manufacturing exemption involves advertising. Advertisers have challenged imposition of sales tax for pre-printed newspaper inserts, contending that the inserts become a component part of the product. Despite the rather obvious fact that inserts are in no way manufactured by the newspaper, which operates only as a deliverer except for mechanically folding the inserts into the paper, some courts have accepted the argument and granted the exemption.[24] Most courts that have faced the issue have not considered pre-printed ad inserts eligible for the exemption.[25] Whether the exemption is granted or not, state court decisions usually turn on specific definitions within state statutes. Not all states define "manufacturing," "component part," or "consumed" in the same way.

Free distribution newspapers and shoppers may have difficulty qualifying for the manufacturing exemption, since the exemption typically requires the manufacture of a product for sale. In one shopper case, the fact that tangible supplies were used in the production of advertising failed to qualify the publication for exemption, in part because selling advertising space is not a sale of tangible property.[26]

Another issue concerns the operation of the general sales tax exemption for newspaper sales. A primary concern of free distribution publications is qualifying for the exemption in the first place; without the exemption, sales or use tax is liable to be imposed based on overall revenues, depending upon specific state law, despite the fact that no retail sale occurs. The majority of cases have upheld narrow exemption definitions and qualifications, either from the statute or as created by an administrative agency. In *In re Village Publishing Corp.*,[27] the North Carolina Supreme Court said that denial of exemption to a shopper with minimal news content was valid. The publisher claimed that classifying newspapers on the basis of the amount of news content was unconstitutionally discriminatory. The court used a rational basis test rather than the compelling interest test from *Minneapolis Star* to uphold the classification.

An almost identical challenge was brought by the publisher of a weekly shopper that was more than 90 percent advertising. California's classification denied sales and use tax exemption to any publication exceeding 90 percent advertising content. In upholding the classification, a state appeals court determined that *Minneapolis Star* was inapplicable since the state rule was based not on content, but on the form or format of the content. The court then decided that the legislature had a rational basis for concluding that newspapers with more news would better serve the public.[28]

The California decision should concern any newspaper manager. Unless challenged and reversed, it paves the way for legislatures to use the sales tax exemption as a lever to control the size of their newsholes. As a matter of First Amendment principle, the decision is unfortunate in any event, ignoring as it does Justice O'Connor's warning that a statute regulating content is presumptively unconstitutional. While the California statute facially only concerned the amount of content, it is settled First Amendment law that government cannot compel that the press use its space in a certain way.[29]

In what, it is hoped, is an isolated case, the *Huntington Advertiser* claimed that its carriers were liable for taxes on retail sales rather than the newspaper. Carriers were technically allowed to set delivery subscription prices but the paper, like most, strongly suggested prices. Suggested prices were almost always the charged prices. The newspaper claimed that the carriers, many of them minors, were independent contractors. The court instead said that the carriers were agents of the newspaper, thereby imposing the tax on the newspaper.[30]

Exemption From Income Taxes

The law concerning tax-exempt organizations is not normally a concern for the commercial, for-profit newspaper. The assumption of this book is that most newspapers have profit as a goal. But thousands of publications are put out by organizations that have applied and qualified for tax-exempt status under federal and state income tax laws. While no commercial newspaper is known to have a tax-exempt status, a number of potentially competing or substituting publications or broadcast outlets are tax-exempt.

Most tax-exempt publications pose no serious competition for newspapers. These include organization newsletters, scholarly journals, and a number of trade or professional magazines, for example. Among the tax-exempt publications, however, are some major consumer magazines, including *Harper's*, *Mother Jones*, *The Progressive* and *Smithsonian*. There are examples as well of magazines and even newspapers organized on a non-profit basis in local markets.[31]

Most publications that are tax-exempt qualified under the federal statutory provisions for educational, literary, or cultural organizations.[32] Qualified entities not only pay no income tax—except perhaps on business activities not directly within an organization's mission—but they are also entitled to receive contributions which other taxpayers may deduct from income.

There is no practical limitation on the number of entities that might qualify. Most publications claim "educational" status, arguing that publication of news and information is necessarily educational. In an attempt to limit the scope of the term "educational," the Internal Revenue Service propounded regulations designed to require that coverage of controversial issues be full, fair and unbiased, sort of a print version of the Fairness Doctrine, but the regulations were declared unconstitutional.[33] With the exception of one case involving a Nazi newsletter, it appears that IRS attempts at direct content regulation are doomed.[34] It is easy to see why. No one, especially judges, is comfortable with the notion of IRS agents acting as arbiters of what benefits the public.

To the extent that the tax-exempt status of some publications acts in effect as a discrimination in favor of a few, and implicitly as discrimination against others, it may be challengeable under *Minneapolis Star*. But no challenge has been brought. Unless a newspaper had evidence that the tax status of a competitor gave it a competitive advantage, there would be little sense in challenging the status in particular or the tax laws in general. Usually one cannot contest the tax status of another party, but in the First Amendment context this general rule may not be enforced because the courts allow broader challeges to tax and regulatory provisions when First Amendment rights are at issue.[35]

Tax-exempt status provides several economic advantages to a publication, the greatest of which is that 'profits' are neither taxed nor distributed to stockholders, but rather are usually directly re-invested into the news product. In theory at least, organizing newspapers as tax-exempt, non-profit entities would have maximum benefit for the intellectual market. Its appeal, though, is limited for obvious reasons.[36]

Business License Taxes

Many local governments impose business license or occupation taxes. These taxes may be imposed on a flat fee basis or may be based on amount of business activity, typically expressed in terms of gross or net revenues. When Los Angeles imposed its city business tax on newspapers and other publications formerly exempt, the Los Angeles *Times* and other area newspapers challenged.[37] The newspapers raised several arguments. They said that the formulas devised for newspaper tax liability were invalid since they singled out the press. They argued that the city must prove a compelling interest to impose the tax in general, and especially as to the formulas. They also argued that the tax law gave too much discretion to city officials, thereby raising the specter of direct content regulation. The California Court of Appeals rejected all the arguments.

First, the business tax applied generally and did not single out the press. That the previous exemption, which *did* single out the press, was revoked in special legislation did not render the tax something other than general. Second, the court concluded that the formulas used by the city were valid because they were based on the peculiar characteristics of all types of businesses, including the press. Given those conclusions, the court determined that proof of a compelling interest was not necessary. The court also decided that certificates required under the law did not create an impermissible discretionary regulatory scheme. Just the opposite was true: all businesses were required to obtain certificates. The challengers had relied upon a previous California case that had struck down a local business license tax that applied to subscription television companies.[38] The general provision in the earlier case, though, contained so many exceptions that the court had concluded the law had a discriminatory effect. No such defect appeared in the Los Angeles tax.

In the absence of a constitutional claim, business or occupation taxes and the amounts assessed under them are virtually unassailable. Any rational basis by a legislative body will be sufficient to uphold a tax. The burden of proving lack of a rational basis is on the party contesting the tax. One court used a rational basis test, the usual standard in tax cases,[39] probably wrongly, in upholding a city business tax that taxed newspapers at a rate higher then other businesses.[40] The result is indicative of the deference courts grant to tax decisions, however.

Federal and State Estate or Inheritance Taxes

Inheritance taxes are relevant to newspapers because of their collateral rather than immediate effects. These taxes, after all, are imposed on owners and heirs of newspaper companies, not on newspapers themselves. Nonetheless, inheritance taxes have played a major role in newspaper economics in this century, resulting in an indirect and unintended regulatory effect.

High tax rates on estates are a major cause of sales of newspapers to groups and conglomerates. The tax laws work synergistically with the interest in growth of newspaper firms. Large estates through the 1970s could face a tax of up to 70 percent. Lowering of the federal rate to 50 percent only modestly reduced the effect. Elderly independent owners, or family members in situations where an independent newspaper is owned by several members of the same family, are given plenty of economic incentive to cash in their one major asset rather than see most of its value used to pay taxes (see Chapter 5). With valuation of and bidding on newspaper properties at unprecedented levels, the allure is especially great; a newspaper's sale value typically far exceeds its book value. The assets resulting from sale may be protected more easily from taxes in a variety of ways than if the original asset had been inherited.

One study concluded that tax laws, especially estate taxes, were the major cause of newspaper ownership changes.[41] Those who desire to stem the progress of ownership concentration might be wiser to concentrate on tax law modification than on application of the antitrust laws (see Chapter 7).

LABOR LAWS AND THE PRESS

The term labor law is usually taken to refer to federal and state regulation of the relationships between employers and employees, especially in the context of collective bargaining. While that remains the usual understanding, *labor law* as used here refers to laws of all types that affect the employer-employee relationship. In addition to such regulatory statutes as the National Labor Relations Act (NLRA),[42] newspaper managers are also affected by state and federal civil rights provisions and also by the common law of contract as it relates to employment.

The common characteristic of all laws affecting employer-employee relations is that they restrain what would otherwise be the virtually unlimited authority of employers to deal with their employees as they wish. Labor law at the federal level is passed pursuant to Congress's authority to regulate interstate commerce. At the state level, the state's traditional justification for passing statutes is that they are pursuant to their "police powers," the general authority to legislate for the good of the citizens.[43] To the extent that state law conflicts with federal law, the federal will prevail under the supremacy clause of the U.S. Constitution.[44]

Federal Labor Law

Two statutes form the heart of federal labor law, the NLRA and the Fair Labor Standards Act (FLSA).[45] Each statute was a product of the New Deal period and, like many of those statutes, acts as an enabling statute which provides for actual interpretation, application and enforcement by an administrative entity. In the case of the NLRA, the National Labor Relations Board is the agency. In the case of the FLSA, the Wage and Hour Division of the Department of Labor is the agency. Both statutes were relatively promptly subjected to First Amendment challenges.

National Labor Relations Act. In the *Associated Press v. NLRB* case,[46] AP argued that the NLRA violated the First Amendment by abridging the freedom of the press. The case arose when a discharged employee, Morris Watson, filed a complaint under the act alleging he had been fired for his activities in attempting to form a union. AP refused to appear and offer a defense at the subsequent hearing, citing its constitutional argument. The Supreme Court, in a 5-4 opinion, limited the notion of press freedom to preventing abridgments of content:

> The publisher of a newspaper has no special immunity from the application of general laws.....The regulation in question here has no relation whatever to the impartial distribution of news.

AP also argued that the act served to deprive it of property without due process of law, an argument shrugged off by the majority as almost beside the point. Attempting to equate operation of the NLRA with a confiscation does seem rather overstated.

In addition, AP argued that the employee's editorial work bore no relationship to interstate commerce. Since the employee's work product made its way into interstate commmerce via AP wires, that argument too was doomed to fail. The AP appeared to be on the verge of claiming that Watson was in effect a managerial employee not covered by the act, an issue of contemporary importance.

The NLRA is an elaborate statute which establishes a framework for recognition of collective bargaining agents, for the conduct of contract negotiations, and for the assessment of each party's behavior during the terms of a contract. Most of the 'law' of federal labor law, then, is private law, found in the contract. The NLRA is primarily concerned with assuring fairness to employees in the formation of the contract. Watson's claim relied on the NLRA's protection for employees taking initial steps toward collective bargaining.

Most NLRA activity concerning the media revolves around allegations of unfair labor practices. Unfair labor practices can range from discharge of an employee for union organizing activity or for published comments critical of the employer[47] to imposition of policies or procedures without collective bargaining.[48] Employers retain extensive power to impose policies. The obligation to collectively bargain over policies arises when the policy may have either an economic or job security effect on protected employees. For example, imposition of an editorial code of ethics was considered within the province of management, but penalty provisions of the ethics code potentially affecting job security were bargainable.[49]

While policies affecting income and job security will be considered mandatory bargaining issues, other policies are likely to be considered permissive bargaining issues. Matters such as vacation and leave policy relate directly to "wages, hours, and other terms and conditions of employment,"[50] and are thus mandatory bargaining issues. Permissive issues would likely include such policies as those relating to smoking in the workplace or drug testing. If a drug testing program contains penalty provisions, the issue may be mandatory. What will be considered an unfair labor practice or a mandatory bargaining issue is hard to predict, however. Each dispute is context-specific, typical of administrative regulatory decision making.[51] One particular unfair labor practice, refusal to bargain collectively, has been interpreted fairly expansively. A refusal to share information may be considered a refusal to bargain. In several cases, the NLRA has been interpreted as requiring employers to provide financial and employment data. One case involved amounts paid by a newspaper to non-union writers. While commanding that names be removed to protect privacy, the NLRB required the financial disclosure.[52] An employer was also required to hand over employee performance appraisals and lists of employee names and job classifications.[53] A claim that the information was confidential was rejected both because there was no evidence of sensitive material, and also because confidentiality was apparently being used as a pretext to refuse to disclose. Even when union employees desired confidentiality of records, the union bargaining agent was entitled to the records.[54]

Another area of dispute concerns which employees are covered by the NLRA. In general, professional employees are not covered.[55] The act defines a professional or managerial employee as one whose work is "predominantly intellectual and varied in character as opposed to routine mental, manual, mechanical, or physical work." Other indicators include the grant of discretionary authority to an employee, inability to standardize work product goals, and specialized education or training. Although this language would appear to place most newsroom employees outside the protection of the NLRA, leaving only the trade unions representing groups such as press operators or delivery truck drivers, the exception for professionals has been limited primarily to managerial editorial employees or to employees whose work is essentially unassigned and unsupervised. A number of cases have examined the distinction. An employee who supervises other employees will normally be outside the act. An editorial writer was considered professional and not covered because her job allowed exceptional discretion.[56]

Fair Labor Standards Act. The FLSA, which established minimum wage and maximum hour limits, was subjected to a First Amendment challenge in *Oklahoma Press Publishing Co. v. Walling*.[57] The U.S. Supreme Court again upheld an interstate commerce regulation applied to the press. Again there was no direct effect on content. The newspaper also attempted to argue that the statute was unconstitutional because small newspapers, mostly weeklies of 3,000 or less circulation, were exempted from the act. The Court rejected that argument, noting that "Nothing...forbids Congress [from exempting] some publishers because of size from either a tax or a regulation which would be valid if applied to all." The congressional intent, obviously, was to safeguard small publishers from the economic effects of the Act. The contention's validity must be doubted following the *Minneapolis Star* case, which expressly forbade overt discrimination in favor of smaller publishers.

Virtually all the key questions under the FLSA since 1946 have concerned whether or not an employee or group of employees is covered by the act. A small number of cases have dealt with employers failing to meet recordkeeping requirements, especially of overtime work,[58] which must be paid minimally at one-and-a-half times regular pay. Small newspapers have been considered notorious at failing to record work hours properly.

Much like the NLRA, the FLSA exempts professional employees from the minimum wage and overtime provisions. It is therefore in an employer's interest to have as much of the workforce considered professional as possible. Employees in titled supervisory and managerial positions are almost always exempt. Employees in the trades are almost always covered. The uncertain ground concerns editorial employees.

The newspaper industry has been active in working to have the definition of professional under both acts include editorial employees.[59] Journalists, the industry has argued, exercise discretion, usually have advanced or specialized training, and produce work product that is not readily quantifiable. Two recent cases have reached opposite results on the issue of whether journalists are professionals under the FLSA.

In *Sherwood v. Washington Post*,[60] a federal district judge granted the newspaper's motion for summary judgment in a case where the newspaper claimed that 99 journalists who had filed for overtime pay were professionals. Judge Gesell reviewed the backgrounds of the journalists, the nature of their jobs, and the amount of discretion they had in performing their duties. He concluded that there was plainly nothing "routine" about them or about their work. The opinion was reversed on technical grounds.[61] The appeals court said summary judgment was inappropriate because premature, and that the journalists must have a chance to establish at trial that they are not covered by the act's definition of "professional." In other words, the appeals court complained that Gesell short-circuited the judicial process, but expressed no opinion on the claim itself.

A conflicting case, *Dalheim v. KDFW-TV*,[62] ruled that journalists in a local television department were not professionals. The judge cited two main reasons: First, that the job duties and work product were not original or creative and, second, that the FLSA places the burden of proof on the employer when exemption is at issue.

Whatever the eventual outcome of cases involving the FLSA exemption, it will likely influence analysis under the NLRA as well.

A last area of dispute, under both acts, is whether or not an individual will be considered an employee for purposes of the statutes. Being categorized as an employee may also matter for purposes of unemployment compensation and workman's compensation statutes under state law. In general, administrative bodies will examine factors such as the nature of the relationship between the newspaper and an individual or group, job duties, amounts of time spent on the job, and pay. Stringers whose full-time work yielded significant weekly pay were deemed employees.[63] Significant contact with a newspaper's editors, via telephone conversations, and evidence of expense allowances may justify a conclusion that a writer termed a freelancer acted more as an employee for purposes of filing a libel suit against the newspaper.[64] Part-time newspaper carriers and drivers are likely to not be considered employees.[65] Carriers are not only affected by part-time status, but many states exempt them from statutory coverage altogether.[66]

Civil Rights Laws

The single most important statute regarding civil rights in the employment context is Title VII of the Civil Rights Act of 1964, as amended.[67] The act prohibits discrimination in employment based on "race, color, religion, sex, or national origin..." Acts prohibited include refusals to hire, discharges, unequal compensation, and unequal conditions of employment resulting from discrimination. Other civil rights acts, state and federal, typically follow the analysis that has been developed in Title VII cases.

For newspapers, two potential areas for discrimination claims dominate. First is sex discrimination. With women making up more and more of the newspaper workforce, significant under-representation of women in higher-level positions and over-representation in lower-level, lower-paying positions could be a problem. The same analysis holds true for employees who are members of racial or ethnic minorities, the second group most likely to bring a claim. Discrimination may be proved either by the existence of patterns that establish a presumption of impermissible discriminatory intent or by evidence specific to an individual showing unequal treatment.

In either type of case, plaintiffs must make a *prima facie* showing that they are within the classes protected in the statute, that similarly-situated persons not in the protected class were treated differently (better), and that an employer engaged in the type of acts specified in the statute. At that point, the burden shifts to the defendant employer to offer a non-discriminatory justification.[68]

Class action or group claims focus on patterns of employment decisions. For defendants, there is no 'safe' level of discrimination, but group plaintiffs must show more than a numerical disparity: the disparities must be statistically significant, allowing an inference of discriminatory motive.[69] Individual claims require a close examination of dealings between the employer and the specific employee. Although most discrimination claims fail because employers are able to establish a job-related basis for a decision, Title VII and other statutes are tilted toward plaintiffs. A newspaper that finds itself a defendant should expect to submit a large amount of documentation. In some states, pro-plaintiff non-trial hearings and meetings in the early stages may serve as much to let an aggrieved employee let off steam as to resolve the legal issues. The press has never challenged application of civil rights statutes on First Amendment grounds.

Title VII has no provisions targeted to newspapers, but it can be applied especially to newspapers. Women, for example, have traditionally been assigned to feature and lifestyle sections (and before that the women's pages), perhaps rendering newspapers more susceptible to a sex discrimination charge based on patterns of employee assignment. The *Detroit News* reached a settlement with a large number of present and former female employees in a class action case based on classifications and lack of promotions. With many newspapers developing and acting on plans to increase minority employment in newsrooms, failure to bring them fully into the workforce at various levels would seem to be inviting trouble.

Case law specific to journalism is scarce. The two best-known cases involving news organizations each demonstrate that the process is harrowing for both sides of the dispute. Four black reporters for the New York

Daily News charged that the newspaper had prevented them from advancing to better jobs. A jury agreed. The trial itself took more than nine weeks, and the dispute lasted more than four years.[70] The second case, brought by discharged local television news anchor Christine Craft, resulted in a deluge of publicity but a legal victory for the station.[71] Craft claimed that she had been discriminated against on the basis of sex and age. The appeals court accepted the station's reliance on audience surveys as sufficiently job-related to undercut the claim.[72]

Common Law Contract and Employment-at-Will

State courts have traditionally held that, in the absence of a written agreement to the contrary, an agreement between an employer and employer is terminable at any time by either party without notice. The employment-at-will doctrine so described was a product of nineteenth century legal interpretation, and has been under attack one way or another most of this century. It should be obvious that the doctrine works primarily to the benefit of employers; few employees will have sufficient bargaining power to prevail over an employer. The federal NLRA and FLSA are two of the limitations on the common law authority of employers, for example.

Many state courts have limited the employment-at-will doctrine. For the many newspapers whose employees are not protected by collective bargaining agreements, protection provided through exceptions to the employment-at-will doctrine may be the only available option. When the doctrine has been limited, it has usually been in one of two contexts. The first type of limitation is based on express promises made by an employer. These may be in writing, as in an employee handbook, or oral. Promises made expressly will be enforceable as in any contract.[73] Obviously, oral promises will be harder to prove, but an oral promise made to several employees is easily proved and might just as well be written out. There need be no evidence of any bargaining or meeting of the minds between the parties. It is sufficient that an employer can be proved to have made the promise.

The second type of limitation on the doctrine is based on public policy as expressed in constitutions or statutes. In general, employment-at-will agreements will be assumed by the courts to be consistent with existing law. A policy or agreement that requires an illegal action by an employee may be set aside as void if the employee challenges. Similarly, no provision restricting an employee from participating in activities the employee is legally entitled to engage in will be upheld in the absence of proof that the provision is directly job-related. In *Minnesota v. Knight-Ridder*,[74] a court upheld a newspaper's ethics code forbidding editorial employees from running for political office. The job-related conflict of interest is apparent.

Contract law can get much more complicated when the contract at issue is with a prize employee. These kind of "personal services" contracts are widespread in broadcast, but relatively uncommon in print. Typical provisions call for an employer to have the exclusive rights to the employee's services, or for a specified portion of services. Another typical provision is a limitation on the employee's ability to move to a competitor. In one television case, though, the limitation defined the entire state as a competing market, and a court voided the restriction as too broad.[75] Such a noncompetition clause will be upheld to the extent it reflects actual competition in the market. What if the market is nationwide?

One newspaper case was a cause celebre more than a cause of action in court. When columnist Mike Royko declared that he would no longer work for the Chicago *Sun-Times* after that newspaper was bought by Rupert Murdoch, the paper threatened to invoke the contract's non-competition clause to keep Royko from jumping to the *Tribune*. Royko argued that the clause and contract were no longer valid because the identities of the parties had changed. Although the two sides never faced off in court, it is difficult to predict who would have won. Personal services contracts, as in professional sports, are generally assignable. But Royko, especially as a columnist, is engaging in activity protected by the First Amendment; to hold him to the contract would require that he speak as an agent of a publisher he opposed in conscience.

NEWSPAPERS AND THE POSTAL LAWS

Postal law offers newspapers a benefit or privilege rather than potential liability. The practice of providing cut-rate mailing privileges to newspapers and other periodicals started in colonial days when Benjamin Franklin was postmaster. In the latter 1700s and through much of the nineteenth century, newspapers traveled through the mails at no cost.[76] Congress eventually devised in the postal act of 1879 the multi-level system of classes for mailable material.[77] Private letters are sent at first class rates. Second and third class were established as subsidized rates. Second class subsidies benefit newspapers, periodicals and similar types of materials, although the public is the primary beneficiary in the eyes of Congress. Third class rates were, until recently, primarily the province of non-profit groups.

For most of its life, postal law was located in government, in the Post Office Department. Following the Postal Reorganization Act of 1970, however, the resulting United States Postal Service (USPS) is a quasi-independent entity. Under the act, each class of mail is expected to bear its own costs.[78] Despite this mandate, subsidy has remained, as year after year Congress appropriates what it refers to as "revenue foregone subsidies." Each of the subsidy classes bears much more of the true cost of service than was true in 1970, however. For large newspapers that rely on the mails, such as the *Wall Street Journal*, a second class increase of just two or three cents can raise cost by millions of dollars. For small, often weekly, newspapers, increased postal costs can cut thinner an already thin profit or operating margin.

USPS proposes rate increases to the independent Postal Rate Commission. The commission has authority to accept, reject or modify rate increase recommendations. Once the rate increase has been approved, there is little chance that it will be reversed in court. The courts will use a rational basis or substantial evidence test, which favors the Postal Service, when weighing any challenge.[79] Despite odds against winning, publishers regularly challenge rate hikes. Strategically at least, going to court might delay the new rates. Second class does pay more of its costs. In 1970, general second class cost a nickel for the first two ounces, but by 1987, the same weight cost 39 cents. Even allowing for inflation, the increase is significant. Specific rates for newspapers and periodicals are lower than general second class rates. An eight-ounce paper mailed within one county travels for just under eight cents; out-of-county costs are almost double.

As in other areas of indirect regulation, there is a long-standing precedent based on a challenge to the statute and regulations. Under the postal laws, second class status is premised on a periodical having a "public character." In 1943, the Postmaster General determined that public character meant "a positive duty to contribute to the public good," and thereafter began actions to revoke the second class permit of *Esquire* magazine. The U.S. Supreme Court declared unconstitutional the discrimination based on an official's discretionary decision that the magazine's contents were subpar.[80] The Post Office and Postal Service have not rendered judgments on quality since.

The rationale behind the second class subsidy was that it would encourage citizens to obtain newspapers, thereby staying abreast of current events.[81] Just like sales tax exemptions, the subsidy is aimed at increasing demand by reducing costs for businesses. The third class subsidy was seen at least initially as a benefit for organizations that were working for the public good, a rationale similar to that underlying grants of tax-exempt status.

Newspapers have historically been most interested in second class. There are really only three issues regarding second class mail. The first two concern qualification for the status. A publication must, first, have a list of paid subscribers. The cost of a subscription must be above a nominal

BUSINESS REGULATION OF NEWSPAPERS 255

rate. The United States Postal Servive requires only that more than 50 percent of a newspaper's mailed copies be paid for. This regulation allows a newspaper to send free total-market type publications in numbers equal to just under half its paid subscription. When the Postal Service attempted to prevent the use of second class for total market publications, it was sued. The two Nashville, Tennessee dailies won on the ground that the change in policy amounted to a reclassification, which may only be done through the Postal Rate Commission. The change had not been the result of a commission recommendation.[82]

A newspaper that is circulated at no cost to readers may qualify if a sufficient number of recipients will fill out cards indicating their desire to receive the publication. The paid subscriber rule was challenged by a free circulation weekly newspaper in *Enterprise, Inc. v. United States*.[83] The newspaper argued that the rule was a facially discriminatory regulation singling out some members of the press for preferential differential treatment, basing the argument on the *Minneapolis Star* case. The court said that the *Star* case did not apply, holding that Congress and the Postal Service need only have a rational basis for the rule to be upheld. The congressional interest in assuring that the subsidy would be available only to newspapers which could demonstrate that readers considered them valuable was a sufficient basis, the court said. The paper also argued that the alternative of having readers fill out requester cards was unreasonable, but the court said otherwise.

The case appears to violate both the *Minneapolis Star* case, by failing to use a compelling interest test, and also the rational basis test. The entire point of a free circulation newspaper is achieve maximum exposure in hopes of reaching readers who will benefit from it. The court's analysis implies that the fact people pay for a newspaper makes it a better newspaper, and therefore more deserving of subsidy. The requester card system is impractical for publishers of free newspapers; imagine the difficulty of getting readers who have gotten used to receiving a newspaper at no charge to fill out a form. Besides, by concluding that paid newspapers have better content than free ones, the court runs afoul of the rule that government must remain content neutral.[84]

The other issue in qualifying for second class status concerns the relative amounts of news and advertising in a newspaper. To get the subsidy, a newspaper must devote no more than 75 percent of its total space to advertising copy on average; if more than half the issues in one year exceed the limit, the permit may be revoked.[85] This provision appears to facially violate the rule requiring content neutrality on the part of government. On the other hand, without such a rule—or the paid subscriber rule—there would perhaps be no way to limit the number and cost of second class permits.

Generally, second class permit holders must presort mail by zip code and pack the mail in bundles. There are separate rates for in-county and distant mailings, with in-county cheaper as an encouragement to community newspapers. In return for handling much of the work, publishers receive expedited service. For daily newspapers relying on the mails for delivery, such "red tag" service is essential.[86] Periodical publishers holding second class permits must also file information forms specifying ownership, circulation and "such other information as the Postal Service deems necessary.[87]

Another area of dispute is third class rates. Newspapers are quite concerned over the spread of direct mail advertising under third class status. Third class has been the fastest growing portion of the mails in the last decade, largely due to the growth of direct mail. In addition, some 300,000-plus non-profit organizations have third class status.[88] Third class direct mail advertisers and other permit holders perform even more detailed sorting and bundling than second class permit holders. The efficiency of these advertisers reduces cost to the point that items mailed almost cover their own cost, despite higher third class rates. Third class rates have been challenged by newspapers as too low, effectively creating an unfair competitive effect as between newspapers and direct mail advertisers,[89] but such challenges have been unavailing.

Third class permits must be granted by the USPS on a non-discriminatory basis just as second class permits are.[90] The cases involved discrimination based on an organization's status as a political party or group, but the principle is similar to that in the *Esquire* case.

NEWSPAPER DISTRIBUTION, CIRCULATION, AND RECIRCULATION

One problem created by umbrella competition is rapid growth in the number of newsracks on city sidewalks. In the downtown areas of even relatively small cities, one may find vending boxes of suburban dailies, satellite dailies, metro dailies, and national dailies, and usually boxes for specialized local publications as well. Partially as a result, the 1980s featured a dramatic increase in attempts by local governments to regulate the placement and number of newsracks. In some instances, cities have even attempted to regulate the appearance of newsracks. In addition to concern over the number and kind of newsracks, cities have been eager to pass regulations that assure newsrack owners bear any risk of injury or financial liability posed by their placement.

There have been dozens of cases brought that are available in the written opinions of courts—and there must be many dozens of disputes more that never made their way into court.[91] The government urge to regulate coincides with a newspaper industry urge to proliferate newsracks. While home delivery circulation has declined significantly the last decade, single-copy purchases, often from newsracks, have increased, especially in the markets with the largest newspapers.[92]

A decade of litigation was capped by a U.S. Supreme Court decision in 1988, the first newsrack case the Court has heard. In *City of Lakewood v. Plain Dealer Publishing Co.*,[93] the Cleveland *Plain Dealer* challenged a newsrack permit ordinance adopted by the suburb of Lakewood. The ordinance required that a newspaper submit applications to the mayor, who was required to "either deny the application, stating the reasons for such denial, or grant said permit..." No reasons for granting or denying a permit were stipulated in the ordinance. Even if the mayor approved a permit, the ordinance required approval by the city's Architectural Board of Review. No newsracks were allowed in residential areas. The ordinance also required that a newspaper provide proof of liability insurance for at least $100,000. Finally, the grant of a permit could be based upon "such other terms and conditions deemed necessary and reasonable" by the mayor.

The *Plain Dealer* claimed that the entire ordinance violated the First Amendment on its face. But the case raised several tricky issues of constitutional law for the Court to resolve. First, the Court had to decide if the newspaper was an appropriate party to bring a facial challenge; in First Amendment cases, a statute or regulation may be challengeable on its face, without waiting for enforcement proceedings, if the statute or regulation is overbroad or vague.[94] By a narrow margin, the seven members of the Court hearing the case (Rehnquist and Kennedy did not participate) agreed that the *Plain Dealer* was entitled to challenge the ordinance. A second tricky issue was the First Amendment status of newspaper distribution. It is well-established that the First Amendment protects publication, the right to gather news, and a right of access to certain places and materials. But does the First Amendment guarantee the right to distribute newspapers in a certain manner? The Court appeared to say it does, invoking arguments from cases on prior restraint to bolster its analysis.

The Court ultimately, though, treated the issue of newsrack regulation under the time, place, and manner test. Generally, government may regulate the time, place, or manner of expression if the regulation is content neutral and is neither vague nor overbroad.[95] The Lakewood ordinance failed because it was vague. It was vague because there were no standards stated for granting or denying a newsrack permit. It was also vague, and perhaps overbroad, in granting "unbounded" discretionary authority to the mayor.

The rules, then, for a newsrack regulation that will be considered constitutional appear to be as follows:

1. The regulation must be content-neutral and narrowly drawn to achieve a "substantial" or "significant" government interest.[96] Such an

interest can include the aesthetics of the community, public safety concerns for pedestrians and motorists, and equitable allocation of scarce space. Mere invocation of the interest by the local government is insufficient to establish the interest as substantial. Real proof that newsracks pose a danger to the interest is expected. Studies of both pedestrian and automobile traffic patterns might prove a safety interest, for example. For an aesthetic interest to be substantial, there must be some aesthetic to preserve.[97] A regulation is narrowly drawn when it is designed to accomplish the stated interest, but does not go farther than the interest. Usually the government must show that the regulation is likely to accomplish the interest as well.[98]

2. The regulation must be written clearly enough that its operation requires no significant interpretation. A first-come, first-served type of policy tends to be clear and also obviously neutral. As *Lakewood* demonstrates, a regulation cannot vest a government official with broad discretionary power. Standards must be stated in the regulation. The regulation must specify procedures for a denial to be challenged and reviewed.[99]

3. The regulation may not favor some newspapers over others, either directly or by operation of the regulation.[100] An ordinance that granted permits only to paid-circulation newspapers would likely violate the First Amendment. Similarly, a high fee structure that results in a competitive harm to smaller newspapers would likely be open to a discriminatory effect claim. That a publication is a shopper and primarily filled with advertising does not make it more subject to newsrack regulation than other publications.[101]

4. Sidewalks will generally be considered public forums. In First Amendment law, public forums are usually government-owned areas that have traditionally been open to use for expressive activity.[102] If the area in which a publisher wishes to place a newsrack is determined to be a public forum, a presumption arises that the First Amendment allows the expressive activity. Among the areas that have been held to be public forums are airport terminals, subway stations, and highway rest stops.[103] The public forum analysis appears to indicate that a city lacks the authority to ban newsracks altogether.[104] But the dissenters in the *Lakewood* case thought that cities retain the authority to ban newsracks altogether.[105]

5. Liability insurance premiums stipulated in the regulation must bear a close relationship to the risks associated with placement of the vending box. It should also be closely related to insurance requirements in analogous settings. A $1 million insurance requirement acts more like a prior restraint than a reasonable manner restriction.[106]

6. To be valid, time, place, and manner regulation must allow reasonable alternatives. The burden is on the government to show that alterna-

tives exist. A newsrack location at a corner without pedestrian traffic would likely be an unreasonable alternative.

7. Newspaper plaintiffs may recover attorney fees in some cases when the regulation is declared unconstitutional.[107]

Some unanswered questions remain. The numerous newsrack cases do not address the question suggested by the *Minneapolis Star* case. Are not these ordinances and statutes by definition singling out the press for negative differential treatment? Under the rule of that case, they would be presumptively invalid under the First Amendment, without regard to the time, place, and manner test. Justice Brennan's prevailing opinion in *Lakewood* accepts the linkage of content effects with cost and inconvenience effects, but did not apply a stricter test. The value of the *Lakewood* case as precedent must also be doubted. With only a 4-3 decision and an argument that rested primarily on giving the mayor too much discretion, the case hardly resolves all the legal issues regarding newsracks.[108]

Similar issues arise when local governments attempt to control circulation by carriers or delivery agents. Fewer cases have arisen concerning delivery, but the basic rules remain the same. When the town of Doylestown, Pennsylvania, attempted to restrict delivery of a free-circulation shopper that contained a smattering of news on the basis of an interest in preventing littering and vandalism, the regulation was declared unconstitutional because it discriminated on the basis of content, was not narrowly drawn, and there were no reasonable alternative methods of circulation available to the shopper.[109]

Newspaper delivery tubes along streets and highways have also been the subject of regulatory attempts. Whether or not the side of the road is considered a public forum has apparently not been decided. But an additional First Amendment argument exists for newspapers to challenge attempts to ban or regulate delivery tubes—the right of the audience to receive the newspaper and the ideas within it.[110] Two Wisconsin papers sued to reverse a Door County zoning board decision that delivery tubes with the names of newspapers on the side are signs for purposes of a county ordinance that bans signs on the side of the road.[111]

State laws mandating the use of recycled newsprint were passed in 1989 in Connecticut and Florida, and other states are considering similar measures. The Florida statute requires that newspapers serve as recycling drop-off sites; it also imposes a 10 percent tax on virgin newsprint. Connecticut's law is less strict financially, but stricter on goals. By 1998, newspapers must be 90 percent recycled. It does, however, create a Newspaper Recycling Task Force, which will include two newspaper representatives appointed by the state house and senate majority leaders. It is uncertain how the push for recycling will develop, and for that matter how these or similar laws will fare when challenged, but one author who examined recycling from a First Amendment perspective anticipates their invalidity.[112] The industry has become actively interested in newsprint recycling for pragmatic reasons in any event. Perhaps the economic viability of recycling[113] will increase along with the industry's voluntary recycling efforts, avoiding a court battle.

SUMMARY

Each of the areas of business regulation reviewed in this chapter impinge on the financial and internal policy options of newspaper firms, effectively modifying the market. Tax law, with its post-World War II history of use as an instrument of social engineering and economic policy, is likely to have the greatest effect on management options. Labor law likely has the second-largest effect. But labor law ground rules have been around so long and changed so little that they are today constraints that are largely internalized by managers, and hence less noticeable. Postal law is much more difficult to assess. In no other area of law has government so clearly, or for so long, encouraged activity in the intellectual market. But the rationale for subsidy is dubious now. Alternatives and substitutes abound. The firms that benefit most are those least in need. Regulation of circulation and distribution concerns overt physical behavior of businesses rather than economic behavior. The constraints are fewer here. Alone among media, newspapers have a right to distribute copies on public ways at no cost.

The freedom to set up newsracks on public sidewalks is an expansive interpretation of the First Amendment. Yet each of the areas of regulation to some extent illustrates the special status of newspapers that separates them from other businesses, making newspaper economics unlike the economics of many other industries. Newspapers may challenge regulation where others might not. Often they win, where others are sure to fail. Government is on notice from the courts to take extra care when regulating newspapers. And newspapers are often the beneficiaries of special treatment unavailable to other businesses. Both the courts and legislative bodies have repeatedly recognized that adding or reducing costs affects the intellectual market. How those costs are added or reduced can make a great difference in the constitutional viability of regulation.

ENDNOTES

1. *Miami Herald Publishing Co. v. Tornillo*, 418 U.S. 241 (1974).
2. Opinion of the Justices, 392 N.E.2d 849 (Mass. 1979); Consumers Union v. Periodical Correspondents Association, 365 F.Supp. 18 (D.D.C. 1973).

3. 301 U.S. 103 (1937).
4. Donald M. Gillmor, Jerome A. Barron, Todd F. Simon, Herbert A. Terry, *Mass Communication Law: Cases and Comment*, 5th ed. (St.Paul, MN.: West Publishing Co., 1990), pp. 713-742.
5. *Advertising Compliance Handbook* (New York: Practicing Law Institute, 1988).
6. *Allied Stores of Ohio, Inc. v. Bowers*, 358 U.S. 527 (1959).
7. Mary A. Anderson, "Taxing Position," *presstime*, March 1987, p. 6.
8. *First Federal Savings & Loan Association v. State Tax Commission*, 363 N.E.2d 474 (Mass. 1977), *affirmed*, 437 U.S. 255 (1978).
9. 460 U.S. 575 (1983).
10. Todd F. Simon, "All the News That's Fit to Tax: First Amendment Limitations on State and Local Taxation of the Press," *Wake Forest Law Review* 21:1 (Spring 1985), pp. 87-89.
11. 460 U.S. at 585.
12. *Consolidated Edison Co. v. Public Service Commission*, 447 U.S. 530 (1980).
13. Simon, *op. cit.*, pp. 80-84.
14. 111 S.Ct. 1438 (1991): *Arkansas Writers' Project v. Ragland*, 481 U.S. 221 (Scalia, J., dissenting).
15. 297 U.S. 233 (1936).
16. "Legislatures chip away at newspapers' tax exemptions," *presstime*, August 1986, p. 40.
17. *Hearst Corp. v. Missouri Director of Revenue*, 779 S.W.2d 557 (Mo. 1989); "Missouri legislature lifts retroactive tax on newspapers," *presstime*, June 1990, p. 65; *see also, Huntington Publishing Co. v. Caryl*, 377 S.E.2d 479 (W.Va. 1988)(sales by route carriers subject to sales tax).
18. Weber, "Florida's Fleeting Sales Tax on Services," *Florida State University Law Review* 15:613 (1987).
19. *City of Baltimore v. A.S. Abell Co.*, 145 A.2d 111 (Md. 1958).
20. *Catholic Archdiocese of Denver v. Denver*, 741 P.2d 333 (Colo. 1987).
21. *Dow Jones & Co., Inc. v. Oklahoma*, 16 Med. L. Rep. 2049 (Okla. 1989).
22. *Golden Triangle Broadcasting, Inc. v. City of Pittsburgh*, 397 A.2d 1147 (Pa. Commonwealth Ct. 1979).
23. *McClure Newspapers v. Vermont Department of Taxes*, 315 A.2d 452 (1974).
24. *In re Appeal of K-Mart*, 710 P.2d 1304 (Kan. 1985); *Allentown v. Call-Chronicle*, 13 Med. L. Rep. 2329 (Pa. Ct.Common Pleas 1987); *Daily Record Co. v. James*, 629 S.W.2d 348 (Mo. 1982).
25. *Hannaford Brothers Co. v. Vermont Department of Taxes*, 15 Med. L. Rep. 1413 (Vt. 1988); Sears, Roebuck & Co. v. Woods, 708 S.W.2d 374 (Tenn. 1986).
26. *Bodenstein v. Vermont*, 510 A.2d 1314 (Vt. 1986).
27. 322 S.E.2d 155 (N.C. 1984), *appeal dismissed*, 105 S.Ct. 2693 (1985).
28. *Redwood Empire Publishing Co. v. California State Board of Equalization*, 255 Cal. Rptr. 514 (Cal.App. 1989).
29. *Miami Herald Publishing Co. v. Tornillo*, 418 U.S. 241 (1974).
30. *Huntington Publishing Co. v. Caryl*, 377 S.E.2d 479 (W.Va. 1988).
31. Todd F. Simon, "Tax-Free Speech: Exempt Organizations, Government

Promotion of Expression, and the First Amendment," Unpublished manuscript, 1985.
32. *Ibid.*; Internal Revenue Code sec. 501(c)(3).
33. *Big Mama Rag, Inc. v. United States*, 613 F.2d 1030 (D.C.Cir. 1980).
34. *National Alliance v. United States*, 710 F.2d 868 (D.C.Cir. 1983).
35. Simon, 1985, *op. cit.*, pp. 50-55.
36. Jonathan Kwitny, "The High Cost of High Profits," *Washington Journalism Review*, June 1990, pp. 19-29.
37. *Times Mirror Co. v. Los Angeles*, 237 Cal. Rptr. 346 (Cal.App. 1987).
38. *City of Alameda v. Premier Communications Network, Inc.*, 202 Cal. Rptr. 684 (Cal.App. 1984).
39. *Regan v. Taxation With Representation*, 461 U.S. 540 (1983).
40. *Thomson Newspapers, Inc. v. City of Florence*, 338 S.E.2d 324 (S.C. 1985).
41. James N. Dertouzos and Kenneth E. Thorpe, *Newspaper Groups: Economies of Scale, Tax Laws, and Merger Incentives* (Santa Monica, CA: Rand Corp., 1982).
42. 29 U.S.C. sec. 151 et seq.
43. John E. Nowak, Ronald D. Rotunda, and J. Nelson Young, *Constitutional Law*, 3rd ed. (St. Paul, MN.: West Publishing Co., 1986), pp. 350-361.
44. U.S. CONST. art. VI, cl. 2.
45. 29 U.S.C. sec. 201 et seq.
46. 301 U.S. 103 (1937).
47. *Cincinnati Suburban Press, Inc. v. Flannery*, 289 NLRB No. 127 (1988).
48. *Newspaper Guild v. NLRB*, 636 F.2d 550 (D.C.Cir. 1980).
49. *Capital Times Co. and Newspaper Guild of Madison*, Local 64, 223 NLRB No. 87 (1976).
50. 29 U.S.C. sec. 158(d).
51. Gillmor *et al.*, *op. cit.*, pp. 574-576.
52. *Brown Newspaper Publishing Co. and San Francisco-Oakland Newspaper Guild*, Local 52, NLRB Decisions 1981-1982, No. 18,401.
53. *New York Times Co. and Newspaper Guild of New York*, Local 3, 1984-1985 NLRB Decisions, No. 16,468.
54. The Detroit News, A Division of the Evening News Association, and Local 22, the Newspaper Guild, NLRB Decisions, 1984-1985, No. 16,562.
55. 29 U.S.C. sec. 152 (12).
56. *Wichita Eagle & Beacon Publishing Co. v. NLRB*, 480 F.2d 52 (10th Cir. 1973), *cert. denied*, 416 U.S. 982 (1974).
57. 327 U.S. 186 (1946).
58. *Donovan v. Reno Builders Exchange*, 26 Wage and Hour Cases 1234 (D.Nev. 1984).
59. "ANPA urges labeling reporters as professionals," *presstime*, April 1986, p. 64; "Definition of 'professional' sharpens," *presstime*, January 1988, p. 52; "Reporters ruled 'professionals'," *presstime*, February 1988, p. 66; Clark Newsom, "Union Decertifications Increase," *presstime*, January 1998, p. 30; Clark Newsom, "The Changing Face of the Newspaper Workforce," *presstime*, March 1987, pp. 26-34.

60. 677 F.Supp. 9 (D.D.C. 1988).
61. *Sherwood v. Washington Post,* 871 F.2d 1144 (D.C.Cir. 1989).
62. 706 I. Supp. 493 (N.D.Tex. 1988).
63. Andrew Radolf, "Philadelphia NLRB says stringers are employees," *Editor & Publisher,* August 13, 1988, p. 28.
64. *Kassel v. Gannett Co, Inc.,* 875 F.2d 935 (1st Cir. 1989).
65. Gene Goltz, "Split Verdict in Employee Status," *presstime,* May 1988, p. 78.
66. Simon, "All the News," *op. cit.,* p. 89.
67. 42 U.S.C. sec. 2000e et seq.
68. George E. Stevens, "Discrimination in the Newsroom: Title VII and the Journalist," *Journalism Monographs,* No. 94, September 1985, pp. 2-4.
69. *Hazelwood School District v. United States,* 433 U.S. 299 (1977).
70. Jan Albert, "The Trial of New York's *Daily News,*" *Columbia Journalism Review,* July/August 1987, pp. 27-33.
71. *Craft v. Metromedia,* 766 F.2d 1205 (8th Cir. 1985).
72. Note, Sex Discrimination in Newscasting, *Michigan Law Review* 84:443 (1985).
73. Annette Taylor, "Newspaper Ethics Codes and the Employment-at-Will Doctrine," Paper presented to the Law Division, Association for Education in Journalism and Mass Communication, Portland, OR, July 1988; Gail Barwis, "Contractual Newsroom Democracy," *Journalism Monographs,* No. 57, August 1978.
74. 5 Med. L. Rep. 1705 (Minn. Dist. Ct. 1979).
75. *Capital Cities Communications v. Sheehan,* 9 Med. L. Rep. 2172 (Ct. Super. Ct. 1983).
76. Jean Folkerts and Dwight L. Teeter, *Voices of a Nation* (New York: Macmillan Publishing Co., 1989), p. 92.
77. 20 Stat. 355.
78. 39 U.S.C. sec. 3622(b)(3) et seq.
79. *Direct Marketing Association v. Postal Service,* 778 F.2d 96 (2d Cir. 1985).
80. *Hannegan v. Esquire,* 327 U.S. 146 (1946).
81. Note, "Second-Class Postal Rates and the First Amendment," *Rutgers Law Review* 28:693, 702 (1975).
82. "Nashville dailies win suit over 2nd-class TMC mail," *presstime,* July 1988, p. 74.
83. 833 F.2d 1216 (6th Cir. 1987).
84. *Pacific Gas & Electric Co. v. Public Utilities Commission of California,* 475 U.S. 1 (1986).
85. Public Law 233, 65 Stat. 672.
86. *Dow Jones & Co., Inc. v. Postal Service,* 656 F.2d 786 (D.C.Cir. 1981).
87. 39 U.S.C. sec. 3685.
88. U.S. Postal Service, "Third Class Nonprofit Permits and Volume by Type of Qualifying Organization" (1986).
89. "ANPA warns of danger to second-class," *presstime,* June 1990, p. 62; "Proposed lower ad-mail rate pits ANPA against direct mailers," *presstime,* April 1990, p. 54.

90. *Spencer v. Herdesty*, 571 F.Supp. 444 (S.D.Ohio 1983); *Greenberg v. Bolger*, 497 F.Supp. 756 (E.D.NY 1980).
91. Wallace B. Eberhard, "Journalism on the Rack: Regulating Newspaper Vending Machines," *Newspaper Research Journal*, Winter 1989, p. 27.
92. "Single-copy sales take up some of the slack," *presstime*, May 1989, p. 81.
93. 108 S.Ct. 2138 (1988).
94. *Maryland v. Joseph H. Munson Co., Inc.*, 104 S.Ct. 2839 (1984).
95. *Heffron v. International Society for Krishna Consciousness*, 452 U.S. 640 (1981).
96. *Jacobsen v. Harris*, 869 F.2d 1172 (8th Cir. 1989).
97. *Southern New Jersey Newspapers, Inc. v. New Jersey Department of Transportation*, 542 F.Supp. 173 (D.N.J. 1982).
98. *Washington Post Co. v. Turner*, 708 F.Supp. 405 (D.D.C. 1989).
99. *Chicago Newspaper Publishers Association v. City of Wheaton*, 697 F.Supp. 1464 (N.D.Ill. 1988).
100. *Jacobsen v. United States Postal Service*, 812 F.2d 1151 (9th Cir. 1987).
101. *New York City v. American School Publications*, 509 N.E.2d 311 (N.Y. 1987).
102. *Widmar v. Vincent*, 454 U.S. 263 (1981).
103. *Gannett Satellite Information Network, Inc. v. White*, 14 Med. L. Rep. 2037 (N.D.N.Y. 1987).
104. *Providence Journal Co. v. City of Newport*, 665 F.Supp. 107 (D.R.I. 1987).
105. *City of Lakewood*, 108 S.Ct. at 2152.
106. *News Printing Co. v. Borough of Totowa*, 511 A.2d 133 (N.J.Super.Ct. 1986).
107. *Chicago Newspaper Publishers Association v. City of Wheaton*, 16 Med. L. Rep. 2207 (N.D.Ill. 1989).
108. Eberhard, *op. cit.*, p. 36.
109. *Ad World v. Doylestown*, 672 F.2d 1136 (3d Cir. 1982).
110. *Booth Newspapers, Inc. v. City of Ann Arbor*, 3 Med. L. Rep. 2180 (Mich.Circ.Ct. 1977).
111. "Newspapers appeal order to remove delivery tubes," *presstime*, June 1989, p. 106.
112. Helen Niemiec, "Press Rolls Over, Plays Dead in New Assaults on First Amendment Protection," Paper presented to the Law Division, Association for Education in Journalism and Mass Communication, Minneapolis, MN, August 1990.
113. *Ibid.*, pp. 18-21.

10

Conclusions

As a discipline of study, economics concerns the allocation of scarce resources to achieve goals. These allocations take place within a set of constraints that affect the amount of resources available and how those resources can be used. These constraints come from the marketplace, where a business must buy raw materials and sell its commodities, and from government intervention. The number of constraints and how much power they divert from the firm affect the structure of the marketplace. A perfectly competitive market structure means individual firms have no power to alter the market, while monopoly market structure means one individual firm controls the market. In reality, most industries fall somewhere between these two extremes.

Generally, newspaper owners and managers have a great deal of discretionary power when it comes to their markets. This power results mostly from being the only newspaper within a geographic area, which is the situation in the vast majority of cities and towns. In the strictest sense, these newspapers are not monopolies, but they do exercise a degree of monopoly power. The existence of other media and competition from newspapers outside the city places limits on the monopoly power.

The freedom of readers to take a newspaper or not is also a constraint. The markets in which newspapers must buy supplies, labor, and technology also constrain the firm's decisions. Finally, governments limit newspaper managers' decisions through their regulation of various business activities.

THE IMPACT OF MARKET AND REGULATORY CONSTRAINTS

The following section will address the constraints that flow from competition, demand, suppliers, and government regulations in order to get a sense of how a newspaper's environment affects its efforts to achieve goals.

The assumption of this analysis is that newspaper firms have three goals: (a) a newspaper firm aims to produce a high profit, (b) a newspaper firm aims to create a newspaper with enough information quality to retain readers across time, (c) a newspaper firm aims to fulfill its social responsibility in the intellectual market at a level that will continue public support for its First Amendment protection. The first goal tends to be a short-run goal that is evaluated every year by looking at revenue and costs. The second and third goals are long-run goals that are extremely difficult to evaluate. The inability to evaluate those goals as easily as profit does not lessen their importance to the long-term survival of newspapers.

Newspaper firms do not attempt to maximize profits in the sense that they produce to the point where marginal revenue equals marginal cost. It is next to impossible to know where this point occurs—even in an industry as simple as shoe manufacturing. The joint commodity nature of newspapers, with the interdependence of three markets, makes such a goal impossible. However, most newspapers seek high profits, but the levels of profit goals vary. The efforts to make high profits are reflected in high return on investment of newspaper firms. In 1986, the average newspaper's profits equaled 27 percent of assets, which was the highest of all communication industries.[1]

High profit goals have led critics to argue that newspapers do not try to produce quality commodities. Unfortunately for readers, many examples of this behavior exist. Some owners and managers cut news-editorial costs to increase profit, but some of these same people will say they produce a quality newspaper. The differences in quality sometimes arise because of differences in managers' perceptions about what constitutes quality and in the minimum quality level necessary to retain readers in local markets. Financial resources also play a role in determining what levels of quality can be reached. Managers with large absolute amounts of resources find it easier to balance potentially conflicting goals than do those with few resources. This explains why large circulation newspapers tend to dominate lists of "best" newspapers.

While the goal of quality information is only difficult to determine because of measurement problems, the third goal is impossible to quantify adequately. A newspaper manager cannot know what level of participation in the intellectual market is necessary to retain public support, or even interest, for the unique role of newspapers in a democracy. However, most editors recognize that opinion material is important in attracting readers, although they may not link that with its role in retaining public support for the First Amendment.

These three goals are assumed here for the sake of analysis. Whether an individual newspaper organization accepts such goals depends on the people who run the newspaper. The important point is that these goals are not independent of each other. Each influences and is influenced by the other. The fact that readers expect all three markets to be served means the goals will have an impact on the long-run prosperity of the newspaper firm.

Often, one goal may be sacrificed to some degree to achieve another goal because managers are allocating scarce resources. Just as decisions concerning different goals are interrelated, short-run decisions affect long-run performance. A decision that accomplishes goals in the short-run may have a negative impact on the same goal during the long-run. With the three assumed goals in mind, the impact of constraints on allocation by newspaper managers will be discussed in relation to demand, supply, competition, and regulation.

Demand

Demand by readers and advertisers constrains newspaper firms to the degree that acceptable substitutes are available. Because newspapers serve three main markets and several advertising submarkets, the substitutability of other commodities varies within a geographic market for the same firm. The resulting complexity in decision making is further exacerbated by the limited ability to measure demand in the information and intellectual markets.

For example, a newspaper considering an expansion of information faces numerous options. The extent of the options can be seen from Table 2.2. This table presents a typology for categorizing information. If you exclude advertising, the table presented six geographic categories, four nature of news information categories, two format categories, and eight topic area categories. Combining these categories results in 384 different types of information from which a manager could select to try to increase readership. These classifications narrow the options, but the question of which content areas to concentrate on remains difficult to answer, especially since each of the information areas will draw its own readers.

Analyzing advertising market decisions is not quite as complex, but neither is it easy. Pricing decisions for various submarkets must reflect the ability of the advertisers to move to other media if they do not like the newspaper's price. But substitutability is a function of price and the nature of media. For years, newspapers in most markets faced few substitutes for run-of-the-paper display advertising. This condition changed with the ability of advertisers to print insert advertising. The resulting cross-elasticity of price demand from one submarket to the other is not always easy to estimate. In this case, the same firm provides space for both submarkets, display and inserts.

In effect, newspaper managers allocating resources face a double constraint from demand, which is exaggerated by the complexity of newspaper markets. The first limitation is the traditional one in economics. A newspaper must produce a commodity that readers and advertisers will pay for or it will not continue in business. The second constraint is one of uncertainty. It is difficult to allocate resources without information concerning what it is that readers will buy. The two constraints are interrelated and would occur even in a simple market; the three interconnected markets of the newspaper industry makes decision making more difficult.

The constraint of meeting demand can have short-run and long-run effects. One short-run effect in the information market is a tendency to react more to readers' immediate wants as determined by surveys. This reaction occurred frequently during the 1980s and usually involves three steps. The process starts with the recognition that circulation is either declining or not increasing with the population. The second step is to conduct a readership survey to determine what the readers want. The third step is to modify the newspaper content to reflect at least some of the survey results.

In the abstract, it does not seem like this process should create difficulty, but it has for three reasons. First, readers' immediate wants do not necessarily reflect their future needs. For example, a family may not pay attention to news about the local school district until it has a child in school. Parents' information wants when their child is two differ from their needs when the child is eight. They may be aware that their wants and needs change, but the awareness is limited when it comes to predicting exactly what types of stories they will desire in six years. In any event, asking readers what they want will likely draw suggestions for feature or entertainment material. Not even editors, much less readers, can predict future news or its value.

Second, the need to consider long-run impact increases the uncertainty about reader demand. Uncertainty is reduced by information, and information about the future is limited. Information about the future is derived by prediction, using statistical methods with current data. Prediction is based on models of behavior. As pointed out, theories and models of behavior concerning newspaper use are scarce and underdeveloped. Attempted to use demographics and psychographics to develop such predictive models have not been totally satisfactory.

Classic microeconomic models of consumer behavior have been inadequate because they assume buyers and sellers have perfect knowledge and that products are perfect substitutes. Even though these assumptions are unrealistic, they need not cause serious problems when price is the key variable. Price is a consistent and easily observable measure for evaluating supply and demand. But with commodities that involve consumer "taste," measurement is a tricky problem. Limited measurement in areas such as quality and taste has stunted development of theories of reader demand.

But the absence of adequate theory is not the only constraint facing newspaper managers in their effort to predict long-run behavior. A lack of understanding of research methods is a third reason behind the difficulty in dealing with changing reading habits. The lack of understanding of research for estimating shifts in demand can cause serious problems for journalists who engage in management. It means they are ill-prepared for participating in long-term planning. Second, it means they may not be in a position to counteract efforts of other managers to overemphasize profit.

Supply

Supply constraints take the form of problems with raw materials, labor, and technology. Of these, raw materials are the easiest to understand. Ink and paper are the basic ingredients of the production process. Ink is of minor importance compared to paper. Paper constrains newspapers through its impact on costs. Increasing newsprint cost means either lower profit or higher prices. Lower profits result in even more scarce resources and tougher allocation decisions. Higher prices mean a potential decline in demand with a possible decline in profit. Whether this profit decline actually occurs depends on the nature of competition in the markets. Monopoly power allows a firm to pass increasing costs to readers.

While increasing newsprint costs can be a short-run headache, newspaper firms can take definite steps to reduce the pressure in the long run. First, the firm can conserve in various ways. Second, it can encourage and participate in community conservation. Third, it can invest money in the long-run development of paper production capacity. Newspaper firms are doing all of these.

Labor supply poses problems similar to those faced in the raw material markets. The need for good journalists, advertising sales people, delivery people, and managers requires competitive salaries. Higher salaries, just as higher newsprint prices, mean either lower profits or higher prices, with the corresponding results. Managers often assume it is easy, however, to dodge the impact of lower labor quality than the impact of inadequate newsprint supply. Without newsprint, there are no newspaper copies. With lower quality journalists, copies are still produced and the ultimate impact is not as obvious. So, cutting labor costs appears to have less of an impact than not having enough newsprint. This is a deception.

Using cheaper labor with weaker skills will have definite long-run, negative effects on a newspaper firm. Over time, circulation will fall from dissatisfaction with news-editorial content and delivery service, and lower-level management with weak skills will make poor decisions. All of these will increase costs and reduce revenues. The newspaper tradition of hiring entry-level journalists at low wages, especially in small and medium markets, expecting them to "move up" to better-paying newspaper organizations, seems inconsistent with sound management in an industry with high profit margins.

Newspaper labor problems have been recounted numerous times in the trade press during the 1980s. The failure to offer salaries competitive with those in public relations, reductions in reporter autonomy, the inability to recruit and retain minority journalists, and the failure to train managers adequately are all recognized problems in the industry. Toward the end of the 1980s, the industry showed movement, at least among larger firms, toward solving some of these problems, but the cumulative impact of qualified people leaving newspaper journalism has yet to be determined.

Technology also affects both costs and revenues. The main way to increase productivity and lower costs is through adoption of better technical methods. Technology is also related to increased revenue by assisting in creating a better commodity. Current constraints on newspaper firms come more from the technology that does not exist than from existing technology. Newspaper managers see great potential in growing technology. The potential can be tapped in two ways: development and adoption of technology. Development of technology means research and development by the industry for the industry, which is taking place to a degree. Adoption means using existing technology to reduce cost or increase revenue.

Because of hidden costs of using technology and lack of predictive ability concerning information demand, adopting technology does not always have the anticipated results. People in any industry often seem to adopt technology because it is there. Managers can become so fascinated by a process that they buy it with little thought to whether or not it will accomplish the goals of the organization. Technological adoption that changes newspaper content or the delivery system should have some basis in reader demand. The fact that something can be done does not mean the average person will pay for it. Similarly, the fact that a technology will reduce cost does not mean employees can or will embrace the new process readily and easily.

Competition

As detailed earlier, competition is a major constraint for newspaper firms in some areas, but not in others. The competition for readers and advertisers occurs through price and content and occurs primarily in the information and advertising markets.

In the advertising market, competition from a multitude of other forms of communication affects the amount of advertising linage and the price that can be charged for it. This varies with the substitutability of other media for the various submarkets of newspaper advertising. The intensity of the competition often grows from the very success of the newspaper. The high price of display advertising helped to push advertisers to inserts and direct mail. The high profit made from classified advertising helped attract shoppers into the industry.

In the information market, the increasing competition for the readers' time and money and the changing nature of the audience have caused leveling in circulation growth. The overall information environment that readers live in can affect the way they expect to receive information and the nature of the content they want to use. As a result of these trends, managers sometimes question the effectiveness of specific newspaper content.

Increased competition for attention means managers must continuingly evaluate their commodity to see if it meets readers' needs and wants. An editor can no longer assume that she or he knows what the reader likes and needs. At the same time, a manager cannot unquestioningly apply the results of a readership survey; what people need and what they want at the time of a survey may not be the same.

In addition to uncertainty about content, the manager is faced with uncertainty about the impact and constraints of various forms of competition. A hundred years ago, newspaper editors and publishers knew their main competition was from the other papers in their market that were on the same publication cycle. All they had to do was produce a better newspaper at a lower price to be successful. Today, competition flows from alternative media and from various forms of newspapers. The new forms of competition create uncertainty about what content newspapers should publish and about the very nature of how readers use newspapers. Despite the uncertainty of demand, the rule of producing a better newspaper holds true. The problem is that managers are not sure anymore what "a better newspaper" means.

Regulation

Some federal and state laws, such as postal regulations and labor law, act as day-to-day business constraints. However, newspapers have generally been less constrained by antitrust laws than most industries. Although the First Amendment has not prevented antitrust enforcement, the special economic status of newspapers has. This special treatment is partially formalized through the Newspaper Preservation Act, which explicitly limits antitrust enforcement.

While the government has been hesitant to pursue antitrust cases, private companies have been involved in such suits. Busterna listed 44 private antitrust cases between 1980 and 1986.[2] Of these 44, only six were won by the plaintiff. These figures do not include the type of situation where a daily uses predatory practices on a weekly and then buys the weekly because the smaller paper does not have the resources to battle or sue. It would appear that even privately instituted antitrust actions are unpromising as a deterrent to illegal business behaviors in the industry.

Despite not being a deterrent, antitrust laws can have some constraining impact on newspapers. The potential for a suit is always present, especially in a market involving two successful groups. This potential does eliminate some of the more obviously illegal practices, such as tying. The disincentive is, of course, directly proportional to the potential for legal action. Just a few actions by the Justice Department would work to constrain newspaper management behavior that is injurious to the readers.

The effects of other areas of regulation and law on newspaper economics and competition are much harder to assess. Only in postal regulation, where the costs from rate increases are easily computed, can effects be assessed readily. The biggest postal subsidy issues for the future are whether or not Congress will continue subsidies and at what levels, and the use of subsidized mailing by competitors. Direct mailers are efficient, if expensive, and draw advertising revenues away from newspaper firms while using a subsidized rate. It is little wonder that the industry opposes third-class rulings that benefit direct mail. Less easy to understand is the opposition of the newspaper industry to letting free circulation newspapers qualify for the second-class subsidy. Should the intellectual market justification for subsidy depend on having a cover price? The answer to this question may change as large groups buy more weekly newspapers.

Tax incentives and postal subsidies both undoubtedly help newspaper firms economically, but it is difficult to estimate the value of that help. Sales tax exemptions reduce tax payments, but no one has shown that exemptions induce people to buy copies of newspapers, which is the rationale. The net effect of sales tax exemption, then, is that newspaper firms clearly benefit, but it is not clear that readers or society at large do. The slight difference in price without sales tax exemption might have no effect on reader demand. In the meantime, newspaper firms' retail and advertising sales remain exempt in most states, an advantage not available to other commodities.

The basic rationale for income tax exemption is the same. Yet there is no study showing that nonprofit, tax-exempt status has encouraged the creation of newspapers or, for that matter, other media, that might not have appeared in the absence of exemption.

Postal subsidy too is based on inducing greater participation in the intellectual market. With an ever-growing number of alternatives in this market, special economic advantages to producers of tangible mailable goods deserves to be reexamined. Its role in the spread of newspapers and magazines during the 19th century is recognized, but the need for it in the late 20th century is undocumented. On First Amendment grounds alone, it patently favors print media, especially newspapers, over nonprint media. No compelling government interest for the distinction is apparent. In addition, this benefit, like others, also has not been studied in an attempt to discover whether or not it actually affects purchase behaviors. If it does not, there is little to justify postal subsidy save tradition and nostalgia.

Labor regulation is changing rapidly in the newspaper industry, as in other mature industries. The percentage of workforce represented by unions, especially among newsroom personnel, is declining, making the National Labor Relations Act and the attendant regulations of the National Labor Relations Board less relevant. At the same time, the education and training of newspaper employees in all departments is more advanced than ever before, requiring that newspaper managers develop skills in interpersonal communication and negotiation on issues that may formerly have been dealt with collectively.

While collective regulation of labor has declined, individual protection has grown, largely as a result of various civil rights laws, but also due to changing judicial interpretations regarding employment contracts. Managers must be aware of and responsive to the rights of employees as individuals. The industry's shift from a collectively represented one should not lull managers into thinking that labor regulation is no longer a concern.

The provisions in several states to require that newspapers use a certain amount of recycled newsprint may represent a major trend for the 1990s, and at the same time a shift in focus for newspaper managers from federal law to state and local law as the basis for regulation. Such a shift should be no surprise after ten years of federal regulatory inaction under presidents Reagan and Bush.

Only one area of regulation appears solid. Newspaper firms have a legal right to place newsracks on public sidewalks. It is not an absolute right, but no precedent allows a local government to ban the boxes altogether. As competition for single-copy sales grows, this legal protection will take on additional significance.

Summary

Despite the high degree of monopoly power some newspapers have (compared to other industries), managers in the business still face many constraints. These constraints are similar to those faced by other industries. Constraints are not negative in and of themselves. Some, such as most regulations, exist to protect the public. Others, such as competition, help managers respond to a changing environment. In all cases, two things are clear. Constraints change with time, and management will always face them.

Newspaper firms face these constraints in both the supply and demand markets. In the supply markets, they have to compete for labor and raw materials to produce copies. They are also constrained by nondirect competition, primarily in the advertising market. Direct mail, television, radio, magazines, billboards, trade shows, and newspapers from other umbrella layers are all after the same pool of advertising money.

Constraints in the intellectual market are primarily self-imposed. Since it is difficult to establish accurately the relationship between supply and demand in the intellectual market, newspaper managers are only vaguely aware of what they should be doing with content to respond to either. This is a vital area to the industry, and as such, it should have periodic evaluation.

Constraints in the information market have more to do with the changing nature of the public than the specific content of newspapers. Declining penetration results more from changes in the way people distribute their time than in a direct substitution of television or radio news for newspapers. Because of this, newspapers may only have a minimal, short-run impact by changing content. It seems unlikely that newspapers will ever return to the high penetration rates of the early 20th century.

Even though newspapers will not regain the levels of penetration held earlier, several steps exist that can help make them more responsive to the constraints that occur in the environment. The following section discusses some of the options newspaper firms have for long-term growth.

POLICY ISSUES IN THE NEWSPAPER INDUSTRY

While the previous section discussed existing constraints on the newspaper industry, this section will review specific areas of policy facing the industry in the future. *Policy* refers to issues of social interest. The issues need not involve regulation or other government concerns. The standard for discussion here is that the issues relate to the special place of newspapers in the U.S. society.

Competition

Without dramatic changes in production and distribution technology, head-to-head competition among dailies within the same city will soon disappear in all but the largest cities. The joint commodity nature of newspapers and the high fixed cost of operating a daily form a one-two punch difficult to survive. The only hope for future direct competition would be significantly reduced fixed cost that would lessen the impact of the joint commodity nature. Such technological changes do not appear on the horizon.

The disappearance of this form of competition does not mean the end of all competition. Deregulation of broadcast television holds promise for developing the role of TV news in the intellectual market. The growing length of newscasts in many markets also may provide increased competition in the information and advertising markets. Advertising competitors, such as direct mail, will continue to emerge because of the profitability of newspapers.

While these developments will certainly affect newspaper management decision making, the positive impact on the public may be limited. Direct mail tends to carry little news or opinion. Even the increased news and opinion information available through TV news will be limited at a local level. Research indicates that most of the increased time is going to national and foreign news.[3] The addition of TV editorials, worthwhile as they may be, will have limited local impact. Access for the public will be limited even if all three network affiliates started running editorials. The stations usually run news concurrently. Since television news is rarely taped, a viewer would have access to only one editorial a day. Alternatives do not serve as substitutes; rather, they compete for time. Any policy of meeting the competition for time and attention by emulating the content of other media will therefore have only limited benefit.

More disturbing, from society's point of view, is what may happen to umbrella competition. Newspaper competition across city and county lines does have an impact on what readers have available in the advertising, information, and intellectual markets.

In the advertising markets, weekly and small dailies in large metropolitan areas offer small businesses advertising that is targeted to their consumers and lower in price than advertising in metro dailies. Competition from a daily outside the immediate city and county forces the hometown newspaper to put greater emphasis on local news and to increase the newshole. The relatively low fixed cost of starting a suburban weekly still provides access to independent voices in a metropolitan area.

Yet, the social advantages derived from umbrella competition may fall victim to the trend toward consolidation. For example, ownership of a large metro daily and suburban dailies in the same area may reduce pressure on the suburban dailies to spend money on their editorial product. Why should the owners of such suburban dailies spend money to take readers away from their own newspapers?

Consolidation of metro dailies with suburban weeklies also could affect readers. In the advertising market, such a combination greatly increases a newspaper company's discretionary power. If a smaller suburban business must buy from two newspapers owned by the same firm, that firm can increase prices. If a new weekly enters a market against a weekly owned by the metro daily company, the latter can use greater financial resources to underprice the independent.

These possibilities are all too real as more large metro dailies connect with suburban newspapers. For example, in 1990 the Chicago *Sun-Times* owned several dozen weekly papers in the Chicago area. Belo Corporation of Dallas owned *The Dallas Morning News* and several suburban weeklies in the area.

Whether or not the potential negative impact on readers of this intercity concentration occurs depends on several factors. Primary among these are the presence of other newspapers in the area and managerial policy. Concentration shifts power from the consumer to the owner. Evidence from many industries indicates that readers and even companies are better served in the long run by competition. The declining market shares by United States automobile companies is a good example of what happens when competition declines and then intensifies again.

The government has the ability to encourage umbrella competition through its antitrust laws, if the application of such laws to the newspaper industry are consistent with appropriate economic theory. The perfect competition models cannot justify action because they cannot explain adequately newspaper market behavior.

Three changes in application of antitrust law to newspapers could help preserve umbrella competition without leading to content regulation. First, recognize the impact in all three markets as being important. The impact of anticompetitive behavior on the business side of newspapers has been recognized as within the range of antitrust since 1945. However, the interconnection of all three markets means the impact of anticompetitive behavior on the information and intellectual markets should be part of the regulatory efforts.

Second, other media are not good substitutes for newspapers in any of the three markets. While some of the advertising submarkets face fairly good substitutes, the particular substitute varies with the type of advertising. This means newspapers, as a whole, face poor substitutes. This means it is the newspaper markets and not all media markets that are relevant for antitrust.

Third, geographic boundaries of newspaper markets are no longer determined by city boundaries. Another geographic designation, such as county or metropolitan area, might be a better definition of geographic market. The designation should be based on statistical evidence of business activity or circulation within an area, not solely on a newspaper's stated market area. The focus should be on where competition occurs rather than where the firms aspired to have it occur.

These ideas would obviously need refining to be applicable in courts of law, but efforts to develop better policy for newspaper markets would benefit the readers and the industry. Without such efforts, the newspaper market will remain largely unregulated, as it has been during the last 20 years. As a result of this nonregulation, umbrella competition may slowly follow direct competition toward extinction. The difference will be that direct competition died from natural monopoly, while umbrella competition died from lack of policy.

Ownership

As pointed out earlier, concentration of ownership continues. This process in itself is not a serious problem; it is the decline of competition that makes such a trend dangerous from a reader's point of view. Compared to other countries, concentration of ownership is still relatively limited in the United States. However, fear that problems could evolve from this trend are not entirely groundless.

Currently the public has little power, through buying decision or government regulation, to affect the growth of concentration. This would hold true even if concentration were greater. The limitations for readers come from limited competition. The limitations for government come from the necessity of examining antitrust action on the basis of geographic and product markets. Direct intervention to prevent concentration is of dubious value and is probably unconstitutional in any event. Critics fear that concentration will negatively affect the information and intellectual markets, but have little but anecdotal evidence to support that fear. Any "deconcentration" law would be based on an assumption that group speakers are less desirable than others, a discriminatory position repeatedly held to violate the First Amendment. The entire case law addressing special protection for the press would have to be reinterpreted to uphold such a law.

Government limitations draw attention to the argument made concerning umbrella competition. Group ownership of two newspapers in different markets has no inherent negative impact on readers. However, group ownership of two newspapers that compete through umbrella competition might. Thus, the growth of groups can and should be controlled if it begins to dilute the socially desirable effects of such competition. But better understanding of the economics of newspapers by judges and lawyers may be sufficient to accomplish this. Wholesale revision of law, with provisions directly aimed at newspapers, should not be necessary.

Subsidy Policies

The newspaper industry should anticipate an assault on its special status in postal and tax laws in the near future. Governments strapped for cash and eager to raise revenue without raising taxes for individuals are already questioning the desirability of sales tax exemptions for retail sales of newspapers. The United States' transition to an economy based more on services assures that the tradition of exempting advertising sales from sales tax will be reconsidered. The almost $120 billion advertising industry is largely untaxed—a huge potential source of revenue.

The postal subsidy for newspapers and periodicals directly contradicts the express command of the Postal Reorganization Act that mail must pay its own way. The newspaper industry has enjoyed almost 20 years of benevolence as Congress has appropriated subsidy funds notwithstanding the act. Still, subsidy rates are closer to true costs than at any time in U.S. history. The two will eventually meet.

The principles underlying subsidy policies hold less water with each passing year. Tax and postal benefits are challenged in court by other media businesses that demand subsidy too—or none. That the government should do nothing to favor some media over others is likely to be the eventual First Amendment approach taken. And since the society cannot afford to subsidize all media, subsidies are likely to disappear.

Labor Policy

The newspaper industry, with total work force approaching half a million employees, is one of the largest in the country. As union representation continues its long decline, newspapers should recognize that employee relations are still subject to considerable regulation. And they should remember that the unions still set the pace in many ways; after all, many firms wishing to avoid union representation of employees can only do so by offering pay, benefits, and conditions of employment as good or better than available under union contracts.

The biggest changes facing managers are the growing professionalism of the work force and increased efforts to protect individuals by law. Federal labor regulation was based on an assumption that most employees were engaged in repetitive production work. That assumption and the definitions developed under it never did apply well to newsroom employees, and probably the professional/managerial exemption will eventually be applied to newsroom employees. Even production and printing no longer requires the repetitive, unthinking work the National Labor Relations Act assumes. As technological advances make each job more individualized, the status of even the traditional trades under federal law may be reconsidered. Whether or not they bargain collectively, newspaper employees of the future will be much more skilled at bargaining individually, a result of better education and training. And they will have civil rights and other laws to back them up.

The biggest labor policy issue, however, is nonlegal, a matter of company policy. The newspaper industry cannot continue to hire cheap. You get what you pay for. Change has already occurred in circulation personnel, with more adult carriers replacing the extremely low-paid newsboy or newsgirl. An uncertain delivery force based on child labor may have worked when newspapers penetrated almost every household, but today circulation from home delivery is too precious. Similarly, newspapers cannot keep paying less than the competition for newsroom personnel. True, there are thousands of eager young graduates of journalism schools. But the costs of newsroom training are high and, with rapid turnover, replacement costs are high too. In the meantime, news content, the single most distinctive feature of the newspaper, stands to suffer from lack of reporter experience or lack of reporter familiarity with the community. The industry has been losing a large percentage of experienced reporters and promising young workers to other fields, especially public relations, and not because all those employees had a deep desire to practice public relations. The problem is exacerbated by the policy in some newspaper chains of moving promising staffers along rapidly to bigger markets and more responsibility. Quality and continuity of coverage in smaller markets is endangered.

Technology

As discussed above, economies of scale from technology are not the prime reason for declining direct competition, but they do contribute. Technology has contributed to growing umbrella competition by lowering costs. The future of competition in the newspaper industry is dependent upon a continuation of cost reduction. Ultimately, barriers to entry can only be dropped when cost savings reach a point that a trailing newspaper in a competitive situation can survive with a very small proportion of advertising.

These cost savings will have to be in the reproduction process and in the delivery process. Obviously, the development of high quality, rapid small printers in the home would have far-reaching consequences on the industry. The likelihood of this happening soon is very small. However, the possibility exists, however slight, that smaller presses located at diverse printing locations might allow competing dailies to exist in some large cities.

This possibility rests on several assumptions. First, as mentioned above, economies of scale from reproduction occur at fairly low levels of circulation.[4] Second, that savings can be made by distributing newspapers from several locations, rather than one or two. This certainly would be true of evening newspapers in large cities. Third, such a printing set-up would help move the deadlines for newspapers closer to the printing time. For evening newspapers, this would make them more competitive with the evening news in timeliness. Fourth, the economies of scale for increasing pages would still be obtainable from these smaller printing locations. Fifth, the smaller printing location would allow for even more local zoning in the content of the newspapers.

The above process is apparently not yet feasible in most U.S. markets. However, research to lower cost through technology holds at least a small possibility for returning to more competitive newspaper markets. After all, few would have suggested in 1970 that network television would be losing viewers as quickly as it did in the 1980s.

Unfortunately, technology does not develop without large outlays of money. Failure rates are high. Yet, the industry will continue to work toward improving technology that will reduce cost because it is still a somewhat competitive industry. However, research and development may be the first casualty if ownership becomes too concentrated. Competition breeds innovation and research development. If competition continues to decline, the incentive to continue development will decline.

This disincentive to invest in development can mean the long-run decline of an entire industry. Other industries that faced little short-run competition found themselves bypassed in the long run because they failed to continue investing in their product or service. Railroads, for example, are a viable alternative to driving and flying, at least theoretically. Yet, the railroad industry in the United States failed to adjust through research as the airplane developed. By the 1980s, railroad passenger travel had all but disappeared in the United States, while remaining a valuable transportation system elsewhere.

The lesson for newspaper companies is that decline of competition does not justify abandonment of technological research, even if that research holds the possibility of increased long-run competition. The industry must develop or those outside the industry will find ways of making it obsolete.

Of course, industry is not the only institution that can engage in research and development. In some parts of the world, the public sector is far more active in research and development. This has not been the tradition in the United States, except when the technology had potential defense application. There is no reason that the federal government could not invest in research and development of mass communication technology, especially in light of its use for public communication. Such developments may well help increase the number of voices in the intellectual market, which is good for society.

As the newspaper industry develops technology to increase revenues and decrease costs, the potential competition from telephone companies is an ongoing concern. The regional bell operating companies and newspaper firms are trying to tap into the small but growing business of electronic information creation and delivery. Newspapers have the advantage of owning companies that create information, but the telephone companies have a virtual monopoly on the delivery system. The debate in Congress and the courts concerns the competitive impact of this monopoly on the electronic information market if the telephone companies are allowed to produce information.

A 1990 appellate court decision required U.S. District Court Judge Harold H. Greene to reconsider his ruling that the telephone companies could carry, but not create electronic information.[5] The fate of this issue will ultimately fall into the hands of the Federal Communication Commission and Congress. A bill was discussed in Congress in June 1990 that would effect a compromise by letting the RBOCs participate more fully but not completely. The resolution of this issue will affect both the information and the advertising markets. The telephone companies already compete for advertising through their Yellow Pages, although they tend to have a different function than newspaper advertising.

Reader Influence

With the decline of direct competition, the growth of group ownership and the current threats to umbrella competition, the readers may wonder what role they play in the future of the newspaper industry. Their role is central, as it has always been. Newspaper managers usually are sensitive to readers. They have to be. The degree of that sensitivity, of course, is determined by the degree of competition from other firms and by the degree of understanding the manger has of the reader.

Interestingly, readers often do not know the power they hold. A large group of offended readers can have a strong impact on a newspaper's policy. The smaller the newspaper, the stronger the impact. This power comes from the readers' ability to not buy the newspaper or the goods advertised therein.

Journalists sometimes fear reader censorship as much as advertiser censorship. Both forms can have negative effects when exercised in a way that deprives others of valuable information. The important question then becomes, how does one encourage readers to demand quality newspapers without becoming a negative force to eliminate unpleasant but important news?

The answer is education. Readers must understand the nature and qualities of good journalism. This can only start with a quality newspaper, but that alone is insufficient. Newspaper and educational institutions at all levels need to foster an appreciation and understanding of good journalism. This is easier to suggest than to carry out, but there are some definite steps.

First, newspaper firms and the industry must continue to develop and invest in education about journalism. This means sending journalists into schools, paying tuition for teachers to learn about journalism, and encouraging universities and colleges to offer and require courses to improve media literacy. *Media literacy* means the ability to understand how media work and how they affect their users. Few high schools or colleges offer much in the curriculum to make students media literate. Students in high school may be dissuaded from taking such courses because they are considered "too light" for a college preparatory program. College students may be dissuaded from taking such a course because advisers consider them too light. College and university journalism and media programs, in turn, may devalue the class by assigning it to inexperienced faculty members and by jazzing up the course without covering media seriously. That media literacy is so little taught and studied is amazing in a society as media-dependent as ours.

Second, newspapers and the industry can invest in a better understanding of newspaper quality. Most good journalists know quality when they see it, but readers may not. The first step to sharing understanding is defining the concept in ways that will allow it to be shared. This means posing and answering questions about what makes quality and how it is achieved.

Third, the staffs of the newspaper should meet with the public to educate them as to what newspapers do and why. These town hall types of meetings can help the long-run viability of a newspaper. Many people have moved away from the "newspaper habit." These types of meetings may help reintroduce it. They might also bring journalists into closer contact with what their readers want and need.

Fourth, journalists and journalism educators must learn to deal better with criticism. Often, as with all professions and crafts, people associated with journalism can become defensive in the face of criticism. While this protects egos, it does not promote understanding and flexibility, essential traits in long-run survival of businesses.

Fifth, the journalistic arrogance that often develops must be eliminated. Readers often perceive journalists as being arrogant. A visit to some newsrooms will give the visitor the same impression. This feeling is manifest in the periodic polls that show people believe the press is too powerful. It results often from the press hiding behind the First Amendment no matter how terrible its mistakes. People will often forgive mistakes more quickly than arrogance or efforts to avoid responsibility for those mistakes.

Perhaps the best demonstration of press arrogance was the overall negative reaction to the 1947 Hutchins Commission Report.[6] Although criticized by much of the press, many of the suggestions made in the report have been adopted to some degree. No matter what an individual thinks of specific suggestions, the point of the report was that the press does not always act responsibly toward its readers, even though it should try. To deny this, rather than attempt to improve performance, does not help newspapers in the long run.

There is a simple formula. The credibility given newspapers by readers is directly proportional to the readers' perceptions of newspapers as responsible social institutions. The perception of newspapers as being responsible is directly proportional to their actual responsibility and the readers understanding of the industry. Although this formula will not explain entirely the source of low credibility, ignoring the relationships in the formula can be hazardous to newspaper firms.

SUMMARY

Many have argued that television has been the most dominant force in mass communications during the second half of the 20th century. It is the only medium in history that can unite people around the globe simultaneously. Yet, as television entered its fifth decade, the attention it received emphasized more how its audience is fragmenting. Technology changed the nature of television forever in the 1980s. The days of nightly massive audiences are gone.

The change illustrated that people want what newspapers have been giving them all along—some control over the information they use. Newspapers have done this by offering a large amount of information from which the reader could select. The newspaper's advantages are illustrated by its longevity as a primary source of public information.

This survival was not by accident. It was anticipated by those who created the First Amendment to protect newspaper journalism from the government. That was during a time when the opportunity to express oneself in print to a significant proportion of an intellectual market was easier to accomplish than it is now. This decline in opportunity reflects population growth more than anything else. To serve the large population, expensive technology that limits access has been used.

In the process of financing that technology and making a profit, newspapers became dependent on advertising. The result has been a decline in the number of print voices within geographic markets. At the same time, the resources available for journalism and the need for information have increased, which reflects an increasingly complex world.

In the face of these changes, managers of newspapers continue to perform the same function: the allocation of scarce resources to obtain goals. The constraints that make these resources scarce have changed with history, but the basic decisions remain the same, just as the three basic markets—information, advertising, and intellectual—remain the same as in the 1830s, when modern newspaper journalism began.

It has become almost faddish to predict the death of newspapers, as we have known them, because of developing technology. Death may come to the printed newspaper, but the forms of information currently used will continue to exist. The important question is whether that death, if it comes, resulted from the natural superiority of some production and distribution technology or because newspaper managers failed to make the decisions that would have preserved the industry.

The argument presented here is that survival of newspapers as important contributors to society and as profitable businesses, in whatever form, rests on adequately serving the advertising, information, and intellectual markets. Despite demonstrable behavior in the industry toward letting the advertising market dominate, survival as a unique institution protected by the Constitution is a function of providing information and opinions that serve a social and personal purpose. In short, the industry will survive in the long run only if the managers who exercise power understand that good journalism is good business.

ENDNOTES

1. *Communications Industry Report: 5th Annual* (New York: Veronis, Suhler & Associates, Inc., 1987).
2. John C. Busterna, "Antitrust in the 1980s: An Analysis of 45 Newspaper Actions," *Newspaper Research Journal*, Winter 1988, pp. 25-36.
3. James M. Bernstein, Stephen Lacy, Catherine Cassara, and Tuen-yu Lau, "The Localism Doctrine and Use of SNG Vehicles: A Study of Geographic Coverage by Local Television News," Paper delivered to the Association for Education in Journalism and Mass Communication, Washington, DC, August 1989.

4. Barry Litman, "Microeconomic Foundations," *Press Concentration and Monopoly* eds. Robert G. Picard, Maxwell E. McCombs, James P. Winters, and Stephen Lacy, (Norwood, NJ: Ablex, 1988), pp. 3-34.
5. "Court Orders Reconsideration of RBOC Leash; ANPA Looks to Judge Greene to Retain It," *presstime*, May 1990, p. 64.
6. The Commission on Freedom of the Press, *A Free and Responsible Press* (Chicago: The University of Chicago Press, 1947).

Author Index

A

Adams, J.B., 66, 67, *88, 89,* 105, *126*
Albert, J., 252, *263*
Allen, D.S., 146, *159*
Altschull, J.H., 111, *128,* 154, *161*
Anderson, M.A., 39, *52,* 209, *213,* 238, *261*
Ardoin, B., 106, *126*
Atwater, T., 102, *126,* 190, *210*
Aumente, J., 177, *185*

B

Bagdikian, B.H., 133, 135, 142, 154, *157, 158, 159, 161*
Barron, J.A., 193, 194, 204, *210, 211, 212,* 230, *235,* 238, 248, *261, 262*
Barwis, G., 252, *263*
Baumol, W.J., 137, 139, *158*
Beam, R., 64, 80, *88, 89,* 102, *126,* 143, *159*
Becker, L., 64, 80, *88, 89,* 102, *126,* 143, *159*
Benham, W., 144, *159*
Bernstein, J.M., 10, *20,* 67, 86, *88, 89,* 101, 123, *125, 129,* 153, *160,* 275, *284*
Bigman, S.K., 101, 112, *125, 128*
Bird, G.L., 106, *127*
Blankenburg, W.B., 18, *22,* 40, *52,* 62, 64, 71, 73, 80, *88, 89,* 96, 109, *125, 127,* 150, 151, 152, *160*
Blanks, S.E., 146, *159*
Blood, R.W., 49, *53*
Bogart, L., 10, 12, *21,* 50, *53,* 64, *88,* 119, *129,* 148, *160*
Borstel, G.H., 112, *128,* 155, *161*
Bossen, H., 174, *184*
Bowers, D.R., 181, *185*
Breed, W., 64, *88,* 94, *125*
Bridges, J., 18, *22,* 102, *125,* 145, *159*

Browning, N., 144, *159*
Busterna, J., 102, 121, *126, 129,* 133, 146, 155, *157, 159, 161,* 193, 198, 200, 205, 207, *210, 211, 212,* 215, 218, 227, 232, *234, 235,* 272, *284*

C

Candussi, D.A., 107, *127*
Carter, M.G., 70, *89*
Cassara, C., 275, *284*
Chamberlin, E.H., 26, *51,* 218, 227, *234, 235*
Christians, C.G., 86, *90*
Coen, R.J., 11, 12, *21*
Compaine, B.M., 133, 134, 139, 141, 142, *157, 158, 159*
Coulson, D.C., 218, 231, *234, 235*
Counts, T., 50, *53*
Cyert, R.M., 138, *158*

D

Danielson, W.A., 66, 67, *88, 89,* 105, *126,* 173, *184*
Daugherty, D.B., 156, *161*
Demers, D.P., 145, 156, *159, 161*
Dennis, E.E., 155, *161*
Dertouzos, J.N., 246, *262*
Devey, S.M., 116, *128*
Donahue, G.A., 13, *21,* 117, *128,* 133, 141, 145, *157, 158, 159*
Drew, D.G., 144, *159*
Drier, P., 150, *160*
Dunwoody, S., 174, *185*

E

Eberhard, W.B., 256, 259, *264*
Einsiedel, E.F., 49, *53*
Entman, R.M., 112, *128*

AUTHOR INDEX

F

Fackler, G.D., 109, *127*
Fawcett, D., 134, *158*
Featherston, J.S., 106, 107, *126, 127*
Ferguson, J.M., 40, *52*, 109, 121, *127, 129*, 151, *160*
Fico, F., 38, *52*, 64, 80, *88, 89*, 105, *126*, 146, 148, *159, 160*, 220, *234*
Fielder, V.D., 49, *53*
Fink, C., 75, *89*
Finnegan, J., 144, *159*
Fishman, M., 94, *125*, 230, *235*
Folkerts, J., 100, *125*, 253, *263*
Fortini-Campbell, L., 27, *52*
Friedman, M., 139, *158*
Fullerton, H.S., 119, *129*

G

Garcia, H.D., 131, *157*
Garrison, B., 173, 174, *184, 185*
Garrison, D., 144, *159*
Gaziano, C., 155, *161*
Gentry, J.K., 68, *89*, 170, 174, *184*
Gerald, J.E., 5, *20*
Ghiglione, L., 139, 142, 143, *158, 159*
Gieber, W., 64, *88*
Gillmor, D.M., 155, *161*, 193, 194, 204, 210, 211, 212, 230, *235*, 238, 248, *261, 262*
Glasser, T.L., 146, *159*
Goltz, G., 10, 13, *21*, 251, *263*
Gordon, G.N., 25, *51*
Greer, D.F., 136, 138, 139, *158*
Gromley, W.T., 120, *129*, 230, *235*
Grotta, G.L., 107, 120, *127, 129*, 143, 151, *159, 160*
Gruley, B., 209, *213*

H

Hahn, T.-Y., 141, *159*
Hale, D.F., 144, 150, 155, *159, 160, 161*
Han, K.-T., 150, *160*
Hansen, K.A., 155, *161*, 173, *184*
Harberger, A.C., 218, *234*
Hart, J.R., 131, *157*
Hartman, B., 101, *125*
Hembree, D., 173, *184*
Henry, S., 173, *184*
Hicks, R.G., 106, 107, *126, 127*
Howard, H.H., 144, *159*
Huck, C.S., 152, *160*

Hurd, R.E., 50, *53*
Hynds, E.C., 86, *89*, 111, *128*

J

Jackson, K.M., 34, *52*, 117, *128*
Jacobson, T.L., 172, *184*
Johnson, R.M., 177, *185*
Johnson, W., 64, *88*
Jones, R.L., 101, *125*

K

Kahaner, L., 122, *129*
Kang, N., 49, *53*
Keir, G.J., 49, *53*
Kenney, K., 172, *184*
Kerr, J., 180, *185*
Kerton, R.R., 109, 121, *127, 129*
Kinter, C.V., 119, *128*
Kwitney, J., 80, *89*, 140, *158*, 245, *262*

L

Lacy, S., 10, 16, *20, 21, 22*, 30, 38, 40, *52*, 64, 66, 67, 80, 85, 86, *88, 89*, 100, 101, 102, 105, 106, 112, 115, 116, 119, 120, 123, *125, 126, 127, 128, 129*, 146, 147, 148, 153, 156, *159, 160, 161*, 172, 181, *184, 185*, 209, *212*, 221, 228, 233, *234, 235, 236*, 275, *284*
Lago, A., 109, 121, *127, 129*, 151, *160*
Laidler, D., 216, *234*
Lau, T., 10, *20*, 101, *125*, 275, *284*
Lavine, J.M., 12, 17, *21*, 175, *185*
Leigh, R.D., 17, *22*
Levin, H.J., 119, *129*
Liebler, C.M., 174, *185*
Lindley, W.R., 68, *89*, 174, *185*
Litman, B.R., 18, *22*, 70, 72, *89*, 93, 94, *125*, 145, *159*, 167, *184*, 280, *285*
Loevinger, L., 141, *159*

M

Machlup, F., 137, *158*, 163, *183*
Maggs, P.P., 188, 203, *210, 211*
Mansfield, E., 165, *184*, 188, *210*
Marby, B.D., 139, *158*
March, J.G., 138, *158*
Marris, R., 138, *158*
Marshall, A., 216, *234*
Martindale, C., 7, *20*

AUTHOR INDEX

Mathewson, G.F., 109, 121, *127, 129*
Matustik, D., 64, *88*
Mauro, J.B., 85, *89*
Mayfield, E.K., 110, *127*, 154, *161*
McClenghan, J.S., 50, *53*
McCombs, M.E., 16, *22*, 32, 49, 50, *52, 53*, 117, 119, *128*, 225, 233, *235, 236*
McGowan, J.J., 16, *22*, 119, *129*
McLeod, D.M., 173, *184*
McManis, C.R., 188, *210*
McNichol, T., 170, *184*
Merrill, J.C., 17, *22*, 110, *127*
Meyer, P., 35, *52*, 80, *89*, 135, 146, *158, 160*
Miller, B.L., 45, *52*, 180, *185*
Milton, J., 5, *20*
Morton, J., 181, *185*
Mullins, L.E., 102, *125*

N

Neuwirth, K., 174, *185*
Newsom, C., 249, *262*
Newsom, D., 120, *129*
Nicholson, W., 58, *87*, 136, *158*, 165, *184*, 216, *234*
Niebauer, W.E., 10, *20*, 101, 104, *125, 126*, 180, *185*
Niemiec, H., 260, *264*
Nixon, R.B., 14, *21*, 101, *125*, 132, 141, *157, 159*, 191, *210*
Noll, R.G., 16, *22*, 119, *129*
Nowak, J.E., 247, *262*

O

Odell, S.J., 17, *22*, 110, *127*
Olien, C.N., 13, *21*, 117, *128*, 133, 141, 145, *157, 158, 159*
Olsen, O., 49, *53*
Oppenheim, S.C., 188, 203, *210, 211*
Owen, B.M., 14, *21*, 91, 109, 113, 121, *125, 127, 128, 129*, 151, *160*, 226, 232, *235, 236*

P

Palmgreen, P., 27, *51*
Parsons, P., 144, *159*
Patkus, J.P., 207, *212*
Peck, M.J., 16, *22*, 119, *129*
Picard, R.G., 46, *52*, 107, 109, *127*, 200, *211*, 218, 233, *234, 236*
Posner, R.A., 189, 190, 199, *210, 211*, 215, 218, *234*

Q

Qin, X., 102, *126*

R

Radolf, A., 11, *21*, 250, *263*
Rambo, C.D., 36, *52*
Rarick, G., 101, *125*
Reagan, J., 120, *129*
Riddle, J., 174, *185*
Rivers, W.L., 86, *90*
Roach, C.B., 154, *161*
Roberts, K., 181, *185*, 230, *235*
Robinson, J., 227, *235*
Rosse, J.N., 16, *21*, 37, *52*, 99, 112, *125, 128*
Rotunda, R.D., 247, *262*
Russial, J., 64, 80, *88, 89*, 102, *126*, 143, *159*
Rykken, R., 67, *89*, 175, *184, 185*, 205, *212*

S

Schechter, R.E., 188, 203, *210, 211*
Schramm, W., 27, *51*, 86, *90*
Severin, W.J., 13, *21*, 27, *51*
Shipley, L.J., 68, *89*, 174, *184*
Shipman, J.M., 173, *184*
Shoemaker, P., 110, 111, *127, 128*, 154, *161*
Simon, T.F., 66, *88*, 105, *126*, 146, *159*, 190, 193, 194, 204, *210, 211, 212*, 230, *235*, 238, 239, 240, 244, 248, 250, *261, 262, 263*
Singletary, M.W., 50, *53*
Slesin, L., 173, *184*
Sohn, A.B., 40, *52*, 85, *89*, 116, *128*, 181, *185*
Soloski, J., 144, *159*
Stamm, K.J., 27, *52*
Standen, O., 179, *185*
St. Dizier, B., 155, *161*
Stein, L., 173, *184*
Stein, M.L., 135, *158*
Stempel, G.H., 15, *21*, 85, *89*, 120, *129*, 230, *235*
Stephens, L.F., 40, *52*, 116, *128*, 181, *185*
Stevens, G.E., 251, *263*
Stevens, J.D., 131, *157*
Stigler, G.J., 23, *51*
Stone, D., 64, 80, *88, 89*, 102, *126*
Stone, G., 13, *21*, 64, 80, *88, 89*, 102, 120, *126, 129*
Sylvie, G., 173, *184*

T

Tankard, J.W., 27, *51*, 182, *186*
Taylor, A., 252, *263*
Teeter, D., 253, *263*
Terrell, P.M., 67, *88*
Terry, H.A., 193, 194, 204, *210*, *211*, *212*, 230, *235*, 238, 248, *261*, *262*
Thomas, L., 190, *210*
Thorpe, K.E., 246, *262*
Thrift, R.R., 155, *161*
Tichenor, P.J., 13, *21*, 117, *128*, 133, 141, 145, *158*, *159*
Tillinghast, D.S., 116, *128*
Trotter, E.P., 64, 80, *88*, *89*, 102, *126*
Truitt, R.C., 174, 178, *184*, *185*
Tuchman, G., 64, *88*, 94, *125*

U

Udell, J.G., 5, *20*, 63, *88*
Ullman, J., 172, *184*
Underwood, D., 4, *20*

W

Wackman, D.B., 17, *22*, 145, 155, *159*, *161*
Ward, J.A., 173, *184*
Wearden, S.T., 135, 146, *158*, *160*
Weaver, D., 49, *53*, 65, 80, *88*, *89*, 102, *125*
Weber, 241, *261*
Weinberg, S., 150, *160*
Westley, B.H., 13, *21*
Weston, G.E., 188, 203, *210*, *211*
Wilhoit, G.C., 65, *88*, 144, *159*
Williamson, J., 139, *158*
Williamson, O.E., 137, *158*
Willoughby, W.F., 101, 112, *125*, *128*
Winter, J.P., 32, *52*, 107, 117, *127*, *128*, 233, *236*
Wood, W.C., 119, *129*
Wright, B.E., 12, *21*, 175, *185*

Y

Young, J.N., 247, *262*

Z

Zang, B., 170, *184*
Zerbinos, E., 100, *125*

Subject Index

A

Advertising, 11–12
   classified, 43, 81–84, 179
   demand, 40–48
   display, 43, 178
   legal, 44
   local, 44
   market for newspapers, 5, 117–118, 121–122, 150–152, 222–224
   national, 44
   price, see Price, advertising market
   run of the paper (ROP) 43–45
   substitutability, 46–48, 117
   types of, 41–42
Advantage Publications v. Daily Press, 199, 201–202
American Newspaper Publishers Association, 9, 11
Anchorage *Times*, 135
Antitrust law, 3–4, 187–209, 272
   collusion, 189, 206–207, 232
   future applications
      direct competition, 228
      intermedia competition, 230–231
      ownership, 231–233, 277–278
      umbrella competition, 228–230
   general justification for, 215–219
   geographic market, 193–196
   justification for applying to newspapers, 226–227
   merger, 194, 206–207
   predatory pricing, 200–203
   product market, 196–199
   price discrimination, see Price, — discrimination
   price fixing, see Price fixing
   refusal to deal, 203–205
   tying arrangements, 205

Arkansas Democrat, 107
Arkansas Gazette, 109
Associated Press v. NLRB, 237, 247–248
Associated Press v. United States, 191–193, 196, 226–227

B

Barriers to entry, 18, 101, 108, 134
   technology, see Technology, barriers to entry
Belo Corp., 276
Buffalo Courier-Express v. Buffalo Evening News, 201, 203

C

Celler-Kefauver Act, 188
Chain ownership, see Ownership, groups
Chicago *Sun-Times*, 253, 276
Chicago *Tribune*, 253
Christian Science Monitor, 37, 113
Circulation, 10–11, 75, 78–80, 97–99, 104–105, 170–171
   control, 73
   distribution regulation, 256–260
   group ownership and, 148–149
Circulation spiral, 18–19, 97–101
Citizen Publishing Co. v. United States, 198, 206–207
City of Lakewood v. Plain Dealer Publishing Co., 257–259
Civil rights laws, see Labor law, civil rights laws
Clayton Act, 188–190, 200, 203, 206
Collusion, see Antitrust law, collusion
Committee for an Independent P.I. v. Hearst Corp., 208
Competition, 270–271
   direct, 10, 94–112, 152–153, 228, 275

291

292 SUBJECT INDEX

intermedia, 85, 119–123, 230–231, 275
intercity, see Competition, umbrella
intensity, 101–102, 172, 221
monopolistic competition, 92–94, 227
oligopoly, 92–94, 107
perfect, 82, 92–94, 107, 215
technology, see Technology, impact of competition
umbrella, 16, 37, 112–118, 194–195, 228–230, 275–276
Common carrier, 110
Consumer's surplus, 216–218
Constraints on managers, 265–274
Content
   bias in, see Objectivity
   degree of interest, 35
   editorial and opinion, 49–50, 74–76, 85–86, 110–112, 155–156, 180
   endorsements, 155
   format, 33–34
   geographic emphasis of, 32, 34, 36, 112–118
   impact of technology, 172–175, 178
   legal regulation of, 240–241, 255
   nature of, 33–34
   quality, 30–32, 38, 64–66, 77–80, 98–99, 102–107, 143, 147–149, 170–172, 180, 221–222, 266–267, 279
   specialization of, 35
   topics, 33–34
Cost(s), 56–74
   average, 56–58
   average total cost, 57–58, 70–71
   average fixed cost, 56–58
   average variable cost, 56–58
   fixed, 56–58, 108, 275
      direct, 62–63, 69
      indirect, 63
   long-run average cost, 167–168, 173
   marginal, 56–58, 70–71
   short-run, 168
   variable, 56–58, 69–70
Credibility, 283

D

Delayed reward, 27
Dallas *Morning News*, 276
Demand, 23–24, 267–269
   advertising market, 46–48
   elasticity, see Elasticity, demand
   inelasticity, see Inelasticity, demand
   income, 23, 26
   information market, 23–40, 48, 102–105
   intellectual market, 48–50
   interaction with supply, see Supply, and demand
   price, impact of, 23–24, 42, 267
   substitutes and complements, impact of, 25–26
   taste, impact of, 23, 26
   theory for media, 30–32, 268–269
Demand curve
   kinked, 31–32, 78–80, 102–105, 148–149
   price, 24–26
   quality of content, 77–80, 102–107
Deregulation, see Regulation
Detroit *Free Press*, 19, 208–209
Detroit *News*, 19, 75, 208–209, 251
Direct mail, 12, 43–44, 84–85, 256, 275
Diseconomies of scale, see Scale, diseconomies

E

Economic markets, 5–6
Economics and Freedom of Expression, 113
Economies of scale, see Scale, economies of
Editor & Publisher, Inc., 9, 11, 36
Elasticity
   demand, 24–25, 47, 77, 93, 107
   cross-elasticity, 26, 47, 231
   supply, 61, 77
   unit elasticity, 24–25, 61
Electronic information services, 176–178
Enterprise, Inc. v. United States, 255
Equilibrium, 59–60
   advertising market, 222–223
   content quality, 77–80, 102–105
   classified advertising, 82–84
   intellectual market, 224–226
Estate taxes, see Taxes, estate
Exclusionary practices, 189, 199–200

F

Fair Labor Standards Act, see Labor law, Fair Labor Standards Act
Federal Communication Commission, 15, 230, 237–238, 281
Federal Trade Commission Act, 188–190
Federal Trade Commission, 188, 190
Financial commitment theory, 102–106, 148–149, 221
First Amendment, 17–19, 49, 87, 153, 216, 224, 266–267, 273

SUBJECT INDEX   293

and antitrust, 190–191
and business regulation, 237–238, 241–242, 249, 255, 257–260
Fixed costs, *see* Costs, fixed

G

Gannett Co., 4, 140
Geographic market, *see* Market, geographic
Goals
   profit maximizing, 136–137
   revenue maximizing, 137–138
   sales maximizing, 138–139
   utility maximizing, 137
Grand Rapids *Press*, 229
Groups, *see* Ownership, groups
Grosjean v. American Press, 240

H

Hart-Scott-Rodino Antitrust Improvement Act, 189–190
Harte-Hanks, 135
Houston *Chronicle*, 135
Hutchins Commission, 49, 86–87, 132, 154, 283

I

Immediate reward, 27
Income taxes, *see* Taxes, exemptions from income taxes
Independent newspapers, *see* Ownership, independent
Inelasticity
   demand, 24, 77
   supply, 61, 71
Information market, 5, 115–117, 120–121, 142–150, 172–178
   demand in, *see* Demand, information market
   price, *see* Price, information market
   supply in, *see* Supply, information market
Inheritance taxes, *see* Taxes, inheritance
Inland Press Association, 63, 69, 175
Inputs, 66–68
Intellectual market, 5–6, 109–112, 118, 122–123, 152–155
   demand, *see* Demand, intellectual market
   supply, *see* Supply, intellectual market
Interaction among markets, 75, 85, 87, 110–111

in antitrust law, 228–230, 276
Interlocking directorship, 149–150

J

Joint operating agreements (JOAs), 10, 96, 99, 207–209
   advertising market, 109
   information market, 105–107
   intellectual market, 112
Joint commodity (product), 18–19, 73, 178, 242, 275

K

Kansas City Star Co. v. United States, 197, 205, 230
Kerner Commission, 7, 86
Knight-Ridder Co., 146, 176
Knoxville *Journal*, 144, 207
Knoxville *News-Sentinel*, 144, 207

L

Labor costs for newsroom, 63–68
Labor law, 246–253, 273, 278–279
   civil right laws, 250–252
   common law contract, 252–253
   employment-at-will, 252–253
   Fair Labor Standards Act, 247, 249–250, 252
   federal, 247–249
   National Labor Relations Act, 247–250, 252
   personal service contracts, 253
Labor supply, 269–270
Leathers v. Medlock, 240
Lorain Journal Co. v. United States, 196, 199
Los Angeles *Herald Examiner*, 19
Los Angeles *Times*, 140, 245
Louisville *Courier-Journal*, 134–135

M

Magazines, 46–47
Management goals, *see* Goals
Market(s)
   advertising, *see* Advertising market
   geographic, 5–6, 40–41, 91–92, 112–115, 229, 276–277
      antitrust and, *see* Antitrust, geographic market
   information, *see* Information market
   intellectual, *see* Intellectual market
   product, 92, 229

294 SUBJECT INDEX

antitrust and, see Antitrust, product market
segmentation, 101
structure, 91–94
McCann-Erickson, 12
Media General, Inc., 135
Media literacy, 282
Merger, see Antitrust law, merger
Miami Herald Publishing Co. v. Tornillo, 17
Microeconomic theory, 55–58, 108, 136, 139
Milwaukee *Journal*, 174
Minnesota Star and Tribune Co. v. Minnesota Commissioner of Revenue, 239–241, 243–244, 249, 255, 259
Monopoly, 92–94, 108–109, 172, 216–218
natural, 18–19, 219–220, 232
predatory pricing, see Antitrust, predatory pricing
Monopoly power, 61, 91, 109, 165, 276
advertising market, 222–224
information market, 220–222
intellectual market, 224–226
unnatural, 219–220

N

National Labor Relations Act, see Labor law, National Labor Relations Act
New York *Daily News*, 251–252
New York *Times*, 15, 37, 113
Newspaper(s), 4–7
alternative, see Newspapers, specialized
circulation, 10–11
dailies, 9–10
departments, 7–8
ethnic, 35–36
general circulation, 6–7, 108
historical trends, 9–10, 14–16
metropolitan dailies, 37, 45, 112–115, 117, 275–276
processes, 7–8, 102
publication cycle, 36
satellite-city dailies, 37, 112–115, 117
specialized, 6–7, 101, 108, 111, 153–154
suburban, 37, 101, 112–118, 275–276
weeklies, 9, 100–101, 108, 112–118, 152, 154, 275–276

Newspaper Preservation Act, 96, 105, 187, 207–209
Newsprint, 69–70
Newsracks, 256–259, 273

O

Objectivity, 17, 110–111
Oklahoma Press Publishing Co. v. Walling, 249
Oligopoly, see Competition, oligopoly
Opportunity cost(s), 87
Ownership, 131–161
antitrust, see Antitrust, ownership
concentration, 132–136, 141, 154, 231–232, 277–278
cross-media, 120–123, 230–213
conglomerate, 10, 133
goals, 105, 136–141, 144
group, 9–10, 132–136, 142–156
independent, 9–10, 141, 143–145
one-owner combinations, 106
privately-held, 139–140
publicly-held, 133, 134, 139–140, 146–147

P

Panax, 142
Paschall v. Kansas City Star Co., 204
Penetration, 10, 38–39, 274
Philadelphia *Bulletin*, 19
Philadelphia *Inquirer*, 105
Postal laws, 253–256
Postal Rate Commission, 254
second class mail, 253–255
third class mail, 253–254, 256
Postal subsidy, 253–256, 273, 278
Predatory pricing, see Antitrust law, predatory pricing
Price
discrimination, 109, 203
fixing, 201
Prices
advertising market, 46–47, 81–85, 108–109, 121–122, 150–153 222–224
group ownership, 151–153
information market, 23–24, 76–77, 97–99, 107
joint operating agreements, 109

milline rate, 42-43, 85, 121-122
monopoly power, 108-109, 220-224
oligopoly, 107
Product (commodity) differentiation, 92-94, 116-117
Production, 7-8, 69-73, 175
Production function, 55-56, 63, 175
Productivity, 56, 65-68, 74, 167
Profit, 68, 77, 97, 229
  controversy, 5, 266-267
  high, 233, 266-267
  group, 133-134
  long-run, 59, 80
  maximizing, 55, 136-140
  monopoly, 216-218
  normal, 59
  nonnormal, see Profit, monopoly
  optimizing, 77
  short-run, 59, 80
Publication cycle, 9, 95, 228, 230

R

Radio, 120-121, 152-153, 176
Readers, 13, 26-32, 116, 149, 180
  civic commitment, 27, 49
  demographics and psychographics, 13, 27, 43
  heterogeneity, 38-40
  homogeneity, 38-40
  influence, 281-283
Reader use of content
  decision making, 28-30
  entertainment, 28-30
  social-cultural interaction, 28-30
  surveillance, 27-29
  timing, 28-30
  utility, 38
Recycling newsprint, 259-260, 273
Refusal to deal, see Antitrust law, refusal to deal
Regional Bell Operating Companies, 122, 177, 231, 281
Regulation, 3-4, 122-123, 271-274
  television, 122-123
Relative constancy, Principle of, 119
Research and development, 270, 280-281
Retail trade zone, 40, 45
Robinson-Patman Act, 188-189, 203

S

Sales taxes, see Taxes, sales and use
San Antonio *Express*, 26
San Antonio *Light*, 26
San Diego *Transcript*, 35
Satellite transmission, 179
Scale
  diseconomies of, 58
  economies of, 58, 70-72, 99, 117, 151, 181, 280
  returns to, 58
Seattle *Post-Intelligencer*, 208
Seattle *Times*, 4, 208
Separately owned and operated newspapers, see Competition, direct
Sherman Antitrust Act, 188-189, 203
Social responsibility, 17
Sociological competition, 106-107
Socialization in newspapers, 144-146
St. Louis *Sun*, 101, 134
St. Petersburg *Times*, 135
Substitutability, 116, 276
Substitutes, 24-25
Supply, 55
  advertising market, 73-74
  and demand
    advertising market, 59-61, 81-85
    information market, 77-80
    intellectual market, 85-87
  elasticity, see Elasticity, supply
  inelasticity, see Inelasticity, supply
  information market, 63-73
  intellectual market, 74-76

T

Taxes, 134, 233, 272-273
  business license, 245
  capital gains, 135
  discriminatory taxation, 239-241
  estate, 246
  exemption from income taxes, 243-245
  inheritance, 134, 246
  sales and use, 241-243, 272, 278
Technology, 62, 163-183
  adoption of, 165-166, 172-173
  advertising market, 168-169
  backshop, 175
  barriers to entry, 100, 164, 168, 180-181, 279

computers, 68
economies of scale, 167–168, 279
future of, 181–183, 270
hidden costs, 172–174, 270
impact of competition on, 164–165
information market, 170–178
optical character reader (OCR), 166
printing, 164–166, 180–181, 279–280
profits, 171
VDTs, 173–175
Television, 41–42, 46–48, 120–123, 152–153, 176, 275
Timeliness, 65
Times-Picayune Publishing Co. v. United States, 196–197
Total market coverage (TMC), *see* Direct mail
Tying agreements, *see* Antitrust law, tying agreements

U

Umbrella competition, *see* Competition, umbrella
United States Postal Service, 253–254
United States v. Times Mirror Co., 194–195, 198, 206, 227–228

USA Today, 6, 15, 37, 67, 113, 140
Use taxes, *see* Taxes, sales and use
Uses and gratification, 27
Utility theory, 30

V

Veco International, Inc., 135
Vertical integration, 232
Videotext, *see* Electronic information service
Viewtron, 176

W

Wall Street Journal, 6, 15, 35, 37, 113, 254
Wants and needs of readers, 30–32, 268
Washington *Post*, 140, 221
Washington *Times*, 19, 134
Woodbury Daily Times v. Los Angeles Times-Washington Post News Service, 195–196, 204–205

Y

York *Dispatch*, 209
York *Daily Record*, 209

Z

Zoning, 44–46, 117–118, 181